Sophocles

CLASSICAL HERITAGE
VOLUME 4
GARLAND REFERENCE LIBRARY OF THE HUMANITIES
VOLUME 1455

CLASSICAL HERITAGE

WARD W. BRIGGS, JR., *Series Editor*

OVID
The Classical Heritage
Edited by William S. Anderson

VERGIL
Edited by Craig Kallendorf

MARTIAL
Edited by J.P. Sullivan

SOPHOCLES
The Classical Heritage
Edited by R.D. Dawe

HOMER
Edited by Katherine Callen King

TACITUS
The Classical Heritage
Edited by Ronald Mellor

Sophocles
The Classical Heritage

Edited by
R. D. Dawe

Garland Publishing, Inc.
New York and London
1996

Library of Congress Cataloging-in-Publication Data

Sophocles : the classical heritage / edited by R.D. Dawe.
       p.   cm. — (Classical heritage ; vol. 4) (Garland reference library
of the humanities ; vol. 1455)
    Includes bibliographical references.
    ISBN 0-8153-0334-3 (alk. paper)
    1. Sophocles—Criticism and interpretation.   2. Greek drama
(Tragedy)—History and criticism.   3. Mythology, Greek, in literature.
4. Sophocles—Stage history. 5. Sophocles—Appreciation.   I. Dawe, R. D.
(Roger David) II. Series.   III. Series: Garland reference library of the
humanities ; vol. 1455.
PA4417.S692   1996
882'.01—dc20   95-53958
                                                      CIP

Printed on acid-free, 250-year-life paper
Manufactured in the United States of America

TABLE OF CONTENTS

SERIES PREFACE

Ward W. Briggs

With the proliferation in the last generation of courses in Western Humanities or Great Books of the Western World, the need to demonstrate the continuity from ancient to modern culture is ever more pressing. Recent years have seen phenomenal interest in the area of studies known as the Classical Tradition, with at least one major journal well established (*Classical and Modern Literature*) and at least one other in the offing. The Institute for the Classical Tradition at Boston University continues to thrive with conferences and publications both here and abroad. The recent bimillennium of the death of Virgil brought forth a number of volumes in his honor and many of their contributions dealt with his *Nachleben*. Much the same will undoubtedly be true of the bimillennium of the death of Horace. Despite this interest, there have been no volumes designed to survey the influence of various ancient authors throughout European and American history.

This series will present articles, some appearing for the first time, some for the first time in English, dealing with the major points of influence in literature and, where possible, music, painting, and the plastic arts, of the greatest of ancient writers. The editors are published authorities on their authors and they provide introductions that summarize the scope of each author's impact on Western literature and art.

INTRODUCTION

Sophocles and Posterity

The influence of Sophocles from the Renaissance to the present day has not been a steady pressure manifesting itself evenly through the centuries, and those who have written interesting pieces on this author during that period have not done so with a view to smoothing the path of any future editor who might wish to place before the public a continuous and developing discourse. The present volume reflects the discontinuity of its subject matter, and the different aspects of the subject itself. There was a time when it seemed the best arrangement might be to keep in separate sections articles or chapters which dealt with a) the content of Sophocles; b) his translators; c) the various approaches to staging. But there was necessarily much overlap, and in the end it seemed appropriate to adopt a system based on chronology: which is not quite the same thing as date of publication. Thus Vidal-Naquet finds himself in an early position, although he has things to say about Freudian interpretations of Sophocles, simply because his article takes as its starting point the Vicenza production of 1585 with which we open.

As one surveys the available literature, it becomes apparent that professional Greek scholars have exhibited relatively little enthusiasm for pursuing the fate of Sophocles' work beyond the Roman period. (Sir Richard Jebb and Wolfgang Schadewaldt are two notable exceptions.) For the most part pieces dealing with Sophocles and X have been written from the standpoint of those who are more interested in X than in Sophocles. This is in the nature of the subject, and does not constitute a bar to inclusion. But there is something else which has acted as such a bar, and since any editor of a volume such as this must feel more regret at what he has had to exclude than pleasure at what he has been able to include, it is necessary to say at once what that something is. Essentially it is a matter of relevance. Commonly an author will be found who is discussing the influence not of Sophocles in particular but of Greek tragedy in general. One might, for example, expect to find a chapter on Hegel's views on Sophocles, but they are distributed through his works in a way that does not lend itself to helpful reproduction. A similar problem presented itself with the unpublished dissertation of a former pupil of mine, Mr. J. M. Parry. His thesis is called *English Attitudes to Greek Tragedy* 1491–1971, and can be found as item no. 8630 in the section in the Cambridge University Library which contains doctoral dissertations: its date is 1973. How useful and entertaining a guide this may be to others who may find themselves drawn into this area of study may be gauged from a few excerpted jottings. How many of us knew, for instance, that Aeschylus wrote "the most indifferent things in a Tragick Huff,"[1] even if we had long suspected that Aristotle is "unenlivened by a single ray of poetic genius and utterly destitute of the colouring of imagination."[2] How should we respond to the sentiment "Who has not read *Oedipus Tyrannus* but sighs when he reflects that Sophocles was not a Christian?"[3] Or to the exhortation of the stage manager: "Now, ladies and gentlemen, remember this is classical. Breadth! Breadth! No particular attention to meanings."?[4]—an exhortation already anticipated perhaps by some of the older school of translators: for what Eduard Fraenkel in the mid-twentieth century rendered as "in harmony therewith say 'woe, woe!', but may the good prevail!" (Aeschylus *Agam.* 158–159) had been more memorably given to us by Potter in the eighteenth century as "Sound high the strain, the according notes prolong, / Till conquest listens to the raptured song."[5] Justified or not, there is a certain charm in seeing and hearing a translation such as that, and there is much to be learnt from the unspoken assumptions that lie behind the various versions offered us over the centuries, as we shall see for ourselves in the two chapters on eighteenth-century French translations of Sophocles and on Hölderlin. It is a pity that limitations of space have made it impossible to include a selection from all the versions on offer. A dip into Francklin (1759) is enough to make some of us wish we had a copy on our own bookshelves for constant reference and delight.

---

[1] R. Rapin, *Reflections on Aristotle's Treatise of Poesie*, made English by T. Rymer (1674) p. 117.

[2] Mrs. Carter, *Letters*, ed. Pennington (1817) II. 22.

[3] *The Harrovian*, April 1828.

[4] *Atlantic Monthly* vol. 116 (1912) p. 663.

[5] R. Potter, *The Tragedies of Aeschylus* (1777).

But it is time to set regrets behind us, and to pass from what we have kept out of this book to what we have let into it, and to give the reader a guide to what is to come. We begin with the year 1585, and a performance in Vicenza of _Oedipus Rex_ in the translation by Orsatto Giustiniani. There exist a number of documents relating to this performance.[6] We have chosen to print the most thoughtful, and least adulatory, the one by Antonio Riccoboni, who with Aristotle's _Poetics_ and commentators on it as his guide finds much to criticize both with the play as Sophocles wrote it and in various aspects of its staging at Vicenza. Some of the criticisms of Sophocles we shall find echoed later; as for the Vicenza production itself perhaps the most important criticism, as we look back in the light of subsequent developments, is the one which complains that the words of the chorus, rightly recognized by Riccoboni as vital, could not be heard for the music to which they were sung. One wonders if this had been a matter of much discussion, for what Riccoboni has to say seems contradicted by the evidence of two other witnesses: first Filippo Pigafetta, "il qual coro con piacevole parlare e armonia adempì l'offizio suo in maniera che s'intendevano schiettamente le parole quasi tutte (the chorus with its graceful delivery and harmony fulfilled its office in such a way that practically all the words were clearly heard)," and second Giacomo Dolfino, who wrote of the music that it was "conveniente assai al soggetto e in maniera tale che per quanto si poteva nel concorso di tante voci s'intendevano distintamente quasi tutte le parole (very suitable to the subject and such that, so far as was possible with so many voices together, practically all the words were heard distinctly)." These are statements from members of the audience, after the event. For a full statement of the producer's original plans and intentions before the event we are still able today to consult the document written by the man himself, Angelo Ingegneri.

The next piece, by Pierre Vidal-Naquet, serves as a partial substitute for the other accounts of the Vicenza performance which we have not, for reasons of space, been able to include, and it also looks ahead to the reception of Sophocles in France, thus providing a link not only with the original excerpts from Corneille, Voltaire, and Brumoy which we print in this volume, but also with the chapter by Suzanne Saïd and Christian Biet on French eighteenth-century translations. Now Vidal-

---

[6] A convenient place to find them is Alberto Gallo, _La Prima Rappresentazione al Teatro Olimpico_, Milan 1973. Those with more opulent tastes may consult the splendidly produced book by L. Schrade, _La Représentation d'Edipo Tiranno au Teatro Olimpico_, Paris 1960. To the bibliography listed by Vidal-Naquet (our next item) we may add now Chapter II of H. Flashar's _Inszenierung der Antike_, München 1991.

Naquet's name is closely associated with that of Jean-Pierre Vernant, and the work of these two scholars has been, in certain circles, highly influential. It will be seen that Vidal-Naquet refers, with no small satisfaction, to his colleague's work of demolition, "*Oedipus without the Complex*," done on Didier Anzieu. M. Anzieu certainly suffered from the fault of being more Freudian than Freud, but hardly merited being taken so seriously, and later in this Introduction we shall find it necessary to question whether the same may not be said of his critic.

For a while we remain in France, and after hearing Corneille explain what alterations he had found it necessary to make in order to produce an *Oedipus* acceptable to the audiences for whom he was writing, pass on immediately to a trenchant critique by the youthful Voltaire of the Sophoclean original. Voltaire does not hesitate to speak of places in the text that "revolted" him, or of "faults." He is always ready to deride, and scores many direct hits. But though he can see what Sophocles lost by proceeding as he did, he does not stop to ask what he might also have gained. Occasionally he misrepresents the facts, as when he says that after the scene with the Corinthian messenger "Oedipe ne soupconne rien encore: il n'a d'autre crainte que d'être né d'une famille obscure (Oedipus still suspects nothing; he has no other fear than that of being born of an obscure family)." Much more often he judges what he finds in the play against the criterion of real-life probability instead of engaging in the sympathetic suspension of disbelief that is called for not merely in the theatre and more generally in literature, but also in opera (especially!), in painting (why has that man got both eyes on the same side of his face?), and in sculpture (why has that woman got a huge hole in her middle?). Voltaire is conscious of this himself, for he speaks of a poet "qui viole les règles du sens commun pour ne point manquer en apparence à celles du théâtre (who violates the rules of common sense so as not to appear deficient in those of the theater)." Where we may listen to him with more respect and less impatience is where we find him declaring, after watching a stage performance, "qu'on peut sans péril louer tant qu'on veut les poètes grecs mais qu'il est dangereux de les imiter (one can without peril extol the Greek poets as much as one wishes, but it is dangerous to imitate them)." That other man of the theatre, Schiller, was, we shall find, to make the same painful discovery. Such criticisms may make us bristle, but they also make us think; and Voltaire's epigrammatic "N'est-ce pas avouer qu'elle est finie qu'être obligé de prouver qu'elle ne l'est pas (Is it not to admit that it is finished, when one is obliged to prove that it is not)?" though directed only at the last three hundred lines or so of *Oedipus Rex*, is the sort of criticism which must haunt us, even after all the most eloquent defences

have been read, when we go through more than one Greek tragedy, most
notably *Ajax*.

More influential than Voltaire's asperities was Pierre Brumoy's
Théâtre des Grecs, first published in 1743, from which we have chosen
to reprint the *Remarks upon Oedipus* which were appended to a translation of the play which it contained. While disavowing the authority of
Aristotle, Brumoy all too plainly feels the Stagirite breathing down his
neck, and like him esteems *Oedipus* as *the* Greek tragedy *par excellence*.
His claim that the unity of time is scrupulously observed is overdone, if
we allow a reasonable period for the summoning of the shepherd from
the mountains to the palace at Thebes. But there are compensating
virtues. A résumé of the plot is saved from aridity by the way in which
Brumoy has constantly before his eyes the *mise-en-scène* and movement
of actors in the theatre; and he makes a point not often made in connection with *Oedipus Rex*, namely that we are treated to a greater *variety* of
persons on stage than we are accustomed to seeing. Whether it was
Voltaire who opened his eyes or not, he is also alive to two cardinal
points in the play's construction: first that Teiresias's revelations
threatened to bring it to a premature close at the end of what he would
style the second act; and that the last part, the fifth act, was something a
number of people might feel we could well do without. (When the
eminent Hellenist D. L. Page used to lecture on this play in Cambridge,
it was his practice to ignore its ending.) But he does his best to defend
the end: "Quelle impression de tristesse ne devoit pas produire un pareil
spectacle!" ("What emotions of grief and tenderness must not such a
spectacle produce!") is said of Oedipus's *adieux* to his children. Brumoy
concludes by examining the question of the hero's guilt, if any, and how
far he deserved his punishment. The general tenor of his remarks does
not differ from what has been written in a thousand, no, ten thousand,
student essays ever since. He does not misrepresent the facts, but what
he does do perhaps is to blur the distinction between artistic traits, such
as the possibility that Oedipus was quick to anger, and the facts of the
myth, which provides Oedipus with his fate before he is even born.

Our next chapter, the one by Suzanne Saïd and Christian Biet,
discloses with detailed illustrations the kind of thing which Brumoy and
two other early French translators and commentators on Sophocles
thought worth their, and their readers', attention. Even though the works
in question span only the years 1761 to 1788, sharply different approaches are detected and analysed. One such difference lies in the way
two of the commentators try to stress the continuity of certain ideas
between the world of the ancient Greeks and our own, while the third
tries to keep them separate, yet only partially succeeds, regarding Antiq-

uity as a sort of chronological bloc all of its own, within which differentiation between the time of Sophocles and the time of e.g. Pliny is
scarcely to be found.

Meanwhile England was keeping step with France. We have
already mentioned Francklin's translation of Sophocles, and now permit
ourselves the indulgence of reproducing prefaces by two other translators, Maurice and Potter, separated from each other by only a decade.
Both give Sophocles full marks. Not only do they adopt a stance
diametrically opposite to Voltaire's: "The successive circumstances of
the play arise gradually and naturally one out of the other" says one, and
the other echoes him; but Maurice at least also contradicts in advance
what Keble was later to say about a vital missing element of humanity,
for he finds in *Oedipus Rex* evidence that "shews Sophocles to have had
an intimate knowledge of the human heart." Not heavyweight contributions to the subject, these two prefaces, but like so much of eighteenth-
century English full of charm and elegance.

So far Italy, France, and England. But the country which has
done most for Greek scholarship is Germany. One of the handful of
books which set into motion that imposing movement of scholarship
which has still not come to a halt was Lessing's *Laokoon*. Our present
selection deals principally, because the material available deals principally, with *Oedipus Rex* and *Antigone*. It is something of a relief then to
be able to turn to a different play, *Philoctetes*, in the excerpt from
Laokoon which we have chosen. We find Lessing extolling, almost fier-
cely, the excellences of the play, and defending it from more modern
assaults and imitations. As a companion piece we take Herder's polemic
against Lessing. There is even more passion behind Herder's words than
there was behind Lessing's, indeed too much. Admiration of Philoctetes
leads to a blackening of Odysseus's character that goes beyond what
Sophocles probably intended, though Herder himself expressly attributes
that polarity to him. It is unfortunate that Lessing's true position is mis-
represented, almost to the point of caricature. But Herder is an important
figure, and what he has to say is, in its most extended form, about the
whole concept, today more questioned than it used to be, of classical
restraint.

We shall take up the thread of critical writing again when we
come to the lectures of A. W. Schlegel. But before then we must spend
an interlude in the company of Hölderlin and Schiller. If one were to ask
someone equally well versed in all the European literatures what name
came immediately to mind in connection with Sophocles' influence, it is
likely enough that the answer would be Hölderlin; and in deference to
this opinion we spend a considerable amount of space on a discussion of

his translations of *Oedipus Rex* and *Antigone*. But before we go closely into the subject it is only prudent to remind ourselves of Hölderlin's severe technical limitations, as seen from the standpoint of a professional Greek scholar, who is likely to rule, rather discouragingly from the Germanist's point of view, that Hölderlin's series of gross and elementary blunders disqualifies him utterly from serious consideration as an interpreter of Sophocles; and in any case we seem often to be talking not so much about Sophocles' influence on Hölderlin as Hölderlin's influence on Sophocles. But it is unlikely that these objections will ever do anything to diminish the powerful and continuing fascination which his translations and revealing mistranslations exercise over the minds of men of letters. To do justice to both sides the present volume includes Schadewaldt's assessment of Hölderlin's linguistic competence[7] before it passes on to the excerpts from the chapter by R. B. Harrison which struggles, with some considerable success, to make intelligible Hölderlin's mystic musings. A hundred years have passed since Voltaire produced his all too rational dissection of *Oedipus Rex*, and the gap separating the two poet/translators is one of unbridgeable width. It is Hölderlin today who excites the greater interest, but the *caveat* needs to be repeated that his command of the Greek language was that of a raw recruit to the subject.

At much the same time as Hölderlin was translating Sophocles, Schiller was composing his *Bride of Messina*. There may be times, as we read the chapter from Prader's *Schiller and Sophocles*, when we feel ourselves closer to the world of *Il Trovatore* than to the drama of classical Athens: but we have Schiller's own words to correct us. Of particular interest is the way Prader brings out the various improbabilities in Schiller's play forced on him by the way he has chosen to lay out the plot. Professional students of Sophocles will see here a kind of parallel with the interpretation of Sophocles himself given by Tycho von Wilamowitz-Moellendorff in his famous book. Prader's conclusion on the relative merits of the two dramatists' handling of comparable plots distinctly favours Sophocles. It is only for reasons of space that we have left out Prader's treatment of the religious and philosophical aspects of Schiller's plays, but here too he finds confusion and from the same cause, namely that Schiller was imitating elements of ancient tragedy without altering them sufficiently to suit the conditions of his own day.

---

[7] A fuller treatment of the same topic can be found in Part Two of Fr. Beissner's *Hölderlins Übersetzungen aus dem Griechischen*, ed. 2 Stuttgart 1961, 65-146. In this respect Hölderlin was not a unique figure: for a discussion of Shelley's mistranslations of Greek see Chapter III of Timothy Webb's *The Violet in the Crucible*, Oxford 1976.

Not that Schiller himself was ignorant of the dangers: a letter he wrote to Joh. Wilhelm Süvern on 26 July 1800 contains the following sentence: "I share with you unqualified admiration of Sophoclean tragedy, but it was a phenomenon of its time that can never come back; and to force the living product of an individual particular 'present' to become the standard and model of a quite different time would mean rather to kill off than to fill with life the art which must always arise and have its effect as something dynamic and living." We have also reluctantly omitted a small section on Schiller's chorus as a vehicle for the gnomic evaluation of the action; and another on the effect on the spectators' senses as they look on and hear the chorus reciting and singing. But the section comparing Schiller's use of the chorus with Sophocles' is indispensable. One may however question, while at the same time feeling every sympathy, the assumption that the choruses of Sophocles were meant to be obscure at first hearing. Today we labour under the handicap of corrupt texts and of metres which so far from being instantly recognisable are more an object of scientific study. If we had the poetry in its pristine state, and had been brought up from the cradle to recite Greek lyric poems, we might find Sophoclean choruses as clear as Schiller's—and certainly clearer than Hölderlin's translations! After another omission, dealing with *The Bride of Messina* on stage, we reproduce Prader's final thoughts on Schiller-v-Sophocles.

One cannot mention the name of Schiller without the name of Goethe coming immediately to mind. Both were practicing creative artists, but both were prepared also to theorize in the manner of a literary critic. Tempting though it would be to move on to Goethe at once, it has seemed more prudent, in the light of the influence he exerted, to print first A. W. Schlegel's lecture on Sophocles. It seems innocuous enough today, yet the book from which it is drawn prompted the following response in England: "Disposed to rationality more than to mysticism, we are apt to doubt when we do not understand . . . We are not fond, moreover, of *a priori* criticism, which makes the gauge first, and then tries the work by it."[8] The modern reader disposed to rationality, if he still exists, might feel inclined to apply these words to structuralism and its foetid offspring, but certainly not to Schlegel. One can hardly assent to the justice of a charge so comprehensively put, but Schlegel is perhaps vulnerable on more limited a front. His description of *Oedipus at Colonus* as evincing "a mature serenity and total freedom from the impetuosity and violence of youth" is not at variance with what countless others have said; yet there is nothing very serene about Oedipus's denun-

---

[8] *Monthly Review* vol. 81, Oct. 1816, p. 113.

ciation of either Creon or Polyneices. And when Schlegel speaks of
Sophocles as "the one whose feelings bear the strongest affinity to the
spirit of our religion" he breathes forth the same sentiments as the con-
tributor to *The Harrovian*, but elicits from us, nearly two centuries later,
little more than a puzzled smile.

Attitudes change, not only in religion. Feminists of today will
swallow hard when they read Schlegel's verdict on the heroine of
Women of Trachis (admittedly the kind of woman who would go looking
for a gas leak with a lighted match): "the female levity of Deianira is
beautifully atoned for by her death." They will bring to it the same for-
bearance they surely bring to Sir Richard Jebb's description of Homeric
women as "essentially feminine, without being insipid or inane."
Schlegel partly makes amends by detecting what many others had not, a
certain hardness in the character of Antigone. Curious perhaps that he
should be alive to this latent characteristic when he had been so unreceptive to the more overt hardness of the aged but still unquestionably mas-
culine Oedipus. Those who are absorbed more in the technical aspects of
Greek scholarship will perhaps judge the single most interesting thing in
Schlegel's survey is his barely overcome reluctance to accept that
Women of Trachis is indeed from the hand of the master; and his concluding paragraph with its suggestion that "Sophocles" may mean
"school of Sophocles" is provocative and disturbing precisely because
we have no certain way of refuting it.

We have already alluded to Tycho von Wilamowitz-Moellendorff's book, and in the brief excerpts from the Eckermann conversations we shall see that Goethe himself was already anticipating one of its
basic tenets; which is perhaps why the later author included a sentence
by Goethe (letter to Eichstädt 1794) as a sort of prefatory motto to his
own monograph. Goethe, like Tycho, laid stress on the way that
Sophocles always had his eyes on the scene he happened to be working
on at the moment, and on the likely effect it would have in the theatre.
Of his more specific criticisms the one impugning Antigone's sophistic
arguments on the claims of a dead brother compared with those of a dead
son or husband, and describing them as "bordering on the comic"[9] is the
most famous. Yet after the best part of two centuries the "competent
philologist" has not yet been found to provide what Goethe yearned for,
the scholarly proof that the lines are spurious, any more than any one

---

[9] Reminiscent of what Schiller had said in a letter to Goethe of 2 Oct. 1797
about *Oedipus Rex*: 'If anybody wanted to retain the essential elements of the actual
story, with different persons and times, what now inspires fear would become laughable.'

has been able to prove what Schlegel suspected, that *Women of Trachis* is not pure Sophocles.

And now back to England, or at any rate Scotland. When Schlegel's lectures first came out in their English translation, a reviewer,[10] after a xenophobic denunciation of Germans in general, conceded that they were not without merit. But when he came to the chapter on Sophocles he had misgivings:

> After all, however, the tragedies of Sophocles, which are the perfection of the classical style, are hardly tragedies in our sense of the word. They do not exhibit the extremity of human passion and suffering. The object of modern tragedy is to represent the soul utterly subdued as it were, or at least convulsed and overthrown by passion or misfortune. That of the ancients was to show how the greatest crimes could be perpetrated with the least remorse, and the greatest calamities borne with the least emotion. Firmness of purpose, and calmness of sentiment, are their leading characteristics. Their heroes and heroines act and suffer as if they were always in the presence of a higher power, or as if human life itself were a religious ceremony, performed in honour of the Gods and of the State. The mind is not shaken to its centre; the whole being is not crushed or broken down. Contradictory motives are not accumulated; the utmost force of imagination and passion is not exhausted to overcome the repugnance of the will to crime; the contrast and combination of outward accidents are not called in to overwhelm the mind with the whole weight of unexpected calamity. The dire conflict of the feelings, the desperate struggle with fortune, are seldom there. All is conducted with a fatal composure. All is prepared and submitted to with inflexible constancy, as if Nature were only an instrument in the hands of Fate . . .
>
> . . . as Aeschylus differs from Sophocles in giving greater scope to the impulses of the imagination, so Euripides differs from him in giving greater indulgence to the feelings of the heart. The heart is the seat of pure affection,—of involuntary emotion,—of feelings brooding over and nourished by themselves. In the dramas of Sophocles, there is no want of these feelings; but they are

---

[10] *The Edinburgh Review* vol. 26 (1816).

suppressed or suspended by the constant operation of the senses and the will. Beneath the rigid muscles by which the heart is there braced, there is no room left for those bursts of uncontrollable feeling, which dissolve it in tenderness, or plunge it into the deepest woe. In the heroic tragedy, no one dies of a broken heart,—scarcely a sigh is heaved, or a tear shed.

The reviewer is conscious of two things above all: he knows that Greek tragedy is not a unified bloc, and that there is something distinctive about Sophocles. What that something is will be the subject of the next essay we print, the one by Thirlwall. But he is also conscious of something else: he detects a certain marmoreal chilliness, a lack of humanity, in Sophocles; and that is a theme which we shall find taken up and developed further by Keble in the essay that comes after Thirlwall's.

Thirlwall's essay *On the Irony of Sophocles* is, like Schlegel's, a general survey from a particular standpoint. It fastens on to what is distinctively Sophoclean in Sophocles, and earns its place in this volume not only for that reason but also for having won the accolade of once being described as "the most exquisite piece of criticism in the English Language."[11] It sets the tone for the standard English view of Sophocles which, in spite of all assaults, has lasted right up to our own times, fortified *en route* by the tacit endorsement of the most influential of all Sophoclean commentators, Sir Richard Jebb. It is perhaps the first major attempt in English, a generation after the death of Porson, to do something about "the melancholy inference . . . that the study of the poet's works with a view to the pleasures of the imagination has not kept pace with the diligence bestowed on them as objects of philological criticism."

Thirlwall's exposition of *Oedipus Rex* is not immune from criticism of detail. Was it a misunderstanding of the function of the "paean" which caused him to write "*but* its strains are still interrupted by the voice of wailing"? What makes him assert that "The royal house has been hitherto exempt from the overwhelming evil" (sc. the plague) and that Oedipus is "himself unhurt," and then use this as a basis for seeing irony: "the spectator has leisure to reflect, how different all is from what it seems. The wrath of heaven has been pointed against the afflicted city, only that it might fall with concentrated force on the head of a single man . . ."? For it is Oedipus himself who as early as v. 60 is telling the "pitiful children" that "there is none of you as sick as I." Certainly there

---

[11] *Guesses at Truth* (1848) 188.

may be poetic irony in those words, but that irony does not reside in the contrast Thirlwall is drawing for us, but in the contrast between an epidemic that defeats medical science and the inherent nature of an Oedipus who, late in the play, will be crying, in Jebb's unfortunate translation, "Say, am I vile?"—sick to the very depths of his being, sick, as we might say today, in his genetic make-up.

Thirlwall however has a gift of making even the mere re-telling of a plot into an enthralling English narrative, using his command of language to generate excitement as he picks out motives or traits of character. Sometimes he exceeds the evidence, as when he speaks of a Philoctetes "impatient of wasting the arrows of Heracles on birds and beasts." But these are small matters. Ample and unhurried though his style seems, Thirlwall is telling us a lot as he moves majestically on his way. Reinhardt's famous *Schein* and *Sein* antinomy is already foreshadowed: "the main theme of the poet's irony is the contrast between the appearance of good and the reality of evil." Then in discussing *Oedipus at Colonus* he shows himself a better critic than Schlegel, detecting in the hero at one time "a somewhat unamiable aspect" amounting to "a vindictive sternness." He does not however overtly cross swords with Schlegel, who appears only later as "a celebrated critic" who suspected the authenticity of *Women of Trachis*, but with Hermann, towards whom he directs a respectful polemic, asking very properly that we do not bring to bear our own modern preconceptions but see the play through the eyes of its ancient audience. Even so one wonders if Thirlwall had entirely convinced himself, when we find such embarrassed comments as "the most obscure as well as repulsive passage in the whole piece, may have had an adequate motive, which we cannot fully comprehend."

More open to view are his doubts over the speech of deception— or not of deception—in *Ajax*. It is his very honesty in dealing with the evidence that makes his tentative conclusion unsatisfactory. No one after him has been any more successful, but we may feel that his own words apply to him as much as to any one else: "What has been said on this subject has for the most part been proposed in the language of apology, and in a tone which now and then raises a suspicion that the advocate is not thoroughly convinced of the goodness of his cause." But when we come to *Antigone*, Thirlwall is once more confident and authoritative, and when he evaluates Creon's proclamation with the words "Nor was the decree a wanton or tyrannical exertion of power" he is free from a common error still to be found today in such phrases as "Creon's vicious law."[12] As for *Philoctetes*, notwithstanding the minor cavil made above,

---

[12] M.S. Silk and J.P. Stern, *Nietzsche on Tragedy*, Cambridge 1981, p. 322. In one of the Eckermann excerpts printed in this book it will be seen how even Goethe believed that Creon acted 'out of hate towards the dead man'.

Thirlwall's examination is masterly.

Like most critics, Schlegel and Thirlwall had been concerned with content rather than language. Criticism of a poet which leaves his actual handling of words untouched must necessarily be incomplete. When we come to Keble we move one step further away still from the actual texture of the poetry. His antennae were not as sensitive as they need to be in a critic of the highest rank: it is curious, for instance, to find him ignoring the guard in *Antigone* when he writes "we find in him (sc. Sophocles) no character like the soldier of the *Agamemnon* or the nurse in the *Choephoroe.*" When he asks "What artist ever handled the Greek tongue with greater power, to make it express whate'er he would?" one suspects the prelate of forcing himself to appear just, but only against his true feelings, and it is not long before he explicitly denies that beauty of language "is one of the very sources and fountain-heads of Poetry." Sophocles is therefore surveyed from a sternly moralistic standpoint, for "the essence of all poetry is to be found . . . in the depths of the heart . . . ," and as for Sophocles "I, indeed, entirely miss in him those glowing emotions of the mind which spring to birth spontaneously." Keble would, so to speak, give Sophocles a high second class degree, but could not in all conscience vote for a first. His observations on the relative coldness of Sophocles *vis-à-vis* some poets who wrote in his own language may be justified, but here, unlike Thirlwall, he is not commenting on what is distinctively Sophoclean in Sophocles. He seems marginally aware that his censures may apply to other Greek poets, for he writes of Sophoclean characters that "They, one and all, simply say and do such things as may assist the plot, or contribute to a discussion on some question of casuistry, such as are constantly met with in the later Greek drama."

Keble cannot quite forgive Sophocles for not being a Christian, indeed for not even being Virgil. Even the motives behind the introduction of the third actor he views with suspicion. Why then do we include this essay in our collection? Because paeans of unmixed praise are no substitute for criticism, and when one lingers over Keble's basic point, it is impossible to repress a feeling that he has put his finger on something we might prefer not to have brought out into the open, but which ought to be. How far his strictures are specific to Sophocles, and not to all classical Greek literature—not just the "later Greek drama"—is again something which could be made the subject of fruitful debate.

The English translation of Keble's lectures from the Latin did not appear until 1912. By that time Jebb's immortal series of commentaries had been completed. But by that time too the theories of Sigmund Freud were already being evolved and disseminated. The times overlap, yet with Freud we seem to have a leap into an entirely new world. Right at the core of Freud's beliefs and teachings was the Oedipus complex, and the question at once arises what bearing, if any, that theory should have on the interpretation of Sophocles' play. Freud believed himself to have detected in the unconscious mind a desire on the part of men to marry their mothers, and a sense of rivalry between men and their fathers which finds expression in a sense of relief when the father dies. It is not only in the extract that we have printed that he quotes Diderot: "Si le petit sauvage était abandonné à lui-même, qu'il conservât toute son imbécillité, et qu'il réunît au peu de raison de l'enfant au berceau la violence des passions de l'homme de trente ans, il tordrait le col à son père et coucherait avec sa mère (if the little savage were left to himself, preserving all his foolishness and adding to the small sense of the child in the cradle the violent passions of a man of thirty, he would strangle his father and lie with his mother)." He was also aware of the couplet in *Oedipus Rex* which says "Many men have, in their dreams, lain with their mothers."

It is important to distinguish between what Freud said about the Oedipus myth and what he said about Sophocles as a playwright using that myth. In essence there is no difference between what he says about Sophocles and what he says in another place about Ibsen: "If we may rely on the fact that the dramatist's conscious creative combination arose logically from unconscious premisses . . ."[13] It was the myth, not Sophocles' play, which gave its name to the theory: "We give the whole of this mental structure the name of 'Oedipus complex' after the familiar Greek legend."[14] The following two quotations may usefully be added to the section we have chosen to reprint in the main body of the book.[15]

> The Greek hero killed his father and took his mother to wife. That he did so unwittingly, since he did not know them as his parents, is a deviation from the analytic facts which we can easily understand and which, indeed, we shall recognize as inevitable.

> One may hear it objected, for instance, that the legend of King Oedipus has in fact no connection with the construc-

---

[13] *The Standard Edition of the Complete Psychological Works of Sigmund Freud*, ed. J. Strachey etc., London 1964, XIV 329.

[14] XX 213.

[15] XXIII 187 and 191.

tion made by analysis: the cases are quite different, since Oedipus did not know that it was his father that he killed and his mother that he married. What is overlooked in this is that a distortion of this kind is inevitable if an attempt is made at a poetic handling of the material . . . The ignorance of Oedipus is a legitimate representation of the unconscious state into which, for adults, the whole experience has fallen; and the coercive power of the oracle, which makes or should make the hero innocent, is a recognition of the inevitability of the fate which has condemned every son to live through the Oedipus complex.

At an early point in this Introduction we alluded to Vidal-Naquet's citation of an essay by Jean-Pierre Vernant attacking the Freudian interpretation of *Oedipus Rex*. Vernant accuses Freud of projecting his own ideas back on to an ancient masterpiece. But if we examine how scrupulous Vernant himself is in the examination of evidence we shall not be over-impressed. In his chapters on *Oedipus without the Complex* and *Ambiguity and Reversal: on the Enigmatic Structure of Oedipus Rex* we find that he speaks of Oedipus as "the object of the prayers of an entire people as if he were a god"[16]; and then writes "In his very first words to him, the priest of Zeus refers to Oedipus as though he were in some way the equal of the gods: *isoumenos theoisi*,"[17] conveniently leaving out the word "not" (οὐκ) immediately preceding. In his second chapter Vernant spends a large part of his time developing an idea touched on in his first, that Oedipus is expelled from the city as a scapegoat: the word for scapegoat, *pharmakos*, is constantly mentioned. For some reason those who belong to the same school of thought as M. Vernant believe that they import some kind of (admittedly much needed) scholarly rigour to their arguments if they substitute transliterated Greek words for the more customary translations: a process which logically has no end, for no words in ancient Greek can mean *exactly* the same thing in modern English or French. This infection is not confined to discussions of tragedy: much modern writing on the Odyssey has banished "return journey" and "household" in favour of an endless dripping of *nostos* and *oikos*. As for the word *pharmakos* itself, a glance in the lexicon will show what company it keeps: it is totally foreign to tragedy. As for the quality of the

---

[16] J. P. Vernant and P. Vidal-Naquet, *Tragedy and Myth in Ancient Greece*, a translation by J. Lloyd (Brighton 1981) of *Mythe et tragédie en Grèce ancienne* (Paris 1973); p. 81.

[17] Ibid. p. 92.

rest of Vernant's argumentation, let us count the number of errors in the following very brief extract.

> Oedipus is described as a hunter on the trail, tracking down and flushing out the wild beast (109–10, 221, 354, 475 ff.) at large in the mountains, pursuing and putting it to flight (469), relegating it to a place far from human beings (479). But in this hunt the hunter ultimately finds himself the quarry: pursued by the terrible curse of his parents (419), Oedipus wanders away, howling like a wild animal (1255, 1265), before putting out his eyes and fleeing into the wild mountains of Cithaeron (1451).

1) Nothing is said of any wild beasts at 109–10, 221, and 475 ff. An ordinary metaphor is being employed, as any policeman might say today "I will track down the criminal" or indeed as any scholar might say "I will track down the reference."

2) v. 354 has no conceivable relevance to the argument.

3) The one who is mentioned at v. 469 as putting the criminal to flight is not Oedipus but "the son of Zeus"; and for what it is worth the chorus say not that the unknown man is in flight but that it is time he was. In v. 476 it is said that "everyone" should track him down.

4) The place far from human beings is where the criminal is already imagined to be, not where Oedipus will relegate him.

5) "Pursued by the terrible curse of his parents (419)" is part of a prediction by Teiresias, not something confirmed by the action of the play.

6) Oedipus does not wander away, howling like a wild animal on his way to Cithaeron. 1255 is another reference of total irrelevance, and 1265 refers specifically to Oedipus's howl of dismay on finding Jocasta swinging from a noose.

7) Oedipus does not flee into the wild mountains of Cithaeron. v. 1451 contains a plea by him that he might be allowed to, and that plea is turned down. The text spends a good deal of time making precisely that point. Consequently the pages filled by Vernant on the subject of Oedipus as a scapegoat have absolutely no bearing whatsoever on the structure of Sophocles' play.

Later on (p. 103) we are given v. 1426 as a reference which "explicitly presents" Oedipus as a "defilement that must be expelled." The text actually says, in Jebb's close translation, "revere at least the all-nurturing flame of our lord the Sun,—spare to show thus nakedly a pollution such as this,—one which neither earth can welcome, nor the holy rain, nor the light. Nay, take him into the house . . ." M. Vernant evidently believes that "expel" is a synonym for "take indoors," and that on Mt. Cithaeron the sun never shines and the rain never falls.

It is difficult to have patience with this kind of thing, and that patience snaps entirely when the name Oidipous, a name which Sophocles himself interprets for us, has its first component element re-interpreted as if it meant "know," so that Oedipus will mean, presumably, "the man with the knowledgeable feet"—a sort of theatrical agent's description of some kind of tragic Fred Astaire; or else, even more hilariously, the name is divided into the exclamation *oi* + *dipous* ("Hi! Two-foot" = "Hi! Shorty"?). Posterity will look back with amazement on an era when these queer fantasies were allowed to flourish. But flourish they do, to such an extent that they have been reproduced as if orthodoxy in many examination answers written by candidates for a degree in classics at Cambridge University, such being the quality of the guidance they receive. But we believe we have by now given sufficient reasons for leaving this unquestionably influential branch of advanced thinking unrepresented in the present collection. Freud's thinking may be speculative, and it may be vulnerable. But he towers above his critics.

No play of Sophocles, not even *Oedipus Rex*, has attracted more critical discussion over the years than *Antigone*, and Käte Hamburger's essay, though it looks at Sophocles anachronistically through the eyes of Anouilh and others, is a stimulating piece of writing characterized by clarity and penetration, and by a corresponding lack of literary-critical mumbo-jumbo. Whether Sophocles really meant to endow Antigone with a death-wish is something over which we may retain some mental reservations; and at the back of our minds may always lurk the thought that perhaps Sophocles himself had not worked out the full implications of what he was saying with the scrupulous care of a modern philosopher. But even in a piece like Hamburger's which aims to sweep away the cobwebs it is reassuring to find old friends: the insistence on the importance of the family takes us, no doubt unwittingly, to the central thesis of Hinrichs' little monograph, the starting point of one of the Eckermann conversations recorded in this book.

How richly provocative of thought the Antigone story has been can be seen not only from its successors on the stage but also from the fact that it has been the inspiration for a novel, Hochhuth's *Die Berliner Antigone*. A novel in which Adolf Hitler makes an appearance is clearly too far from Sophocles to justify the inclusion in this book of a critical essay comparing the modern novel with the ancient play, but those who are sufficiently curious to wish to pursue the matter can turn to Lutz Lenz's piece in *Antike und Abendland* XXII (1976) 156–174. Equally it did not seem appropriate to include the influence of *Oedipus Rex* on a comedy, Kleist's *Der Zerbrochene Krug*, about which H. M. Wolff wrote in *Modern Language Notes* LIV (1939) 267–272. It is enough merely to mention the existence of such things.

Next to Anouilh and *Antigone* we set Cocteau and *Oedipus Rex.*
Pantelodimos stresses for us the vitality inherent in the myths of the family to which Oedipus belonged, and the fascination those myths had for
Jean Cocteau. Some of the time we see him as translator, with a penchant for abridgement, and wrestling like so many of his predecessors
with the problem of what to do with the chorus; and then, later, we see
him moving into a realm of creative art that is all his own, no longer
adhering to original texts but playing about with the theme of those texts
and recombining them into something that goes far beyond them, like
some violinist building a cadenza with his own stamp upon it out of a
concerto that has long stood in the standard repertoire.

Lastly we join Schadewaldt again, in a historical survey of a hundred years or so of staging Sophocles. We have seen Schiller despairing
of success in transplanting the drama of ancient Athens to the stage of
his own time. But Schadewaldt has a different tale to tell, of an *Antigone*
performance put on by Ludwig Tieck in 1841, in a translation by Donner
and with the considerable advantage of music by Mendelssohn. From
1866 to the turn of the century Adolf Wilbrandt evidently had much success with Sophocles productions. How then was Wilbrandt successful
where Schiller was not? At least part of the answer comes in diagnosing
elements in ancient tragedy as peculiar to their own time, and then proceeding as follows: "This dead part must be determinedly swept aside,
cut, or reworked, in order to faithfully preserve the real 'life' of those
immortal dramatic works of the Greeks." Some might say that this was
cheating, though Schadewaldt himself by the end of his piece and clothing himself in that vagueness of expression for which the German language is famous—a trait which Goethe had deplored in the case of Hinrichs—has also renounced any attempt to recreate Greek tragedy as it
was. Any such attempt to imitate in, say, the Vienna Burgtheater of
today the conditions of the theatre of Dionysus two and a half millennia
ago is obviously doomed. But is it too much to hope that more such
attempts might be made in Greece itself in its open-air theatres or places
of spectacle, eschewing the practice of June 1986 where a conference on
the ancient drama held at Delphi was accompanied by performances in
the race-course of *Women of Troy* where the fashion was for the actors to
spend a lot of their time on all fours?—though the curiosity of this was
exceeded by one Japanese producer's vision of Euripides which reduced
the role of Helen to a gramophone record of an American pop song sung
as a sort of postscript to the other scarcely less remarkable goings-on.
Killing a work of art stone dead and trampling on the corpse in the name
of breathing fresh life into it is no fit occupation for any one.

ACKNOWLEDGMENTS

Thanks are due to all those who, holding the copyright to pieces reprinted or translated in this book, generously gave their permission to have them reproduced; their names will be easily inferred from the list of contents. Thanks are also due to the Cambridge University Library and the Ambrosian Library of Milan for their co-operation.

Both the general editor of the series and the editor of this particular volume have had a stab at translating the Italian, French, and German chapters, but have often been in doubt as to how far the originals should be adapted to a neutral English style, and how far the national, and at times historical, idiosyncracies of the authors represented should be allowed to retain their own distinctive flavour. Our perplexities would have been much graver still if we had not been able to call on expert advice: in some cases the persons named have written a whole first draft, in others they have tied up loose ends. Our thanks then to Miss Naomi Candlin and Dr. Lucia Travaina (Italian); to Michael Armstrong, Oliver Paulin and Prof. Roger Paulin (German); and to Edward Reed, James Mann, Miss Jenny Mander and Mlle. Pauline Marchand (French). I am uncomfortably aware of having made unreasonable demands on the services of some of those named, and am made more uncomfortable still by a powerful feeling that my demands should have been pressed to lengths more unreasonable still if errors, stemming from a deficient knowledge of the relevant languages, were to have been completely eliminated. I am especially grateful to Dr. R. B. Harrison for the salvaging operation he undertook as he went through the disaster area constituted by my efforts to translate the excerpts from Hölderlin contained in the sections reprinted from his book.

R. D. Dawe

Antonio Riccoboni, "Letter Describing the Performance of *Oedipus Rex* at Vicenza in 1585" is reprinted in translation by permission of the Biblioteca Ambrosiana, Milan.

P. Vidal-Naquet, "Oedipus at Vicenza and Paris: Two Stages in a Saga," first appeared as "Oedipe à Vicence et à Paris: deux moments d'une histoire," *Quaderni di storia* 14 (1981) 3–21.

Pierre Corneille, "Preface to Oedipus" was published as *Preface à Oedipe* (Paris 1659).

F. M. A. de Voltaire, "Letters on Oedipus, Letter III: Containing the Critique of the *Oedipus* of Sophocles," was published as *Lettre III contenant la critique de l'Oedipe de Sophocle*, Paris 1719.

Pierre Brumoy, "Remarks upon Oedipus," is from *The Greek Theatre of Father Brumoy*, translated by Mrs. Charlotte Lennox (London 1759) 68–78; from *Réflexions sur l'Oedipe* (ed. 1 1730. ed. 2 1749) 362–382.

Suzanne Saïd and Christian Biet, "What Lies behind the Notes: The Translations of the *Antigone* of Sophocles in the 18th Century," was first published as "L'enjeu des notes: Les traductions de l'Antigone de Sophocle au XVIIIᵉ siecle," *Poétique* 58 (1984) 155–169.

Thomas Maurice, "Preface: The *Oedipus Tyrannus* of Sophocles," is from *Poems and Miscellaneous Pieces with a Free Translation of the Oedipus Tyrannus of Sophocles by the Rev. Thomas Maurice A.B. of University College, Oxford* (London 1779) 149–152.

R. Potter, "Preface: *The Tragedies of Sophocles*; *Oedipus, King of Thebes*," from *The Tragedies of Sophocles translated* (London 1788) i–iv, v–viii.

Gotthold Ephraim Lessing, "From *Laokoon*" is from *Laokoon*, Berlin 1766, ed. 2 1788, ed. 3 1805, translated by Sir Robert Phillimore, (London 1874) 38–47.

Johann Gottfried von Herder, "From *Kritische Wälder: Erstes Wäldchen*" sections 2 and 5 (Riga 1769) 15–73.

Wolfgang Schadewaldt, "Hölderlin's Translations," is from "Hölderlins Übersetzung des Sophokles," *Sophokles Tragödien,* deutsch von F. Hölderlin, herausgestellt und eingeleitet von W. Schadewaldt (Frankfurt am Main 1957), reprinted in *Hellas und Hesperien* (Zürich and Stuttgart 1960; ed. 2 1970) 278–287. Reprinted by permission of Artemis & Winkler Verlag.

R. B. Harrison, "Sophocles and Hölderlin," is excerpted from Chapter V of *Hölderlin and Greek Literature* (Oxford 1975) 160–61, 166–92, 197–219. © Oxford University Press 1975. Reprinted by permission of Oxford University Press.

Florian Prader, *"The Bride of Messina,"* was published as "Die Braut von Messina," chapter V of *Schiller und Sophokles* (Zürcher Beiträge zur Deutschen Literatur und Geistesgeschichte 1954) 56–58, 79–81, 85–91, 94–96.

August Wilhelm von Schlegel, "Life and Political Character of Sophocles—Character of his Different Tragedies" is Lecture VII of *Über dramatische Kunst und Litteratur* (Heidelberg 1809–1811; ed. 2 1817) translated by John Black (London 1815, revised ed. 1846) 96–110.

Excerpt from *The Conversations of Goethe with Eckermann and Soret,* translated from the German by John Oxenford, London 1850 (1827) 365–74, 381–83.

Connop Thirlwall: "On the Irony of Sophocles," from *Philological Museum* II (Cambridge 1833) 483–538.

John Keble, "Lecture XXVIII," the English translation by E.K. Francis (Oxford 1912) 200–23, of *Praelectiones Academicae Oxonii habitae annis 1832–1841* (Oxford 1844).

Sigmund Freud, "The Oedipus Complex," from *Introductory Lectures on Psycho-Analysis,"* translated by J. Rivière (London 1922) 277–84.

Käte Hamburger, "Chapter 10 of *From Sophocles to Sartre,"* a translation by Helen Sebba (New York 1969) 147–66, from *Griechische Dramenfiguren antik und modern* (Stuttgart 1962) 189–212.

Démetrios N. Pantelodimos, "The Descendants of Labdacus in the Theatrical Works of Jean Cocteau," was published as "Les Labdacides dans le Théâtre de Jean Cocteau," *Festschrift für Konstantinos J. Merentitis* (Athens 1972) 331–343.

Wolfgang Schadewaldt, "Ancient Tragedy on the Modern Stage," was published as "Antike Tragödie auf der modernen Bühne," *Sitzungsberichte der Heidelberger Akademie der Wissenschaften* 1955–6, 622–50.

Letter Describing the Performance of
Oedipus Rex at Vicenza in 1585

Antonio Riccoboni

Most distinguished Mr. Mayor,

    I left your Excellency so soon that I was not able to give you my opinion regarding the tragedy performed there, as you seemed to want me to. I now say to you that those men of the Academy did most wisely in dignifying that magnificent theatre of theirs with a tragedy of Sophocles so highly esteemed by Aristotle, and with that tragedy which above all the others has been most praised. And it was very appropriate that that great poet, who, as Aristotle testifies, instituted the ornamentation of the stage, should be honoured with the magnificence of such a theatre. And so beautiful a theatre, truly royal, which fully proclaims the generosity of the gentlemen of Vicenza, worthy work of their compatriot, the famous Palladio, chief of modern architects, exactly merited being glorified by *Oedipus Tyrannus* of Sophocles; the tragedy which Aristotle himself shows to be beautiful for its *peripeteia* and recognition. He quotes the *peripeteia* of Oedipus as the finest in that place: "ut in *Oedipode*, cum venisset nuntius tanquam letitiam allaturus Oedipodi eumque metu liberaturus adversus matrem, ut aperuit quisnam esset, contrarium fecit (As in *Oedipus*, when the messenger came as if to bring Oedipus happiness and release him from the fear he had *vis-à-vis* his mother, on revealing who he was did the opposite.)." And of the recognition, he writes thus: "Ac pulcherrima agnitio est, cum simul peripetiae fiunt, ut se habet in *Oedipode* (And the finest recognition is when reversals happen at the same time, as is the case in *Oedipus*.)." And elsewhere "omnium autem optima agnitio est, quae ex ipsis rebus est, facta consternatione per verisimilia, ut in Sophoclis *Oedipode* (But the best recognition of all is the one which arises from the actual events, astonishment coming through things that are likely, as in Sophocles' *Oedipus.*)." One adds to the beauty of a tragedy so constructed that, what is terrible and pitiful being characteristic of the tragic poem and being capable of finding expression in two ways, the one less fine by means of the theatrical resources, the other better with the construction of the story, *Oedipus* expresses it in the better way, Aristotle writing as follows: "Ac licet quidem terribile et miserabile ex apparatu fieri, licet vero etiam ex ipsa constitutione, id quod prius est et poetae melioris, oportet enim etiam sine apparatu fabulam sic constitutam esse, ut audiens res quae fiunt et horreat et misereatur ex ijs quae contingunt, in quas perturbationes cadet ille qui *Oedipodis* fabulam audiat (What is terrible and pitiful may arise from the theatrical resources, but may arise also from the actual construction of the story, which is preferable and the mark of the better poet; for the story should be so constituted, even without theatrical resources, that the person who hears of what happens feels horror and pity at those events—that agitation of mind that anyone falls into who hears the story of *Oedipus.*)." Nor will I omit to say that, there being four degrees of the tragic situation: "cum scientes faciunt, cum ignorantes faciunt, cum ignorantes inibi sunt, ut faciant, sed non faciunt, cum scientes non faciunt (When people act with knowledge; when they act in ignorance; when they are on the point of acting but do not act; when they, with knowledge, do not act.)." The second and third are approved by Aristotle as better, as those which render the tragedy beautiful; and this tragedy is an example of the second grade, of which one reads these words: "Ac licet agere ita ut ignorantes rem agant atrocem, postea vero amicitiam agnoscant, ut Sophoclis *Oedipus* (And the action may be such that people do a dreadful deed in ignorance, but later recognise that those dear to them are involved, as Sophocles' *Oedipus.*)." Also of relevance to the beauty of the same tragedy is its brevity, since just as tragedy is preferred to epic in this respect, as having a shorter construction, so also this tragedy deserves to be praised because, although in the translation made from Greek into Vulgar Latin it has been necessarily lengthened somewhat and it has been very solemnly recited, it has still not reached a length of four hours. "Finis imitationis" says Aristotle, "est in minore longitudine. Nam strictius est iucundius quam id quod multi temporis mixtionem habet. Dico autem, quemadmodum si quis componeret *Oedipodem* Sophoclis in quot versibus *Ilias* est (The aim of the representation is achieved in a shorter length, for what is tightly organised gives more pleasure than that which involves a long period: I mean, as if one were to compose Sophocles' *Oedipus* in as many verses as the *Iliad.*)."

But what need is there to prove at length what is very well known: that this is one of the most beautiful tragedies that have ever been written? I do it, my most distinguished gentleman, not only to praise the judgement of the gentlemen of the Academy of Vicenza who chose such a beautiful tragedy, but also to come to this dilemma: that either Aristotle was a fool to praise something that did not deserve great praise, or if in Vicenza it did not have the success you were expecting, that did not happen because it was not excellent or through some deficiency of the subject, as it seems that some have spread abroad and as Signor Giovanni Dolfino assured me, but for some other reason. Let us therefore consider a little the criticisms which are made both of the poem and its representation, and let us see of what moment they are, so that your Excellency and I may decide, if there was little success (which I do not say but others do) on whom the blame must be laid; and let all of this be between ourselves, as I would not like what I do as a favour to you to be misinterpreted. Only when they print all this matter, as has been said to me, will you be able, if you so decide, to warn some of those gentlemen of the Academy, so that they can divest themselves of some of the blame that could be laid on them, pleading impossibility, or something else, and so that it does not seem that they have not seen certain things. And it will be at the discretion of your Excellency either to suppress all these comments of mine or to allow some of them to be known without naming me; for I want to contribute to the increase rather than the diminution of the honour of that honoured Academy. And perhaps (to give my opinion too in this matter) if these comments are worth it, it would be better to let the thing pass in silence without a lot of printing, since printing it gives to the world all the more reason for speaking. *Sed ipsi viderint* (but let them see it themselves) since no other motive makes me speak other than sheer zeal for their honour.

Now there are four principal criticisms of the tragedy: one is born rather from a contradiction there seems to be in Aristotle regarding the tragic *persona*, than from any deficiency of Sophocles; the second is made and examined by Aristotle; the third has been made by the excellent doctor, Signor Mercuriale; the fourth by some others.

First, then, one doubts whether the person of Oedipus is suited to tragedy. It is well known that Aristotle teaches that the material of poetry being either of people better or worse or similar to us and of average circumstance, tragedy is distinguished from comedy because the former represents the better, the latter, the worse, and that in this respect Sophocles is the same artist as Homer, since both represent the good; and elsewhere that tragedy being the representation of the better, tragic poets must imitate the good painters who, painting the pictures of certain people, paint them in the best way, and *pulchriores fingunt* (portray them as finer), and in another place, that Sophocles represented people *quales esse oportebat* (as they ought to be), having regard for morality's foundation, but Euripides *quales erant* (as they were). Thus one infers that Oedipus should be among the number of the better people. Nevertheless it seems that he is among the average people and of average goodness and badness and similar to the common condition of men, given that Aristotle, where he speaks of the constitution of tragedy as being beautiful, as if forgetful of himself, writes that neither the very good nor the very wicked are suited to the business of tragedy, which is terrible and pitiful, but the average and those of average goodness and badness, giving rise to just that terror and pity for people similar to us to whom those misfortunes happen which can happen to ourselves. He adds that Oedipus was of these average people; and speaking of the morals of the tragic hero, he looks for not only good, appropriate and fair morals but also those similar to the common morals of men. To this truly great contradiction, than which there is perhaps none greater in the whole of the *Poetics* of Aristotle, Ludovic Castelvetro replies that Aristotle using the words μιμεῖσθαι βούλεται (wishes to represent) is right that tragedy wants to represent the better, but does not do so always, indeed very often represents those similar to us or men of the present age; to which response, taking it to be more ingenious than true, I would say that tragic characters must be better as regards mind and intention, as indeed were Oedipus and Jocasta, but as regards misfortune and disaster, which determine the terrible and the pitiful, they must be similar to us; that is, as Aristotle says: "qui neque virtute praestant et iustitia (who are not pre-eminent for virtue or justice)" for the shocking act which they fall into "neque vitio praestant et iniustitia (nor are they pre-eminent for wickedness or injustice)" because they do not act by choice but by error. And thus Oedipus, as regards his mind, was one of the better sort, but as regards the deed committed in error, he was one of those similar to us.

But I come to the second criticism; Aristotle writes in this way: "At sine ratione in rebus nihil esse oportet, sin minus, id extra tragediam sit, ut quae sunt in *Oedipode Sophoclis* (But there must be nothing irrational in the plot; failing that, it must be outside the tragedy, like the things in Sophocles' *Oedipus*.)." He seems to be excusing that which is unreasonable in Sophocles' *Oedipus*, because it is outside the tragedy, that is outside the day of the tragic action and happened before that day. Castelvetro thinks that Sophocles is excused for having made Oedipus ignorant of how Laios, the king of Thebes, was killed, and for having made him so negligent that he did not try to find out who Laios was and how he died; Castelvetro is mistaken, given that Oedipus knew that

Laios had been king of Thebes before him, as is apparent from the prologue in the following way:

"CRE. Fuit nobis, o rex, Laius olim dux terrae huius, priusquam tu hanc gubernares urbem.
OED. Novi audiens, non enim audivi unquam."
("CREON. Laius, your Majesty, was formerly the ruler of our land, before you took over the city's government.
OEDIPUS. I know: so I heard—for I never saw[1] him.")

What is more, he knew how he had died, as we read in the first episode:

"CHO. Occisus esse dictus est a quibusdam viatoribus.
OED. Audivi et ego, sed qui viderit, nemo videt."
("CHORUS. He was said to have been killed by some travellers.
OEDIPUS. I heard that too, but no one sees anyone who saw it.")

What then does Aristotle mean? He means, in my opinion, what is read in the second episode: that Oedipus was ignorant not of who Laios was and how he died, of which things he was truly not ignorant, but where and when and with how many companions, that is, that he was killed "in triplici via terrae Phocidis (on a branching (triple) road in the land of Phocis)" and at precisely the time that he in such a place had killed one person with as many companions as Jocasta said had been killed with Laios; from which he became fearful that he himself could have been Laios's killer. And indeed it was likely that before that day of the tragedy he had spoken to Jocasta about such things, and could have made the same conjecture as he made ultimately, and begun to recognise the truth. This truly strange situation Aristotle admits to be unreasonable. Nevertheless he excuses it by saying that it is outside the tragic action and happened before the day of the tragedy. In the exodus, after the news that Jocasta has hanged herself and Oedipus has gouged out his eyes, the way in which Oedipus appears on stage, blinded and with the blood from his eyes still on his face, and remains on the stage for a long time lamenting up to the end of the tragedy, this, says the most excellent Mercuriale, is almost impossible, and without doubt it is hardly likely that someone should have gouged out his eyes without being in such tor-

---

[1] The Latin text printed above is in error: *audivi* should have been *vidi*, and this is what we translate. The mistake has a curious parallel in the Greek manuscripts in the next citation, where the true text should be 'no one saw the one who *did* it.'

ment that he cannot walk and talk at such length, the pain of those whose
eyes have been gouged out being acute and horrific. I would reply:
however much this passes the limits of possibility and probability
according to the doctors, nevertheless it is possible and probable in the
opinion of the crowd, to whom the poet is directing himself, who do not
see so easily into the reasons for things. Moreover, Oedipus, judging
himself deserving of every ill, can bear it more easily, and admitting that
he suffers justly that which he suffers and unburdening himself with
words makes himself more capable of suffering, this criticism too I
object to.

Others say that these ancient matters of oracles, of monsters like
the Sphinx and similar happenings far from what we are used to happening in our times, are not suited to meet success with us and that this tragedy, containing such things, is not to be wondered at if it was not as
pleasing as expected. I think that these people are mistaken, because
although these things are old, they are not for that reason so beyond popular belief as not to be credible, and although they no longer relate to
our times, nevertheless that solution of Aristotle's holds good. "Qualia
erant, non qualia sunt (the kind that were, not the kind that are.)."

For this reason, my most excellent sir, it seems to me that everything else can be borne except this; that such a tragedy, so famous and
celebrated by the writings of the most famous men—that such a man
Aristotle was no-one will deny—did not have much success because of
some imperfection it had, it being utterly perfect both for the eight characteristics of the plot which is complete, of the right length, unified,
possible, not episodic, admirable, well constructed, full of passion, and
for the excellently expressed morals, according to the testimony of
Aristotle, good, appropriate, similar, equal, and for the meaning—or
shall we say discourse—which with logic, rhetoric and emotions can give
every satisfaction. As for the language, in the style in which it is written,
one cannot desire better; no wonder, Sophocles being called for the
beauty of his language "Apis attica (The Athenian bee)." And in the
translation made from Greek into the vulgar tongue, although I have not
yet seen it written but only heard it, still it seems to me to have been
reasonably well treated, contrary to murmured criticisms. Only one thing
seemed strange to me, not because of the gentleman who translated it but
of the majority of those who recited it, the fact that it seemed to have
been rendered not in verse but in prose: they broke up the verses so
much without giving them any cadence. This means of reciting goes
against the nature of poetry which uses verse as its proper instrument for
the natural representation of speaking. For it is not likely that in prose
people would speak to one another so loudly that they can be heard by

an audience, unless by chance they are mad or deaf; but so well in verse that it is nearly singing, and therefore finds the vocal level suited to the audience's understanding. And however much iambic verse has been accepted in Greek and Latin tragedies and comedies for being near to prose, and so in the vulgar tongue, blank verse without rhyme, nevertheless it must seem like verse, so that, as I have said, the speaking is realistic. This was very badly observed in the recitation of the said tragedy.

And these are the essential parts of what makes tragedy: namely, the story, the morals, the speech, the elocution, and they belong to poetry and are indispensable. Therefore, if song is called by Aristotle "maximum condimentum (the main seasoning)" and it is said that the spectacle "allicit animos (charms the mind)," nevertheless they are called parts without art and not integral to poetry, belonging to other arts, and are said to be consequences of poetry rather than integral and necessary in it. Of the theatrical resources one reads thus "et apparatus allicit quidem animos, sed maxime est artis expers et minime proprius poeticae. Nam tragediae vis et sine certamine et histrionibus est. Praeterea vero potentior est circa fabricam apparatuum ars illius qui scenam conficit quam ars poetarum (Spectacle certainly charms the mind, but has absolutely no share in the art, and has nothing to do with poetry. For the effect of a tragedy exists even without performance and actors. Moreover the art of the person who makes the scenery has more influence than the art of poets when it comes to the creation of things for theatrical display.)." Of the song and spectacle together, the following: "Iam vero haec oportet servare et ad haec ea quae sub sensum cadunt consequentia poeticae praeter illa quae sunt ex necessitate; etenim secundum ea sepenumero contingit peccare. Dictum autem est satis de ipsis in editis libris (But now we must observe this carefully, and in addition the things which impinge on the audience's perceptions that follow from the poetic art as well as those which are unavoidable. For by those rules it frequently happens that people commit offences. However enough has been said on precisely that in my published books.)."[2]

The gentlemen of the Academy have then been greatly helped in the matter of these two parts, and at their great expense, both by the work of the excellent architect Palladio, who made the theatre truly worthy of praise and admiration, and also by the famous musicians; and in this they certainly merit the greatest praise, having done what a king could scarcely have done and having shown a most generous spirit. But

---

[2] The translation given is open to question. So too is the Latin itself, but the Greek text it purports to render is itself suspect.

perhaps some things have been misunderstood, which I shall discuss briefly. And first I will offer for consideration the parts of the whole enumerated by Aristotle: prologue, episode, exodus, choral part, which is either parodos or stasimon, in which is considered also the commos; these parts are ordered thus: prologue, parodos, first episode, first stasimon, second episode, second stasimon, third episode, third stasimon, exodus. Now since the theatrical resources contain all these things and embrace all those that are put before our eyes: scene, people, clothes, I will put forward some reservations one by one.

In the first part of the prologue, then, the stage had two altars, one on either side, with several priests accompanied by a good number of young boys, all of them crowned with branches; suppliants, they were seated round those altars, which were called the altars of Oedipus. I doubt much of this. For what purpose did those altars serve where they were sitting? Why were they sitting round the altars and were not instead on their feet or kneeling on the ground to sacrifice or pray? The king appears and does not name altars but only "ἕδρας" which means thresholds or steps, and says below: "ὑμεῖς μὲν βάθρων ἵστασθε (You, stand up from the plinth)"; only the priest, having left another multitude crowned in the squares and in the twin churches of Minerva and in the prophetic ash of Ismenos, and having come with his company to wait for the king, says "ὁρᾷς μὲν ἡμᾶς ἡλίκοι προσήμεθα βωμοῖσι τοῖς σοῖς (You see the ages of those of us who sit at your 'βωμοί.')." I suspect that the word βωμός has not been understood, which, though it sometimes means the altar—from which possibly the error arose—is also the same as ἕδρα and βάθρος [sic] and means τὴν βάσιν (the plinth), very close to Homer, in whom Sophocles was very well versed, as is apparent from his many imitations; the evidence of Ammonius points in the same direction, who in his book Περὶ ὁμοίων καὶ διαφόρων λέξεων (On similar and differing expressions) writes thus: παρὰ δ᾽ Ὅμηρον [leg. Ὁμήρωι] ὁ βωμὸς καὶ τὴν βάσιν σημαίνει· χρύσειοι δ᾽ ἄρα κοῦροι ἐυδμήτων ἐπὶ βωμῶν· ἀντὶ [leg. ἀντὶ τοῦ] ἐπὶ βάσεων (In Homer βωμὸς also means "plinth," "golden youths on well-made βωμοί," for "plinths.").

The king appeared and, as in the third episode, the queen, most regally dressed in gold clothing. It seemed strange to me that in such calamitous time of pestilence they should dress so grandly, since even among royal clothes there is some differentiation, some being more bright and others less so and their being obliged to wear the less bright ones in calamitous times. And if some say that this is a convenient way of giving greater hope to people of better times, it seems to me that hope should be given by other means than clothes, and that in a time of such misery and calamity one ought not have gone to the extreme of such solemn pomp, but should have to a certain extent renounced such pomp, so that the people should not say: "the king and queen celebrate while we remain in continual misery."

But let us grant them this pompous mode of dress, corresponding more perhaps to the magnificence of the gentlemen of the Academy than to a time of disaster. The second part of the tragedy is the parodos, which is defined by Aristotle in the following way: "Chorici autem parodus prima dictio integri chori, stasimum vero cantus chori sine anapesto et trocheo (Of the choral element, a parodos is the first utterance of the whole chorus, a stasimon a choral song without anapaests or trochaics)"; these feet were suitable for dance. From this it is understood that the parodos had dancing but the stasimon did not. Here one must note that, there being three instruments of imitation: the tempo of the dance, the harmony of the music and singing, and the speaking, Sophocles instituted three types of actors in the chorus, as Aristotle writes in the *Poetics* and Diogenes Laertius in the *Life of Plato*, so that some played, others sang and certain others danced. These three sorts of actors were used principally in the parodos which had movement for its appearance on stage, the other choruses being stasima and stationary without any movement and with only singing and music. Nevertheless the parodos in this tragedy was represented with only one type of actor, who only sang: thus Sophocles was denied dance and music. Further, in ancient times the chorus sang and made music in such a way that what it sang was understood, whereas that chorus only made heard the harmony of the voices alone without the words being understood. It greatly prejudices the tragedy, not understanding what the chorus says. I will not omit to say that in Greek one reads "χορὸς ἐκ Θηβαίων γερόντων (Chorus of Theban old men)," nevertheless in this there were the figures of little children and young women.

One has the impression that the first episode joins on to the parodos with Oedipus saying "αἰτεῖς· ἃ δ' αἰτεῖς (You ask, and as for what you ask . . .)" and what follows, that is, as it is read in the commentary on the performances of Sophocles published by Ioachinus Camerarius "Audio praeces tuas, quod si quae dicam exequi voles, ego quidem qui nunc primum hoc factum narrari audio, inveniam ad salutem viam (I hear your prayers: if you will carry out my instructions, I, who now for the first time hear the tale of this deed, will find a path to safety)." As if Oedipus were on stage while the chorus sang and once the chorus finished, in line with what had been sung, began to speak with one member of the chorus. But I do not wish to argue about this. I will just say that that member of the chorus with whom he spoke seemed very strange in putting himself at a distance most affectedly from the crowd of the chorus and putting himself on a level with the king, in such a way as to represent a particular interlocutor and not a member of the populace who would intervene in the action, being able to stand fittingly in his rank and position himself, so that when the opportunity came of speaking he could do so as an ordinary person without separating himself from the others. Further, I am not certain that it was a single member of the chorus and not more, of whom very likely now one, now another, spoke. Here one must observe what Aristotle writes: that, the chorus being either not part of the whole when it begins to sing, or part of the whole when it is made part of the action, Sophocles deals with this better than Euripides, in as much as Euripides has the chorus speaking what any other person could easily say, but Sophocles only what is appropriate for it, portraying a people and making it part of the action.

In the same episode Tiresias appeared, differently dressed from what Julius Pollux writes, namely: "τὸ ἄγρηνον ἦν πλέγμα ἐξ ἐρίων δικτυῶδες περὶ πᾶν τὸ σῶμα, ὃ Τειρεσίας ἐπεβάλλετο, ἤ τι ἄλλο μαντικόν (The robe was woven out of wool, net-like, covering the whole body, which Teiresias put on, or something else associated with sooth-sayers.)." The first stasimon did not seem stationary because the chorus, after positioning themselves in the form of a moon, and with the song finished, so as to give space to the interlocutors spaced themselves out in a quite ugly fashion, and then came together past that person who separated himself from the others, as I said above. In this way it was not truly stationary; and one can say the same of the second and third stasimon; and there was only singing and no music, and a constantly uniform singing which did not let the words be understood, and which resembled brothers or priests singing the lamentations of Jeremiah.

In the second episode appeared among others Jocasta, who should have been very old, having been first wife of Laios, with whom, as Diodorus writes in his fifth book "cum diutius caruisset liberis, tandem peperit eum qui Oedipus dictus est (After being without children for a long time, finally gave birth to the one called Oedipus)," and then of Oedipus with whom she gave birth to Polynices, Eteocles, Antigone and Ismene; and Oedipus being already old when he was led into exile by Antigone after having blinded himself—this points very much to the old age of his mother Jocasta. In spite of this, this Jocasta seemed a young girl, quite a pretty young thing, whose face could have been made pale in some way and grey hairs put on her head.

I will not forgo making a little digression on the matter of this second episode, regarding which, when Aristotle cites a place in the third Book of the *Rhetoric*, Vittorio thinks that Aristotle commits an error of memory, and I think, with Maggioragio, that he can be defended. The words of Aristotle are these: "In logis (he understands dramatic poems with action like tragedies and comedies) et epicis est specimen orationis, ut provideant qua de re sit oratio et non suspensa sententia sit, quod enim indefinitum est, cogit vagari, qui igitur dat principium tanquam in manum facit ut haerens sequatur orationem: Ob id "iram, dic dea"; "Dic mihi, musa, virum"; "Praecipe mihi sermonem alium ut ex Asia venit in Europam bellum magnum"; et tragici indicant in dramate, quamvis non statim ut Euripides, sed in prologo tamen indicant, ut et Sophocles: "Mihi pater fuit Polybus"; et comedia similiter (There is a kind of speech which lets people look ahead to the subject matter of what will be spoken about, and its purpose will not be left hanging in the air; for what is undefined forces people to drift about, so that the person who puts the beginning of the story into the hands of the reader, as it were, makes it possible for him to follow what is said without losing touch. For that reason we get "Tell me, goddess, of the anger . . ."; "Tell me, Muse, of the man . . ."; "Teach me a different tale, how a great war came from Asia to Europe." And the tragic poets give indications in their plays, if not at once, like Euripides, then in their prologues, as Sophocles: "my father was Polybos;" and similarly with comedy.)." Aristotle gives the name prologue to the exposition of the subject, wherever the opportunity comes of making it, even if it is made most of the time in the first act, which for this reason is called the prologue. But it is not prohibited for it to be made also in the other acts if the opportunity arises, as Sophocles did in the second episode of this tragedy, and as proems, which are similar to the prologues, are made not only at the beginning, where they have their proper place, but also sometimes in the middle of the piece, since a given part of the piece, on a particular subject, coming in the middle, may have its own proem. There is a difference, therefore, between epic and dramatic prologues: the former are always made immediately in the beginning, but the latter not *statim* (at once), that is in the first act most of the time but sometimes also in the others. In this way it seems to me that Aristotle can be defended. Nevertheless Vittorio writes as follows, quite modestly as is his usual way: "id mihi scrupulum non parum affert, quod explicatio haec generis fortunarumque Oedipodis extra prologum a Sophocle inducitur, in tertio enim actu tragediae posita est, quare vereor ne μνημονικὸν ἀμάρτημα sit (I am considerably worried by the fact that this exposition of Oedipus's birth and fortunes is introduced by Sophocles outside the prologue, for it is placed in the third Act of the tragedy. So I am afraid that it is an error of memory.)."[3]

---

[3] The line 'my father was 'Polybos' occurs as v. 774 of *Oedipus Rex*, i.e. half-

But let us return to the point. In the third episode came two shepherds: one of Polybos, king of Corinth, the other of Laios, king of Thebes, who were dressed much below the condition of royal shepherds. The first had been sent also as ambassador of Corinth, the other had been held in service to the Theban king as a loyal person; so it seemed to me they should have been better dressed. In the exodus appeared two young boys who represented Antigone and Ismene, both very small; so that the continuing tragedy entitled *Oedipus at Colonus* would have had little sense if Antigone, if she had been so small, could have conducted her old father from Thebes to Athens. The tragedy seemed less terrible and pitiful for having been recited with little passion, where the commos was not seen in the people of the chorus and the stage, but with certain muted gestures that did not stir one greatly. The commos, a most important part of tragedy, is thus defined by Aristotle: "Commus est lamentatio communis chori et a scena (The commos is a general lament by the chorus, and from the stage.)."

But I have perhaps written too much, and pray your Excellency to excuse and attribute all this to the desire that I have to do something that pleases you. In this, if with these long comments of mine I cause you too much annoyance (they would be even longer if I were not writing to a most intelligent person like you and to whom it suffices merely to touch on things), at least my intention must be accepted as good, as I pray you to do, and kissing your hand I recommend myself to you in gratitude.

From Padua the first day of Lent, 1585

Your Excellency's most devoted servant,

Antonio Riccoboni

---

way through the play. The quotation from Aristotle is from *Rhetoric* 1415a.

Oedipus at Vicenza and Paris:
Two Stages in a Saga

Pierre Vidal-Naquet

In the never-ending saga of Oedipus, the *Oedipus* of Sophocles, though Oedipus has largely outgrown him, I have chosen to give prominence to two critical moments.[1] Strictly speaking, that word is a fitting tag only for the first subject of my reflections, namely the performance on Sunday 3 March 1585, which inaugurated the Teatro Olimpico at Vicenza. On that day Orsatto Giustiniani's translation of Sophocles' *Oedipus Tyrannus* was performed. The theatre itself had been built through the good offices of the Accademia Olimpica of Vicenza, from the plans of one member of the Academy, Andrea Palladio.

The second "moment," on the other hand, extends throughout a whole century and even beyond. It has its beginnings in the first French translation of Sophocles' work by André Dacier in 1692 and can be traced through a whole range of translations and adaptations, of which only Voltaire's in 1718 is well-known, up to an end which can be set for the sake of argument at the posthumous publication of *Oedipe-Roi* (1818) by Marie-Joseph Chénier, who had died in 1811.

But, leaving aside for the time being the arbitrary nature of such a choice, why make these two moments the subject of study? What light

---

[1] This article, give or take a few details, reproduces the one I presented at Bologna, at the Palazzo Montanari, on 17 May 1980, at a colloquium on the *Oedipus Rex* arranged by the ATER (Association théatrale d'Emilia-Romagna) of Modena. I warmly thank the organizers for their invitation, and the participants for their observations. I have since then had the opportunity to present these observations at Namur, at the Congress of the Federation of Teachers of Greek and Latin, in February 1981.

could this study possibly shed on Sophocles' *Oedipus Rex*, performed at Athens around 420 B.C.?

I part company here with the almost innumerable scholars who judge themselves capable of being in direct contact with that moment of Athens' history: I cannot but admire their confidence. Two sorts of justification remain for the work of which I here present a sketch.

For one important group of philologists and sociologists, like Jean Bollack and his friends, the work of an historian is seen as a stripping-down enterprise: ancient grammarians and modern philologists have accumulated around the text a whole series of layers of interpretation and successive corrections which must be removed, much as one peels an onion, so that Sophocles' naked text can be reached. But what text are we talking about? No tape-recorder captured the performance in Athens, and the saga of the tradition—and with it the first "variants"—began as soon as scribes began copying out the manuscripts. The naked text is not that of Sophocles, but that of a scribe or a Byzantine editor, e.g. Manuel Moschopoulos. Even the very famous Laurentian MS., that paradigm of "transliteration" (the process by which the text is copied out in minuscule from a version written in uncial), allows us at the utmost to get at the fifth-century A.D. "codex" of which it is a copy. Beyond that one must postulate a "volumen" of the high imperial period, which is not the text of Sophocles, but the interpretation of a philologist of Hadrian's era. And, if we are assuming that the departures from Sophocles began as soon as the tragic text entered the school syllabus, joining the literary canon, in other words, a "classical" text, we must keep in mind that tragedy did not become "literature" only with the *interpretatio romana*, in the form of Seneca's *Oedipus*; that the three great tragedians had already been designated as such by Aristophanes in the *Frogs* (406); and that the texts became classical in the strict sense of the word from the day when, at Lycurgus' instigation, the Ecclesia decided to register the text of the tragedies of Aeschylus, Sophocles, and Euripides in the archives "with prohibition on modifying this text in performance."[2] That is surely a crucial date in the transformation of Greek civilization into a civilization of the written word,[3] but it is one century later than the majority of the works.

In any event, were we to have in our possession Sophocles' own manuscript and a film of the first performance, our problem would only be transferred. To set the principle of a unique, archetypal "meaning" which we would only have to wrest free from the ruins of successive

---

[2] Plutarch, *Lycurgus*, 15.

[3] The works of E. Havelock draw our attention to this transformation.

interpretations would, I fear, not be to return to historical fact, but to blinding intuition, whose impossibility I have postulated. There is no one who has not yearned to recover the spirit of the fifth century, but this cannot be done except through the medium of successive interpretations of which even our own form part from the very moment of their formulation.

Approaching the problem from another angle, there is of course among the interpretations of Sophocles' work which have marked our era that of Freud.[4] Some years ago Jean-Pierre Vernant aimed a crushing refutation against that interpretation.[5] But in truth the force of the refutation stemmed in part from the weakness of the pleading. Didier Anzieu had been rash enough to try to prove[6] that Oedipus' own adventures could be explained by the "Oedipus Complex." Each of Oedipus' errors, according to this interpretation, is a symptomatic act "which reveals that he is unconsciously obeying his desire for incest and parricide."[7] Vernant had no trouble replying to this with one of his ten arguments that, in the tragic Oedipus' emotional life, the character who matters is not Oedipus' true mother, Jocasta, but his adoptive mother, Merope, and that Sophocles took great care not to make the slightest allusion to any degree of sensuality in the relationship between Oedipus and Jocasta. But not all those who narrated the myth took such precautions, and moreover the Freudians had already preempted both Vernant and Anzieu, whose undertaking was quite useless from the Freudian standpoint. How could Oedipus have an "Oedipus Complex" since he is Oedipus? To quote Jean Starobinski: "Oedipus therefore does not have a subconscious since he is our subconscious, by which I mean, one of the major roles which our desire has assumed. He himself does not need depth since he is our depth. Whatever the mystery of his story, its meaning is clear and without gaps. Nothing is concealed: there is no need to plumb Oedipus' motives and driving forces. It would be ridiculous to attribute a psychology to him: he is already the instance of a psyche. Far from being the possible object of a psychological study, he becomes one of the functional elements around which a science of psychology sets out to build

---

[4] At the colloquium in Bologna, it was Sergio Molinari who discussed Freud and the *Oedipus Rex*; see his book *Notazioni sulla Scienza dei Sogni in Freud*, Bologna 1979.

[5] *Oedipe sans complexe*, "Raison présente" 4 (1967) pp. 3–20, reprinted in J.-P. Vernant and P. Vidal-Naquet, *Mythe et tragédie en Grèce ancienne*, Paris 1979(4), pp. 77–98.

[6] D. Anzieu, *Oedipe avant le complexe ou de l'interprétation psychanalytique des mythes*, "Temps Modernes" 245 (October 1966), pp. 675–715.

[7] J.-P. Vernant, *Mythe et tragédie*, p. 91.

itself."[8]

But to what era do this *him* and *us* belong, which punctuate Starobinski's argument? For us, in the twentieth century, who have read Freud and possibly are patients of his followers, Oedipus is an archetype and an "instance of a psyche." But was he already that in 420 B.C.? Or did you have to step back from Sophocles' *Oedipus* to an earlier one, perhaps the Oedipus of the *Odyssey* (11.271ff.), who continues to reign after the revelation, or of the *Iliad* (23.679), who falls in the war? Or on the contrary do you have to go forward until Euripides' *Phoenissae* (410 B.C.), in which Jocasta survives and Oedipus, blinded, remains locked up in his castle while Eteocles and Polynices fight and then kill each other? Alternatively, do you have to go even further forward in time until the Oedipus of the *Story of Thebes* or the Judas of medieval legend who, just like him, kills his father and sleeps with his mother?[9]

Of course, Oedipus could also be that abstract king whose story can be summarized in a few lines. But this abstract, this being of reason, supposing he exists, can only be reached through tales which are so many texts. I would therefore like to present here two moments in the history and "workings" of a text.

Let us consider then at the outset what took place at the "Teatro Olimpico" on 3 March 1585 during the carnival period in Vicenza: the performance of *Edipo tiranno*. It is an event which we know fairly well, essentially thanks to records preserved at the Ambrosian Library in Milan and to the two works of Leo Schrade and Alberto Gallo, which have drawn on these documents and reconstructed the event.[10]

It really was an astonishing performance, worthy of the astonishing monument it inaugurated, an "ancient theatre" built between 1580 and 1585. Thanks to Filippo Pigafetta, the famous traveller born of a well-to-do family in Vicenza, who drafted the morning after an account of the proceedings addressed to an anonymous "Illustrissimo signore e padrone osservatissimo,"[11] we are pretty fully acquainted with the facts and we know that it was an immense success. The play lasted for three

---

[8] J. Starobinski, *Préface* to E. Jones, *Hamlet et Oedipe*, trans. A.M. Le Gall, Paris 1967, p. xix.

[9] L. Constans, *La Légende d'Oedipe*, Paris 1881, pp. 93–103.

[10] L. Schrade, *La Représentation d'Edipo Tiranno au Teatro Olimpico* (Vicence 1585), a study followed by a critical edition of the tragedy of Sophocles by Orsato Giustiniani and of the Chorus' music by Angelo Gabrielli, CNRS, Paris 1960; A. Gallo, *La prima Rappresentazione al teatro Olimpico con i progetti e le relazioni dei contemporanei*, preface by L. Puppi, Il Polifilo, Milan 1973 [hereafter *Représentation* and *Prima Rappresentazione*]. A second performance took place 5 March 1585.

[11] Text in *Prima Rappresentazione*, pp. 53–58; cf. *Représentation*, p. 47–51.

and a half hours, but the spectators began to arrive nine and a half hours before the beginning of the performance. Pigafetta concluded his account by saying: "It is the case that, after the ancient Greeks and Romans, the people of Vicenza have been able to realize a tragic poem sooner and better than every other nation. It has been such a success that they have become not only the first, but also the best." So it was a unique privilege for the people of Vicenza: they had revived ancient tragedy in its original setting, an ancient theatre, and were not only the "first" since Trissin's *Sofonisba* had been played half a century beforehand, but also, thanks to Palladio and to *Oedipus the King*, the best.

Prima facie an ancient historian is in his element when faced with this moment in the saga of the *O.T.* Everything happens *as if* it were an intensely political event, in the full sense of the word. In 1591 G. Marzari published in Venice his *Historia di Vicenza*. The work is divided into two sections: the first recounts the events in chronological order; the second is a list, a catalogue, of important men of the town. In this second part Palladio and others responsible for the event of which I speak have their place. The first book ends with the creation in 1555 of the "Accademia Olympica," which was to undertake the erection of the "superbissimo teatro" which is their country's glory, and which can vie "with every other theatre, both ancient and modern, built for the staging of plays." Better still—and here we find ourselves at the very heart of a patronage-centred culture on the Greco-Roman model, in the world described by Paul Veyne,[12] a scholar of the eighteenth century, Count Montenari, informs us, basing himself on the Vicenza archives, that the theatre was constructed "at the private expense of the Academicians and those who wished to obtain citizenship of the city."[13] Citizenship was granted in return for a *private* gift for a public monument . . . a sure sign that we are right in the middle of a Hellenistic period.

Orsatto Giustiniani's translation is pervaded by the same sense. The least that can be said is that it does not neglect—it sometimes even emphasizes—the civic dimension of Sophocles' text. Beginning with the title, whatever you may say, Sophocles' *Tyrannos* is not a "king" as our translations would have it. An element, indeed a majestic element, of the Italian texts is the lengthy dialogue which brings the opposing forces of royal hero and city face to face. Let us give some examples: in Tiresias's speech: φανήσεται Θηβαῖος (453), Oedipus "will reveal himself to be a

---

12 *Le Pain et le Cirque*, Paris 1976.

13 Comte G. Montenari, *Del Teatro Olimpico di Andrea Palladio*, Padua 1749(2), p. 3. Montenari relies on a supplication addressed "a Deputati al governo di essa Città" urging the grant of the "Cittadinanza" to twelve people, which was later done in 1581.

Theban," is translated as "esser di Thebe cittadin [be a Theban citizen]."
At the beginning of the messenger invocation, Ὦ γῆς μέγιστα τῆσδ' ἀεὶ
τιμώμενοι (1223), "you whom this land has always held in most
honour," becomes through a remarkable amplification

> O Principali Cittadini soli
> Ornamento e sostegno
> De la Città di Thebe;   (1288)

πᾶσι Καδμείοισι "to all the Cadmeans," becomes simply "a tutti i cittadini"; ἐκ χθονὸς (1290), "out of this land," is rendered by "fuor di
questa cittade." Finally the closing invocation of the chorus: Ὦ πάτρας
Θήβης ἔνοικοι (1523), "inhabitants of my homeland, Thebes," is
rendered by "O di questa mia patria incliti e degni Cittadini [famous and
worthy citizens of this my country]." Again, there is a difference to be
seen: it is indeed the citizens who are being addressed, but above all a
select group among them.

But was it really a question of citizens? Patrician, senator, and
politician, Orsatto Giustiniani was indeed one of the "Principali Cittadini," not of Vicenza however, but of Venice. Vicenza had been
annexed by Venice in 1404, and was now part of the "mainland," or
what the ancients would have termed the *chôra*; it is no more than a
ghost of a town, which has no place as an autonomous political factor in
the history of the sixteenth-century Italy.[14] In fact, the town historian,
Marzari, congratulates himself on the assistance given to the Accademia
Olimpica by practically all the nobility of Lombardy and the Marches of
Treviso,[15] a nobility having very little in common with the citizenry,
since it comes not only from the "Marches of Treviso," but from Lombardy itself.[16] The municipal authorities had indeed made available the
plot on which the theatre had been built, but they were nothing more
than a municipal council strictly governed by Venice. Moreover Pigafetta indicates that the military authorities were present, along with a few

---

[14] Thus, in A. Visconti's substantial *L'Italia nell'epoca della Controriforma
dal 1516 al 1713*, Milan 1958, I found two references to Vicenza, to the effect that Palladio had worked there (p. 128), and that there was a wool-producing industry there (p.
229).

[15] *La Historia di Vicenza*, Venice 1591, p. 160.

[16] The Cinquecento in Venice is a period which saw a distinct resurgence of
the aristocracy: cf. A. Ventura, *Nobiltà e popolo nella società veneta del '400 e '500*,
Bari 1964, pp. 275-374; on Vicenza, cf. p. 279-280 and 362-363; however, from the
indications given in this book we can deduce that the "cittadinanza" was still regarded
as a privilege. I thank my colleague A. Tenenti for having brought this book to my
attention.

(Venetian) senators, but without the mayor of the town, "The distinguished Captain was present with some senators, and the Mayor stayed away."[17]

We even have a very detailed piece of criticism of the performance of 3 March 1585, presented as a letter to the Podestà (mayor) of Vicenza, from Antonio Riccoboni,[18] but I must confess that the political dimension of this critique, if indeed it exists, escapes me totally.

For the governing stratum of Vicenza, this performance and the theatre itself are really a kind of projection of an ideal. The founder members of the "Olympic Academy," and notably Gian Giorgio Trissino, humanist and tragic author, are, so to speak, aristocrats who got Palladio, himself the son of a modest craftsman in Padua, to join them. Knowledge of the ancient world in Vicenza does not lead to political power but to something resembling a metaphor of political power. This is what allows, for example, Filippo Pigafetta to describe the principal member of the Academy as follows: "The principal of the Academy is the illustrious Count Lunardo Valmarana, who has the spirit of Caesar and was born for enterprises of great courage."[19] The rest of the text, however, tells us what were the "courageous enterprises" of Count Valmarana: to have welcomed into his palace at Vicenza the most serene Empress and to have granted the privilege of his gardens, compared quite naturally to the "gardens of Sallust" (*horti Sallustiani*) in ancient Rome, to strangers passing through his town.

The Olympic Theatre itself is a monument to the glory of Academicians who are depicted in ancient costume on the front of the stage, while the upper motifs were taken up by the Labours of Hercules. James Ackerman noted the point well: "The allegorical figures proposed in Palladio's drawings were transformed by vote of the Academicians in the spring of 1580 [immediately after the death of Palladio therefore] into heroic likenesses of themselves; just at the moment when Vicenza's noblemen had to abandon all hope of ever being heroes in fact."[20] The

---

17 *Prima Rappresentazione*, p. 56.

18 *Ibid.*, pp. 39–51; cf. A. Gallo, *ibid.*, pp. xxii and xxviii who mentions a document from the archives of the Academy: "Il podestà ripugna la rappresentazione," and believes that "this behaviour is difficult to understand," but also it represents a personal decision rather than a political stance.

19 *Ibid.*, p. 55.

20 Ackerman, *Palladio*, Harmondsworth 1977, p. 180; one could naturally find fault with this "just at the moment." I have consulted on the subject of Palladio and his theatre the following works: L. Magnato, *The Genesis of the Teatro Olimpico*, Journal of the Warburg and Courtauld Institutes XIV (1951), pp. 209–220; L. Puppi, *A. Palladio*, London 1975; R. Schiavo, *Guida al Teatro Olimpico*, Vicenza 1980; H. Spelmann, *Andrea Palladio und die Antike*, Munich and Berlin 1964; the essential documentation is to be found in the corpus of G. Zorzi, *Le Ville e i Teatri di A. Palladio*, Vicenza 1969.

theatre itself is described in the same account as "a sort of academic discourse in three dimensions, a learned reconstruction of the ancient Roman theatre based on a lifetime of study of monuments and texts."[21] The erudition of Palladio is very real, but his theatre is by no means a dissertation in three dimensions.

Leaving aside the difficult debate over what can be ascribed respectively to Palladio, who drafted the plan, and to V. Scamozzi, who executed it, L. Magagnoto appears to have proved[22] that one of the most alluring features of the theatre to our eye, namely the street drawn in perspective and which splits in two the stage wall, stems from a misinterpretation of a passage in Book V of Vitruvius.[23] Palladio is also conspicuous for having removed the preferential seats of which the Roman theoretician had talked. Each spectator—aristocrat—is equal to the others.

But there is something more important: this Greek tragedy, translated into Italian (Tuscan), and chosen as being, according to Aristotle, the best, in preference to any ancient or modern tragedy, and also in preference to a pastoral,[24] is being performed in a Roman theatre. Vitruvius' doctrine on Greek theatre could not have been further from the minds of Palladio and Scamozzi. Furthermore, it is on a reduced scale and a contemporary, G.V. Pinelli, put it succinctly when he said: "Il teatro troppo piccolo [too small]."[25] It is also the case that the auditorium was covered, and if the covering, which has, since 1914, given way to the open sky, was in 1585 a painted canvas,[26] it was not daylight which lit up the actors and the Chorus, and that inaugural performance took place at night. All this was entirely in harmony with a humanist ethic which imitates antiquity while being fully conscious that it is not antiquity.

---

[21] J. Ackerman, *Palladio*, p. 34.

[22] In the article cited above, n. 20.

[23] *De Architectura*, V, 6.8: "secundum autem spatio ad ornatus comparato"; *secundum* was for a long time understood to mean "behind" and not "beside."

[24] References to Aristotle are pervasive and can be found in Pigafetta and in Riccoboni; cf. *Prima Rappresentazione*, pp. 39–42 and 54. On the choice of a Greek tragedy as opposed to a pastoral or an Italian tragedy, cf. F. Pigafetta, *Prima Rappresentazione*, pp. 53–54 and A. Gallo, *ibid.*, pp. xix, xxi.

[25] *Ibid.*, p. 59; Pinelli in any event was not present on 3 March 1585; cf. A. Gallo, *ibid.*, p. xxiii; the capacity of the theatre was sometimes overestimated by contemporaries. G. Marzari (*Historia di Vicenza*, p. 117) declared it capable of holding 5000 spectators, which is an enormous exaggeration: cf. *Représentation*, p. 48.

[26] The detail is little known; the principal document is a cameo by Antiodeus, which represents none other than *Oedipus Tyrannos*; cf. R. Schiavo, *Guida*, pp. 127–132.

It remains for us to say how the performance of 1585 related to Greek dramaturgy of the fifth century B.C. As it happens, we are reasonably well informed about the intentions and achievements of the producer, Angelo Ingegneri from Ferrara, and about the debates which he prompted, since, in addition to the accounts of his contemporaries, we have the actual text of his proposal.[27]

The stage setting is, properly speaking, no more "archaeological" than the theatre itself. But for us the problem is in isolating the element of intentional *reconstruction*, what was voluntary divergence (for the purposes of translation to the modern setting), what was conscious modernity.

The reconstruction could, of course, be nothing other than dictated by books. This was so on a detailed level, e.g. at the beginning of the play when the curtain fell. "First a very pleasant smell of perfumes could be felt, to make it understood that in the city of Thebes which was being depicted fragrances were spread abroad according to ancient history to soften the anger of the gods":[28] though this may amount to little more than a commentary on verse 4 of *Oedipus Rex*: Πόλις δ'ὁμοῦ μὲν θυμιαμάτων γέμει, "et la Cittande di vapori odoriferi ripiena," in the words of Giustiniani.

As regards the choruses which Angelo Gabrieli set to music[29] and which Riccoboni compared to the Lamentations of Jeremiah,[30] it must surely be unconsciously that they were transformed into intermezzi separating the Acts. Moreover, the small numbers forming the chorus (15) in comparison with the huge apparatus of the production produce what amounts, in many ways, to a curious mélange of scrupulous archaeology and semi-conscious innovation.

For the greatest innovation of the spectacle is in the voluntarily regal air of luxury which it was given. If the link between the chorus and the city is better expressed in the translation than in the production, the

---

[27] It is reproduced in *Prima Rappresentazione*, pp. 3–25; on the production see especially L. Schrade, *Représentation*, pp. 51–56.

[28] F. Pigafetta, *Prima Rappresentazione*, p. 56; the curtain which hides the stage was lowered, not raised; cf. Pigafetta, *ibid.* and L. Schrade, *Représentation*, p. 49.

[29] Cf. Schrade, *Représentation*, pp. 65–77; I say unconsciously, because the producer, Ingegneri, really did believe that the Chorus was the incarnation of man on the stage: "Il Choro, rappresentante tutta la Terra," op. cit. *indra*, no. 40, pp. 18–19; "terra" therefore means the city.

[30] *Prima Rappresentazione*, p. 49; L. Schrade (p. 76) notes that "amongst all the observations, for the most part obtuse, that Riccoboni made . . ." this one at least is not devoid of meaning, since Gabrieli's music can indeed have drawn inspiration from the polyphonic versions of the Lamentations.

royal nature of the characters is superabundantly underlined. Thebes is, according to Ingegneri, "the famous city of Boeotia and seat of empire."[31] Oedipus must "be of greater stature than all the others";[32] he is accompanied on each of his entrances by an entourage of 28 people, the number falling to 25 for Jocasta and 6 for Creon, who is only a prince.[33] Ingegneri specifies in his scheme that the costumes must be Greek, and not Roman, with the exception only of those of the priests.[34] But the dress he thus terms Greek seems to have been plucked from an Orient more familiar to the Venetians of 1585 than the Orient of Greece or even Byzantium: the Turkish Orient. It is amusing to compare the following sentence of Ingegneri: "The King's guard will be of men all clothed in the same colours, in the Greek style," with this one of Pigafetta: "The King with the guard of twenty-four archers clothed in the costume of the *solachi* of the great Turk . . ."[35]

But, in spite of Ingegneri's wishes, is Rome ever in fact very far away? There is little doubt that Seneca's *Oedipus* is present behind that of Sophocles. Laius' anonymous shepherd in Sophocles is called "Forbante" (Phorbas) by Ingegneri, in keeping with the Latin model.[36] The regal luxury is more in keeping with the imperial or papal tradition[37] than with what was known in the sixteenth century of the Greek tradition. One of the contemporary critics, Sperone Speroni, objected to this "regal majesty" in the name of tragedy and history. It was a time of plague, a time for "supplication, not pomp,"[38] and he asserts, getting his eras a little confused, that barbarian kings wear a white band around their heads and Greek kings bear only a sceptre, as one can see in Homer. As for Jocasta, her attire should have the simplicity of Penelope's, and two attendants suffice her.[39]

But the essential point remains that all are acutely conscious of their status as moderns. Ingegneri's text here is irreplaceable.[40] The

---

[31] *Prima Rappresentazione*, p. 9.

[32] *Ibid.*, p. 10.

[33] These are the figures retained by A. Gallo, *ibid.*, p. xiv, and L. Schrade, *op. cit*, p. 53; the data recorded are somewhat contradictory and the figures occasionally a bit lower.

[34] *Prima Rappresentazione*, pp. 13–15; the priests' costumes seem to be inspired from the traditional dress of Jewish priests in Renaissance art.

[35] *Prima Rappresentazione*, pp. 15 and 56 respectively.

[36] *Ibid.*, p. 12.

[37] A solemn mass was sung on 4 March 1585 by the Academicians.

[38] "Il re e tutto il popolo era in stato di supplicare e non di pompeggiare" (*ibid.*, p. 31).

[39] *Ibid.*

[40] Ingegneri is an important theoretician of theatre production and the author

stage-setting includes the *apparato*, costumes, movement of the *ensemble*, ceremonial; it also includes (apart from the music) the *action* which is itself divided in two: "The action consists in two things: in voice and in gesture."[41] The voice is addressed to the ear, gesture to the sight. If it is legitimate for the actors to be dressed "à la grecque," the modern art of acting precludes their wearing the mask, since the action is not principally accomplished with arms and legs but with the face and the eyes: "Gesture consists in the appropriate movements of the body and its parts, and particularly of the hands, and much more of the face and, above all, of the eyes."[42] As a result, the mask, whose role in ancient theatre was perfectly well known to Ingegneri,[43] is deliberately excluded from the performance of 1585. By this awareness the performance escaped the clutches of a more or less imaginary archaeology to make of this Greek masterpiece, imposed on the academicians of Vicenza by the *Poetics* of Aristotle, a critical moment in a saga that was happening now.

Now let rather more than a century go by, and let us leave Vicenza for Paris. In 1692 André Dacier published a translation with commentary of Sophocles' *Electra* and *OT*.[44] In many respects this translation, which some others were to follow,[45] marks a turning point upon which we ought to ponder.

1. As Marie Delcourt pointed out,[46] this version marks the victory of Sophocles over Seneca, of whom two recent and almost complete translations existed in Corneille's lifetime. There were to be no further translations of Seneca's *Oedipus* until 1795.[47] The only discernible hint

---

of several specialist works (cf. L. Schrade, *Représentation*, pp. 51–52); his most important work, published at Ferrara in 1598, is entitled: *Della poesia rappresentativa e del modo di rappresentare le favole sceniche*; it contains a general discussion based on the production of *Edipo Tyranno*, notably p. 18.

[41] *Prima Rappresentazione*, p. 8. This division stems from Aristotle, *Rhetoric* III.1403b 20–1404 a 8 and *Poetics* 26, 1461 b 26–1462 a 4, on the subject of which read A. Lienhard-Lukinovitch, *La voce e il gesto nella retorica di Aristotele*, in Società di linguistica italiana, *Retorica e scienze del linguaggio*, Rome 1979, pp. 75–92.

[42] *Ibid.*, p. 18.

[43] *Ibid.*, p. 8.

[44] A. Dacier, *L'Oedipe et l'Electre de Sophocle, tragédies grecques traduites en Français, avec des remarques*, Paris, 1692.

[45] By Boivin (with *The Birds* of Aristophanes), Paris 1729, by R.P. Brumoy, in the *Théâtre des Grecs*, Paris 1730 (re-edited by Rochefort and Laporte du Theil in 1785), by Rochefort with the whole of Sophocles, I, Paris 1788, pp. 3–133.

[46] Marie Delcourt, *Étude sur les traductions des tragiques grecs et latins en France depuis la Renaissance*, Brussels 1925, p. 5.

[47] By M.L. Coupé is a translation of *Théâtre de Sénèque*, Paris 1795, I, pp. 309–400; the commentary is interesting in that it suggests the creation of "tragic novels."

of Seneca's clandestine presence in the adaptations of Sophocles' play
are given by means of characters like "Phorbas" or "Laius' Shade."
2. Without relying on a new edition of the text—none saw the
light of day before the "professors' revolution" at the end of the eighteenth century[48]—this translation still managed to mark a break with the
"beautiful infidelities" of Arnaud d'Andilly and Perrot d'Ablancourt. As
René Bray put it: "When at the end of the century Dacier and Mme.
Dacier translated Aristotle, Anacreon, Plato, Plutarch, Horace, Plautus
and Terence, and Sophocles, they did it as philological scholars, not as
authors in search of inspiration and rhetoric."[49]

3. This translation is the starting point, almost the origin, the
ἀρχή of an astonishing number of adaptations, parodies, and reflections
on Sophocles' play and on the Oedipus theme, which form one of the
least known aspects of eighteenth-century literature and philosophy.
Almost neglected until the present day,[50] this topic has been
examined in depth by the young scholar, Christian Biet,[51] who has
identified no less than 17 adaptations (of which two are parodies and two
operas), which are strung out between 1718 and 1811.[52]

4. It is remarkable, finally, that the Dacier translation was
intended to be an item related to the long-running debate of the ancients
and the moderns, and Dacier energetically embraced the side of the
ancients. The result was the opposite of what had been anticipated, as
much on a general level as on that of the drama of Oedipus. The change

---

[48] Brunck's edition, prefaced by J. Schweighäuser, was published at Strasburg
in 1779, that of F.A. Wolf at Halle in 1787.

[49] R. Bray, cited by R. Zuber, *Perrot d'Ablancourt et ses "belles infidèles."*
Traduction et critique de Balzac à Boileau, Thesis, Paris 1968, p. 19; the references
here could be multiplied, for example, G. de Rochefort in his "Observations sur les difficultés qui se recontrent dans la traduction des Poëtes tragiques grecs," published as an
introduction to *Théâtre de Sophocle* I, Paris 1788, pp. xxi–xliii, explains that the
readers most to be feared "are the semi-scholarly. Those create a sensation in the world;
they are scattered in society, they are taken at their word; they pass for scholars in the
eyes of the superficial. They have no fear at boldly making judgements at the first
glance upon a work whose gestation has been lengthy"; henceforth the enemy is the
"honest man."

[50] There is little to quote from other than a dissertation from Bochum (1933):
W. Jordens, *Die Französischen Oidipusdramen. Ein Beitrag zum Fortleben der Antike
und zur Geschichte der Französischen Tragödie.* Even W. Jordens only found five
adaptations in the 18th century.

[51] Ch. Biet, *Les Transcriptions théâtrales d'Oedipe-Roi au dix-huitième siècle,*
a 3e cycle thesis under the supervision of J. Chouillet, University of Paris III, Paris
1980; I had the honour of being one of the judges of this work, and I have since had
more than one opportunity to discuss its conclusions with the author.

[52] I shall cite a number of these adaptations later on, but it is for Ch. Biet to
publish the file which he has assembled. [See now *Oedipe en monarchie, Tragedie
théorie juridique à l'âge classique* (Paris: Klincksieck, 1994).-Ed.]

which arose from the work of the Daciers[53] was in the very status of translation in the literary Republic, being subjected henceforth to an imperative for precision to the point, at times, of literalism. Pierre Coustel, in 1687, explained that the translation of a profane text is subject to a criterion of aesthetic expansion: "If one only translates literally, one offers a weak, base, and tiresome translation: one without beauty, without colour, without life; it no more resembles the original than a dead man resembles a living one." But he made one exception to this rule, the Bible: "One must nevertheless make an exception of Holy Scripture, which should always be translated as literally as possible, because the order of words is often a mystery."[54] Translating Sophocles literally entails a twofold effect. On the first, more logical than historical, plane, it may suggest that it is a sacred text, just like the Bible; on the second, both are to be deemed profane. Whatever the situation, it is marked initially by a foray into a forbidden domain. More than that, this more or less literal translation of Dacier's was to provoke in turn, without paradox, adaptations which were not at all so, and it is a resolutely modern Oedipus who forms the backdrop to the ideological and political debates of the century.

Voltaire, the author of the first of these *Oedipus* plays, which was a huge success in 1718, the greatest in the history of French theatre in the eighteenth century, expresses the matter rather well in a letter addressed to the Jesuit R. P. Porée, "I was full of my reading of the classics and of your instruction, and I knew very little of the theatre in Paris; I set to work almost as if I had been in Athens. I consulted M. Dacier, a local. He recommended that I introduce a Chorus into each scene as the Greeks had done. It was akin to advising that I parade around Paris in the garb of Plato."[55]

It goes without saying that I do not intend here to make a systematic study of these plays, which could scarcely be more than a

---

[53] See Noémi Hepp, *Homère en France au XVIIe siècle*, Paris 1969.

[54] P. Coustel, *Régles de l'Education des Enfants où il est parlé de la manière dont il faut se conduire, pour leur inspirer les sentiments d'une solide piété et pour les apprendre parfaitement les Belles Lettres*, 2 vols., Paris 1687, pp. 193–4; I owe this reference and many others to Ch. Biet; on the problems posed by the translation of the Bible, see M. de Certeau, *L'Idée de traduction de la Bible au XVIIe siècle: Sacy et Simon*, "Recherches de science religieuse" 66, 1978, pp. 73–92; I have borrowed this important statistic from him: from 1695 to 1700, of the 60 Parisian editions of the Bible, 55 were in French; half a century earlier the proportion was reversed. The two authors studied have different, not to say opposite, ideas on what a translation should be. See also M. Delcourt, *op. cit., supra*, n. 46, who insists on the cardinal role of Daniel Huet (pp. 155-157).

[55] *Oeuvres complètes* de Voltaire, Edition Besterman, 86, Geneva 1969, p. 49 (for the date, cf. p. 50).

summary of Christian Biet's study. I shall restrict myself, therefore, as regards this corpus, to the formulation of a few general remarks.

In the first place, this corpus has the mark of an intensely intro-spective multi-referential group. In a study recently translated into French,[56] Hans Robert Jauss considered why a play like Goethe's *Iphigenia in Tauris* had now lost all impact. He suggested that it might in part at least be due to the twin frames of reference employed by Goethe, references, on the one hand to ancient tragedy, and on the other to French classical tragedy, which are today wholly inaccessible. There is no doubt that this double scheme left its mark also on Voltaire and his successors; moreover, it was accompanied by a running reference to the current political and ideological situation with the effect that the plays quickly became unreadable, because incomprehensible. A historian would, of course, react differently: one of the peculiarities which many of the plays present *to our eyes* is their insertion often explicitly, some-times implicitly, into an aesthetic, ideological, and cultural debate con-stantly in flux. That is true of Dacier's translation which has appended to it a detailed commentary. That is true of Voltaire, whose *Oedipus* is accompanied by a whole series of letters, the earlier ones of which he wrote himself, and which contain "a critical appraisal of Sophocles' *Oedipus*, Corneille's, and his own."[57]

It is hardly surprising, since it is a work of scholarship, that R.P. Brumoy's volume *Théâtre des Grecs*, in his edition of 1785,[58] should comprise at once the translation of the text of Sophocles, some reflec-tions on this play by the translator, some extracts, still due to R.P. Brumoy, of plays by Seneca and Corneille, an anonymous summary of Giustiniani's *Edipo Tiranno*, of which it was still known in 1785 that it was "performed with much pomp and ceremony at Vicenza by the Academicians," and a detailed analysis of Voltaire's play. All perfectly normal one may fairly say, and one could make the same observation for the *Electra* or the *Antigone*. What is much more surprising is that a gen-tleman like the Count de Lauraguais should publish in 1781 a tragedy in five acts called the *Jocaste*, preceded by a 183-page discourse on the

---

[56] "De l'Iphigénie de Racine à celle de Goethe," in *Pour une aesthétique de la réception*, trans. Cl. Maillard, preface by J. Starobinski, Paris 1978, pp. 210–262.

[57] *Lettres écrites par l'auteur qui contiennent la critique de l'Oedipe de Sophocle, de celui de Corneille et du sien*, Paris 1719, reprinted in Voltaire, *Oeuvres*, II, Paris 1877, pp. 11–46. For the year 1719 alone, Ch. Biet mentions no less than six publications debating the new Oedipus, cf. R. Pomeau, *La Religion de Voltaire*, Paris 1969 (2nd ed.), pp. 85–91, and J. Moureaux, *L'Oedipe de Voltaire. Introduction d'une psychocritique*, Paris 1973.

[58] Volume 3, published by the Messrs De Rochefort and du Theil of the Académie royale des Inscriptions et Belles Lettres.

Oedipus-plays in which a comparative study is made of Sophocles, Corneille, Voltaire, Houdar de la Motte and Lauraguais himself.[59] *Oedipus* is a play which cannot be presented on its own. Rather, it is a quite exceptional pretext for aesthetic experimentation. Houdar de la Motte, who was a great advocate of the "modernists" but also the adapter of the *Iliad*, rendered two successive versions of it in 1726, one in prose, the other in verse. The first was rejected by the French actors, which explains the composition of the second.[60]

But the most astonishing case is probably that of M. de la Tournelle, by profession Commissioner for War, a friend of the Academician Boivin, and translator of Sophocles and Aristophanes. This character is the author of a (lost) *Anthology* which contained no less than nine plays on the subject of Oedipus. Four of these, published in 1730–1731, feature in the Parisian libraries: *Oedipe ou les Trois Fils de Jocaste, Oedipe et Polybe, Oedipe ou l'Ombre de Laius, Oedipe et toute sa famille.* They made a double and systematic exploration, an exploration at the same time of the dramatic opportunities offered by Oedipus' family, both natural and adoptive,[61] and a psychological exploration of the emotions which could be attributed to this interesting family. One sufficiently surprising example is that of the *Trois Fils de Jocaste*, a play adapted simultaneously from the *Oedipus Rex*, the *Seven Against Thebes* of Aeschylus and the *Phoenissae* of Euripides. In it, "Polinice" kills Etéocle, Jocaste kills Polynice (in an unprecedented innovation) and then kills herself with Oedipus. To quote Christian Biet: "The ending does not issue in any political power: nothing is left." That serves to remind us in one word, "power," of the political problems set by the whole body of these adaptations.

Up to a point this was already a problem for the ancient tragedy, this dialogue between a hero drawn from the depths of the age of myth and the modern democratic city: *Oedipus Rex* is a three-cornered drama played between the tyrant, the Chorus, voice of the city, and the seer, Tiresias, in whom is vested the power to reach the gods.

---

[59] In the catalogue of the Bibliothèque Nationale, and in the *Bibliographie de la Littérature française* of Cioranescu, n. 53638, this essay is attributed to G. de Rochefort; I do not know upon what grounds this attribution is founded; in any case, the text is presented as that of the author of *Jocaste*; on Lauraguais, the study of P. Fromageot, *Les fantaisies littéraires, galantes, politiques et autres d'un grand seigneur. Le comte de Lauraguais (1733-1824)*, Revue des Études historiques 80, 1914, pp. 15-46, does not mention *Jocaste*.

[60] These are found in volume IV, pp. 3-68 and VIII, pp. 459-519, of the *Oeuvres* of A. Houdar de la Motte, Paris 1754; see also in VIII, pp. 377-458, the "Quatrième discours à l'occasion de la tragédie d'Oedipe."

[61] The reflection on the relationship between Oedipus and his adoptive father Polybus seems to me practically unique.

All the transcriptions are bound to give an account of this political debate, which is already the object of a radical transformation in Corneille's *Oedipe* (1659), a tragedy in which the authority of the tyrant and the legitimate power confront each other without the *demos* being in the least involved.[62]

It is by means of such set-tos, much more than through a direct reflection on incest and parricide, that the Oedipus plays of the eighteenth century join in the great debates of the time. The heroes of the drama are to be the people, priests, and king. In Dacier's time one cannot speak yet of a set-to. Through a twofold misinterpretation which was to have a lasting effect, Dacier makes of Zeus' priest who addresses Oedipus at the beginning of the Sophocles' play, a "high priest" on the Jewish model, and if in his realisation the play begins with the "assembly of the people," he immediately entrusts the political, the "popular" role, to a chorus of "sacrificers" which he has invented for the purpose and which "serves to inspire the people with the emotions they ought to have."[63]

It is with Voltaire that the chorus reasserts its autonomy as a separate political force, but a very moderate one, for Voltaire, while accepting that such a political dimension is a necessary element of tragedy from which it is impossible to escape, viewed it with much suspicion and sought to reduce its effect as far as possible. Let us hear how he defined this minimum: "The plot of an interesting play usually requires that the leading actors have secrets to confide to one another. And the means to tell their secrets to a whole people . . ." And again "There are still today some scholars who have the courage to assert that we have no conception of real tragedy, since we banished choruses from it. It is as if in the same play we were required to represent Paris, London and Madrid on the stage, solely on the basis of our forefathers' custom when theatre became established in France." Voltaire concluded "So I shall always believe, until the result proves me wrong, that one cannot take the risk of introducing a chorus into a tragedy without the precaution of putting it in its proper place." The final decision involves dual considerations simultaneously and inextricably of an aesthetic and political nature. As far as beauty is concerned, the playwright admits the chorus "only when it is necessary for the embellishment of the stage," while, on the political plane, both ancient and modern, the chorus . . . only befits

---

[62] S. Dubrovsky, *Corneille et la dialectique du héros*, Paris, 1963, pp. 337–339; A. Stegman, *L'Héroïsme cornélien, Genèse et signification*, I, Paris 1968, pp. 618–619.

[63] A. Dacier, *op. cit.*, pp. 149, 169, 198.

plays which involve a whole people,"[64] which, as Voltaire admits, is preeminently the case in the *Oedipus Rex*.

Voltaire, quite remarkably, was to remain in isolation on this point in those early years of the century. If we collect in two chronologically separate groups the Oedipus-plays of the eighteenth century, the one dating more or less from the Regency period and comprising between 1718 and 1731 no fewer than 11 plays, and the other dating from the end of the eighteenth and beginning of the nineteenth centuries, represented by six plays, it becomes apparent that of the first group only Voltaire gives a political chorus to his play, while the Jesuit, Folard, who published a rival *Oedipus* to the philosopher's in 1722, goes only as far as a chorus of children. Of the six plays in the second group, only one, that of N. G. Léonard[65] which was only published in 1798—the author died in January 1793—has a chorus reduced to its most simple expression. In all the other plays, the chorus fulfils an important role, and in Marie-Joseph Chénier's work it appears in every act and in every scene. No doubt the antiquarian traditions which characterized both the end of the century and the empire have their part to play in the reintroduction of the chorus, but that explanation has its limitations. It is in fact hard to resist seeing in this very real rising of the role of the chorus the signs of a raising of the political stakes—a reading of the plays amply confirms this—in the modern (democratic) sense of the term. Admittedly, we did not need the Oedipus plays to be apprised of this fact, but it is always interesting to have confirmation, however indirect.

How did the eighteenth-century theoreticians frame the problem? Neglecting everything which—whatever one may say—ensures that the chorus is not entirely identifiable with the city, if only because as a body it was, generally speaking, composed of persons foreign to or beyond the city (women and elders),[66] they deliberately and to much greater effect than many of the philologists of the nineteenth or twentieth centuries concentrated on the conflict between prince and city in Greek tragedy. In 1730, in his "Discourse on the Parallels of Theatre," R. P. Brumoy has a splendid page on kings and tragedy. "The Greeks," he said, "only want to see kings on stage to be able to gloat over their hum-

---

[64] These quotations are taken from the 6th letter on *Oedipus* (1729), "which contains an essay on the Choruses," in *Oeuvres complètes*, II, Paris, Garnier, 1877, pp. 42–44.

[65] N.G. Léonard, *Oedipe ou la Fatalité* in *Oeuvres*, I, Paris 1798, pp. 51–91.

[66] The only exceptions among the preserved plays are the *Ajax* and the *Philoctetes* of Sophocles and the *Rhesus*, which has come to us with the works of Euripides: in these three plays the chorus is comprised of adult soldiers or sailors.

bling, because of their implacable hatred of their supreme dignity."
When Rochefort and Du Theil reprinted this text, they protested in a
footnote: "all this paragraph needs to be read with caution."[67] In 1788,
in the chapter which he devoted to Greek tragedy in his *Voyage of the
Young Anacharsis*,[68] Father Barthélmey wrote: "Contemporary republi-
cans always contemplate with malign joy the rolling of thrones in the
dust."

In terms of individuals, the political characters of the *Oedipus
Rex* are the King, the Queen, the High Priest. Naturally, of course, one
must add Creon, alternately a retiring brother-in-law and a haughty
pretender. All are taken from Sophocles, with the possible exception of
the High Priest, who is transformed and supplemented, sometimes confused with Tiresias, sometimes distinct from him.[69] The parody performed in 1719 and ascribed to Biancolelli, an actor of the Duc
d'Orleans,[70] makes Tiresias the village schoolmaster, while in another
parody, which pointedly aims at Houdar de la Motte, Legrand replaces
the gods and their oracle by an old rabbi and a witch.[71]

The same chronological juxtaposition which was operative in the
presence and absence of the chorus is operative again here: in Voltaire's
Oedipus and the plays inspired by it and which owed their genesis to a
time of particularly public religious conflicts (between Jesuits and
Jansenists, for example), it is priests (and behind them, their God), who
are the principal targets. Posterity is only familiar with two lines of
Voltaire's play, partly borrowed from Jocasta's criticism of the seers:[72]

> Les prêtres ne sont pas ce qu'un vain peuple pense,
> Notre crédulité fait toute leur science.
> (The priests are not what a foolish world thinks they are.
> Their "science" is made up out of our credulity.)

---

[67] Brumoy, *Théâtre des Grecs*, Paris 1785, I, pp. 186–187.

[68] IV, ch. 71, p. 32.

[69] The two characters are distinct in the plays of Voltaire, and Buffardin
d'Aix, *Oedipe à Thèbes ou le fatalisme*, Paris 1784, of Marie-Joseph Chénier, in the
Oedipe-Roi of Bernard d'Héry, London and Paris 1786, in the *Oedipe à Thèbes* of
Duprat de la Touloubre (opera), Paris 1791, in the *Oedipe ou la Fatalité* of N. G.
Léonard.

[70] P. F. Biancolelli (*alias* Dominique) and A. F. Riccoboni, *Oedipe travesti*, a
comedy by M. Dominique, Paris 1719.

[71] M. A. Legrand, *Le Chevalier Errant, Parodie de l'Oedipe de Monsieur de
la Motte*, Paris (1726?).

[72] *Oedipe-Roi*, 707–710; 857–858; 946–947; on Voltaire's battle as he wrote
the *Oedipus* against the "terrible God" and the "cruel priest," see R. Pomeau, *La Religion de Voltaire*, 2nd d., pp. 85–91.

The play ends, very overtly, on an encomiastic note with a eulogy of the enlightened despot, in the form of the "legitimate" king, Philoctetes.

At the end of this century, quite naturally, it is the offending king and the incestuous queen who are on trial, for good or ill. Thus in 1786, in a play by one Bernard d'Héry,[73] the tragedy opposes the "high king," to the "high priest" and the chorus of citizens. The Greek theme is interpreted as meaning the king's sacrifice for his people. At the end of the play the people (the Chorus) ask Oedipus to stay, whatever the cost.

In 1791, Duprat de la Touloubre broke off his opera before the death of Jocasta and the self-mutilation of Oedipus in order, says the author, "to close the spectacle brilliantly." The play has been interpreted as "an obstinate defence of the Father King on trial" (Ch. Biet). Finally, Nicolas G. Léonard presented in 1793, not long before his death, the king as victim of a popular rebellion. The chorus' elimination from the play cannot then be accidental. As for the Republican, M.-J. Chénier, he presented an Oedipus in opposition "to the right of each inhabitant of the city to speak and proffer opinions" (Ch. Biet).

The truth is, the author's personal feelings, however clear, are of little consequence. What does matter is this progression, this metamorphosis of the royal character. From an internal debate about his function, which characterized the *Oedipe* of Corneille and of Voltaire, we have moved on to a religious and political conflict between a king and his people. This is a long road which has been trodden from Voltaire to Chénier, but all along the way a common language has been kept, and that is what had to be brought out.

Today we can smile at that multiple Oedipus of the Century of Enlightenment, as we can smile at the Oedipus of 1585 with his cohort of 28 archers and courtiers. They too, however, have contributed in their own way to the moulding of our own Oedipus.

---

[73] *Oedipe-Roi*, a lyric tragedy in five acts, London and Paris, 1786.

From *Preface to Oedipus*

Pierre Corneille

Furthermore, I will not conceal from you that having chosen this subject, confident that I would have the approval of all scholars, who have
regarded it as the masterpiece of antiquity, and that the thoughts of these
great minds who have dealt with it in Greek and Latin would make it
easier for me to complete it quickly enough to have it put on during
Carnival, I still could not help trembling when I have looked at it close
up, with a little more leisure than I had when choosing it. I realised that
what had passed for miraculous in those distant times could seem
hideous to ours, and that this eloquent and strange description of the
manner in which this unfortunate prince pokes out his eyes, and the
spectacle of these same eyes from which the blood trickles down his
face, which occupies the whole fifth act in these incomparable originals,
would offend the delicacy of our ladies, who make up the most beautiful
part of our audience, and whose disgust easily brings on the censure of
those who accompany them; and that, finally, love having no part in this
subject, nor women any role, it was devoid of the principal ornaments
which ordinarily win us public opinion. I have endeavoured to remedy
these faults as best I could, by sparing my audience on the one hand this
dangerous spectacle, and in adding on the other the happy episode of the
love of Theseus and Dirce, whom I make the daughter of Laius, and sole
heiress to his crown, assuming that her brother, who had been
abandoned to the wild beasts, had been devoured by them as people
believed; I have cut the number of oracles, which could be tedious and
give Oedipus enlightenment as to his identity; I have rendered the
response of Laius, called up by Teiresias, obscure enough in its clarity to
make a new knot of intrigue, and one which perhaps is no less fine than
that of our ancients; I have even sought reasons to justify what Aristotle

finds without reason and which he excuses as coming at the beginning of the story; and I have arranged it so that Oedipus, even though he remembers having fought three men at the very place where Laius was killed, and at the same time as his death, so far from believing himself its author, believes he has taken revenge for it on the three brigands to whom the common rumour attributes it. This has made me lose the advantage I had promised myself of often being only the translator of those great men who have preceded me. As I have taken another route from theirs, it has been impossible for me to follow in their footsteps; but, to make up for this, I have had the honour of making most of my listeners admit that I have written no play where so much skill is to be found as in this one, although it is only a work of two months, which French impatience made me rush through a proper eagerness to execute the favourable orders which I had received.

Letters on Oedipus

F. M. A. de Voltaire

LETTER III

CONTAINING THE CRITIQUE OF THE *OEDIPUS* OF SOPHOCLES

Sir, my want of erudition does not permit me to examine "whether the tragedy of Sophocles makes its imitation by its speech, cadence, and harmony: what Aristotle expressly calls agreeably seasoned speech." Nor will I discuss "if it is a play of the first type, simple and involved: simple because it has only one simple catastrophe; and involved because it has the moment of recognition with the *peripeteia*."

I will give you a simple account of the places that have shocked me, and upon which I need enlightenment from those who, knowing the ancients better than I, can better excuse their defects.

The scene opens, in Sophocles, with a chorus of Thebans prostrate at the foot of the altars; who, by their cries and tears, ask the gods for an end to their calamities. Oedipus, their liberator and king, appears in their midst.

"I am Oedipus, he tells them, a name well known to all." There is some likelihood that the Thebans were not unaware that his name was Oedipus.

With regard to this great reputation he boasts of, M. Dacier says this is skilful of Sophocles, who in this way wishes to give a foundation to the character of Oedipus, who is proud.

"My children," says Oedipus, "what is it that brings you here?" The high priest answers him: "You see before you young people and old men. I who speak to you am the high priest of Jupiter. Your city is like a ship buffeted by the tempest; it is ready to be swallowed up in the deep, and has not the strength to rise above the waves crashing down on her.'' From this the high priest takes the opportunity to give a description of the plague, about which Oedipus was as well informed as he was of the name and position of the high priest of Jupiter. Moreover, does this high priest make his homily truly moving by comparing a plague-stricken city, littered with the dead and dying, to a tempest-tossed ship? Did not this preacher know that one weakens large things by comparing them to small?

All that is hardly proof of this perfection to which it was claimed, some years ago, that Sophocles had carried tragedy; and it is not apparent that one is so greatly mistaken in this century to withhold one's admiration from a poet who uses no other artifice to make his characters known than to have one say: ''I am Oedipus, a name well known to all''; and the other: ''I am the high priest of Jupiter.'' This crudity is today no longer regarded as a noble simplicity.

The description of the plague is interrupted by the arrival of Creon, the brother of Jocasta, whom the king had sent to consult the oracle, and who begins by saying to Oedipus:

> My lord, we once had a king who was called Laius.
>> OEDIPUS.
> I know, although I never saw him.
>> CREON.
> He was assassinated, and Apollo wants us to punish his murderers.
>> OEDIPUS.
> Was it in his house or in the countryside that Laius was killed?

It is already contrary to the notion of verisimilitude that Oedipus, who has been king for such a long time, should not know how his predecessor died; but that he did not even know whether it was in the country or in town that this murder was committed, and that he should give neither the least reason nor the least excuse for his ignorance, I confess that I do not know any term to express such an absurdity.

It is a fault of the subject, it is said, and not of the author: as if it were not up to the author to correct his subject when it is defective! I know I can be reproached with pretty much the same fault; but I will not spare myself any more than I do Sophocles, and I hope the sincerity with which I shall admit my faults will justify my boldness in picking out those of an ancient author.

What follows seems to me equally far from common sense. Oedipus asks if nobody returned from Laius's retinue from whom one might ask for news of it; some one replies that "one of those who accompanied this unfortunate king, having escaped, came to tell in Thebes that Laius had been assassinated by robbers, who were not in small but large numbers."

How can it be that a witness to the death of Laius would say that his master was overwhelmed by numbers, when the truth is, however, that it is one man alone who killed Laius and all his attendants?

The supreme example of contradiction is when Oedipus says in the second act that he has heard it said that Laius was killed by travellers, but that there is no one who says he saw it; and Jocasta, in the third act, speaking of the death of this king, explains herself thus to Oedipus:

"Be quite sure, my lord, that the one who accompanied Laius reported that his master had been assassinated by robbers; he could not change now, or say otherwise; the whole city heard him as I did."

The Thebans would have been far more to be pitied, if the riddle of the sphinx had not been easier to solve than all these contradictions.

But what is still more surprising, or rather what is not at all, after such faults against verisimilitude, is that when he learns that Phorbas still lives, Oedipus does not think only of having him fetched, but amuses himself by making imprecations and consulting oracles, without giving the command to bring before him the only man who could throw light on the mystery. The chorus itself, which is interested in seeing an end to the misfortunes of Thebes and which is always giving advice to Oedipus, does not give him that of interrogating this witness of the death of the late king; it only begs him to send for Tiresias.

At last Phorbas arrives in the fourth act. Those who do not know Sophocles no doubt imagine that Oedipus, impatient to know the murderer of Laius and to restore life to the Thebans, is swiftly going to interrogate him upon the death of the late king. Nothing of the sort; Sophocles forgets that vengeance for the murder of Laius is the subject of the play: not a word is said to Phorbas about this adventure; and the tragedy ends without Phorbas having even opened his mouth about the death of the king, his master. But let us continue our examination of Sophocles' work.

When Creon has informed Oedipus that Laius was assassinated by robbers who were not in small but large numbers, Oedipus replies, according to several translators: "How could robbers have undertaken such an attempt, since Laius had no money on him?" The majority of other commentators understand this passage differently, and have Oedipus say: "How could robbers have undertaken such an attempt, if they had not been given money?" But that interpretation is hardly more reasonable than the other: one knows that robbers do not need to be promised money to engage them in committing a crime.

And since commentators often have the power to make their authors say everything they want, what would it cost them to give them a little good sense?

Oedipus, at the beginning of the second act, instead of summoning Phorbas, has Tiresias brought before him. The king and the soothsayer begin by getting angry at each other. Tiresias finishes by telling him:

"It is you who are the murderer of Laius. You believe yourself to be the son of Polybus, king of Corinth: you are not: you are Theban. The curse of your father and mother once took you far from this land; you came back to it, you killed your father, you married your mother, you are the author of incest and parricide; and if you find that I am lying, say I am not a prophet."

All that hardly resembles the ordinary ambiguity of oracles; it would be difficult to explain oneself less obscurely; and if you add to the words of Tiresias the charge that someone when drunk once made to Oedipus, that he was not the son of Polybus, and the oracle of Apollo who predicted to him that he would kill his father and he would marry his mother, you will find that the play is entirely finished at the beginning of this second act.

New proof that Sophocles had not perfected his art, since he did not know how to lead up to events, nor how to hide under the thinnest veil the catastrophe in his plays.

Let us go further. Oedipus treats Tiresias as *crazy* and as an *old magician*; however, unless he was out of his mind, he ought to regard him as a true prophet. Ah! with what astonishment and with what horror should he not be struck on learning from the mouth of Tiresias all that Apollo had once predicted for him? What self-examination should he not make on learning of this fatal correspondence which exists between the charges made to him at Corinth but that he was only a suppositious son, and the oracles of Thebes who tell him he is Theban? Between Apollo who predicted to him that he would marry his mother and that he would kill his father, and Tiresias who informs him that his frightful destinies are fulfilled? However, as if he had lost the memory of these appalling events, no other idea comes to him than to suspect Creon, his *old and faithful friend* (as he calls him), of having killed Laius; and that, without any reason, without any grounds, without the least daylight to authorize these suspicions, and (since we must call things by their name) with an extravagance of which there is scarcely an example among the moderns, nor even among the ancients.

"What! you dare to appear before me! he says to Creon; you have the audacity to enter this palace, you who are surely the murderer of Laius, and who have manifestly conspired against me to rob me of my crown!

"Let us see, tell me, in the name of the gods, have you noticed some cowardice or madness in me, to have undertaken so daring a plan? Is it not the most foolish of all enterprises to aspire to royalty without troops and without friends, as if, without this help, it was easy to ascend the throne?"

Creon answers him:

"You will change your mind if you will give me the time to speak. Do you think there is any man in the world who would prefer to be king, with all the terrors and all the fears that accompany royalty, to living in the lap of tranquillity with all the safety of a private person who, under another name, would possess the same power?"

A prince who would be accused of having conspired against his king, and who had no other proof of his innocence than the verbiage of Creon, would have need of his master's clemency. After all these grand speeches, foreign to the subject, Creon asks Oedipus:

"Do you want to drive me from the kingdom?
OEDIPUS.
It is not your exile I want; I condemn you to death.
CREON.
Before then you must let it be seen whether I am guilty.
OEDIPUS.
You talk like a man resolved not to obey.
CREON.
It is because you are unjust.
OEDIPUS.
I take every precaution.
CREON.
I should as well.
OEDIPUS.
O Thebes! Thebes!
CREON.
I have the right to cry "Thebes! Thebes!" too.

Jocasta enters during this fine conversation, and the chorus begs her to take the king away: a very wise proposal, because, after all the follies Oedipus has just committed, it would be no bad thing to lock him up.

JOCASTA.

I will take my husband away when I have learned the cause of this disturbance.

CHORUS.

Oedipus and Creon have had words together about very uncertain reports. People often take offense over unmerited suspicions.

JOCASTA.

Was that on both sides?

CHORUS.

Yes, Madam.

JOCASTA.

What words have they had then?

CHORUS.

It is enough, madam. The princes have not pushed the matter further, and that is sufficient.

Indeed, as if that were sufficient, Jocasta does not ask the chorus any more.

It is in this scene that Oedipus recounts to Jocasta that one day, at table, a drunk man accused him of being a suppositious son. "I went, he continues, to find the king and queen: I questioned them about my birth; they were both very vexed about the charge made against me. Although I loved them with much tenderness, this wrong, which had become public, did not cease to lie on my heart, and give me suspicions. I left then, without their knowing, to go to Delphi: Apollo did not deign to answer my question precisely; but he told me the most frightening and appalling things one has ever heard spoken of: that I would without fail marry my own mother; that I would set before men's eyes an unhappy lineage that would fill them with horror, and that I would be the murderer of my father."

There again the play is finished. It had been predicted to Jocasta that her son would soak his hands in the blood of Laius, and would bring his crimes as far as the bed of his mother. She had had this son abandoned on Mount Citheron, and had had his heels pierced (as she admits in this same scene): Oedipus still carries the scars from this wound; he knows he has been charged with not being the son of Polybus; is not all that, for Oedipus and Jocasta, a demonstration of their misfortune? And is there not a ridiculous blindness in doubting it?

I know that Jocasta does not say at all in this scene that she had one day to marry her son; but that itself is a new fault. Because, when Oedipus says to Jocasta: "It was predicted that I would defile the bed of my mother, and that my father would be slaughtered by my hands,"

Jocasta should answer at once: "As much had been predicted for my son"; or at least she should make the spectator feel that she is convinced, at this moment, of her misfortune.

Such ignorance in Oedipus and Jocasta is only a gross artifice of the poet, who, to give his play the proper length, puts off to the fifth act a recognition already manifest in the second, and who violates the rules of common sense so as not to appear deficient in those of the theater.

This same fault remains throughout the whole course of the play.

This Oedipus, who could solve riddles, does not understand the clearest things. When the Corinthian shepherd brings him the news of the death of Polybus, and informs him that Polybus was not his father, that he was abandoned by a Theban on Mount Cithaeron, that his feet were pierced and bound with straps, Oedipus still suspects nothing; he has no other fear than that of being born of an obscure family; and the chorus, always present in the course of the play, pays no attention to everything that ought to have instructed Oedipus about his birth. The chorus, which one takes for an assembly of enlightened people, shows as little insight as Oedipus; and, at the time when the Thebans should be seized with pity and horror at the sight of the misfortunes they witness, it exclaims: "If I can judge the future, and if I am not mistaken in my guesses, Cithaeron, tomorrow will not pass without your making known to us the birthplace and the mother of Oedipus, and our leading dances in your honor as thanksgiving for the pleasure you will have given our princes. And you, prince, of which of the gods are you then the son? What nymph has had you of Pan, god of the mountains? Are you the fruit of Apollo's loves? because Apollo too takes pleasure in the mountains. Is it Mercury or Bacchus, who also stay on the summits of the mountains? etc."

At last the one who formerly abandoned Oedipus arrives on the stage. Oedipus questions him about his birth; a curiosity that M. Dacier condemns after Plutarch, and that would seem to me the only reasonable thing Oedipus has done in the whole play, if this proper desire to know himself were not accompanied by a ridiculous ignorance ridiculous about itself.

Oedipus then knows at last his whole fate in the fourth act. So there again the play is finished.

M. Dacier, who has translated the *Oedipus* of Sophocles, claims the onlooker awaits with much impatience the part Jocasta will take, and the manner by which Oedipus will execute upon himself the curses he has pronounced against the murderer of Laius. I was led astray on that point by the respect I have for this learned man, and I was of his opinion when I read his translation. The production of my play has completely disabused me; I recognize that one can without peril extol the Greek poets as much as one wishes, but that it is dangerous to imitate them.

I had taken from Sophocles a part of the account of the death of Jocasta and of Oedipus's catastrophe. I felt that the attention of the spectator diminished as did his pleasure in the account of this catastrophe: minds, filled with terror at the moment of recognition, no longer listened except with disgust to the end of the play. Perhaps the mediocrity of the verses was the cause of it; perhaps the spectator, to whom this catastrophe is known, regretted hearing nothing new; perhaps also terror having been pushed to its utmost, it was impossible for the rest not to seem listless. However that may be, I felt myself obliged to cut out this account, which was not more than forty lines; and in Sophocles, it takes all the fifth act. It seems entirely reasonable that one should not permit an ancient two or three hundred useless lines, when one does not permit a modern forty of them.

M. Dacier warns in his notes that Sophocles' play is not finished in the fourth act. Is it not to admit that it is finished, when one is obliged to prove that it is not? One does not find oneself required to make similar notes on the tragedies of Racine and Corneille; there is only *Les Horaces* that would need such commentary; but the fifth act of *Les Horaces* would appear any the less flawed.

I cannot keep myself from speaking here of a place in the fifth act of Sophocles, which Longinus admired, and which Despréaux has translated:

> Hymen, deadly Hymen, you have given me life,
> But into these same flanks where I was confined
> You made this blood return from which you had formed me,
> And that way you produce both sons and fathers,
> Brothers, husbands, wives and mothers,
> And everything that the malign fury of fate
> Ever brought to light in the way of shame and horror.

Firstly, it should have been stated that it is in the same person that one finds these mothers and these husbands; because there is no marriage that does not produce all that. In the second place, today one would not forgive Oedipus for making so curious a search into the circumstances of his crime, and thus combining with it all the horrors; so much exactitude in counting all their incestuous titles, far from adding to the atrocity of the action, seems rather to weaken it.

These two lines of Corneille say much more:

It is they who made me the assassin of my father;
It is they who made me the husband of my mother.

The lines of Sophocles are those of a declaimer, and Corneille's those of a poet.

You see that, in the critique of the *Oedipus* of Sophocles, I have only striven to point out the defects that are for all times and all places: contradictions, absurdities, vain declamations, are faults in every country. I am not surprised that in spite of so many imperfections, Sophocles won the admiration of his century; the harmony of his lines and the pathos that reigns in his style could seduce the Athenians, who, with all their understanding and all their good breeding, could not have had a correct notion of the perfection of an art that was still in its infancy.

Sophocles was close to the time when the tragedy was invented; Aeschylus, contemporary with Sophocles, was the first who thought of putting several personages on the stage. We are as moved by the grossest sketch in the first discoveries of an art, as by the more accomplished beauties once perfection is known to us. Thus Sophocles and Euripides, as imperfect as they are, had as much success among the Athenians as Corneille and Racine among us. We should ourselves, in finding fault with the tragedies of the Greeks, respect the genius of their authors: their faults are attributable to their era; their beauties belong only to them; and no one can believe that if they had been born today, they would have perfected the art which they practically invented in their time.

It is true that they have fallen far from this high esteem in which once were held: their works are today either unknown or scorned; but I believe this oblivion and this scorn belong to the number of injustices of which our era can be accused. Their works deserve to be read, without doubt; and, if they are too flawed to be approved, they are too full of beautiful things for one to scorn them entirely.

Euripides especially, who seems to me so superior to Sophocles, and who would be the greatest of poets if he had been born in a more enlightened time, has left works which reveal a perfect genius, despite the imperfections of his tragedies.

Ah! what idea should one not have of a poet from whom Racine himself has borrowed ideas? The places where this great man has translated from Euripides, in his inimitable role of Phèdre, are not the least beautiful in his work.

Gods, why am I not seated in the shade of the forests!
When will I be able, through a noble dust,
To follow with the eye a chariot flying in the race-course?
. . . Insensible, where am I? and what have I said?

> Where have I let my wishes and my mind go astray?
> I have lost it, the gods have robbed me of its use.
> Oenone, blushing covers my face;
> I let you see too much my shameful sorrows,
> And my eyes, in spite of me, fill with tears.
>
> *Phèdre*, I, iii

Almost all this scene is translated word for word from Euripides. However, the reader need not, seduced by this translation, imagine that Euripides' play is a good work: that is the only fine part of his tragedy, and even the only reasonable one; for it is the only one Racine has imitated. And as one would never think of approving the *Hippolytus* of Seneca, although Racine has taken from this author the whole declaration of Phèdre, so one should not admire the *Hippolytus* of Euripides for thirty or forty lines which have been found worthy of being imitated by the greatest of our poets.

Molière sometimes took whole scenes from Cyrano de Bergerac, and would say by way of excuse: "This scene is good; it rightfully belongs to me; I recover my goods everywhere I find them."

Racine could say pretty well as much of Euripides.

For myself, after having said a lot of bad things about Sophocles, I am obliged to tell you everything good I know of him: in that respect very different from the cavillers, who begin by praising a man, and end by making him ridiculous.

I admit that perhaps without Sophocles I would never have come to the end of my *Oedipus*; I would never have even undertaken it. I first translated the first scene of my fourth act: that of the high priest who accuses the king is entirely his; the scene of the two old men belongs to him as well. I would like to have other debts to him, I would admit them with the same good faith. It is true that, as I owe beauties to him, I also owe faults, and I will speak of them in the examination of my play, where I hope to give you an account of mine.

Remarks upon Oedipus

Pierre Brumoy

The Oedipus of Sophocles has been always considered as the master-piece of antient tragedy, as the Iliad of Homer is in epic poetry, and the Laocoon and Venus of Medicis in sculpture.

This universal esteem, from time immemorial, is warranted by the imitations, and even by the criticisms that have been made of this work. For who ever thinks of imitating or criticising what is in itself of little value? It is well worth our pains therefore to search into the most secret causes of this general applause: yet without pretending to disguise those defects which are obnoxious to criticism, and to compare the model with the copies that have been made of it by persons who are now dead, and of whom only we are at liberty to speak freely. Such will be the subject of these reflexions.

In order to penetrate into the causes of that pleasure which this piece has never failed to give, it is not necessary to go far into the deep researches of Aristotle; nor to examine, if it be *simple and implex*; and in what sense it be so: whether the catastrophe be single; and if it unites the recognisance with the *peripetie*. When we write for our countrymen we should write in their language, without subjecting ourselves to the restraint of foreign expressions. It will be easily perceived, that nothing can be more regular than the plan of Oedipus: that the unity of place is exact and natural: that the unity of action is no less so: and that the unity of time is so scrupulously observed, that the action of the play takes up no more than the representation. It would be needless also to point out to the judicious reader, that inimitable art with which the scenes, and each part of the whole piece is connected with the other; so that if any thing was taken away the whole would fall, like a vaulted edifice, where the stones mutually support one another. But to proceed to something of greater importance: for, however necessary and beautiful these qualities are which we have already mentioned, and which are so seldom found together in dramatic compositions, yet it must be acknowledged, that they are not the only ones which constitute a good tragedy: and it is certain, that a tragedy may have all these without being perfect. A building, for example, may have great regularity, great symmetry of parts, yet have neither an advantageous situation, nor a noble air, nor magnificent furniture, nor that elegance and propriety which must contribute to its perfection. Art is one thing, and the delicacies of art another. M. d'Aubignac wrote a tragedy according to the rules; yet it was good for nothing. The reason is, that he play'd the game mechanically, without being able to catch the spirit.

Nothing can be imagined more happy than the subject of Oedipus. It is allowed to be excellent even in our days. What can be grander or more interesting than that the preservation of a whole kingdom should depend upon the discovery of a secret, and the punishment of a crime, the author of which is found to be a great king, who labours with the utmost solicitude to discover the one and punish the other? What more capable of raising curiosity than the enquiries into this secret, and this crime? What at length more striking than the discovery of both, by those very means from which greater obscurity might be expected? But let us enter into the detail, and follow the plan.

The opening is so wonderful, that it is equally impossible to express as not to feel its beauty. It is one of those magnificent pictures which would be worthy of the pencil of Raphael. That square, from which a great number of streets are seen at a distance; that palace and portico, which make the back-ground of the picture; that altar, which smokes with incense; that good king, who is met by a company of children, youths, and priests, who all, with branches in their hands, implore his compassion: those temples; those statues of the Gods; and those crowds of people who surround them. This is a speaking spectacle, and a picture so beautifully disposed, that even the attitudes of the priests and of Oedipus express, without the help of words, that one relates the calamities with which the people are afflicted, and the other, melted at the melancholy sight, declares his impatience and concern for the long delay of Creon, whom he had sent to consult the Oracle. Could Creon come more seasonably? He is expected: they count the moments with anxiety: the safety of the state depends upon the answer he brings. He appears: he is pressed to speak: he endeavours to give them hope; but the ambiguity of the Oracle lessens, in some degree, the comfort they derived from his words. Oedipus however retires, fully determined to obey the Oracle, if it be possible, and to discover who was the murderer of Laius. This scene is the beginning of the intrigue; this is the entrance to that theatrical labyrinth in which Oedipus is so soon to lose himself, in order to be found the most wretched of mankind. The first act is concluded with the invocation of the Chorus, which ought certainly to reconcile us to Chorusses: at least, it convinces us, that Sophocles has, in this first picture, displayed all the riches of the most finished design, and all the correctness of the most glowing colours.

The disposition of the second act is the necessary consequence of the preceding. Oedipus appears again; not merely as a king, who weeps over the miseries of his people, but as a king who is active for their relief; as a legislator, whose first act of obedience to the Oracle, is to oblige all his assembled subjects to agree with him in imprecating the most horrible curses on the unknown criminal.—What a change! when, at the unravelling the intrigue, he discovers that he has himself pronounced his own sentence! They consult; they deliberate: the smallest circumstances are thoroughly examined. Tiresias comes; but not uncalled: for Oedipus thinks of every possible expedient to satisfy the Oracle. It would seem, that the piece is now upon the point of being finished, and that the Prophet will explain the whole mystery. He does so indeed: but what probability is there that he should be believed either by Oedipus, the people, or the audience? Oedipus is supposed to be the son of Polybus, not of Laius. Hence arises that beautiful contest between the King and the Prophet; in which the haughty, inquisitive, and impetuous character of Oedipus shows itself. The declaration made by Tiresias becomes an affair of state. The unravelling, which was believed to be so near, is farther off than ever; and the Chorus, thrown back into their former uncertainty, are not able to guess who this criminal is who is sought after so carefully.

In the third picture, Creon, accused of conspiring with Tiresias, justifies himself to no purpose. The rage of Oedipus increases. Jocasta appeases him. She exhorts him to despise the accusations of the Prophet, who charges him with the murder of Laius: and, to discredit the veracity of oracles, she relates the prediction which Laius had received, that he should be murdered by his son. She goes on to acquaint him with the fate of that unhappy son, and the manner in which Laius was murdered in the road to Daulia. How beautiful is this management! The discourse of Jocasta produces an effect quite contrary to what she designed. Oedipus, instead of being comforted, trembles with his apprehensions. He remembers, that he had slain an old man, in the same circumstances Jocasta has described. He begins to suspect, that it is possible he may be the murderer he is in search of: and it may be observed in what manner the intrigue and the solution are so artfully mingled together, that as the plot is entangled it is disentangled at the same time, and entangled again, by two contrary effects produced at once by the same means. This is perceived in the sentence pronounced against the unknown criminal: in the interviews with Tiresias, with Creon, and afterwards with Jocasta; and at length appears plainly in the discourse of the shepherd, upon which all the hopes of Oedipus are founded. For he passes continually from fear to hope; sometimes confounded and dismayed; sometimes half encouraged: never wholly free from his suspicions, and always full of eager curiosity to know his birth. It is these circumstances which make the great movements of the theatrical balance.

In the fourth design, we see the inquietude of Oedipus is increased; and that his doubts concerning the murder of Laius are so forcibly impressed upon his mind, that Jocasta, to free him from this restless state, becomes, from irreligious and profane, as she at first appears, all on a sudden extremely pious. She goes to consult the Gods. This is an admirable character. In the first act she despises the Gods, and their Oracles: in the second, she is a zealot. The peculiar circumstances she is in produce both these dispositions. As she is going to the temple, to perform her devotions, she meets with the Corinthian shepherd, who removes all her fears concerning the destiny of Oedipus. Farewell piety: she forgets the Gods. Her suspicions are banished by the apparent inconsistency of the Oracle; which had predicted to him, that he should kill his father: and she is informed, that Polybus, his father, is dead. Ought the words of Tiresias then, who accuses him of parricide, to be regarded? But Oedipus, impelled by that curiosity which so strongly marks his character, forces the shepherd, by repeated questions, to acknowledge, that Polybus was not his father. He is now thrown back into all his former suspicions. The Corinthian explains himself by degrees: but Oedipus learns neither the name, nor the quality of the person to whom he owes his birth. He had been exposed while an infant. This is all he is told. Hitherto he believes himself to be the son of this shepherd, or of some other slave: and the error he is in hinders him from being alarmed at the consternation of the queen, already acquainted with the whole mystery, and at her precipitate departure. There is a necessity for having recourse to Phorbas; who at length appears; and, by his reluctance to answer the questions that are proposed to him, unfolds the fatal secret. Thus Oedipus, by his restless curiosity to discover the whole mystery, discovers it at length, to his misfortune. He finds he has murdered his father, and been the husband of his mother. What an intrigue, what an unravelling is here! How complicated both! But what an involution of both one and the other, and what a chain of events, which, like waves, destroy one another!

In the fifth and last picture, we have on one side a relation of the fatal death of Jocasta, by her own hands. On the other, Oedipus bleeding from his wound, who comes to vent his sorrows and despair. He blushes while he unveils the enormity of his crimes, or rather the horror of his destiny, by the punishment he has inflicted upon himself. He would have the one compared with the other; and he even paints his crimes, as greater than his misfortunes. Punished by his own hands, and bound by the sentence he has pronounced, he thinks little of his fall, from the highest prosperity to the last degree of wretchedness. His fate, so full of guilt, is ever present to his mind. The most forceable expressions seem to him but poorly to represent his misery; and the striking contrast of a king, who, from happy and beloved, becomes in one day the execration of his people and the out-cast of the earth, although pitiful, gives in his opinion, but a slight idea of what he feels.—Laius, Jocasta, Citheron, are the names he calls upon incessantly. He dares not pronounce that of father, or of husband. But returning tenderness makes him wish to take an everlasting leave of his daughters. The children are brought to him: he holds them close embraced in his arms: he bathes them with bloody tears. What emotions of grief and tenderness must not such a spectacle produce! Creon at length endeavours to persuade him to retire into his palace; and can no otherwise suspend the violence of his despair, than by promising him to obtain, as a favour from the Gods, that banishment to which he had condemned himself.

Let us now take these several paintings, and reunite them together; and we shall find, that they all form but one tragic picture. A mere painter can represent a single instant only. Tragedy reunites several in one point of view. It is the same picture, diversified from one end to the other. The same dispositions, the same proportions, the same end. In the Oedipus of Sophocles the general disposition is above all criticism: the proportions are scrupulously exact, and the end so grand and striking, that it becomes the true source of that pleasure which this piece inspires. By the end I mean that inexplicable interest which at first excites curiosity, and increases it in proportion as it satisfies it. Whoever reads Oedipus, and is in the least degree attentive to his own emotions, will find, that he passes from fear to hope, and from hope to fear, to arrive at last to compassion mixed with terror: happy effect of that interest which is diffused throughout the work, like life in every part of the body! The character of each personage in the drama is strongly marked, and so well supported that they all in concert contribute to those alternate emotions, occasioned by the two Oracles. A very simple movement, for a machine, which, by its effects, appears to be composed of innumerable parts, and yet has in itself nothing of complication. All is useful, all necessary: there is not one superfluous scene: not one episode; nor the smallest part that could be retrenched. In a word, it is interesting to the highest degree; and what is it that charms us in all the beauties of nature, or of art, but that affecting quality? It makes the grace and soul of tragic beauty: and this it is that has united all the suffrages in favour of Oedipus; except of those, perhaps, whose imaginations are not strong enough to transport them to the theatre of Athens, and to make them for a moment forget that of Paris.

But we will now take a view of the objections which may be made to this tragedy of Sophocles. I shall forbear to mention such as turn upon the obscurity of the text, the manners of the Greeks, and such trifling matters. They do not deserve to be enquired into: and the only answer that ought to be given is, to refer those by whom they are made either to the text, or to the Athenian *pit*. It will be sufficient to repeat one of this kind, and which seems to be the most reasonable.—Why did not Oedipus kill himself? The answer is easy.—He had no weapon. It was not the custom to wear any. He asked for arms: his attendants refused to bring them; and opposed the madness of his grief. Thus reduced to use as a weapon whatever first presented itself, he snatches a clasp from the robe of his dead wife, and with it he tears out his eyes. A punishment which bears so much the greater conformity to his misfortunes, as it appears to him to be more dreadful than that death which he envies Jocasta. Nothing can be more simple than the solution of this question; and Sophocles has taken care to furnish it.

He is reproached with a more capital fault than this, which Aristotle has observed. How was it possible to suppose that Oedipus could either neglect to revenge the death of Laius, or be ignorant of the manner of it? He had been married to Jocasta several years; was it not highly probable, that he would be informed of every circumstance relating to the murder of his predecessor, and that he would cause a strict search to be made for the perpetrators of so horrid a crime? Aristotle[1] indeed, who has observed, endeavours to excuse this fault, by saying, that it is a circumstance foreign to the piece: that it does not enter into the composition of the subject; and that Sophocles, finding himself under a necessity of making use of this improbable circumstance, has, with great judgment, avoided placing it within the action of his piece, in which he ought to be imitated by all tragic poets; who in the like difficulty ought to make whatever is improbable, or without reason, either precede or follow the action. But even this excuse shews, that it is much better to avoid an improbability, though it does not enter immediately

---

[1] Poetics, chap. 15 & 16.

into the action: and this fault, though canonised by Aristotle, is not less a fault. But it will be more readily pardoned, as it is the source of all the marvellous in the tragedy; since every thing depends upon that happy ignorance of Oedipus, who, in seeking what he is ignorant of, finds more than he would have been willing to know.

M. Dacier sees but this one fault in the whole play. Others, less ardent in their admiration of Sophocles, see an act too much in it. And this is the fifth. The piece, say they, is finished in the fourth act, after the discovery made by Phorbas and the Corinthian shepherd. There is indeed some foundation for this charge. Oedipus knows his birth. The criminal is discovered. The sentence he pronounced is fallen upon himself. Yet it cannot be said, that the action is absolutely terminated, for these reasons. First, the Oracle of Apollo is not obeyed; for it was not only necessary, that the criminal should be discovered, but that he should be banished likewise. Now this must be done by the king and the people: for they made the law. The decision of the people therefore, and of Creon, who sees himself raised to the throne by the misfortunes of Oedipus, must be waited for. Secondly, it was so unlikely that this criminal should be found to be the king himself, that it cannot be supposed the sentence should be executed behind the scene, as it would have been, had the criminal been only a private person. The nature of the crime, and the criminal, certainly suspends, and in some degree prolongs the action. Thirdly, besides the murder of Laius, the perpetrator of which is discovered, there is also a complication of fatal accidents which must be revealed, in order to come to this first crime: I mean, parricide and incest: accidents which, having made part of the intrigue, ought also to make part of the *dénouement*, or untying it. The spectator surely would not have been satisfied, if he was left ignorant of the destiny of Jocasta, Oedipus, and his family, who are all involved in the same misfortune, by the discovery of more than they sought to know. The discovery ought always to be conformable to the intrigue. The concatenation of the two Oracles, and the two crimes, one of which leads to the knowledge of the other, must all be unravelled; and this could not be done completely, unless the spectator is informed, that Jocasta is punished; and that Oedipus, now the most miserable of mankind, is preparing to undergo the sentence he pronounced; that he is deprived of sight by his own hands; and that at length his hapless posterity is drag'd down the precipice he led them to. I add moreover, that the end of the piece being a double affair of state, in which the preservation of the people is concerned, and the race of Laius for ever deprived of the kingdom, it is necessary that the event should be conformable to this end, as the unravelling of the intrigue should be conformable to the intrigue itself.

After all, if the critics will obstinately maintain, that this fifth act may be wholly omitted, without any prejudice to the piece, yet it cannot be denied, that it is admirably well blended with it. It is so pathetic, and heightens in such a manner the agitation of the drama, that it well deserves our indulgence, in not examining too rigorously, if its connexion with the rest be necessary, or only barely useful at best. We would have readily pardoned the two last acts of the Horatii of Corneille, if they had been as happily added as this last act of Oedipus with the rest.

The first thing that strikes, and which I have reserved for my last examination, is the subject itself: the foundation of which seems faulty in the opinion of many. What is the crime of Oedipus? they say. An insolent fellow reproaches him to his face with his being a foundling, and not the son of Polybus. Upon this he goes to consult the Oracle of Delphos. The God, instead of answering his question, predicts to him, that he shall murder his father, and be the husband of his mother. Oedipus, by the silence of Apollo, being confirmed in his opinion, that Polybus is his father, is so truly virtuous, that, to avoid the possibility of accomplishing this horrible prediction, he banishes himself from his country, wanders as chance directs, and at last arrives at Thebes. There fortune smiles upon him. He confounds the Sphinx; becomes king of Thebes, and the husband of Jocasta. And most certainly he is ignorant, that it is his mother who is his wife. In all this, if there be any crime, it is Apollo, and not Oedipus, who is guilty. Yet it is Oedipus who suffers for this crime. And by what a dreadful punishment! We will answer these articles severally. And, first, it is clear, that, laying aside all theology, either pagan or Christian, Sophocles has made Oedipus criminal. But in what does his guilt consist? it will be asked. I answer in this, that he murdered an old man in the road to Delphos. It is true he thought himself insulted by that old man. This circumstance extenuates, but does not acquit him of guilt: for a moderate man would have examined into the nature of the dispute, and have taken care to be informed of the rank of the person to whom he was required to give way. Yet more, although as a good king he loves his people, yet he has the vices of a private man, and even of an imprudent king. He is choleric, proud, and inquisitive, to excess. Such is the picture which Sophocles has drawn of him. Oedipus therefore is not an irreproachable prince. Nor would the rules of tragic art have permitted, that a perfectly virtuous man should be loaded with misfortunes. I acknowledge, that Oedipus seems not to merit those miseries to which he ignorantly condemned himself. But it is this which makes the delicacy of the art, which consists in setting to shew a man whose crimes are small, and misfortunes great. As to the involuntary

crimes of Oedipus, Apollo has predicted them, and they are ratified by
Fate. Such is the pagan theology. Inevitable destiny is the great hinge
upon which it turns. It would be an injury to the reader to load these
remarks with a great number of extracts from antiquity, which are easy
enough to compile, but very tiresome to read. A very superficial knowledge of the Greeks and Latins is sufficient for this purpose, and without
going further than the tragic poets, who are better commentators upon
each other than their several commentators upon them, we shall find no
tragedy in which destiny is not regarded as the soul of all that passes
here. Yet free will is not without a place in this strange theology; for
they make a proper distinction between voluntary crimes and those
which proceed merely from the force of destiny. It is very probable, that
by setting the true value of terms, the Greeks will be found to acknowledge a real free will, and only an imaginary destiny, especially when
they speak as philosophers. Their justice in distributing rewards and
punishments shew[s] this more plainly than their writings, and it appears
even in their writings, of which Plato's are a proof. But as the poets in
their tragedies address themselves to the people, and consequently adopt
a popular manner of speaking, they allow a great deal to fate and very
little to free will, without considering how difficult it is to reconcile
these two opinions. In effect, notwithstanding the lights we derive from
Christianity, we find, that self-love has such influence over us, that we
excuse our errors and vices by this popular language: *It was my destiny;
my stars would have it so.* Some distinction must therefore be made
between the different manners of speaking on this subject. But, without
entering into the examination, we may lay it down as a certain principle,
that among the antients fatality was the prime mover of all great events.
In this supposition, if we would receive pleasure from a Greek drama,
we are obliged for a few moments to adopt their system. It is absurd
indeed; but we must forget it is so, since it did not appear such to the
Grecian spectators, with whom we mix. If we should represent a French
prince on our theatre avowing these pagan notions, he would be hissed;
but Augustus might do so, and there would be no impropriety in it. Let
us be equally just to Oedipus, and not condemn him on the very principle which renders him most interesting.

One perceives by this, the passions are much interested. We need
only unfold, if it be possible, this secret sentiment. If Oedipus was a
flagitious wretch, who voluntarily abandoned himself to all those crimes
which he commits, without being able to avoid them, he would raise
indignation in us equal to that we feel at the recital of those wicked
actions whose authors are condemned to the severest punishment, and
whose memory we would erase from mankind. If he was absolutely per-

fect, this indignation would not be less; but it would fall upon the Gods, who decree those miseries which he has not merited. But Oedipus being criminal but in a small degree, and miserable in a very great one, with excellent qualities, and some virtues, he excites in us a mixed sentiment, or rather a sentiment of a particular kind. For this double indignation is then changed into compassion for Oedipus, and fear of the Gods, who punish even involuntary crimes in a person who is not wholly free from guilt. Hence arises that sympathetic concern for ourselves blended with our compassion; which restrains us from committing the same faults that we see are productive of such fatal consequences. This is the pure doctrine of Aristotle, or rather that of nature, or true wisdom. We have remaining some French tragedies of this kind, among others the Phedra of Racine, which shall be spoke of in its place. Racine has not neglected to place the incestuous passion of Phedra to the account of destiny, for the reasons I have already mentioned. We will now proceed to the other plays upon this subject.

Euripides wrote a tragedy upon the story of Oedipus. But there are only a few fragments of it remaining, from whence we cannot form any judgment of it.

What Lies behind the Notes:
The Translations of the *Antigone* of
Sophocles in the 18th Century

Suzanne Saïd and Christian Biet

There is currently a renewed interest in translation and its problems. But up to now little account has been taken of notes in considering what is at stake and the strategy of translation. We will attempt here to do this by examining the notes of three great annotated translations of the *Antigone* of Sophocles:

— *Les tragedies de Sophocle*, trans. by M. Dupuis (or Dupuy) L., of the Academie royale des Inscriptions et Belles-Lettres, Paris, 1761, vol. 2 (cited as Dupuis).

— *Le Théâtre des Grecs*, by R. P. Brumoy, new edition by MM. de Rochefort and Du Theil for the first three volumes and by M. Prevost for the others, Paris, 1785-9 (cited as Brumoy₂).

— *Le Théâtre de Sophocle*, translated entirely with remarks and an examination by M. de Rochefort, Paris, 1788, vol. 1 (cited as Rochefort).

Why Antigone?

If we have chosen these three translations, it is first because of their date. These three works all appear in the second half of the 18th century, that is to say at a time when translators attempt to get themselves recognised and to give respectable foundations to their art. It is also because these translations form a coherent body. Brumoy₂ and Rochefort actually refer several times explicitly to Dupuis, whether to criticise or commend him. All three refer equally to the first edition of *Le Théâtre des Grecs* of R.P. Brumoy, Paris 1730 (which we will desig-

nate henceforth as Brumoy₁) whether to complete it (Dupuis), to follow
it up (Brumoy₂) or lastly to criticise it (Rochefort). Whatever the case,
these three translations, with their text, their notes and their commentary, derive directly from the text of 1730. So Brumoy₁ closely combined a summarising commentary, which gave the *idea* of the text, with
direct translations of the Greek which guaranteed the *exactness* of the
translation, and with citations from the *Antigone* of Rotrou (1639) who
demonstrated its *beauty* in the theatre. The ensemble of these three versions constituted for him alone a perfect translation, at once beautiful
and faithful, ancient and modern. The successors of Brumoy₁ renounced
this impossible dream. They required a more exact translation; and this
exactness could be obtained only *through the means of notes* which made
possible the integration of knowledge accumulated by the Academie des
Inscriptions. But none the less they did not simply give up the idea of
putting their translations at the service of a moral and aesthetic ideal;
which the notes, those too, will undertake to keep in mind as they
examine the text and set it against the French theatrical tradition.

Why the notes?

Like the prefaces or the observations, the notes first of all allow
the identification of the real sources of a translator who ceases for a
moment to disappear completely behind the author. The dual system of
notes adopted by Dupuis invites us to distinguish clearly between two
very different publics. On the one hand, the layman "whom the translator must keep foremost in mind in his work."[1] It is for them that the
notes, usually brief, situated at the bottom of the page, are intended. On
the other hand, there are "the specialists who intend to compare the
translation with the text."[2] It is to them that are addressed the 55 notes
relegated to the end of the text. But with Brumoy₂, as with Rochefort,
there exists but one type of notes at the bottom of the page. Does that
mean that the distinction between the two publics has completely disappeared? No, because in the *Observations sur les difficultés qui se ren-
contrent dans la traduction des poètes tragiques grecs* (observations that
are found in successive editions of the *Théâtre des Grecs* of R.P.
Brumoy and in the *Théâtre de Sophocle* of Rochefort), it is equally
emphasised that the translations, which "are made for those who do not
understand the language being translated," are of interest also to "the
learned people who can pass judgement on them" (Cf. Brumoy₂, p.
325).

---

[1] Cf. the "Avertissement" of Dupuis.
[2] Ibid.

The notes also let us penetrate behind the scenes of the translation. When they treat the readers as scholars who compare the translation to the text, they quote the Greek or approach it through the intermediary of a Latin translation or a more literal French "translation."[3] It thus gives us a "this side" of the translation. When it is intended for the less knowledgeable, it goes "beyond" and develops the translation by the summoning up of "some particulars necessary for the understanding of the text"[4] concerning "the art and the intention of the poet, the customs of the country or the customs of the time" (cf. Rochefort, p. XLII). They show therefore, by the very effort that they make to fill it in, the gap that remains between "the manuscript in one language" and "the discourse formulated in the first place in another," to take up the terms of the article "Traduction" of the *Encyclopédie*.[5]

So then, dual public, dual function for the notes? That would be too simple. When looked at closely, the notes reveal themselves as the privileged domain of ambiguity and free play:

— typographically they present themselves as something other than the translation. They are often just another form of it;

— the notes claim to eliminate the distance between the text of origin and the translated text, Antiquity and the 18th century. Most often they reveal it;

— they would like to seem objective and scientific. In fact, they often permit the diversion of the discourse toward ideological ends.

I. THE NOTE OR THE OTHER TRANSLATION

The distinction which the typography establishes between translation and note is sometimes just an illusion. In Dupuis' edition the notes in effect make it possible to present alternative solutions. Sometimes the translator leaves to the typography, and to it alone, the task of marking his preference between two solutions, since he introduces the second by a simple *or*. Thus in vv. 473–475, the text translates: "Oui, mais sachez qu'on vient souvent à bout de la dureté la plus opiniâtre," but the note at the bottom of the page proposes also: "*ou* qu'elle réussit mal." The second translation presented as a note can also diminish the boldness that the translator exhibits in the text. When Dupuis proposes an original translation for vv. 1317–1318, he makes use of the notes 53 and 54 to

---

[3] Cf. *Encyclopédie ou Dictionnaire raisonné des sciences, des arts et des métiers par une société de gens de lettres; mis en ordre et publié par M. ***, Neuchatel, 1765, art. "Traduction," p. 817.

[4] Cf. Dupuis in his "Avertissement."

[5] See *supra* no. 3.

recall that another interpretation, having either the authority of the ancient commentators or the approval of modern translators, is equally possible. The note can, in short, as in v. 791, present by using an *otherwise*, a different sense even while recalling the translator's preference for the "first sense" which "appears more natural" to him. There is no sign, after Dupuis, of this lack of differentiation between text and note. Given the place of this translation in the series, one can see there a sign of the time when the note is still looking for its true status in relation to the text.

As a rule however, and this as early as Dupuis, the distribution of the translations between the text and the notes justifies itself by a difference of kind. To take up a distinction worked out by the *Encyclopédie*,[6] one can say that the text is the place of the *translation*, whereas the note is the place of the *version*. The former, "more subject in its expressions to the nuances and idioms" of French places itself by the side of the target language. The latter, "more literal, more tied to the ways of going about things proper to the original language" comes closer to the source language. The note therefore permits the translator to fill the gap which separates the French from the Greek with an equivalent so literal that it can be introduced with the formula "the Greek says that . . .,"[7] but also sometimes to mark it by reminding us that "the Greek expression is even stronger" (Cf. Dupuis, p. 217, n.a.). But this function of the note, which is extremely developed in the edition of Dupuis (16 examples), tends to disappear when one comes to Rochefort (4 examples) et Brumoy₂ (2 examples), doubtless because the translator becomes more sure of his rights *vis-à-vis* the original. The translation ends up by actually becoming the true text and by serving as the standard. To introduce a literal translation, one finds Rochefort penning an unexpected but revealing expression: "le texte *ajoute* que . . ." [the text *adds* that] (p. 370, n. 1).

II. THE NOTE AND THE TEXT

A. *The Note and the Greek*
The favoured location of literal translation, the note is also the only place where the Greek text ever appears. The three translations of *Antigone* which we are studying do not figure in some bilingual editions

---

[6] Ibid.

[7] Dupuis also introduces the literal French translation by the formula Gr., followed by the text in French, for example p. 272, n.a. One finds the same thing with Brumoy₂, p. 216, n. 1: "Le grec porte . . .", and p. 263, n. 2: "Gr.: . . ." See finally Rochefort, p. 299, n. 2: "Le grec dit . . ."

which would be the ancestors of the existing "Collection des universités de France." The Greek appears there only occasionally, and always in the form of fragments that are reduced at times to one or two words and never exceed four or five verses; and its presence is always tied to the existence of a textual problem or one of translation.

Textual problems. But with Dupuis as with Brumoy$_2$ who usually borrows his erudition from Dupuis,[8] this text is the one from the *éditions* (essentially that of H. Estienne[9] for Dupuis and that of Vauvilliers[10] for Brumoy$_2$) and not the one from the manuscripts;[11] and the translator is untroubled except when there is a divergence between the editions being used.[12] Everything apparently changes with Rochefort, who inserts references to manuscripts on a large scale and sometimes even gives their listing.[13] So is the translator suddenly changed into an editor? No, but the edition has changed. Rochefort has in his hands the edition of Brunck[14] which has just appeared, and it is with him as intermediary that he has access to the manuscript tradition.[15] He acknowledges moreover in his preface "all that he owes in the way of enlightenment to the magnificent edition of Mr Brunck" and cites it abundantly in the notes.[16]

---

[8] See for example Brumoy$_2$, p. 263, n. 1, and Dupuis, no. 34.

[9] *Tragoediae VII, graece (et Ajax atque Electra latine) una cum omnibus graecis scholiis, et cum Latinis J. Camerarii. H. Stephanus*, in –4°, 1568. It is this text which is adopted by Tonson and Watts *Tragoediae Septem (gr. et lat.) cum selectis variis lectionibus*, London, 1747) to which Dupuis refers for the verse numeration in his preface. Dupuis refers also to the first edition of the text of Sophocles (*Sophoclis Tragoediae septem cum commentariis (graece) Venetiis in Aldi romani Academia*, 1502). Finally, he knows the editions of Grotius (*Excerpta ex tragoediis et comoediis graecis emendata et latinis versibus explicata*, Paris 1626) and of Johnson (*Tragoediae Septem (gr. et lat.): additae sunt lectiones variantes et notae Th. Johnson . . .*, Glasgow, 1745).

[10] *Tragoediae VII (gr.) cum interpretatione lat. et scholiis veteribus ac novis. Editionem curavit J. Capperonnier, eo defuncto edidit, notas, praefationem et indicem adjecit J. Fr. Vauvilliers* (Paris, 1781).

[11] Note 49 of Dupuis shows this well. This translator actually presents as an error of the scholiast what is in fact the text of the manuscripts, and opposes it to a text which is a correction adopted by editors.

[12] See Dupuis n. 10, 11, 13, 17, 34, 41; and Brumoy$_2$, p. 213, n. 1, and 263, n. 1.

[13] Cf. p. 322, n. 1: "Manuscrit du Roi, cote 7212."

[14] By common consent of modern scholars (e.g. J. E. Sandys, *A History of Classical Scholarship*, ed. 3, London, 1967, vol. II, p. 395), this edition opens a new era in the history of the text of Sophocles by suppressing the interpolations of Triclinius and by returning to the edition by Aldus and to the Parisinus A.

[15] As is shown by formulas like "I read as does Mr Brunck . . ." (p. 299, n. 3) or "It appears that one must read as does Mr Brunck . . ." (p. 323, n. 1), etc.

[16] The other editions (be it Aldus or Vauvilliers) play no more than an episodic role.

This scientific concern however has its limits. The principles on which the translators (including Rochefort who did not follow Brunck "with free abandon" and permitted himself to "not be always of the opinion of the author," cf. p. XLIII) base themselves to establish the text when they discuss it have nothing rigorous about them. They only very rarely appeal to the rules of how the language functions, to the immediate context, to parallels and to the scholia. In certain cases they do not even go to the trouble of justifying their preferences. Dupuis, for example, is content with a "I would like better . . ." or a "what is better"—more categorical still. More often the translators condemn the transmitted text for logical reasons (because an idea is "out of place," cf. Dupuis, n. 28, or because a word "does not mean anything here," cf. Dupuis, n. 11) or aesthetic (because "nothing is more insipid," cf. Dupuis, n. 34). Lastly they adduce, like Rochefort, probability and the proprieties. Probability, when he attributes v. 572: "Cher Hémon, que ton père tient peu compte de toi!" to Antigone against the authority of Brunck and the reading of the manuscripts (which give it to Ismene), and so allows the heroine to make known her fondness (for Haemon) with this single word" (cf. p. 340, n. 1). Propriety, when he justifies in v. 735 a correction whose principal merit is "to soften the reply of Haemon, who would sin through harshness and the lack of seemliness" (cf. p. 350, n. 1).

Translational problems. For the Greek text, by its mere presence, permits Dupuis and Rochefort to refute the interpretations of the scholiasts or Latin translators. It also permits them to justify a translation in giving the construction of a passage, in re-establishing in its entirety an elided form or a passage with a word understood, in specifying the meaning of a form, particle or adjective. It permits them, in short, to specify, thanks to comparisons and parallels, a sense "more in conformity with the thought and the ordinary style of the poet" (cf. Dupuis, n. 4). By contrast, in the works of Brumoy$_2$, whose erudition is second hand, the Greek only appears through the quotations made by previous scholars, be it Dupuis, or more still, Vauvilliers.[17]

An argument for a translation or, more often still, a decisive polemic instrument, the Greek appears also in order to mark the limits of the translation. It indicates a word or expression which the translator admits not having rendered.[18] It also marks the distance that separates the "translation" from a literal "version" (cf. Dupuis, n. 7, 9) or from a text which "appears altered" (that is why only the 'idea' is kept, cf. Dupuis, n. 34). It intervenes, in short, to mark the limitations that the

---

[17] Cf. p. 256, n. 1; p. 286, n. 1.

[18] Cf. Dupuis, n. 3; and Rochefort p. 389 n. 1.

target language imposes on the translator and to excuse the length or the fullness of a translation.[19]

B. *The status of Latin*

If, in a general way, Greek appears little, Latin, from Dupuis to Rochefort, itself tends to disappear, both as a language of substitution and as a language of translation.

In the notes at the bottom of the page in Dupuis, the Latin served as a substitute for the Greek. After expressions like "le *texte grec* porte . . ." or "*grec*," one would see the appearance of Latin phrases which were a literal translation of the Greek and took the place of the text.[20] In the works of Rochefort, with one exception (cf. p. 304, n. 1), it is always the literal *French* translation which takes the place of the Greek text.[21]

Moreover, for Dupuis, all the previous translations of the *Antigone* of Sophocles were in Latin (he never refers back to the French translation of Baif).[22] But for his successors, the appearance of a contemporary French translation made the reference to Latin translators unnecessary. Rochefort cites only once "les versions latines" (cf. p. 354, n. 1).

If Latin loses its status as the language of translation from Dupuis to Rochefort, it still remained a necessary bridge between the Greek and the French. In the works of the one, as in the works of the other, the note sometimes justifies the French translation by giving, after the Greek translation and its construction, its "version latine."[23] But in this function Latin begins to find a competitor in a literal translation in French. The phenomenon already appears with Dupuis,[24] but it is more clearly noticeable in the works of his successors. Thus, from Dupuis to Brumoy$_2$, one sees the disappearance of the Latin translation in the note that specifies the sense of v. 722.[25] Even in the works of Dupuis one finds the worth of Latin as a language of translation called into question. Indeed this scholar contrasts a Greek "which unites at the same time

---

[19] Cf. Dupuis, n. 35, 50; and Rochefort, p. 389, n. 1.

[20] Cf. p. 217, n.a; p. 229, n.a.; p. 240, n.a.; p. 242, n.a.; p. 259, n.a. and 51.

[21] See for example p. 299, n. 2. It is the same for Brumoy$_2$ (for example p. 216, n. 1).

[22] Paris, 1573.

[23] Cf. Dupuis, n. 1, 2, 10, 19, 32, 33, 36; and Rochefort, p. 329, n. 1; p. 344, n. 1; p. 350, n. 1, and p. 354, n. 1.

[24] Cf. p. 253, n.a., and p. 267, n.a. It can also happen that he juxtaposes a Latin "version" and a French "version," p. 282, n.a.

[25] Cf. Dupuis, n. 33; and Brumoy$_2$, p. 256, n. 1.

elegance and conciseness, energy and grace" with a "Latin expression" which "is thin, without fire, without elegance, and weakly expresses only a part of the ideas which the text presents" (cf. n. 35).

So the presence of Greek and Latin in the notes ostensibly serves some scientific requirements. But in reality these two languages allow the imposition of a sense and are the instruments of a strategy that goes beyond them. And they fill this role each in its own way. Greek, simply by its presence, is an argument of authority, in the first instance for the use of scholars (in the notes at the end of Dupuis' book), then for the use of everyone, and so for those who do not know it; thus making its effect even stronger. As for Latin, it is clear that it loses its role as indispensable interpreter between the two languages. It is no longer required in order to decipher the Greek or to anticipate the French.

III. THE NOTE AND THE CONTEXT

Notes are not only the place where the sense of the text is construed. They are also what makes possible the clarification of the text by an ancient context which is not always the one expected.

A. The Sophoclean corpus

One could think *a priori* that the commentary on a tragedy of Sophocles would give a favoured place to the works of this author. Originally, nothing of the sort. It is only in note 4, to establish the sense of v. 59, that Dupuis bases himself on vv. 79 and 906 of *Antigone* to show that his interpretation is "in conformity with the thought and ordinary style of the poet." If he refers elsewhere (cf. n. 20 and 32) to Sophocles to clarify the sense of a word or justify a construction, he uses him as one witness among others of the state of the Greek language, on a par with Herodotus or Isocrates.

On the other hand, in the edition of Rochefort, which constitutes the *first complete translation* of the works of Sophocles and presents at last "all of his masterpieces, collected and reproduced by the same hand" (cf. p. 1), the notes are one way of making the unity of the author perceptible, henceforth guaranteed by the coherence of the translation. They refer to notes on other tragedies of Sophocles like *Ajax* and *Oedipus at Colonus* (cf. p. 299, n. 1 and p. 366, n. 1). They cite a mannerism of Sophocles, whether for style ("One finds many examples in the works of Sophocles of these ironic epithets"[26]) or for characterisation ("When Sophocles wanted to make Oedipus unhappy, he took care to present him

---

[26] Cf. p. 299, n. 1. See also p. 399, n. 1, concerning a figure of rhetoric.

as a tyrant who abuses his power. Here he uses *the same behaviour* in relation to Creon [. . .]," cf. p. 318, n. 1). They also indicate variations in the treatment of the same myth by contrasting *Oedipus at Colonus* with *Antigone* with regard to the death of Oedipus (cf. p. 301, n. 1). In thus explaining a particular tragedy by using the entirety of Sophocles' work, they make it possible to see his plays as a coherent whole.

B. *The civilization of antiquity*

Furthermore, notes make it possible to put the text of the tragedy into contact with an Antiquity which is first an ensemble of legends well known to the readers. They do this without doubt to clarify the translation. Thanks to quotations from Homer and Euripides, but also (and above all) from Apollonius, Diodorus, Apollodorus, Pausanias or even from a Latin author like Virgil,[27] Dupuis explains the mythological allusions which the text of *Antigone* contains. But he also gives his reader a veritable course in mythology, comparing the version kept by Sophocles with a series of others, on the subjects of Lycurgus, Menoeceus, the sons of Phineus, Danae, or Niobe.[28] But if the text thus becomes a pretext for mythology, the mythology itself is sometimes only a pretext for settling a quarrel between scholars and for displaying the stupidity of a colleague. And Dupuis criticises the Abbot Faydit who had dared to reproach Virgil for an anachronism when he placed Lycurgus before the Trojan War.[29]

There are a good number of mythological notes to be found in Rochefort's edition. But never are they anything but a summary of those of Dupuis,[30] and the precise references are replaced by vague allusions to "some traditions." Rochefort cites nothing beyond Homer and Pausanias and restricts himself as a rule to introducing such or such a version of the legend by an "it appears that . . ." This vagueness is not to be explained simply by a lesser erudition. It seems rather to ensue from a weakening of the credit accorded to the myths. Rochefort also does not hesitate to criticize them in the name of reason (cf. p. 358, n. 1), something Dupuis never did. Comparison of the notes which the two translators devote to the legend of Niobe[31] is, from this point of view,

---

[27] Cf. n. 39: Homer; n. 52: Euripides; n. 38: Apollonius; n. 39, 40: Diodorus; n. 39, 40, 52: Apollodorus; p. 259, n.a.: Pausanias; n. 39: Virgil.

[28] cf. n. 39: Lycurgus; n. 52: Menoeceus; n. 40: the sons of Phineus; n. 38: Danae; p. 259, n.a.: Niobe.

[29] In his *Remarques sur Virgile et Homère et le style poétique dans l'Écriture Sainte*, Paris 1705-1710. See Dupuis n. 39.

[30] Cf. p. 364, n. 1 ("As Mr Dupuy observed in note 38); p. 365, n. 2 (cf. Dupuis, n. 39), and p. 366, n. 2 (cf. Dupuis, n. 40).

[31] Cf. Dupuis, p. 259, n.a.; and Rochefort, p. 358, n. 1.

very revealing. What Dupuis does is to cite exactly the passage from
Pausanias where Pausanias evokes Niobe and Mt. Sipyle. Rochefort, by
contrast, rapidly summarizes it before becoming indignant towards the
obscurantism that this narrative shows, saying: "How many similar
traditions have been invented or adjusted according to the configuration
of places." Equally, with regard to the Bosporus:[32] where Dupuis
provides one mythological note (on the legend of Phineus), Rochefort
gives two notes, one mythological note which is a rapid summary of that
of Dupuis and a geographic note on the Bosporus which shows a new
interest for *realia*. If Rochefort, like his predecessor, continues to use
the note as an instrument of instruction, he no longer makes it serve for
lessons in mythology. He prefers to speak of history of religions and to
treat for example the status of the sun in the mysteries (cf. p. 378, n. 1).

The note is, in this way, the occasion for displaying the scholarship of the translator and at the same time establishing his authority. But
it must be recognised that, from Dupuis to Rochefort, the content of the
scholarship changes. In Dupuis, who sees himself "an academic
scholar," the erudition is strictly philological. This translator devotes for
example a three page note (p. 48) to establish the meaning of ξίφος and
ἔγχος in tragedy, so taking sides in the dispute which recently compared
"two learned academicians, MM. Fourmont the elder and Abbot Sol-
lier." Rochefort, on the other hand, is interested foremost in geography.
He discusses the situation of the Bosporus of Thrace or the city of Nyssa
in Ethiopia (cf. p. 336, n. 1, and p. 377, n. 2), basing himself on a
recent work, the translation of the *Histories* of Herodotus with historical
and critical remarks, an essay on the chronology of Herodotus and a
geographic table, by Father H. Larcher (1786). He also asks questions
about civilization, by asking himself, for example, with regard to v.
1038, about the kinds of *electrum* with which the ancients were familiar
(cf. p. 370, n. 2).

In short, from Dupuis to Rochefort and Brumoy₂, the notes make
it possible to relate the text to a classical culture perceived as a
homogeneous unity and reconstructed by means of quotations from
authors of every era, Greek as well as Latin.

In this way Dupuis relies on Athenaeus to see in v. 1167 of
Antigone: "For when one has lost pleasures, I hold that one no longer
lives: one is but a body without soul" a maxim which "serves as a guide
to Epicurus to make the sovereign good reside in pleasure" (cf. p. 282,
n.a.). He discovers in a letter from Cicero to Atticus (12.4) the thought
which Antigone expresses in vv. 74–75 (cf. n. 5). He points out a pas-

---

[32] Cf. Dupuis, n. 4, and Rochefort, p. 366, n. 1 and 2.

sage from an ode of Horace which expresses literally the same idea as the Ode on man from *Antigone* (cf. n. 34).

In the same way Rochefort likes to point out, in the text of Sophocles, the paraphrasing of a maxim attributed to Chilon or Bias (cf. p. 309, n. 1). He does not hesitate, *à propos* the criticism of tyranny which finds expression in *Antigone*, to recall the accusations of Plato against the poet-friends of tyrants (cf. p. 332, n. 1).

But above all it is Brumoy$_2$ who is fond of following, through Greek or Latin authors, the different formulations of an idea or sentiment which he finds in the text of Sophocles. He takes up Dupuis' parallels from Cicero and Horace to add to them two references to the *Moralia* of Plutarch where the sentiment expressed by the text of Sophocles would be "perfectly developed".[33]

The Ancients then form a unity for the three translators of the 18th century. But the notes show that the relation kept up with them changes completely from Dupuis (and Brumoy$_2$), to Rochefort. For the first two, whose place is in the continuation of the *Théâtre des Grecs* of Father Brumoy (Brumoy$_1$), there is nothing specific to antique civilization, and the note permits a bridging between the Ancients and the reader. At the very time that Brumoy$_1$ seems most to be drawing the attention of the public to the *antique* character of the Farewells to the Sun of Antigone when speaking of "these complaints *in the manner of the Ancients* which the Latin people call *novissima verba*," he immediately erases the barrier created between different civilizations by drawing a parallel with the Old Testament and comparing the farewells of Antigone "to the tears shed by the daughter of Jephtha when she went to the mountains to mourn her virginity before being sacrificed" (cf. p. 193–195). In the same way Dupuis does not content himself with comparing the justification which Antigone gives for her act in vv. 904 *sq.* with what the wife of Intaphernes says in Book III of Herodotus' *Histories*; he quotes an example borrowed from the history of England of Rapin-Thomas "who provides a rather similar way of looking at things" (cf. n. 37). One finds in Brumoy$_2$, with regard to the same passage, the same adducing of an antique text (the reference to the treatise of Plutarch *On Brotherly Love* substituted here for Herodotus), and a contemporary reference, with the same allusion to the history of Robert le Roux (cf. p. 269, n. 1). On the other hand Rochefort, who keeps the parallel of the wife of Intaphernes and Herodotus, but eliminates all modern reference, signals through the note everything that separates the mentality of the

---

[33] Cf. p. 215, n. 3; p. 263, n. 2; p. 269, n. 1 and p. 272, n. 1 (see Dupuis n. 5 and 34).

Ancients and the Moderns, by pointing out that the feeling which inspires Antigone "appeared natural *in the eyes of the Ancients*" (cf. p. 362, n. 1). In the same way, even when Dupuis and Brumoy$_2$ were intent on indicating, with regard to vv. 74–75, the permanence of an identical idea, from Sophocles to Cicero, and so implicitly giving it the status of eternal truth,[34] Rochefort by contrast prefers in the note which he devotes to this passage (cf. p. 303, n. 1), to underline everything that is specific to Greek religion. Thus the note no longer serves to bring Greek civilization close to the reader; it removes it to a distance and makes it an object of study.

This consciousness of a difference between the Ancients and the Moderns which seems to characterise Rochefort is also found in the field of literary criticism when it is expressed in the notes. While Brumoy$_2$ (cf. p. 219, n. 1), after Brumoy$_1$ (cf. p. 180), is conscious of the continuity of literary practice (he points out, with regard to an allegory contained in the *parodos*, that "these kinds of figures are very frequent in the works of the Greek poets," but does not forget to add that a "modern Latin poet uses this successfully" and that "P. Corneille retained this allegory in his translation"), Rochefort on the contrary indicates what is specific to the ancient poets who "used not to tie themselves down to following in one tragedy the same tradition which they had adopted in another," for "they were only looking to stir the emotions" and "they were being asked for moral truths rather than historical truths" (cf. p. 301, n. 1).

But this same Rochefort, who uses imperfect tenses in this way to contrast the Ancients with the Moderns, none the less continues to consider Antiquity as an entity and to neglect the chronological distances. In fact, when he discusses the question of knowing if ordeals were known to the Ancients, he quotes indiscriminately Homer, Plato, Aristotle, the Greek historians, Pliny and the commentary on Virgil by Servius (cf. p. 315, n. 1). What is more, when he criticises Plato for having reproached all the poets for having fawned on tyranny and thus mistakenly putting Sophocles in the same boat as Euripides, he suggests explanations which show a complete disregard for chronology since they assume an Aristotle anterior to Plato. This philosopher would actually have been careful to render justice to Sophocles, "because Aristotle did before him" (cf. p. 332, n. 1).

When they speak Greek or Latin, when they discuss Sophocles or Antiquity, the notes, while pretending to *justify* the translation and to *clarify* it, *authenticate* or even *magnify* it through Greek quotations; they

---

[34] Cf. Dupuis, n. 5; and Brumoy$_2$, p. 215, n. 1.

also make it more *assimilable* thanks to the Latin; they *integrate* it into a Sophoclean corpus which they form; lastly they make it serve towards *classical instruction* and the knowledge of a Greco-Latin culture whose special characteristics they gradually emphasise.

IV. THE WAY THE NOTES ARE DEPLOYED

Up to now we have taken the notes at their face value. But that is to forget that in the first place they make up a complex educational and scholarly apparatus which makes it possible, at the least cost, to pose and resolve aesthetic and ideological problems which are primarily those of the 18th century. They appear when the text is no longer "smooth," when some uneven aspects make the translator hesitate, surprising the reader and running foul of adverse criticism.

On the aesthetic plane, the note becomes the *place of a judgement* which can no longer, as for Brumoy$_1$, be exercised in the text itself.

First it permits the translator to side explicitly with or against what the text says. Thus, with regard to the unity of time, Brumoy$_1$ was praising Sophocles for having "indicated exactly from the first scene" that "the time when the action begins is as night is ending" (cf. p. 175). Its successor, Brumoy$_2$, repeats this observation, but places it in a note and attaches it to v. 16 (cf. p. 212, n. 1). The note thus relates the text of Sophocles to a model and uses it to legitimise rules which were in decline at that time. Conversely, the translator does not hesitate to make use of the note to censure his author in the name of verisimilitude. In the scene of the guard, Dupuis, at the same moment as the guard relates how he caught Antigone in the act, writes in the notes: "We have to suppose that all the deeds detailed in the narrative happened during the time the chorus used to sing the preceding two strophes and antistrophes. They only contain forty short verses. That is very little" (cf. p. 227, n.a.).

One can even follow, through the successive notes of different editions on the same verse, the different manifestations of an identical, though weakening, prejudice. All the translators of the 18th century are equally offended by v. 88 of *Antigone*: "Your heart is aflame for a purpose which ought to chill you" and the appearance of the antithesis of fire and ice in a tragedy. To begin with, Brumoy$_1$ settles the problem in the text itself thanks to a quotation from Rotrou who simply eliminated the image and translated: "How you throw yourself into dangers" (cf. p. 179). Dupuis, who translates: "There is much heat there for an enterprise as futile as it is frightening," restores one of the two terms of the antithesis to his text, while giving in his note the Greek text and his Latin version. But the note not only enables him to point out a gap between text and translation; it also permits him to justify it, as he censures Sophocles: "If such is his idea, the allusion is frigid" (cf. p. 204 and n. 7). Brumoy$_2$ faithfully follows Dupuis, whose note moreover he cites (cf. p. 216). The way Rochefort gets round it is more complex (cf. p. 304).

What he does is retain the antithesis, while modifying the terms, for he translates: "You show much life on behalf of a body that is lifeless." And he uses the note first, like Dupuis, to draw attention to the gap (he gives the Latin "version" of the Greek), then to justify the modification which he introduces, "by changing the expression a little," of an "antithesis which can appear in bad taste." But unlike his predecessors, he is also looking for understanding, and through understanding for a way to excuse the offending passage, as the rest of the note shows: "in any case this utterance of Ismene was possibly a proverbial expression that had lost in actual usage what for us can cause offence." Thus the note legitimises the translation while safeguarding the text with the reference to the socio-linguistic context: to a Greek proverb, identical with a French proverb; and the aesthetic difficulty is smoothed out.

One can in short show how the notes form a system, since one criticism expressed in the works of one, with regard to a particular verse, is taken up again in the works of another in the notes at the end which amount to a commentary on the entirety of the scene.

The second entrance of the guard who speaks to Creon saying: "King, you can't swear to anything" (v. 388), had everything to shock spectators who required from tragedy a language exempt from all triviality. Dupuis translates the verse exactly, at the risk of infringing the law of translation—one must avoid formulas that are too well known—and that of the tragedy—sublime style. But, thanks to the note, he can reveal his distaste for an expression which is somewhat trivial (cf. p. 224, n.a.). Brumoy$_2$, who makes all triviality disappear from the text and translates: "Great King, mankind is master of nothing for sure," uses the note to restore it and to sanction it at the same time, giving a literal and annotated translation of the Greek: "Also," he says rather trivially, "man should not swear to anything." At the same time, the note allows him to justify in some degree Sophocles' lapse with a psychological analysis: "This was a man seized by fear and dread and who, in despair at the thought of being charged with announcing bad news, did not even dare to let it be apprehended in advance, and caused it to be dragged out of him in dribs and drabs. Act I, scene IV. Here this same guard is animated by another feeling entirely: the joy of having found the guilty party, of not being able to be accused of any complicity. This joy transports him [. . .]" (cf. p. 233). In the edition of Rochefort, who translates exactly, the note has disappeared. But it is clear that its content has been retrieved and even developed in the two long notes placed after each of the two appearances of the guard (cf. p. 321, n. 1 and p. 327, n. 1). In the first, Rochefort clearly expresses his criticisms with regard to a scene where "an over-familiar nature prevails," where "the tragedy seems [. . .] to leave behind the dignity that accompanies it to lower itself to the tone of comedy." And if he pretends to justify Sophocles and a scene which would be a rest in the tragedy, it is so that he can all the more condemn a "faulty artistic technique [. . .] which one does not find in the most perfect pieces of the same poet." Unlike his predecessors, Rochefort thus places himself here in a synchronous perspective, and criticises Sophocles by reference to Sophocles himself. In his second note he remains equally in the frame of Greek Antiquity by contrasting Sophocles with the Homeric model: "Sophocles, following Homer's example, was trying to paint faithfully the manners of the least important characters that he placed on stage; and without a doubt he regarded this naïveté of the soldier who is finishing his speech as a characteristic trait which completed his portrait. But there would be a comment to make on the subject. The soldier's thought is natural; but the lack of caution he shows in making his thoughts known is not natural at all. Homer *has a much better grasp of observing the proprieties* in even those traits which seem most carelessly to have run off his pen. When Achilles weeps over the body of Patroclus, Homer says that Achilles' slaves, while appearing to lament the fate of his friend, were lamenting their own sorrows. Here are the laws of propriety and truth, equally observed at the same time. In Homer, it is the Poet who observes and discloses the secrets of his thought. In Sophocles, it is the character who naively says what he thinks, and what the Poet alone must have observed." The note then makes it possible to draw attention to the historical distance which separates the Greek text from the reader, while giving him the means to bridge the gap by setting the text back into its framework. We are very far from the superior tone of Brumoy[1] who, retracing in his manner the history of the genre from its origin up to his era, explained the disappearance of "these antique pieces whose naive refinement did not appear to the Greeks unworthy of tragedy" (cf. p. 182) through the influence of Latin theatre and Seneca.

If the notes often speak of aesthetics, that is not only because they permit the translator to call to mind tragic standards by pointing out their infraction: it is also to conceal problems which are more acute and to divert the reader's attention. For *Antigone* is not only a tragedy whose aesthetics can be discussed: it is also a work capable of troubling a reader who lives in a monarchy with its furious attacks against the tyrant

Creon. The translators of the 18th century were under no illusions about this. Most often, they eliminated the most awkward elements in the translation itself. They sometimes as well made use of the notes to *rectify* that which could be *badly* interpreted.

The problem arises as early as v. 31, at least from Rochefort on, for his predecessors spoke without hesitation (and without notes) of the "good-natured Creon" or of the "kindness" of this king.[35] But the last of the translators of Sophocles in date, while using the adjective "generous" of Creon, shows himself more circumspect, as evidenced by the note (cf. p. 300, n. 1): "One finds many examples in the works of Sophocles of these *ironic* epithets which we thought had to be preserved." The aesthetic argument serves here as a screen and mask for the disrespect.

The note can also take over from the translation in order to correct the text by drawing attention to a stylistic detail or a general problem of aesthetics.

In this way, in v. 470, the words which Antigone speaks to Creon: "But the madman could well be the very one who is calling me mad," could indeed seem shocking. Dupuis (cf. p. 228) attempts to water down this virulence in his translation: "If my conduct seems to you *rash* and foolish, *I venture to say* that these reproaches rebound on your own head." Brumoy[2], who translates exactly: "If you impute conduct like this to madness, it is only in the eyes of a madman that I shall be mad," diverts attention from politics towards literature thanks to a note (cf. 238) which cites Rotrou with praise: "Rotrou is just as forceful when imitating this response." Rochefort, who translates: "This accusation could well be that of an unsound mind,"[36] uses the note (cf. p. 330, n. 1) to focus the reader's attention on the precise problem of translation. "If it was a question of *disguising* one's author and not of *translating* him, it would have been easy to *tone down the harshness* of these expressions." But at the same time he waters down the substance of the text by putting the stress on "the harmony and grace of the Greek which somewhat rectifies the element of excessive harshness which this expression has for our ears and our usages." It is clear that the note here only speaks of ears in order the more easily to obscure the usages.

In vv. 308–309, Brumoy[2] softens Creon's threats to the guards: "Death by itself will not suffice for your punishment: strung up alive you must first acknowledge your insolence," suppressing in his transla-

---

[35] Cf. Dupuis, p. 199; and Brumoy, p. 212.

[36] Rochefort's original text was not available to me. The article by Saïd and Biet reads "Cette accusation pourrait bien être celle d'une insensée." The feminine "insensée" is scarcely credible, and I give what I suppose to be the sense intended.— R.D.D.

tion all explicit allusion to the hanging: "I shall not be content with taking your life. I shall first exact a *lengthy vengeance* for this outrage." Rochefort, who translates: "Death by itself will not be enough for your punishment. You will have to be hung up in the air alive and in that way make me reparation for such an offence," by contrast uses the note (cf. p. 318, n. 1) to divert the mind of the reader from political criticism and direct it towards the problem of the tragic fault by comparing it with *Oedipus Rex*: "When Sophocles wanted to make Oedipus wretched, he took care to present him as a tyrant who abuses his power: here he uses the same procedure for Creon. To see him so unfortunate at the end of the play would be too revolting if he had not shown himself blameworthy during the course of the action."

But if the note masks, it can also emphasise. In vv. 506–507, Rochefort, when his predecessors are content to translate, draws the reader's attention to the critique of tyranny, while pretending to conjure away the political question in favour of a literary debate. The verses of Sophocles become in effect the elements of a dispute in the heart of the Republic of Letters, and illustrate the permanence of the rivalries between writers, whether Greek or French: "One does not understand how Plato, in book VIII of the *Republic*, accusing Euripides of having fawned on tyranny, could include all the Poets in this general reproach and expel them all from his Republic. Was he then ignorant of the violent digs which Sophocles incessantly made against tyranny? Or because Aristotle had done justice to this great Poet, was Plato not anxious to do the same? This motive, which does no honour to philosophy, might not be without foundation or precedent" (cf. p. 332, n. 1).

Lastly, notes make it possible to pose incidentally problems of universal morality. For the readers of the 18th century, there was actually something surprising, even shocking, in the justification which Antigone gives for her act in vv. 904 sqq., when she declares that she has done for a brother what she would not have done for a husband or children. The translators applied themselves first to mitigating the offence by a series of comparisons with Antiquity or modern history. Dupuis (cf. n. 37) thus recalls that "the wife of Intaphernes adduced the same reason which Sophocles puts in the mouth of Antigone" and, for good measure, adds that the history of England furnishes "a rather similar way of looking at things." But that does not prevent him from expressing, in the same note, his disapproval, saying: "A strange morality, whatever one says about it, and scarcely worthy of tragedy." Once more, when morality shocks, aesthetics condemn. Brumoy[2] (cf. p. 269, n. 1) takes up Dupuis' note with the same references, without this time overtly condemning Sophocles' text. With Rochefort (cf. p. 362, n. 1) there is, in the first instance, the same recourse to universal human nature: "The feeling which inspires it is *natural*," but, very quickly, the perspective is modified: "or at least so it appeared in the eyes of the Ancients who seemed to put less ostentation in their sorrow, but also put more truth in it." This inescapably forces the reader to reflect on his own morality and its relativity. In this way the distance is marked out between a "natural" Antiquity and a "regulated" 18th century.

What lies behind the notes: their dual working
The appearance of notes in a series of translations in the second half of the 18th century corresponds to a sudden awareness of the actual operation of translation and its limits. In effect they are written in the gap which always separates the copy from the original. But they form a skilful device for filling it. It is moreover a double device: on one hand, the literal translation which they give often makes it possible to establish a transition between the Greek and the French; on the other, a series of references makes it possible to reconcile with the original a translation which they clarify and enrich. The notes therefore place themselves at the service of Sophocles. But it would also be true to say that they let Sophocles serve them. What they do is to achieve control of a text which they bring back into an order which is in the first place that of the trans-lator, of his language and of his aesthetic and moral values, every time that he looked like deviating from it.

The notes are also, paradoxically, the place where the subjectivity of the translator and the point of view which dictates his interpretation of the text most show themselves, at the very time when they are parading their objectivity. They profess to be scientific, speak scholarly lan-guages, Latin or even Greek, accumulate quotations and references. But all of that apparatus is put to the service of a vision of the text which he is imposing on the reader.

In appearance split, they are in fact convergent and com-plementary, and constitute an effective method for unifying the transla-tion. Separated from the text, in reality they make a pair with it. It is the notes which one must look at first to decipher the meaning of the whole and to identify the translator's system of reading and interpretation.

Preface: The *Oedipus Tyrannus* of Sophocles

Thomas Maurice

The Tragedy of which I have attempted to convey the beauties into the English language in a free translation, stands amidst the foremost of the classical productions of antiquity. Of tragical writing it has ever been esteemed the model and the master-piece. The grandeur of the subject is not less eminent than the dignity of the personages who are employed in it; and the design of the whole can only be rivalled by that art with which the particular parts are conducted. The subject is a nation labouring under calamities of the most dreadful and portentous kind; and the leading character is a wise and mighty prince, expiating by his punishment the involuntary crimes of which those calamities were the effect. The design is of the most interesting and important nature, to inculcate a due moderation in our passions, and an implicit obedience to that providence of which the decrees are equally unknown and irresistable.

So sublime a composition could not fail to secure the applause, and fix the admiration of ages. The philosopher is exercised in the contemplation of its deep and awful morality; the critic is captivated by its dramatic beauties, and the man of feeling is interested by those strokes of genuine passion which prevail in almost every page—which every character excites, and every new event tends to diversify in kind or in degree.

The three grand unities of time, place, and action, are observed with scrupulous exactness. However complicated its various parts may on the first view appear, on a nearer and more accurate examination we find every thing useful, every thing necessary; some secret spring of action laid open, some momentous truth inculcated, or some important end promoted: not one scene is superfluous, nor is there one Episode that could be retrenched. The successive circumstances of the play arise gradually and naturally one out of the other, and are connected with such inimitable judgment, that if the smallest part were taken away the whole would fall to the ground. The principal objection to this tragedy is, that the punishment of Oedipus is much more than adequate to his crimes: that his crimes are only the effect of his ignorance, and that consequently the guilt of them is to be imputed not to Oedipus, but Apollo, who ordained and predicted them, and that he is only *Phoebi reus*, as Seneca expresses himself. In vindication of Sophocles, it must be considered that the conduct of Oedipus is by no means so irreproachable as some have contended: for though his public character is delineated as that of a good king, anxious for the welfare of his subjects, and ardent in his endeavours to appease the gods by incense and supplication, yet we find him in private life choleric, haughty, inquisitive; impatient of controul, and impetuous in resentment. His character, even as a king, is not free from the imputation of imprudence, and our opinion of his piety is greatly invalidated by his contemptuous treatment of the wise, the benevolent, the sacred Tiresias. The rules of tragic art scarcely permit that a perfectly virtuous man should be loaded with misfortunes. Had Sophocles presented to our view a character less debased by vice, or more exalted by virtue, the end of his performance would have been frustrated; instead of agonizing compassion, he would have raised in us indignation unmixed, and horror unabated. The intention of the poet would have been yet more frustrated on the return of our reason, and our indignation would have been transferred from Oedipus to the gods them-selves—from Oedipus, who committed parricide, to the gods who first ordained, and then punished it. By making him criminal in a small degree, and miserable in a very great one, by investing him with some excellent qualities, and some imperfections, he at once inclines us to pity and to condemn. His obstinacy darkens the lustre of his other virtues; it aggravates his impiety, and almost justifies his sufferings. This is the doctrine of Aristotle and of nature, and shews Sophocles to have had an intimate knowledge of the human heart, and the springs by which it is actuated. That his crimes and punishment still seem disproportionate, is not to be imputed as a fault to Sophocles, who proceeded only on the antient and popular notion of Destiny; which we know to have been the basis of Pagan theology.

It is not the intention of the Translator to proceed farther in a critical discussion of the beauties and defects of a Tragedy which hath already employed the pens of the most distinguished commentators; which hath wearied conjecture, and exhausted all the arts of unnecessary and unprofitable defence. The Translator is no stranger to the merits of

Dr. Franklin; whose character he reveres, and by whose excellent performance he has been animated and instructed. He thinks it necessary to disclaim every idea of rivalship with an author of such established and exalted reputation. The present translation, though it be executed with far less ability than that of Doctor Franklin, may deserve some notice, because professedly written on very different principles. The Doctor was induced by his plan, and enabled by his erudition, to encounter all the difficulties of *literal* translation. This work will be found by the reader, what it is called by the writer, a *free* translation. The Author was not fettered by his text, but guided by it; he has however not forgotten the boundaries by which liberal translation is distinguished from that which is wild and licentious. He has always endeavoured to represent the sense of his original, he hopes sometimes to have caught its spirit, and he throws himself without reluctance, but not without diffidence, on the candour of those readers who understand and feel the difference that subsists between the Greek and English languages, between antient and modern manners, between nature and refinement, between a Sophocles who appeals to posterity, and a writer who catches at the capricious taste of the day.

Preface: *The Tragedies of Sophocles*

R. Potter

Sophocles, the son of Sophilus an Athenian, was born at Colonus, and educated with great attention. Superior vigour and address in the exercises of the Palestra, and skill in Music, were the great accomplishments of young men in the states of Greece; in these Sophocles excelled; nor was he less distinguished by the beauty of his person. He was also instructed in the noblest of all sciences, Civil Polity and Religion; from the first of these he derived an unshaken love of his country, which he served in some embassies, and in high military command with Pericles; from the latter he was impressed with a pious reverence for the gods, manifested by the inviolable integrity of his life. But his studies were early devoted to the Tragic Muse; the spirit of Æschylus lent a fire to his genius, and excited that noble emulation which led him to contend with, and sometimes to bear away the prize from his great master. He wrote one hundred and thirteen tragedies, of which seven only have escaped the ravages of time; and having testified his love of his country by refusing to leave it, though invited by many kings, and having enjoyed the uninterrupted esteem and affection of his fellow citizens, which neither the gallant actions and sublime genius of Æschylus, nor the tender spirit and philosophic virtue of Euripides could secure to them, he died in the ninety first year of his age. The burial-place of his ancestors was at Decelia, which the Lacedemonians had at that time seized and fortified; but Lysander, the Spartan Chief, permitted the Athenians to interr their deceased Poet; and they paid him all the honours due to his love of his country, his integrity of life, and his high poetic excellence.

Æschylus had at once seized the highest post of honour in the field of Poetry, the true Sublime; to that eminence his claim could not be disputed. Sophocles had a noble elevation of mind, but tempered with so fine a taste and so chastised a judgement, that he never passes the bounds of propriety: under his conduct the Tragic Muse appears with the chast dignity of some noble matron at a religious solemnity; harmony is in her voice, and grace in all her motions. From him the theatre received some additional embellishments, and the drama, what made it more active and more interesting, the introduction of a third Speaker: but his distinguishing excellence is in the judicious disposition of the fable, and so nice a connexion and dependence of the parts on each other, that they all agree to make the event not only probable, but even necessary; this is peculiarly admirable in his Oedipus King of Thebes; and in this important point he is far superior to every other dramatic writer.

Aristotle, who formed his judgement from the three great Athenian Poets, particularly from Sophocles, observes that Tragedy after various changes, having now attained the perfection of its nature, aimed at no further improvements. The latter part of the observation was at that time just; it continued just more than two thousand years; but of perfection who shall decide? The great Critic did not conceive that Nature could produce a Poet who, without any knowledge of his laws, or of those Grecian models, should exalt Tragedy to an excellence of which neither he nor they had any idea. Shakespear had a genius ardent and sublime as that of Æschylus, his diction is equally great and daring, his imagination was richer and more luxuriant, his observation of the living manners and his knowledge of the human mind more comprehensive; hence his wonderful power over the passions. It is a proof of the commanding force of genius that, as the Agamemnon of Æschylus, with all its faults, excells any thing that remains to us of the Grecian drama, so there are many tragedies of Shakespear, though with more and greater faults, which are superior to the Agamemnon. Nature may yet produce another Poet blest with the powers of Shakespear and the judgement of Sophocles; and the Critic, who shall see this, may then say with Aristotle, "Tragedy has now attained the perfection of its nature:" in the mean time we glory in our countryman, and look back with reverence on the three great Poets of Athens. The sublime and daring Æschylus resembles some strong and impregnable Castle situated on a rock, whose martial grandeur awes the beholder, its battlements defended by heroes in arms, and its gates proudly hung with trophies. Sophocles appears with splendid dignity, like some imperial palace of richest architecture, the symmetry of whose parts, and the chast magnificence of the whole delight the eye, and command the approbation of the judgement. The pathetic and moral Euripides hath the solemnity of a Gothic Temple, whose storied windows admit a dim religious light, enough to show us its high embowed roof, and the monuments of the dead which rise in every part, impressing our minds with pity and terror at the uncertain and short duration of all human greatness, and with an aweful sense of our own mortality.

In works of literature the public is little interested in the motives of the writer; yet some account of this translation may be necessary: it was often requested of me immediately after the publication of Euripides; but I wished to leave Dr. Franklin in the undisturbed possession of his well-acquired reputation, and declined the attempt, till a person of illustrious rank, and more illustrious for mental accomplishments, did me the honour to desire that I would give the English reader all that remains of the tragic Muse of Greece; a request from such a person, and the manner in which it was communicated to me, could not be refused. I undertook the work as a task, sensible of its difficulty, and even despairing of my power to express the propriety, the sweetness, the harmony, the force, and the dignity of Sophocles: as I advanced, I was not wholly dissatisfied with my self; from a task it became an amusement, and then a pleasure to me. This translation professes to be faithful to the original; and I flatter my self that it is in no small degree correct; this it owes to a learned friend, who did me the favour to revise it; with his taste and judgement I am well acquainted, and I confide in his integrity. My own attention and exertions have not been wanting, as it has been my ambition to make it worthy of the noble person to whom it owes its existence, and of the public to which it is now presented.

Preface to *Oedipus, King of Thebes*

The polished citizens of Athens applauded this tragedy; and it has been universally esteemed as the most perfect composition that ever graced their theatre; the judgment of Aristotle and of the best criticks hath justified this general approbation. The reader will observe the wonderful conduct of the poet. The judicious preservation of the Unities, to use the language of criticism, produces such a propriety, such a connexion and dependence of what follows on what is past, that every circumstance seems to arise from the nature of things, and impresses on the mind the idea of reality. The discovery that Oedipus is himself the person darkly hinted at by the oracle, the nice gradations by which this discovery is carried on, the alternate light and shade thrown over it, from the ambiguous answers of Tiresias to his clearer declarations, from the encouragement to the alarms which he receives from Jocasta, from the momentary conviction of its impossibility given him by the Corinthian to the full evidence of the fact, keep the mind in awful suspense, till the distressing certainty breaks in upon it at once, and overwhelms it with terror and pity. This drama resembles an eruption of Mount Ætna; at first clouds of smoke darken the sky; these are dispelled by a dreadful explosion of flames; then the threatening symptoms abate; thus smoke and flame and serenity succeed each other, till the mountain in an instant discharges its torrent fires, which rush down with resistless fury, roll over palaces, temples, and cities, and carry with them deflagration, ruin, and horror.

Aristotle observes that in the most excellent tragedy, which should be imitative of what produces terror and pity, persons illustrious for their good qualities ought not to be represented as fallen from a prosperous to an adverse fortune; for this would raise neither terror nor pity; but lead to impiety. Poetic. c. 13. The precept has been controverted, perhaps with reason; yet cricticks have taken occasion to show how faithfully the poet has adhered to this rule, by charging Oedipus with impiety, pride, choler, violence, and intemperate curiosity. It may not therefore be improper to examine this character, as it is drawn by Sophocles. At the first appearance of Oedipus we are warmly interested in his favour; he is an illustrious and honoured king; anxious for the welfare of his realms, and prizing it more than his own life; his addresses to the oracle at Delphi, his attention to the answers of the god, and the respect with which he receives Tiresias, are undoubted indications of his piety. As a king, he is the benevolent father of his people; as a man, generous, intrepid, and wise; as an husband, affectionate and mild; as a father, tender as the pathetic pencil of Euripides could have pourtrayed him. His anxious endeavours to discover the murder of Laius are occasioned at first partly by his reverence of the oracle, and partly by his own sense of justice; his further inquiries proceed from a delicate and exquisite sensibility. The poet, to attain his end, has judiciously blended this with a certain "firey quality," which blazes out on every occasion; and, though it shows a generous rather than a ferocious mind, naturally leads him into every ill, which the oracle and his destiny had rendered inevitable; for as this instigated his abrupt departure from Corinth, so it inflamed his resentment of the insult offered him in the narrow road "where three ways met;" from which fatal encounter all his misfortunes arose; yet even in this, the barbarous manners of the times considered, he is to be deemed unfortunate rather than criminal. His anger against Tiresias was excited by the prophet's refusal to declare the guilty person; he considered his silence as injurious to himself and to his country; his anger therefore arose from a generous motive: when at length Tiresias was provoked to speak, and pronounced Oedipus himself to be the murderer, conscious of his innocence (for he then thought himself innocent), abhorring the malignity of the accusation, and persuaded from concurring circumstances that the prophet had been suborned by Creon, the one must appear to him as an impostor and a mercenary wretch, the other as a dark designing villain, who had fabricated this charge to deprive him of his crown and his life: he is enraged, but not inexorable; at the intercession of his friends, even whilst he is under this persuasion, he dismisses Creon with impunity. "The stroke, that inflicts the deepest wound on a virtuous and ingenuous nature, is the accusation of guilt." Richardson on the character of Imogen. As circumstances were continually opening, which gave this accusation an increasing force that alarmed even his own mind, neither nature nor reason could suffer a person of so animated a spirit to rest, till he had drawn aside the mysterious veil, and discovered all the horrors of his fate.

Where then was the guilt of Oedipus? We are to look for it not in his conduct, but in his fate. He was, as Seneca finely expresses it, *Phoebi reus.* Before his birth Apollo had foretold that he should murder his father and marry his mother; and his destiny led him, against every effort of a virtuous mind, involuntary and unknowingly to accomplish the oracle; and, what is still worse, he was equally obnoxious not only to human, but even to divine justice, as if he had committed these crimes with a daring and impious intention. Such as the religious belief of Athens even in the days of Socrates: we have little cause to think our reasoning powers stronger, but we feel our understandings more enlightened than were those of the Grecian Sages. We know whence we received this light, let us therefore be thankful for it.

The scene is at Thebes before the palace of Oedipus.

From *Laokoon*

Gotthold Ephraim Lessing

I. How wonderfully the poet has known how to strengthen and deepen the idea of bodily pain! He chose a wound (for the circumstances of the story may be considered by us as dependent upon his choice, inasmuch as, on account of these advantageous circumstances, he chose the whole story),—he chose, I say, a wound and not an internal malady, because he was able to make a more vivid representation of the latter than of the former, however painful it may be. The inward sympathetic fire which consumed Meleager when his mother sacrificed him by the burning of the fatal log to the wrath of his sister, would have been less adapted to the theatre than a wound. This wound, moreover, was a divine punishment; a poison worse than any to be found in nature incessantly raged within him, and it was only the vehement access of pain which had its appointed limit and then the wretched man fell into a stupefying sleep, in which he was obliged to refresh his exhausted nature in order that he might again enter upon the same path of suffering. Chateaubrun represents him as wounded only by the poisoned dart of a Trojan. From such a common occurrence what extraordinary result is to be expected? In the wars of ancient times everybody was exposed to it; how came it to pass that in the case of Philoctetes alone the consequences were so dreadful? A natural poison working for nine years without causing death is infinitely more improbable than all the fabulous wonders with which the Greek has ornamented his story.

2. However great and horrible he made the bodily sufferings of his hero, he felt nevertheless that they alone would not be sufficient to excite a marked degree of sympathy. He combined them with other evils, which, considered in themselves, were not calculated to excite especial emotion, but which, through this combination, wore so melancholy an

aspect as to cause a sympathy in their turn with the bodily pains. These evils were an entire privation of the society of man, hunger, and all the distresses of life to which, in such privation and under an inclement sky, a man would be exposed. Let any one only reflect upon the condition of a man in such circumstances. But give him health, strength, and industry, and he becomes a Robinson Crusoe who makes little claim upon our sympathy, although we are far from being indifferent about his fate. For we are rarely so delighted with human society that the repose, which out of it we enjoy, does not appear fascinating to us, especially if we add the conviction, with which every one flatters himself, that he will learn by degrees to dispense with assistance from others altogether. On the other hand, let a man have the most painful and incurable disease, but surround him with pleasant friends, who will not let him be in need of anything—who lighten, so far as in them lies, his suffering, in whose presence he may utter freely groans and lamentations—there will certainly be a sympathy with him, but it will not last long, and at last we shrug our shoulders and advise him to be patient. It is only when both predicaments concur—when the solitary man has no control over his body, when the sick man receives as little from others as he does from himself, and when his cries perish in the desert air—it is then that we witness all the misery which can befall human nature smite with collected force the wretch, and every fleeting thought by which we place ourselves in his position excites shuddering and horror. We see nothing before us but despair in its most ghastly form, and no sympathy is stronger, none melts the soul more completely; than that which mingles itself with the representation of despair. Of this kind is the sympathy which we feel for Philoctetes, and most strongly in that moment when we see him deprived of his bow, the only thing which had enabled him to support his miserable life. Oh! that Frenchman who had no understanding to perceive this, no heart to feel this; or, if he had, could have been petty enough to have sacrificed it all to the wretched taste of his own countrymen. Chateaubrun places Philoctetes in the society of other persons. He makes a princess's daughter come to him in the desert island, and this is not all, but she brings a mistress of the ceremonies with her, of whom it is difficult to say whether the princess or the poet stood most in need. He leaves out altogether the excellent dramatic incident of the bow; but he makes beautiful eyes take the place of it. In truth, the bows and arrows would have appeared ridiculous to the young French hero. On the other hand, nothing is more serious to him than the wrath of the beautiful eyes. The Greek tortures us with the harrowing reflection that poor Philoctetes will remain without his bow in the desert island and perish miserably. The Frenchman knows another way to our hearts. He makes us fear that the son of Achilles will depart without his princess. This is what the Parisian critics call to triumph over the ancients, and one of them proposed to call the Chateaubrunian piece *la difficulté vaincue*.

3. Next to the general effect let any one consider the only scene in which Philoctetes is no longer the deserted sick man—where he hopes soon to leave his wretched desert and return to his kingdom; where, moreover, all his misfortune is confined to his bitter wound. He whines, he screams, and undergoes the most ghastly convulsions. Here, properly speaking, arises the objection of violated decorum. It is an Englishman who makes this objection,—a man, moreover, whom one would not lightly charge with false delicacy. As has been already remarked, he has good ground for his objection. All feelings and passions, he says, with which others can very little sympathise, become repulsive when they are too vehemently expressed.

"It is for the same reason that to cry out with bodily pain, how intolerable soever, appears always unmanly and unbecoming. There is, however, a good deal of sympathy even with bodily pain. If, as has been already observed, I see a stroke aimed and just ready to fall upon the leg or arm of another person, I naturally shrink and draw back my own leg or my own arm, and when it does fall I feel it, in some measure, and am hurt by it as well as the sufferer. My hurt, however, is no doubt excessively slight, and, upon that account, if he makes any violent outcry, as I cannot go along with him, I never fail to despise him."

Nothing is more deceitful than general laws for our feelings. Their tissue is so fine and complicated that the most cautious speculation can scarcely seize upon any single thread and follow it through all its entanglements; and if we could do this what should we gain? There is in nature scarcely any one unmixed feeling; with every individual one a thousand others spring up at the same time, the least of which alters entirely the ground of the feeling, so that exceptions grow upon exceptions, which end in confining the presumed general principle to the experience of a few particular instances. We despise those, says the Englishman, whom we hear violently screaming from corporeal suffering. But not always: not for the first time: not when we see that the sufferer does all in his power to stifle his anguish; not when we know him to be in other respects a man of firmness; still less when we see amid his sufferings proofs of his steadfastness, when we see that his anguish can force him to scream but to nothing further; that he would rather subject himself to a larger continuance of his suffering than make the slightest change in his manner of thinking, in his resolutions, although in such a change he might expect the end of his suffering. All this is to be found in Philoctetes. Moral greatness consisted, in the opinion of the ancient Greeks, as much in an unchangeable love to friends as in an unalterable hatred to enemies. This greatness Philoctetes throughout all his sufferings possessed. His sufferings had not so dried his eyes that he could not shed tears over the fate of his old friend. His pain had not made him so abject that in order to obtain his liberty he would forgive his enemies and lend himself to the execution of all their selfish projects; and would the Athenians have despised this rock of a man because the waves, which could not shake his purpose, made him cry aloud? I acknowledge that I have little taste for the philosophy of Cicero; least of all for that which he ostentatiously displays in the second book of his Tusculan Disputations upon the endurance of bodily suffering,—one would suppose that he was training a gladiator, so vehement is he against the outward expression of bodily suffering. In that expression he appears to find only impatience, without considering that it is frequently quite involuntary, but that true courage can only show itself in the actions of a free will. In the tragedy of Sophocles, he hears nothing but the complaining and screaming of Philoctetes, never considering the constant manliness of his conduct in other respects. How otherwise would he have found occasion for his rhetorical onslaught on the Poets? "They would make us effeminate while they introduce to our notice the bravest man crying aloud." They must let him cry: for a theatre is no arena. It is the part of the venal or condemned gladiator to do and suffer everything with decorum. From him no loud cry must be heard, in him no convulsion of pain must be seen. For his wounds, his death, must divert the spectator; therefore Art must learn to hide all feeling. The slightest expression of it would have awakened sympathy, and frequently sympathy excited would have made a speedy end to the cold ghastly performance. But the emotion which should not be excited here is that which is the very purpose of the tragic scene, and which requires an exactly opposite behaviour. The heroes of the theatre must manifest feeling, must utter their anguish, and allow nature herself to work in them. If they betray that they are acting under control and restraint, they leave our hearts cold, and prizefighters in buskins can, at the utmost, but excite our wonder. This appellation all the persons of the so-called tragedies of Seneca deserve; and I am firmly of opinion that the Gladiatorial shows were the principal cause why the Romans in their tragedies remained so far below mediocrity. The spectators learnt in the bloody amphitheatre to mistake all that was natural. A Ctesias could indeed have studied his Art there, but a Sophocles never. The most tragical genius accustomed to these artificial death scenes must have been corrupted into bombast and rhodomontade. But these rhodomontades were as incapable of inspiring a true heroic spirit, as the lamentations of Philoctetes were of causing effeminacy. The lamentations are those of a man, but the acts are those of a hero. Both compose the manly hero who is neither effeminate nor hardened, but at one time appears as the former, at another as the latter, even as nature, principle, and duty alternately require. It is the sublimest subject which wisdom can produce, and Art can imitate.

It is not enough that Sophocles has secured his sensitive Philoctetes against contempt; he has also wisely forestalled all the objections which otherwise might have been brought against him by the Englishman. For, although we do not always despise the man who screams from corporeal suffering, it is nevertheless incontestable that we do not feel for him so much sympathy as this scream seems to demand. How then should those comport themselves who have to do with the screaming Philoctetes? Should they be moved in a high degree? That is contrary to nature. Should they show themselves as cold and embarrassed as men are actually wont to be in such circumstances? That would place them entirely out of harmony with the spectators. But, as has been observed, this also has been forestalled by Sophocles; namely, by causing the attendant persons to have their own interests; so that the impression which the scream of Philoctetes makes upon them is not the only thing which concerns them, and the spectator does not so much heed the disproportion of their sympathy with the scream, as observe the change which arises, or ought to arise, in their own feelings and projects through this sympathy, whether it be weak or strong. Neoptolemus and the Chorus have deceived the wretched Philoctetes; they are aware of the despair into which their deceit has plunged him; for now a terrible access of his malady comes on before their very eyes: if this access does not excite any remarkable sympathetic emotion in them, it can, at least, compel them to retire into themselves, to have respect for so much misery, and not to increase it by treachery. This the spectator expects, and finds his expectation fulfilled by the noble-minded Neoptolemus. If Philoctetes had retained the mastery of his suffering, Neoptolemus would have retained the mastery of his dissimulation. Philoctetes, whose suffering makes him incapable of dissimulation, however necessary it may seem in order that the future companion of his travels may not repent of his promise to take him with him, Philoctetes, who is all nature, brings back Neoptolemus to his own nature. This return is excellent, and the more affecting as it is the result of pure humanity. In the French tragedy the fine eyes come into play. But I will spend no more thought on this parody. In the Trachiniæ Sophocles has made use of the same stroke of art, namely, of connecting with the sympathy excited by the scream of corporeal suffering another emotion in the spectator. The suffering of

Hercules is not an exhausting suffering; it drives him to the verge of madness, in which he is snuffing up revenge and nothing else. Already he has in this rage seized upon Lichas and shattered him to pieces on the rocks. The Chorus is composed of women; it is all the more natural that fear and dread should overpower them. This fact, and the waiting to see whether a god will yet hasten to the help of Hercules, or whether Hercules will sink under his affliction, cause the only general interest, to which sympathy contributes a very faint shading. So soon as the result is decided by the intelligence from the oracle, Hercules becomes tranquil, and astonishment at his last resolution takes the place of all other emotions. But it is especially necessary to remember, in comparing the suffering Hercules with the suffering Philoctetes, that the former is a demigod and the latter a man. The man is not ashamed of his lamentation, but the demigod is ashamed that his mortal part has so much influence over his immortal part as to make him whine and whimper like a girl. We moderns do not believe in demigods, but yet the least hero with us must feel and act like a demigod.

Whether the actor can bring the scream and the contortions of pain so home to us as to create an illusion I will neither affirm nor deny. If I find that our actors cannot do this, I should wish first to know whether a Garrick would not be capable of it, and if he should not succeed, should still remember that the scenic apparatus and declamation of the ancients reached a perfection of which now-a-days we have no notion.

From *Kritische Wälder: Erstes Wäldchen*

Johann Gottfried von Herder

"Laokoon suffers as Sophocles' *Philoctetes* suffers." Mr. Less-ing[1] commences with this comparison and argues that it is no com-parison: that Sophocles' *Philoctetes* does not simply sigh with worry and anxiety but cries aloud and screams with wild curses; that he fills the desolate island with these awful cries, and makes the theatre too echo with the sounds of anger, misery and despair. Winkelmann therefore first cannot have read it properly, and secondly made a false comparison and drew a false conclusion.

Sophocles' *Philoctetes* can decide—how does he suffer? It is remarkable that the impression I was left with by this play long ago is the same as the one for which Winkelmann argues: the impression of a hero who in the middle of pain fights his pain, holds it back with hollow sobs as long as he can and when finally the "Ah!", the terrible cry of pain, overcomes him, he still only lets out single, surreptitious sounds of anguish and keeps the rest hidden within his great spirit. Let us look up Sophocles; let us read as if we were seeing, and I think we will perceive this Philoctetes that Sophocles created, and Winkelmann puts before us, just as he was created.

At the beginning of the third Act his pain takes him by surprise—but does he scream and cry? No: he reacts with a sudden silence, a dumb dismay, and when that finally gives way, with a hollow twisted "Ah!" that can hardly be heard by Neoptolemus.[2] "What is the matter with you?" he asks, "Nothing bad: go now, my son" answers Philoctetes, and

---

[1] Lessing, *Laokoon*, p. 3.
[2] *Phil.* 730–733.

how else but with a face full of love, full of reserved heroism? That is how the scene of silent suffering proceeds: the concerned, the restless, the questioning Neoptolemus, and Philoctetes,—who does not scream and rage, who suppresses his pain, for a long time tries to hide it even from Neoptolemus, and only ever when he is right in the middle of it cries aloud to the gods with a fearful ἰὼ θεοί ("O Gods . . ."). And this silent scene of suffering, what effect must it have had on the spectator? He sees Philoctetes suffering, silent, showing his suffering only with contorted gestures and a suppressed "Ah!"; and who does not feel this suppressed "Ah!" more than the bellowing cry of Mars, who, wounded in battle, shouts aloud with the cry of ten thousand men—or why not rather of ten thousand bulls? In the one case one is frightened, in the other one feels: dismayed in sympathy with Philoctetes like Neoptolemus, afraid, not knowing where one is, what is to be done or how one ought to help. At his sad "Ah" one approaches him: "How is it, then? You are in pain. You say nothing. You are suffering! Why so uncommunicative? Are you being tormented? Why do you sigh to the gods?" And Philoctetes answers with a twisted smile, with a face in which pain and courage and friendliness are mixed: "Me? No! I feel it getting less severe. I am praying to the gods for a successful sea trip." What a Greek Garrick is called for, to dispense here the due measures of pain and courage, of human feeling and heroism.

Finally overcome by the pain, he succumbs—but in sounds of bellowing despair, of frenzied cries? Not at all! In a solemn ἀπόλωλα, τέκνον. βρύκομαι, τέκνον. παπαῖ, ἀπαπαπᾶ . . .(I am finished, my son. I cry aloud, my son—Ah, ah, ah . . .)" those are his drawn-out cries of woe! He asks for the heroic remedy, to cut his foot off; he moans. Nothing more? No, nothing more! He broke out, as Neoptolemus says, only in ἰυγὴν καὶ στόνον, in groans and sighs and Ah! how that must affect us! His deformed foot, his twisted face, his breast heaving with sighs, his side racked with moaning, his half Ah! . . . The poet goes no further: and in order to forestall any exaggeration of expression, he lets Philoctetes fall into a delirium from the pain! So much has he suffered, so far has he concentrated his efforts, that he goes wild.

He comes to himself! he recovers! but the illness returns like a lost traveller: black blood gushes forth: his ἀπαπαπᾶ [a cry of woe] starts again: he pleads, groans; a curse on Ulysses, rage with the gods, a call to death, but all merely in fits and starts, only moments! The pain recedes; and look! he uses the moment of recovery to get ready for the third attack. It comes, and as theatrical expression can scale no greater height, Sophocles makes him do everything that he can make him do without making him shriek: rave, groan, plead, curse, breathlessly come to himself, and—fall asleep. An agonizing scene! perhaps the highest in expression ever called for by a tragic play, and only attainable by a Greek actor.

But in this painful scene, what is the highest in expression, what is its prevailing note? Shrieking perhaps? So far from that, that Sophocles seems to have taken no greater care than to avoid this becoming the prevailing note. Where are "the lamentations, the shrieking, the wild curses, with which his pain filled the camp and disturbed all the acts of sacrifice, all the holy acts, and echoed terribly throughout the desolate island."[3] Where are they? In the theatre? Yes, but in the narrative[4], in the narrative of his enemy Ulysses, who wishes to justify himself for leaving him abandoned; but not in the action, not as if this shrieking were the main expression. Another writer, an Aeschylus for instance, would certainly have put more stress on it and perhaps, as with his Eumenides, have frightened a pregnant woman into a miscarriage. With an exaggerated new tragedian Philoctetes' bellowing would certainly have started behind the scenes, and he would burst on to stage with disorderly, wild cries, as for example Hudemann's Cain heralds himself before his entrance with his club in a very pretty and novel *coup de théâtre*, throwing it before him and falling full length into the theatre after it. But with the wise Sophocles?—How has he measured out the sound of fear? How meticulously has he prepared for it! How long suppressed it! How often interrupted! How constantly soothed! The entire scene could be called a picture of pain through all its stages from the silent to the completely deafening, that at the same time, as it were, kills itself; but taken altogether still the picture of *restrained* and not *unbridled* pain—that is unquestionably what is in Sophocles from beginning to end.

Hence too the brevity of the action, which is short in words, but long in performance. If it depended here on "the shrieking, on the woeful exclamations, on the frequent 'Ah's' that *burst from him* and are *abruptly broken off*" as Mr. L.[5] will have it, then I know of nothing that must either proceed in more rapid succession or else make the spectator exasperated. But the restraint, the painful suffering, the long, silent struggles with the agony which are finally concluded with a surreptitious ὤμοι, μοι (= Ah, me); these stretch out, these linger, and they are the prevailing note of the entire scene. Add to that the relaxing chorus which sings a lullaby to Philoctetes as he falls asleep, a soothing song in gentle

---

[3] *Laokoon*, p. 3.

[4] Sophocles *Phil.* Act 1.

[5] *Laokoon*, p. 4.

slow measures, and which here does not simply finish off the Act, but is itself part of the Act; for the sleeping Philoctetes lies before the audience's eyes; add this, I say, and it is a long, whole, complete Act that fills my soul: but not through the bursting out, but through the holding back of the "Ah!" And so Winkelmann can say with justification: Laokoon suffers as Sophocles' Philoctetes suffers: but the former only as a statue, where the sigh lasts for ever, for ever trapped in the breast, and the latter as a tragic character which finally closes the long sigh with an Ah! and must greet the returning pain with an Ah!, that roams over one string of lamentation, but with discontinuous, slowly returning, rising and falling half tones of suppressed pain. Sophocles was, then, the same wise master in his *Philoctetes* as Polydorus was in his Laokoon, and in both of them is displayed, only according to the difference in their subjects, the same kind of wisdom that looks for quiet, suggestive expression, and avoids what is exaggerated. And that is what Winkelmann is saying!

*   *   *

But Philoctetes?—Mr. Lessing has devoted a long section[6] to defending Sophocles for bringing physical sufferings on stage and making a hero shriek in this suffering. The whole defence is from the viewpoint of a dramaturgist, and in its manner of exposition betrays the author of *Dramaturgy*; it is a pity, though, that it is based on an entirely incorrect presumption: that in Sophocles' *Philoctetes* shrieking is the *prevailing note* of the expression of his pain, and therefore the *main means* of engaging sympathy—which is not so. And then it is a pity too that it is taken merely as dramaturgy, as a design for the drama. Better in my opinion to abandon oneself to the impressions made by the performance, and to justify nothing as a dramaturgist, but to note genuine impressions as a Greek spectator.

And what roughly are these impressions? If any Greek play is written to be performed and not to be read, that play is *Philoctetes*: for the entire effect of the tragedy rests on the life of the performance. Let us approach the Athenian stage then with our eyes and minds. The scene opens[7]: a shore with no trace of man: a lonely uninhabited island in the middle of the ocean's waves:—how have these travellers been driven off course here? What will occur in this desolate wilderness? —Here, we learn, is Philoctetes, Poeas's famous son: poor lonely man! utterly bereft

---

[6] *Laokoon*, p. 31–49.
[7] Soph. *Phil.* Act I.

of human company, banished here to perpetual loneliness—how will he spend his days? —And he is unwell—unwell in the foot with a festering sore! —Still more pitiable recluse! Who will look after you here, make you food, clean you and dress your wounds?—and how did you get here? Ah, marooned—without mercy, without help—and because of a crime, because of stubbornness? No: because of his pitiful cries! Ah! those inhuman people, what else can the sick, wretched man do but moan and cry? But not to allow him even this relief, not to tolerate this tiny irritation, to maroon him! Who did maroon him? The Greeks, his people, his companions. Perhaps this happened through some wicked individual? No, on the order of the Greek general, from—Ulysses himself. And this same Ulysses can tell us such a story so coldly, he can break off so indifferently; he has only to see the island, to have new designs against him—oh the wicked man! Who would not have sided with a poor, lonely, deserted invalid, with whom no one has shown sympathy, against the faithless man who was the instrument of his misfortune?

Now we get a closer look at the poor man's dwelling—a deserted cave!—Are there still some household utensils and food in there? Trampled grass—a pitiful animal's den!—here is where the hero must lie, without whom Troy cannot be taken: a beaker made of wood, some things to make fire with, that is the king's entire treasure—and ye gods!—here are rags, full of pus, testimony to his illness! He is away— how far can the poor man hobble? Without doubt he had to—for food perhaps! Perhaps for a soothing herb! If only he could find it! If only someone saw him! Meanwhile[8] the scene of deceit continues, as Ulysses brings Neoptolemus to the point where this good-natured, honest man, the son of the noble Achilles, is to take prisoner a stranger, a wretch, by trickery, through lies and intrigues. I know that Sophocles, even more than other Greeks, hates those immoral monsters in the same way as he is capable of hating moral ones, and that he presents only people in his plays, not angels or devils; but Ulysses, as he appears here, is not simply Homer's cunning schemer: he is a seducer who openly discloses the basic principles of faithlessness that do away with all virtue, and— shame on the villain!—with whom depravity has already found its voice in *principles*. Sophocles then prefers to incur the reproaches of morality-pedants, who want everything said on stage to be the equivalent of Pythagoras' moral sayings: he prefers to paint his Ulysses in somewhat blacker colours than he is accustomed to use—in order to win our sympathy all the more for the poor Philoctetes, who has been deceived by him and is going to be deceived again.

---

[8] Sc. 2.

The chorus and Neoptolemus are now[9] engaged in impressing on us more deeply this pity for Philoctetes; they again go through the previous marks of his distress, increase their number through surmise, and—then in the distance a groan can be heard! Neoptolemus' behaviour shows that it is groaning, not roaring as he, dismayed at his instructions, does not know where it is coming from. The "Ah" comes closer, it becomes moaning, a deep pitiful "Ah!"—only now is it distinct! You were right: Philoctetes must come and—Ah!—though a shepherd comes with the sound of pipes—Philoctetes comes with the sound of distress— he enters! or rather he creeps forward, to—

Now will he throw himself down on the stage with a roar, so that Peter Squenz can say: "dear Lion, roar once more!" Who could have excused the roaring, of which there is so little trace in the Greek, to the artistic judges! Philoctetes talks to the stranger throughout a long Act[10] without thinking of crying aloud: Sophocles has even left backstage the "Ah" that before had been heard from a distance. Wise Sophocles! How shall I think the man effeminate, how shall I think his "Ah!" contemptible, which he only groaned when he thought he was alone, and immediately hides before the strangers and can always conceal in conversation? The sufferer is a hero.

And Sophocles takes meticulous care over this character. He must first of all be made more a friend of our minds[11] before our bodies could sympathise; and how concerned is the poor man about the strangers? Nothing is further from his thoughts than that they should be ensnaring him; the honest fellow takes them for travellers driven off course, for people who deserve his sympathy—this friend of mankind! He sees the Greek clothes, a bitter reminder for him of the faithless Greeks; but he has forgotten this. How he wishes that they were Greeks: how he longs to hear the sound of Greek again! That is an honest Greek, who can take an interest in Greeks.—He hears Greek: poor Philoctetes has forgotten all his severe pain for joy. He gets to know Achilles' son, the son of his dear friend: he becomes more open; he tells him his story, as moving as if *Penia* (Poverty) appeared herself. He is a friend of his friends: he offers the dead Achilles his tears of friendship; he forgets himself, and sighs over a dead man who is happier than he. He is a friend of his friends: Achilles' son sees him taking a heartfelt interest at the very moment when he is ensnaring him. He grieves over the death of the heroes, and—even more noble—he grieves simply because they are

[9] Scene 3.
[10] Act 2.
[11] Act 2, scene 1.

brave men: the worthless he curses! How Philoctetes has won our interest, as a friend of mankind, as a Greek with body and soul, as a hero!
And is this hero to moulder on a desolate island, far from the rivalry
with other heroes? A painful absence, when the others were doing deeds,
when the others died with laurel leaves, while he is to cry "Ah" from a
wound that is no hero's wound. He, a spirit so Greek, must waste his
life far from his fatherland, far from his loving father, who has perhaps
already gone to the spirit world: he, an honest man betrayed,—Oh Neoptolemus, you mean to abandon him! Oh that Philoctetes implore him! He
does so, and so passionately: he lays siege to his heart from so many
sides that the plea of the chorus, "have pity on him!", becomes our
protest too. We are angry with Neoptolemus, that his disgust at the illness still causes objection and love him when he—promises him he will
not deceive him after all! See how he entreats him, how he thanks him,
how he finally even invites him to his cave and—

Now[12] comes the disguised merchant. He hears "he is to go to
Troy, Ulysses promised the army openly" and—he hardly thinks the
merchant worth an answer. A single heroic exclamation "Ye gods! This
wretch, this faithless person has ventured to swear to bring me into the
camp?" betrays all Philoctetes' heroic soul: it speaks forth:[13] it wants to
go to the ship: this noble soul believes Neoptolemus, trusts him with his
weapons, and trusts himself to him in his illness. How I feel for Philoctetes! But for him, as one who shrieks? Not at all! For him, as the hero,
the Greek, the nobleman—and then the one pitiable in the highest
degree, made more pitiable still through the plans people have for him.
We still only sympathise with his spirit through our imagination, and
only now is the rare scene of illness to come. The chorus[14] prepares for
it with a song to the utterly miserable Philoctetes, and it comes.[15] I have
already gone through it and do not need to repeat it. It annoys me when
on the one hand people try to make it a simple cry for help and on the
other hand, like, for example, among the admirable French, Brumoi,[16]
make it nothing but a cross-bar, an insertion to ensure there were five
full acts. What a silence must have descended on the stage in Athens
when this Act took place!

The scenes of physical suffering are over, and I will go no further. I therefore return from the Athens stage back to where I left Les-

---

[12] Act 2, scene 2.

[13] Act 3.

[14] Act 3.

[15] Third scene.

[16] *Théâtre des Grecs*, Vol. 2, p. 89.

sing—how greatly we differ over the impression this play is meant to make. Only one of us two can be correct, and the other has not been able to use his imagination enough so as not to read, but to see. I will take great care that this charge should not apply to *me*.

Mr. Lessing makes "the idea of physical suffering"[17] the main idea of the play and searches for the subtle means[18] by which the author has skilfully strengthened and extended this idea. I confess that, if this were the main idea of the tragedy, then some of means adduced by Mr. L. would have had little effect on me. The impression of physical suffering is far too confused and, as it were, physical, for it, for example, to allow the question:[19] Where is the seat of the pain? Outside or inside? What does the wound look like? What type of poison is at work inside it? If the description of physical pain were so weak as to need to be strengthened by things like that, then the theatrical effect is lost; and in that case it is better that I proceed to examine the wound myself like a surgeon. No! The idea of suffering should be theatrical, and so I want nothing but theatrical strengthening—it is from a distance, from the twisted facial expressions, from the sounds of misery that, if pain is the main idea of the play, I want to get to know it, and then it makes no real difference to me why someone is screaming, and gesticulating, whether over a lame foot or a wound inside the breast. The director loses everything if he strays from the theatrical view, and, to strengthen it and to make it seem plausible presents us with a certificate from a surgeon— what kind of illness it is, that it is a real wound, that it is a poison which could cause so much pain. Sophocles is supposed to have thought over something like that, or not thought it over. Enough: if something like that needed to work on me, to reinforce my idea of pain—well, Adieu, theatre! I will be in the hospital.

Theatrical effect then! And by what means can I be moved, if the main theme of the play is physical pain? What then are the principal means of arousing sympathy? I know of nothing else but the usual expressions, shouting, tears and convulsions. Mr. Lessing[20] also lists these and takes great pains[21] to explain that decency is not affronted, and their decisive effect. Very good! But if the whimpering, the screaming, the dreadful convulsions are the means, the principal means by which to implant the idea of physical suffering in me and to touch my heart, what

---

[17] *Laokoon*, p. 3, 4, 31, 32.

[18] p. 33–49.

[19] p. 33–34.

[20] p. 3, 52, 34.

[21] p. 41–49.

then can be the best effect of this shrewd blow? With physical suffering I can only have physical sympathy: that is, my fibres, through participation, go through a similar tension of pain, and I suffer with him physically. And would this sympathy be agreeable? Nothing could be less so; the cries for help, the convulsions, run through all my limbs, I feel it myself; the same convulsive movements make themselves felt with me, as if on a string tuned to the same pitch. It does not concern me if that man lying there in convulsions and whimpering is Philoctetes: he is an animal, like me: he is a human being: the human pain shatters my nerves as when I see a dying animal, a dead man's death-rattle, a tortured being that feels like me. And where is this impression even slightly satisfying or agreeable? It is painful, even the sight of it, the thought of it, very painful. At the moment the impression is made, one does not think of artistic deception, or of any pleasure in the forces of imagination: Nature, the animal, suffers inside me, for I see, and hear, an animal of my own kind suffering.

And what kind of gladiator's spirit would be called for to endure a play in which this idea, this feeling of physical pain, was the main idea, the main feeling? I know of no third case apart from these two: I am either taken in by the illusion, or I am not. In the first case, even if it is only for a moment that I mistake the actor, and see someone convulsed, screaming, and in agony, woe betide me! It goes through my nerves. I cannot watch the artistic deceiver who for my pleasure, to all appearance, intended to string himself up, for a moment longer once the illusion is dispelled, once he really chokes. I cannot watch the tight-rope dancer for a moment longer once I see him fall and plunge on to the sword lying beneath, once he is lying there with shattered feet. My eyes cannot bear the sight of Philoctetes once I think of him as the suffering Philoctetes. Only a gladiator's soul can want to make a study of this illusion of physical pain, as in that Dying Gladiator: how much life is there still in him? Only a monster can, as in the story about Michelangelo, crucify a man to see how he dies.

Mr. Lessing may say[22] that "nothing is more fallacious than to try to give general laws for the emotions." Here the law resides in my immediate feeling itself, and in fact in the feeling that deviates as far as possible from general grounds, that is inherent in me as a sympathetic animal. As soon as the suffering body of Philoctetes is the principal object of my vision, it remains the case "that the nearer the actor gets to nature, the more painful must the assault be on our eyes and ears."[23] A

---

[22] p. 42.
[23] p. 32.

sea of unpleasant emotions will come over me, with not a pleasant drop mixed in. The presentation of artistic deception?— It is ruined by my illusion: I have nothing but the sight of a man in convulsions, with whom I almost convulse myself in sympathy; of a man moaning, whose "Ah!" cuts me to the heart. It is no longer a tragedy, it is a ghastly pantomime, a sight to shape the souls of gladiators. I make for the door.

But now let us posit the second case, that the Greek actor with all his use of make-up, stage properties and declamation cannot bring the cries and convulsions of pain to the point of illusion (something that Mr. Lessing does not venture to assert[24]), granted then that I stay a cool spectator. In that case I cannot think of any more revolting pantomime than the aping of convulsions, the bellowing cries, and if the illusion is to be complete, a loathsome stench from the wound. The theatrical ape Philoctetes will hardly then be able to say to the spectator what the real Philoctetes says to Neoptolemus: "I know! You have thought nothing of it all, neither my cries nor the loathsome stench have aroused your disgust."[25] With a pantomime that is repulsive and unfortunately fails to deceive, that is inescapable.

I look up the Literary Papers[26] and find the first of their authors, in his basic philosophy, of my opinion in another similar case. He is investigating "Why the imitation of disgust can never please us" and gives as the cause "because this repellent feeling only strikes our lower senses, taste, smell and touch: the darkest senses which have not the least share in the fine arts; because secondly the feeling of disgust is repellent not because of the representation of reality, as with other unpleasant impressions, but is immediate as we look at it; and because finally in this feeling our spirit recognises no perceptible admixture of pleasure. It altogether excludes then what is disgusting from Imitation in the fine arts, and the highest degree of the horrific from pantomime representation in tragedy, because for one thing the deception involved would be difficult, and for another pantomime on the tragic stage would have to stay within the limits of an ancillary art." I wish the philosophic D. had been able to express himself on the objection I raise, as the physical pain of Philoctetes has more than one of these grounds against it. Its deceptive representation can only excite the darkest sense, that of animal sympathy: one's feeling about it is always Nature, and never Imitation: it has nothing pleasant with it: it is scarcely capable of Illusion. It makes the tragic stage into pantomime, which, the more com-

---

[24] p. 49.

[25] Soph. *Phil.* Act 4 Sc. I.

[26] Briefe, die neueste Literatur betreffend, part V, pp. 82–84.

plete it is, the more diffused. Quite simply physical pain cannot be the principal idea of a tragedy.

And yet Philoctetes is in Sophocles, in one of the stage's masterpieces. "How much", says Mr. Lessing,[27] "would appear irrefutable in theory if genius had not succeeded in proving the opposite in practice." Scarcely, I think. What is truly irrefutable in theory, and does not just appear so, will never be refuted by a genius, particularly when the theory rests on our sincere feelings. I am sorry for the trouble Mr. Lessing takes to justify Sophocles and to refute the Englishman Smith. Neither requires it, and if they did, if Sophocles' main aim was to attain his tragic goal through expressions of physical pain, then L. would have said little with all the good things he says.

But Sophocles, the tragic genius, felt far too much against attaining this goal, and went along a quite different path, which could not fail him, and one which Mr. L., apparently, has seen from a side angle. I must recapitulate some points from the previous impression I have already furnished.

1) The first idea we get of Philoctetes is the idea of a man abandoned, sick, pitiful, a recluse betrayed by men, a Robinson Crusoe, whose miserable cave we are shown. This situation Mr. Lessing sets out with his customary forcefulness.

2) The wretched man must suffer one more fresh blow from the craftiness of his old enemy: here our sympathy smoulders, and the contrast between Ulysses and Neoptolemus makes the whole scene human.

3) The chorus and Neoptolemus drive the arrows of sympathy deeper into our hearts: they sing of their pity in full measure. How curious we are now to see the man, who here in the desert island plays a singular scene, and for whom fresh misfortune lies in store. In the whole of this Act there is still no Philoctetes to be seen: still less is the representation of his physical pain the main idea. In this Act Sophocles has taken care in three ways to give us a lengthy preparation for Philoctetes before he comes on: to represent what is hardest and most untheatrical in narrative and not in action: to secure our hearts and imagination on his side, so that we first—may learn to stand even the sight of him. And as if there was still not sufficient preparation for that, a distant muttered "Ah!", coming closer, has to announce the wild man, and—

1) Now, with the appearance of the stranger, the sighs are gone, completely gone. Why is that? Why does Sophocles leave them so completely behind the scene? First he has to secure him not merely from contempt: from his whole first appearance Philoctetes is a suffering

---

[27] *Laokoon*, p. 33.

hero. I do not know why Mr. L. does not pursue this *first impression* as the hero appears: we have barely heard him moaning in the distance, now we see him enduring pain. At the very moment of biting back pain, he stands and speaks, friend of mankind, Greek, hero—why has Mr. L. not more explored the interest which he, as a Greek, as a sympathetic friend of the strangers, as the honourer of Greek heroes, evokes? One can hardly have more sympathy for him than one is already disposed to.

2) And he goes on to display a side of greatness. The one who has just now been crying hears of Ulysses' fresh treachery, and how is the crying wretch suddenly transformed into a hero?

3) Into a hero, who remains *vis-à-vis* his enemies a man of unquenchable pride: the original trait of Greek greatness, "love for one's friends, unalterable hate for one's enemies."[28] And who but an honest man can trust his arrows and his life in such a noble spirit to Neoptolemus? Such a man is not only secured on all sides from our contempt: he has our whole heart.

4) The chorus prepares us for the scene of pity, and its tone is clearly one of respect for a hero who is there enduring pain, and who has endured it for such a long time, not who is there screaming. —How little, how little then after all is Sophocles' Philoctetes on stage with his principal characteristic, the man whom L. is accustomed to characterise as ghastly. He is still always the great enduring hero: and that in two long Acts!

And the idea of his pitiful state, and of Neoptolemus' promise, almost begins to vanish. Is it almost that we have been told too much of his pain, is it almost that the pain may well have diminished in nine years? Could we not then see him suffering for ourselves? If there is nothing other than what we have seen, then—and now comes the attack. It is simply an attack, and I do not know how Mr. L. celebrates the choice of a *wound*[29] that could after all have brought no other advantage than to extend a wretched "Ah!" for five Acts long. Sophocles knew how to choose something better—a short seizure. He puts it in the middle of the play, for it to stand out. It comes suddenly; the poison is made all the more striking as being a punishment from the gods, not just an illness that has crept up on him: it comes in fits and starts, so as not to tire the spectator by persisting. It bursts out in frenzy to turn the spectator's mind from the pantomime more towards the suffering soul. For a long time it is suppressed by Philoctetes, and is accompanied only by isolated sounds of misery in the middle of conversations. It ends in a quiet sleep,

---

[28] *Laokoon*, p. 43.

[29] p. 33.

and that is the first time we are able to think over what Philoctetes has endured. One can make no greater mistake over the whole scene than to take it as the pantomime of a physical pain, or mistake the whole play more than to have Philoctetes there to shriek and yell over his words. The attack is over, and after it, no more than before—but really I am not to write a commentary on Sophocles—whoever wants to form a judgement, let him read!

Hölderlin's Translations

Wolfgang Schadewaldt

Style of the Translation: Limitations

For an elementary understanding of Hölderlin's translations of
Sophocles, we must first shed some light on the many oddities and
obscurities that along with much that is simple and beautiful the
unprepared reader encounters, especially in the *Antigone*. These puzzling
eccentricities do not derive from Sophocles' original text. He, especially
in contrast to his predecessor Aeschylus, speaks a Greek that is hard and
clear, a language that does not avoid elevated colloquialisms and that,
even where it rises to a bold pregnancy of expression (as above all in the
choral odes), never lacks the brightness of the clear Greek daylight.
What is obscure and incommunicable in Hölderlin derives from the fact
that his knowledge of the Greek tragedians was acquired unconven-
tionally, on solitary paths, in isolation. In this isolation, wherein lay the
courage and the energy necessary for independence, Hölderlin won
through to the most astounding insights into the nature of Greek tragedy;
we will have more to say about this. But on the other hand, his isolation
limited and restricted his basic work as translator, the comprehension
and reproduction of the original Greek words in their precise original
sense. This is so far-reaching that to speak of Hölderlin's work as
"translation" perhaps does as little justice to Sophocles as it does to the
characteristics of Hölderlin's achievement.

To begin with externals, we must first realize that the text of the
1804 first edition (the manuscript of the poet himself has not yet been
found) was distorted in the most grotesque manner by misprints.
Hölderlin himself noted this while correcting the galleys, and his dis-

couragement at this depravation of his work continued to trouble him
even during the years of his insanity: he once remarked late in life
(Winter 1842–43): "I tried to translate the *Oedipus*, but the bookseller
was a ____!" In April 1804 Hölderlin himself prepared a list of errata,
which has survived and gives us an idea of the extent of the damage
done to the sense of many passages by the misprints with which the text
is riddled. One finds such things as "In *Ruh* umirrend (wandering in
peace)" instead of Hölderlin's correction "In *Mühn* umirrend (wandering in toil)" (*Oedipus* 709) or even "*Arges* Vieh ("wicked cattle)"
instead of the correct "*Berges* Vieh (mountain cattle)" (*Oedipus* 1047).
Not a few of these misprints were emended conjecturally by the editors
Wilhelm Böhm, Norbert von Hellingrath, Franz Zinkernagel, and
Friedrich Beißner, and we ourselves in this edition found it necessary to
make new corrections in certain passages and in others to propose our
own conjectures. But considering the corrupt state of the first edition, we
will still have to come to terms with the fact that much of what is puzzling in the text derives from yet unrecognized typographical errors.

Moreover, Hölderlin's work was hampered from the start by the
fact that a Greek text of Sophocles such as those that we possess today in
various editions, a text edited and purified of errors with extreme
philological care, was not available to him. If we ignore the early
attempt of Martin Opitz in the seventeenth century, Hölderlin was one of
the first Germans, after the work of Johannes Elias Schlegel (1739),
Steinbrüchel (1760), Goldhagen (1777), Tobler (1781), and Christian,
Graf zu Stolberg (1787), who made any attempt at a translation of
Sophocles. Modern philological methods of manuscript recension and
modern editorial techniques were, in his day, still in their infancy. And
if the aids of textual restoration and textual exegesis were at that time
extremely scarce, so too any widespread sense of what trust one might
place in a text, and what one might demand of it, was entirely lacking.
Furthermore, in his isolation during those years Hölderlin was ignorant
of the then latest text of Sophocles—that of Brunck (Strassburg 1786),
which for its time was excellent. Hölderlin apparently used one or
another of the then available English editions, especially for the *Oedipus*
(as Friedrich Beißner has established), but in the important later period
of his work in Stuttgart and Nürtlingen, he translated primarily from the
old edition produced in 1555 by the Giunti, the family of printers that
had worked originally in Florence and later in Venice; this "Juntine"
edition was found among Hölderlin's books at his death. But this edition,
which had not yet made use even of the important 1553 text of the
French Humanist Turnebus, was full of old corruptions: false readings
and especially false punctuation which distorted the sense. Hölderlin fol-

lowed this text without question as *the* text of the poet. Many of the oddities in his translations are due to his being misled by this faulty Greek text. In addition, it often occurred that when Hölderlin sought to extort some meaning from a false reading in his Greek text, he mistranslated, and thus the error was compounded. For example, we read in Hölderlin's *Antigone* 684 (Creon): "Mag sie das wegsingen *bei dem Bruder* (May she sing it away *with her brother*)" instead of Sophocles' "May she call upon *Zeus*, the protector of blood relation." In the Juntine edition "Zeus" (Δία) had been incorrectly printed without its initial capital letter. Hölderlin mistook this for the preposition διά, translated what was originally "Zeus" as "bei," and then rendered the "protector of blood relation" (ξύναιμον) as "Bruder." Or in the second choral ode of the *Antigone* (387), Hölderlin writes "wo das *Schöne* / mit ihm ist (if beauty is with him)" (Juntine: τὸ μὲν καλόν) instead of precisely the opposite in Sophocles: "the dishonorable" (τὸ μὴ καλόν in other manuscripts). Or Hölderlin's *Antigone* 989: "Aber des Schicksals ist furchtbar die Kraft. / Der *Regen* nicht, der Schlachtgeist / Und der Turm nicht, und die meerumrauschten / Fliehn sie, die schwarzen Schiffe (But terrible is the might of Destiny. Not the rain, and the spirit of battle, and not the tower escape it, or the ships that are storm-tossed.)." How is *rain* exposed, along with the spirit of battle, the tower, and the ships, to the power of Fate? Well, "rain" (ὄμβρος) is the Juntine's false reading; as the philologist Erfurdt correctly saw, the reading must be "fullness of might" (ὄλβος).

A further grievous obstacle to Hölderlin's work as translator was his limited knowledge of Greek—limited even for his time. In his youth he had of course studied Greek in the monastery schools at Denkendorf and Maulbronn, but the instruction in Greek that he received was merely what was common in those schools before the reform of classical teaching in Germany. Later, at the University of Tübingen, Hölderlin's circle of friends considered him a "solid (fermer)" Grecian. He heard lectures on Euripides from Conz, and, at the same time, while writing his M.A. thesis together with his friends Schelling and Hegel read Plato, especially, in the original. But his mind, in all these studies, was not content with the letter of the text; he sought to appropriate Greek thought and the Greek sense of form, and the knowledge that he thus acquired was anything but a schoolmasterly competence; it was, rather, capricious, stubborn, eccentric. As his confidence in dealing with Greek texts increased, his understanding of the language evolved into a unique Graeco-Hölderlinian language system. It seems that, the more he read in the Greek authors, the less use he made even of the aids that were available to him. If he ever opened the earlier translations of Sophocles—

Steinbrüchel or Tobler—he quickly, and surely not without justice, laid them aside. What Norbert von Hellingrath says primarily of Hölderlin's translations of Pindar—" . . . a strange union of intimate knowledge of the Greek language, a lively grasp of its beauty and its character, with ignorance of the simplest rules and a complete lack of grammatical exactitude . . ." "To scarce another was the dead language so intimate and alive, to scarce another . . . was Greek grammar and all philological apparatus so alien"—is in every respect true of Hölderlin's translations of Sophocles.

The eccentricity of Hölderlin's knowledge of Greek first of all affects his understanding of individual Greek words. He does not connect a word with its proper signification, or he does not discover the word's proper shade of meaning in its particular context. Thus he falsely understands "doer" (ἐργάτης) as "Meister (master)" (*Antigone* 263), "blemish" (ἄγος) as "Verbot (prohibition)" (266), "hesitation" (ὄκνος) as "Mühe (toil)" (253), "Frost" (πάγος) as "Hügel (hill)." In the "earlier readiness" of Oedipus (48) he finds an "alter, wilder Sinn (old wild thoughts)." In Hölderlin Oedipus says to Jocasta (786) not the correct "let it not be forbidden you . . ." but "Erniedrige dich nur jetzt allzusehr nicht (now abase yourself not all-too greatly)"; to Creon he says (625) "Will einer schnell, der Schlingen legt, *entwischen* (would one who lays snares quickly escape me)" instead of just the contrary: "act against me." Often the wrong meaning of a word remains firmly fixed in his mind for years. Thus the Greek word for "wetness," "water," "spring" (νᾶμα) becomes, in his translation of Euripides' *Bacchae*, "Wald (forest)" (where he probably has in mind the Latin *nemus*, "grove"), and later in his *Antigone* (1178) the famous spring Castalia becomes "Kastalias *Wald*."

The chief characteristic of Hölderlin's faulty understanding of Greek words, here as in his translations of Pindar, is the extremely frequent confusion of words on the basis of similarity in sound. For example, he often interchanges the words "lieben," "fragen," and "reden" ("love," "ask," "speak") (Greek ἐράω, ἐρωτάω, and ἐρέω). He confuses ἔλουσα "I washed" and ἑλοῦσα "having taken" (*Antigone* 934), αὐδάω "I speak" and ἀοιδιάω "I sing" (*Antigone* 235), and takes βιῶναι "to live" as a form of βιάω "I use violence against" (*Oedipus* 1509). And because to him χολή "gall" is the same as χόλος "anger," in *Antigone* 1047 "hoher *Zorn* ward umhergesät (lofty rage was scattered roundabout)" instead of the concrete expression "gall (from the bowels) gushed forth." He confuses πορθεῖν "destroy" with πείθειν "persuade" (*Antigone* 312), κηδεμών "one who cares for" with ἡγεμών "leader" (*Antigone* 571), πατάξαι "to smite" with πατέω "I tread"

(*Antigone* 1142), and so he writes the strange phrase "Doch wenn einer / Mit Wahn mir auf den Mut *tritt*, wird das schwierig (yet it is hard when one in madness treads upon my spirit)" in place of Sophocles' "But to offer resistance and *smite* the heart with ruin, is terrible." Greek δῆλος "obvious" is equated with δεινός "formidable" (*Antigone* 336) but also with δειλός "cowardly," and thus Hölderlin's Oedipus says (685) "*Feig* bist du, wenn du traurig weichst, und wenn du / Schwer über deinen Mut *springst* (cowardly you are, when in sorrow you yield and when you leap heavily above your spirit)" [for Sophocles' "With loathing, clearly, you yield, but it is difficult for you when you have *passed through* your anger [i.e., gone too far in anger]," where in the second part of the sentence περάω "I pass through" has merged with πατέω "I tread." In Greek τῆλε is "distant," but οἱ ἐν τέλει are "the authorities;" transformation of the latter into the former leads Ismene in the prologue of the *Antigone* (69), instead of professing her obedience to "those who are in authority," to acknowledge in Hölderlin's version the power of "sie, die da ferne gehen (they who go far)": Hölderlin was thinking of the mysterious goddesses of vengeance. The verb form ἀμπλάκω comes from ἤμπλακον "I lost, had no part in;" Hölderlin connects the word now with ἁμαρτάνω "I err, sin" and now with Latin *amplexus* "embrace," and so we read first (*Antigone* 576) "hab ich *Schuld*, daß du stirbst? (is the guilt mine that you die?)" instead of the correct "shall I be *excluded* from your lot?" and later (946) "Wenn diesen ich *umarmt* (if him I embraced)" instead of Sophocles' "If I lost this man." Let us conclude this series of examples, which would not soon be exhausted, with a few especially remarkable cases. The priest in Hölderlin's *Oedipus* says (19): "Das andere *Gezweig* / Häuft sich *bekränzt* auf Plätzen (The other branch, garlanded, throngs the squares)." This strange "garlanded branch" came into existence because Hölderlin took φῦλον "people" for φύλλον "leaf." In Sophocles it is the people of Thebes, sitting in the squares (markets), who are "garlanded." Later Oedipus, shortly before the final revelation of his past, asks the old shepherd (1193): "Was hast du's dann gegeben diesem Alten da (Why did you give it (the child) then to this old man?)" The shepherd replies, "Aus *Mitleid*, Herr, ich dacht, ins andre Land werd er's fortbringen, von wo er selber her ist (From *pity*, my lord; I thought that he would carry it to that other land, whence he himself also comes)." Hölderlin's Oedipus: "Wo kamst du denn zusammen mit dem Greise? (How came you together with the old man?)" The servant: "Er *wohnte*, Herr, also wollt in andres Land / Er ferne ziehn, daselbst (He dwelt, my lord, as if he wished to remove far hence to a distant land.)." Hölderlin has confused the Greek κατοικτίσας "having pitied" with κατοικίσας "having settled," and he has also refashioned the previous verse to bring it into harmony with this misunderstanding. And finally *Oedipus* 897 in Hölderlin: "Das wohlanständige aber in der Stadt, das *Altertum*, / Daß nie es löse der Gott, bitt ich (But what is of good report in the city, antiquity—that the god may never abolish it, is my prayer)," instead of, in Sophocles, "Yet this is for the city's good, this *emulation* [lit. "wrestling"]; that the god may never set it at nought is my prayer." Hölderlin's "well-respected antiquity" derives from his confusion of πάλαισμα "wrestling" with παλαιότης "ancient-ness."

The great number of these verbal confusions—which of course entails an equally great number of distortions in understanding of the original—is especially remarkable in view of the fact that it was Hölderlin above all who, in the important second period of his labours, strove for the greatest possible word-for-word literalness in his translations of Greek originals. It was his aim—and this is the greatness of his undertaking—not simply to "put Sophocles into German" somehow, but rather, by imitation of the forms and characteristic expressions of Greek saga, to enrich his own German language system. But in this undertaking he was not seldom thwarted by the sort of verbal confusions described above.

Thus in *Antigone* 263 he supposes that "der erste Tagesblick (daylight's first glance)" is an exact imitation of ἡμεροσκόπος; but ἡμεροσκόπος means, concretely, "the sentinel of the day's first watch." In *Antigone* 1020, misled by the letter of the Greek τηλεπόροις, he does not shrink from writing the strange phrase "in fernewandelnden Grotten (in distant-wandering caverns)"; but the Greek expression means "extending far into the distance." And this hyper-literality, which yet misses the actual sense of the Greek, is also the basis for the odd expression used by Ismene at the beginning of the *Antigone* (verse 21): "Was ists? du scheinst ein rotes Wort zu färben (What is this? You seem to dye a red word)." The Greek phrase, rendered as literally as possible, would be: "It is clear: you *empurple* a word." "Empurple" is here a verbal formation like German "blauen" (e.g., "der Himmel blaut [The sky is blue]") and refers to the gloomy reddish color which the sea assumes at the approach of a storm. In German, approximately: "Dunkel wälzest du in dir ein Wort (Darkly you revolve a word within you.)."

To go further and speak of sentences and their parts as well as the relations of these parts to each other, of the connections of main clauses and subordinate clauses, and of how Hölderlin conceives of all this, would lead us far afield. Just as Hölderlin confuses words, so he confuses similar grammatical forms with each other; he establishes false

connections of thought by separating phrases that belong together and by
connecting phrases that do not; he obscures the logical progression of the
thought in a given passage, a progression which in Sophocles is as
strictly thought through as it is lively, with a mere "auch (also)" or
"und auch (and also)." A few examples only must suffice. In *Antigone*
452, the Watchman says of Antigone, who has been caught: "*Sie leug-
net' aber nichts mir ab und war / Lieblich zugleich und auch betrübt vor
mir* (But nothing she denied to me, and stood before me at once amiable
and sorrowful)"—though Sophocles, if one has regard to his actual
sentence structure, does not at all evoke the image of an "amiable and
sorrowful" Antigone, but instead has the Watchman say that Antigone's
refusal to lie was to *him*, the Watchman, at once welcome and grievous.
Or *Antigone* 1307: "*Doch das allzugroße Schweigen / Scheint bei
vergebnem Schreien mir bedeutend* (Yet silence all-too great seems, with
vain crying, significant)." The proper connection of thought gives us:
"Excessive silence seems to me *just* as suspicious *as much vain crying.*"
Or finally *Antigone* 1091: Tiresias: "*Um wie viel gilt jetzt mehr
Gutmütigkeit als Wohlsein?* (How greater now is kindliness than
prosperity?)" The partitive genitive has been misunderstood as a genitive
of comparison; in Sophocles Tiresias says: "How true it is that *the sublimest of possessions is insight.*"

   With all of this we have not yet touched upon those obscurities
and deviations from Sophocles' meaning that in Hölderlin's translations,
and especially in the *Antigone*, result from his passing from the role of
translator to that of interpreter. The incommunicable element of his language is especially evident in such interpretive translations, and it sets us
the oddest riddles. In Sophocles' *Antigone* (389) the Watchman, when in
contrast to his earlier expectation he cheerfully comes before Creon with
his prisoner, says, "Often *second thoughts* expose our first opinion as a
liar." Hölderlin's *Antigone* has instead a phrase that remains a riddle:
"*Bildung lacht aus die Meinung* (Education laughs opinion to scorn)." In
Antigone 563 he translates "Hades and the gods below" as "denen, *die
durchgängiger Weise sind* (those who are of a thorough nature)"; he
means "the dead." In *Antigone* 702 he significantly understands κόσμος,
in Sophocles "order," as "world": "*So sichre du, die eine Welt dir
bilden* (Then secure those that fashion a world for you)" instead of
Sophocles' "Thus that which is set in order must be defended." Or in
Antigone 773, Sophocles' Creon says to his son Haemon: "If I intervene
on behalf of my lordship (ἀρχάς), am I at fault?" Hölderlin significantly misunderstands ἀρχάς as "beginning": "*Wenn meinem
Uranfang ich treu bestehe, lüg ich?* (If I stand true to my first beginning,
do I lie?) Or Antigone in her great parting speech (923 ff.): "*Da werd*

ich reisen / Den Meinen zu, von denen zu den Toten / Die meiste Zahl, nachdem sie weiter gangen (gestorben, dahingegangen), / *Zornigmitleidig dort ein Licht begrüßt hat* (Then shall I journey to mine own, of whom the greatest number, when they have passed farther, a light, with anger and pity, has there welcomed to the dead)." Sophocles here has merely: "To my own, of whom the greatest number *Persephassa has received* among the dead." Hölderlin knew of an ancient mystical interpretation of Persephassa, the queen of the dead, as "corrupter of light," and from this he has taken his "zornigmitleidig" and "Licht" (φάος and πέρθειν).

As a final example, let us observe how Hölderlin in this late era has interpreted the Greek νύμφη "young woman" as "water," because the Greeks saw in springs, as also in mountains and trees, the fresh life energy of young divine women. Thus to Hölderlin the final choral ode of the *Antigone* (1162 ff.), addressed to Bakchos, takes this shape: "Namenschöpfer, der du von den *Wassern*, welche Kadmos / Geliebet, der Stolz bist . . . (Creator of names, who are the pride of the waters that Cadmus loved)" instead of Sophocles' "Bearer of many names, O thou the pride of the Cadmean *maiden*" (that is, Bakchos' mother Semele). But the first antistrophe of this choral ode goes on to speak of the twin peaks of Parnassus, where the nymphs of the *Corycian* stalactite cavern dance as Bacchae and Maenads. Hölderlin conceives of these nymphs too as "water," and the *Corycian* cavern, because of similarity in the sound of the words, becomes for him *Cocytus*, the river of the underworld, and so we read in his translation (1176): "am / *Kokytos*, wo die *Wasser* / Bakchantisch fallen und / Kastalias *Wald* auch (by Cocytus, where like bacchants the waters fall, and also Castalia's grove)" (this last, as we have seen, is for "Castalia's spring").

The last instances cited bring us, of course, into the realm of creative translation, the feature that lends inner necessity and—in the real sense of the word—significance to the many obscurities that limit the value of Hölderlin's translations, considered merely as translations; this point will soon occupy us further. But if we first review the characteristic faults of Hölderlin's translations, we find that, all in all, misunderstood words, verbal confusions, and uncomprehended connections of thought so permeate the two dramas that on the average every fourth or fifth line is affected in one way or another. That is: the German text of Hölderlin approximates only gropingly and very vaguely to the original Greek text of Sophocles as it unfolds with crisp precision in the speeches of the characters and the choruses of Sophocles himself. The general and the specific constraints under which Hölderlin translated Sophocles prevent us, in many individual instances as well as throughout long passages, from finding out from Hölderlin just what Sophocles said and had his personages say, speaking naturally and specifically from his own specific world. Insofar as we care deeply about Sophocles' original meaning, this difference must be stated clearly at the outset.

But this is not the last word, it is rather only the first word, on Hölderlin's accomplishment. The limited knowledge of Greek that prevented his translations from being "correct" in the everyday sense has yet opened many possibilities for the translator-poet. Since as a translator he was obliged to make his own way upon utterly untrodden ground, he might be expected to take uncertain steps and to stumble. But in so doing he avoided the well-trodden road of translators' conventions, and his treatment of Sophocles' original text remained original. With all his failures to understand words and grammatical rules and his lack of experience in the routines of understanding, Hölderlin was preserved in his innocence, as it were, from all the translators' routine that makes the usual translations of his time and of later times so correct and so insignificant. He instinctively grasped in particular the "resonance" of Sophocles' speech in its concreteness and profundity, in that serious sense of responsibility for language which does not first have to discard all poeticizing follies. His successes were outstanding successes: the choral odes and the great speeches in their hardness, density, and concreteness. Read for example the great speeches of Oedipus, above all the narration of his history (*Oedipus* 798 ff.), the splendid antiphonal songs in the *Oedipus* and the *Antigone* (*Oedipus* 1320 ff., *Antigone* 811 ff.), and Antigone's parting words (922 ff.). As a translator of Sophocles, Hölderlin can be—to use a simile—compared with those excavators on Greek soil who were yet unschooled and unmethodical but who, in the greatness of their instincts and the fullness of their hearts, went to work quite alone; many of their procedures were violent, they even destroyed a great deal, but nonetheless they truly penetrated into the depths and so showed the way, for those who followed them, to all that awaited discovery.

But we go further and venture to say that the limited means used by Hölderlin in his translations evolved into a unique instrument for that transforming appropriation which is the essence of all creative preservation. The overwhelming majority of Hölderlin's linguistic errors are creative errors: errors in verbal particulars, behind which yet stands a general truth, whether because the error has led the translator astray to a new and personal verbal vision or because the process of erring was creatively directed from the first. We may be justified in requiring of *common understanding* that it rise cumulatively from particulars securely and precisely grasped to an essential whole. But there is also an understanding characteristic of genius, an *anticipatory understanding*, which proceeds from a bare minimum of given data directly to the center and, sensing the reality of a thing, grasps its essence. This was Hölderlin's style of understanding. From what he understood of Sophocles' original text he pressed forward, by virtue of an experience of God that was vouchsafed to none but him in all the isolation of his life's journey, toward a conception of the nature of tragedy that was then and still remains unexampled. On this conception rests an interpretation of the meaning of the *Oedipus* and the *Antigone* which was then, and long remained, unparalleled. Hölderlin gave expression to this sense of the tragic expecially in his notes to the two tragedies, notes written in a barely accessible style. And we too must first grasp this sense if we wish to experience the true essence of Hölderlin's translations and all that they embody.

Sophocles and Hölderlin

R. B. Harrison

I. *Oedipus der Tyrann* and *Antigonä*[†]

"Hölderlin's translations," writes Karl Reinhardt, "are fundamentally different from everything to be found anywhere else in translation from Greek, and not only from Greek. Sophoclean tragedy is for him a piece of Divine Creation, to be rescued and brought to fresh life. No by-product, but one of his major works."[1] Indeed, in one sense the Sophocles translations may be regarded as the culmination of Hölderlin's work, for they represent the final fruit of his efforts to understand the process by which the reunion of man with the divine and the regeneration of society could take place.

The attitude of many of Hölderlin's contemporaries is indicated by the letter of the younger Voß to Abeken: "What do you say to Hölderlin's Sophocles? Is the man raving or is he only pretending to be?"[2] In fact the translations are far from being merely the confused product of a mind on the point of total collapse, but it is only a knowledge of Hölderlin's earlier thought that makes it possible to appreciate fully his interpretation of the tragedies. We must therefore first trace in outline

---

[†] References to Hölderlin's works are to Hölderlin, *Sämtliche Werke* Grosse Stuttgarter Ausgabe, ed. Friedrich Beißner (Stuttgart, 1943–).

[1] "Hölderlin und Sophokles," in *Hölderlin: Beiträge zu seinem Verständnis in unserm Jahrhundert*, p. 292.

[2] Quoted by Schadewaldt, "Hölderlins Übersetzung des Sophokles," in *Hellas und Hesperien*, p. 769.

the development of those aspects of his thought which form the basis of
the translations, and we shall then be in a position to examine a number
of passages from the translations themselves, not in order to point out
how Hölderlin fulfilled his wish "to represent Greek art in a more lively
fashion than usual to the public by laying more stress on the Oriental element which it disowned, and correcting artistic error where it occurs"
(*Br.* 241, VI.434),[3] but in order to show how, sometimes led astray by a
corrupt text, more often simply mistranslating, he interpreted Sophocles
in the light of his own ideas.[4]

* * *

There seems no doubt that Hölderlin planned to translate all of
Sophocles' seven extant tragedies. *Oedipus der Tyrann* forms "the first
volume of the translation of Sophocles' tragedies" (*Br.* 246, vi. 439),
and *Antigonä* was also ready for the "Jubilatemesse" held at Leipzig in
spring 1804, when they were both published by Friedrich Wilmans under
the title *Die Trauerspiele des Sophokles*. There is reason to believe that
the *Ajax* would have formed the third volume, for the play was clearly
very much in Hölderlin's mind when he was writing the "Anmerkungen
zur Antigonä" [Notes on *Antigone*] in which, in three passages, the
structure of *Antigone* is made clearer by comparing it with that of
Oedipus Tyrannus and *Ajax*. *Oedipus Coloneus*, of which Hölderlin also
translated two short passages, is mentioned once (v. 268ff.).

From the *Ajax* he translated three choric passages, which he
wrote without gaps on two sheets of paper (v. 511). Despite the evidence
that the *Ajax* was to form the third volume of Sophocles' tragedies it
seems therefore that here Hölderlin was not immediately concerned with
a translation of the whole play, but was selecting his favourite passages,
a supposition which is confirmed by the fact that a part of each of them
appears in his earlier work. Ajax's prayer for death in the first episode
includes his farewell to nature, and the opening lines of the first
stasimon are formed by the words addressed to Salamis by his companions. In addition to these passages, which we have already discussed,

---

[3] Bießner, *Hölderlins Übersetzungen aus dem Griechischen*, pp. 138 ff.,
shows in a series of examples how Hölderlin aimed "to lay more stress on the 'Oriental'
. . . by striving for passionate intensity." Cf. Reinhardt, op. cit., pp. 293 ff.; Binder,
"Hölderin und Sophokles," *Hölderlin-Jahrbuch* 16 (1969/70), 21 ff.

[4] The text which Hölderlin used for *Oedipus der Tyrann* and *Antigonä* has not
been traced, though Beißner, op. cit., pp. 65 ff., argues that it was published between
1779 and 1786 and was possibly an English school edition. For their revision in 1803
and for the last three choruses of *Antigonä* he used the Juntine edition published in
Frankfurt in 1555 (II.451).

the second stasimon includes the motto of "The Blind Singer," ἔλυσεν αἰνὸν ἄχος ἀπ᾽ ὀμμάτων Ἄρης (*Aj.* 706), which Hölderlin also uses in terms of his own thought. The distress which the god of violent death has cleared like a cloud from the eyes of his Salaminian followers is Ajax's intended suicide. In the context of the poem, however, it is the blindness which represents the darkness of the godless era and which is cured with the dawning of the divine day:

> Tag! Tag! du über stürzenden Wolken! sei
> Willkommen mir! es blühet mein Auge dir.
> [Day! Day! You above the plunging clouds! I welcome you!
> My eye blooms for you.]
>
> (II. 54 f.)

The scenery of the Trojan plain in the first of these passages seems to have held a special fascination for Hölderlin, for it appears not only here and in the penultimate version of *Hyperion*, but also in the last strophe of "Mnemosyne." The nature of its attraction for him emerges most clearly in the translation:

> Ihr Bäche, die ihr ins Meer fließt und ihr Höhlen am
> Meer und du
> Mein Hain, de hänget über dem Ufer . . .
> [You streams which flow into the sea and you caves by
> the sea and you, my holy grove which hangs over the
> shore]
>
> (v. 277 (*Aj.* 412 f.))

In each of the three aspects of the scene which Ajax addresses Hölderlin sees an expression of that unity of land and sea which, it has been suggested, was in his mind in his translation of the words addressed by Ajax's companions to Salamis.

The streams which flow into the sea (πόροι ἀλίρροθοι)[5] are also pictured at the beginning of "Der Archipelagus": "from Kalauria fall / Silver streams, as in times past, into the old waters of the father." They

---

[5] Although Jebb, *The Ajax*, p. 72, believes the words mean here, as they do in Aeschylus, *Persae*, 367, "the paths of the sounding sea," in this case the Hellespont, Liddell and Scott in the earlier editions of *A Greek-English Lexicon* support Hölderlin's interpretation and translate: "seaward flowing streams." However, the seventh edition (1883) adopts Jebb's interpretation, which has been retained in the edition revised by H. Stuart Jones (1940). The other meaning would naturally have occurred to Hölderlin since it makes this aspect of the scene parallel to the other two.

play an important part in the unifying cycle in which the cloud-borne waters which the "Sea God" sends over the land descend in rain, and then, carried by "Mäander," "Kayster," and the "majestic Nile," return to their source, "like the wandering son when his father calls him" (II. 103f.). While in the case of the streams it is thus possible to show how the translation echoes the thought of Hölderlin's earlier work, the "caves by the sea" of the Troad are themselves mentioned in a variant of "The Wandering," where, in answering the question "But where are you living, my dear kin?," the poet mentions all those features contained in this passage of the translation:

> Dort an den Ufern, unter den Bäumen
> Ionias, in Ebenen des Kaisters, an den Grotten der See
> Des Tenedos gegenüber
> [There on the shores, under the trees of Ionia, on the
> Cayster's plains, by the sea-grottoes opposite Tenedos.]
> (II. 140, 174)

In the words "holy grove which hangs over the shore" (νέμος ἐπάκτιον) Hölderlin ignores the basic sense of νέμος (pasture)[6] and expands ἐπάκτιον (on the shore) in such a way that he conjures up "a picture which had long been a favourite," reminiscent above all of the opening lines of "The Middle of Life":

> Mit gelben Birnen hänget
> Und voll mit wilden Rosen
> Das Land in den See.[7]
> [With yellow pears and full of wild roses
> the land hangs into the lake.]
> (II. 117)

It is in essence the same picture as Hyperion recalls in his last letter to Bellarmin:

---

[6] Cf. the verb νέμω (pasture, graze flocks). This emphasis is understandable since the idea of woodland was always associated with the word and became the sole meaning of the Latin *nemus* in poetic usage.

[7] Zuntz, *Über Hölderlins Pindar-Übersetzung*, p. 60, who, however, does not investigate the basis of the attraction which this picture had for Hölderlin. He refers both to these lines and to the incomplete line of "But when the heavenly ones . . ." : "Mountain hangs [over] the lake" (II. 222). Cf. also *Ant.* 1181 f. (1132f.), v. 253: "And green shore, / hanging full of grapes" (χλωρά τ᾽ ἀκτὰ πολυστάφυλος).

> Once I was sitting far away in the country, by a spring, in
> the shadow of ivy-green rocks and overhanging flowering
> bushes. It was the most beautiful noontide that I know of.
> Sweet breezes were blowing and in the morning freshness
> the land was still gleaming and the light was smiling
> calmly in its home in the Aether. (II. 158)

The breezes of "Aether" and the light of the sun, the two aspects
of heaven, are united with the earth to form "the world eternally at
one," which is completed by the unity of land and water created by the
shrubs' hanging over the spring. The unity, emphasized in the structure
of the last sentence by the way in which "the Land" is embraced by
"sweet breezes" and "the light," is so complete that in this setting Hyperion seems to hear Diotima's voice.

For Hyperion a river lacking the overhanging trees which provide
an expression of the unity of land and water is incomplete: "Like a
stream past parched banks, where no willow leaves are reflected in the
water, life ran past me, devoid of all beauty" (III. 42). Conversely, the
beauty of a branch is for him so enhanced by its reflection in water that
he ascribes such beauty to the trees of "the ante-chamber of Elysium,"
where he imagines his spirit played with Diotima "to the pleasant sounds
of the spring, and under branches, as we see the branches of the earth
when, made beautiful, they gleam from the golden stream" (III. 70).
That this unity of trees and water was equally an essential feature of
Hölderlin's ideal landscape can be seen in his letter to his sister from
Hauptwil, in which the two features are introduced separately and then
seen in union. He describes how the Alps descend into the valley,

> this friendly valley, its sides everywhere crowned by
> evergreen copses of fir, and in its depth crossed by the
> water of lakes and streams, and there I dwell, in a garden
> where beneath my window willows and poplars stand by a
> clear stretch of water which delights me at night with its
> rippling sound when everything is still, and I compose and
> muse with the clear starry sky before me.[8] (Br. 228, VI.
> 414)

The one advantage which we have when studying the unpublished
as opposed to the published Sophocles translations is that, since the man-

---

[8] In "Andenken" the stream is overlooked by "a noble pair / of oaks and silver
poplars" (II. 188), and in "From the Abyss . . . ' a "Nußbaum" [walnut tree] bends
over springs (II. 250).

uscripts, which are not fair copies, have survived, we can examine the alterations which Hölderlin made. In this case he began with a completely literal translation: "O holy grove by < the shore> " (v. 511). It is therefore clear that the expansion into the picture we have been discussing was consciously carried out: "you / my holy grove, which hangs over the shore." The further addition of the pronoun "you," strongly stressed by the enjambment of the two lines, and of the emotional possessive "my," which has no equivalent in the Greek text, serves to emphasize Ajax's loving relationship with nature.[9] In Hölderlin's eyes the ideal for man is loving union with the total unity of nature.

We have seen that the Greek gods whom Hölderlin regarded as most important were Apollo and Zeus. It is not surprising therefore that he should have chosen to translate the second stasimon of the *Ajax*, in which the chorus celebrate Ajax's ostensible abandonment of his decision to die, for in it both Apollo and Zeus are invoked. The extent to which he approached the Greek text with his own ideas in mind can be seen in the lines addressed to them.

The Greek sailors invite Apollo to be present at their dance of joy:

> Ἰκαρίων δ᾽ ὑπὲρ πελαγέων
> μολὼν ἄναξ Ἀπόλλων
> ὁ Δάλιος, εὔγνωστος,
> ἐμοὶ ξυνείης διὰ παντὸς εὔφρων.[10]

In his interpretation of Greek religion Hölderlin saw Apollo as the personification of the sun, and the use of the epithet "Delian" in this chorus, recalling the sun-worship on Delos which Hölderlin had described in *Hyperion* (III. 15), must have been an added incentive to see Apollo as the sun here too:

> Und du der aufgeht über den Ikarischen Wassern
> König Apollon

---

[9] Cf. the addition of the possessive adjective, receiving from enjambment an emphasis similar to that given here to "you," in the change of "Am Feigenbaum / Ist mir Achilles gestorben (by the fig tree Achilles died and is lost to me)" to "Am Feigenbaum ist mein / Achilles mir gestorben (by the fig tree my Achilles died and is lost to me)" ("Mnemosyne," II. 817 f.).

[10] "May you, Apollo, coming over the Icarian waters, be with me ever kind." The Greek text given is that of the Juntine edition of 1555, which was found among Hölderlin's books and which he used for his *Ajax* translations as well as for the revision of his two completed translations (II. 451).

Delischer gutbekannt,
Sei mit mir allzeit günstig.
[And you who rise over Icarian waters, King
Apollo, well known to the Delians, be with me
ever propitious.]
                                              (v. 280 (*Aj*. 702 ff.))

In Ajax's prayer for death Hölderlin translated μολών (coming, going)
correctly (v. 277 (*Aj*. 404)), but his rendering of it here with the words
"der aufgeht (who rise)" (he first wrote "aufsteigend [mounting]" (v.
513)) is a small but significant alteration of Sophocles' meaning in terms
of his own thought. The invitation to Apollo to be present has become a
prayer for the sun-god's favour.

The same sort of transformation can be observed in the lines
addressed to Zeus:

νῦν αὖ
νῦν, ὦ Ζεῦ, πάρα λευκὸν εὐ-
αμερον πελάσαι φάος
θοῶν ὠκυάλων νεῶν.[11]

These lines were more difficult to translate: πάρα, as the accent shows,
is not the preposition, but an abbreviation for the verb πάρεστι, and
θοῶν is the genitive plural of the adjective, not the nominative singular
of the participle, which could only mean "sharpening." Nevertheless, it
is characteristic that as a result of the misunderstanding of these two
words Hölderlin's version should be consistent with the thought of the
rest of his work:

Nun Auch
Nun Zeus erschein' am weißen Lichte
Des schönen Tages treibend
Die schnellen Schiffe.
[Now too, now Zeus appear in the white light
of the fine day, driving the speedy ships.]
                                              (v. 280 (*Aj*. 707 ff.))

Zeus, the personification of "Aether," the single term which includes the
destructive lightning and the life-giving rain and air, is seen here as air
in motion, as the wind.

Hölderlin sees the chorus turning to the gods in song to share
with them the joy caused by the ending of their anxiety. This action is so

---

[11] "O Zeus, now it is again possible for the bright light of happy days to come
to the swift, speeding ships."

similar to his own attitude that it is easy to understand how he interpreted the functions of Apollo and Zeus here in his own terms. In fact the Greek sailors do not regard Apollo and Zeus as being responsible for their happiness, but rather Ares, the god of bloodshed and violent death: "Gelöst hat den grausamen Kummer von den Augen Ares (Ares has loosened the grim worry from our eyes)." For Hölderlin, however, unity with the powers they represented is the necessary condition of all joy and song. Addressing "Aether" and "Helios" he writes:

> Ihr guten Götter! arm ist, wer euch nicht kennt,
> Im rohen Busen ruhet der Zwist ihm nie,
> Und Nacht ist ihm die Welt und keine
> Freude gedeihet und kein Gesang ihm.
> [You good gods! Poor is he who does not know you:
> in his rough heart Discord never rests,
> and the world is night to him, and no joy flourishes
> and no song, for him]
> ("Die Götter," II. 16)

Similarly Hölderlin's view of the special position of the hero is apparent in the first of the three passages translated, where Ajax immediately justifies his prayer for death:

> Denn
> Von Himmlischen das Geschlecht nicht und nicht bei
> Alltäglichen Menschen bin ich werth
> Nach einer Hülfe zu schauen.
> [For not from the race of the heavenly ones, and not
> from everday men do I deserve to look for any help.]
> (v. 277 (*Aj.* 398 ff.))

For Sophocles there are two categories: θεοί and ἀμέριοι . . . ἄνθρωποι, gods and men who last but a day.[12] Hölderlin, however, recognizes a tripartite division, as is apparent, for example, when he asks for the beaker to be filled with wine,

> Daß ich den Göttern zuerst und das Angedenken der Helden
> Trinke, der Schiffer, und dann eures, ihr Trautesten! auch
> Eltern und Freund!
> [That I may first drink to the gods and to the memory

---

[12] In *Ant.* 818 (789 f.), v. 238, Hölderlin gives ἀμέριος its proper meaning, translating the same words, "entschlafende Menschen (men who pass away)."

of the heroes, the mariners, and then to yours too, you
dearest ones, parents and friends!]

("Der Wanderer," II. 83)

He thus sees the hero Ajax in a category between men and gods, for, as
he makes clear in the case of Achilles, the hero may be "'born <to
live> for a short time,' according to Homer" ("Über Achill" (I), IV.
224),[13] but he is not "everyday," for Hölderlin a synonym of
"commonplace" and an antonym of "holy," the epithet of the gods;[14] the
reason why the "Divine Youth" appears so seldom in the *Iliad* is that
"der Idealische durfte nicht alltäglich erscheinen (the ideal should not
appear everyday)" ("Über Achill" (2), IV.225).

For Hölderlin the hero differs from "everyday mankind" in the
special relationship which he has with the divine. In the early poems it is
the hero's parentage that is the basis of this relationship, but men too
strive to bridge the gulf between the human and the divine. Hercules, for
example, is addressed as "high demigod," "son of Kronion," but his
immortality can be shared by those who emulate his deeds ("An
Herkules," I. 199f.). Similarly the comfort which the "noble son of the
gods" Achilles receives from his divine mother can also be found by a
mortal in divine nature ("Achill," I. 271). As a result the hero's status is
later seen to be independent of his birth. When at the beginning of the
fourth triad of "Der Rhein" Hölderlin writes:

> Halbgötter denk' ich jezt
> Und kennen muß ich die Theuern,
> Weil oft ihr Leben so
> Die schnende Brust mir beweget,
> [I think now of demigods, and I must know these
> dear ones because often their life moves my
> longing heart,]
>
> (II. 146)

it is Rousseau whom he takes as an example.

Rousseau, though open to the divine, is able to withstand its
destructive revelation. In the "Grund zum Empedokles" the hero is seen

---

[13] Cf. *Il.* I. 352: μινυνθάδιος. Empedokles too is in his own words "born only
<to live> for a short time" (*Emp.* I, iv. 71). He must die "because the gods all loved
him too much" (IV. 85).

[14] Cf. "An die Madonna," II. 216: "Heilig sind sie / Die Glänzenden, wenn
aber alltäglich / Die Himmlischen und gemein / Das Wunder scheinen will . . . (Holy
are they, the shining ones, but when the heavenly ones are to appear everyday, and the
miraculous commonplace . . .)."

as a mortal who exposes himself to the divine power and seeks union
with it at the cost of his own life, in order that a wider reconciliation of
God and man may take place. Not only are Empedokles, Oedipus, and
Antigone heroes in this sense, but so is Ajax. He too is a victim of "the
fire from heaven," for whereas "our tragedy is that we depart from the
realm of the living packed quite quietly into some container or other, not
that consumed in flames we pay for the flame which we had no power to
contain" (Br. 236, VI. 426), it is the latter that is the subject of Greek
tragedy. Ajax, like Antigone, follows the "tearing spirit of the times,"
"the spirit . . . of the world of the dead" ("Anm. Ant." v. 266), and it is
to this "World of the Dead" that the opening words of his prayer are
addressed:

> Io Nacht, mein Licht, o Erebos glänzend mir
> Nimmt mich, nimmt
> Mich Einheimischen, nimmt mich.
> [O Night, my light, O Erebos, shining for me,
> take me, take me to dwell with you, take me.]
>   (v. 277 (*Aj*. 394 ff.))

He despairs of securing "this surest stay [i.e. security in life] in the face
of passing time", which Danae achieves ("Anm. Ant." v. 268), but
which Empedokles rejects: "my stay is not to last for years" (*Emp. III*,
IV. 130); "my stay, like the stream which the frost has enchained"
(*Emp. I*, IV. 79).[15] He therefore continues:

> Wohin muß einer entfliehn
> In dem, wo geh ich hin
> Und bleibe?
> [Where must a man escape to in this,
> where do I go from here and stay?]
>   (v. 277 (*Aj*. 403f.))

The rhythm of Hölderlin's translation of ποῖ μολὼν μενῶ gives special
emphasis to "bleibe (stay)" (in the *Ajax* translations there is only one
other line which is as short), and in this context the word has the same
sort of ambiguity which it has when Empedokles complains, "Nun wein
ich, wie ein Ausgestoßener, / Und nirgend mag ich bleiben (Now I cry,
like one exiled, and nowhere may I stay)" (IV. 19).

---

[15] Cf. "Der gefesselte Strom," II. 67: "Since nowhere may he stay."

Until now the beauty of nature has assured Ajax of this
"staying," for he has been able to regard himself as included in its unity,
and thus to feel in contact with the divine. He addresses those features of
the Trojan landscape which we have already examined:

> Viel viele Zeit und lange
> Habt ihr mich aufgehalten, bei Troja,
> Nun nicht mehr, nicht mehr
> Athem hohlend.[16]
> [Much, much time and long have you held me up
> in Troy, now no longer, no longer drawing breath]
> (v. 277 (*Aj.* 414 ff.))

In his earlier rendering of these lines in *Hyperion* ("ihr habt mich lange
behalten [You have kept me (= been my home) long]) Hölderlin gave
the verb κατείχετε the sense which was clearly intended by Sophocles.
His selection here of another of its senses is significant, for as a result he
uses a word which had for him a special connotation. Empedokles
employs it when he tells Pausanias, "Halte nur / Mein Schiksaal mir
nicht auf (Only do not hold up my fate)" (*Emp. III*, IV. 128), and after
asking, "Gedachtet ihr, / Es halte der Stachel ihn auf? (Did you suppose
the goad would hold him up?)" Panthea reveals her understanding of his
fate:

> es beschleunigen ihm
> Die Schmerzen den Flug.
>
> Sind nicht, wie er, auch
> Der Heroen einige zu den Göttern gegangen?
> [The pain speeds his flight . . .
> Are not, like him, some of the heroes gone to the gods?]
> (*Emp. II*, IV. 116f.)

Thus towards the end of *Oedipus der Tyrann*, where Oedipus begs
Creon,

---

[16] The thought and vocabulary of this passage have a striking parallel in "Der
Adler," [The Eagle] II. 229 f.: "Wo wollen wir *bleiben*? . . . Will einer wohnen, / So
sei es an Treppen, / Und wo ein Häuslein *hinabhängt / Am Wasser halte dich auf. /
Und was du hast, ist / Athem zu hohlen* (Where shall we *stay*? . . . If one wishes to
dwell, then let it be on steps, and where a little house *hangs down by the water make
your stay*. What you have is *to draw breath*)" (my italics).

Bei Göttern! da du mir das Streben aufhielst . . .
Gehorche mir.

* * *

Wirf aus dem Lande mich, so schnell du kannst,
[By the gods! Since you hold up my efforts . . .
Obey me. . . . cast me out from the land as quickly
as you can]

(*Oed. Tyr.* 1451 ff. (1432 ff.), v. 188)

Hölderlin gives his own interpretation of the clause ἐπείπερ ἐλπίδος μ᾽ ἀπέσπασας.[17] Creon has tried to restrain in Oedipus "the . . . effort to have control over himself" ("Anm. Oed." V. 199), the desire for complete knowledge about himself which must end in union with God. In the same way, unlike Dionysus, "who / holds up the passion for death of peoples" ("Der Einzige" (II), 158), the beauty of nature is no longer able to restrain in Ajax the urge towards complete union with the divine.

In the first stasimon the chorus deplore the fate which has befallen Ajax and suggest that death would be a lesser evil than his present madness:

Denn besser ists zu schlafen in der Hölle, denn
Nichtstaugend Krankseyn, wenn vom heimatlichen Geschlechte
Der mühebeladnen Achäier einer kommt
Und nicht des angebornen
Zorns mächtig, sondern außer sich ist.
[For to sleep in Hades is better than illness good for nothing,
if one comes from the native race of the trouble-laden Achaeans
and is not in control of his innate anger, but is outside himself.]

(v. 279 (*Aj.* 635 ff.))

Most significant is Hölderlin's rendering in the last two lines of the words

οὐκέτι συντρόφοις
ὀργαῖς ἔμπεδος, ἀλλ᾽ ἐκτὸς ὁμιλεῖ.

The omission of a noun after the preposition ἐκτὸς made it all the easier for him to think of Ajax as undergoing the same fate as the Lycians in

---

[17] "Since you diverted me from my uneasy foreboding."

Xanthos.[18] When during a seige by Brutus the city caught fire these heroes were seized by "the passion for death": "and were all outside themselves,"

> Denn selbstvergessen, allzubereit, den Wunsch
> Der Götter zu erfüllen, ergreift zu gern
> Was sterblich ist, wenn offnen Augs auf
> Eigenen Pfaden es einmal wandelt,
>
> Ins All zurük die kürzeste Bahn.

[For forgetful of self, all too ready to fulfil the wish of the gods, that which is mortal, when, eyes open, it once walks on its own paths, grasps too gladly the shortest road back into Totality.]

("Stimme des Volks" (II), II. 51 ff.)

Such is Hölderlin's interpretation of Plutarch's account: "But the Lycians were suddenly possessed by a dreadful impulse to madness, which can be likened best to a passion for death" (*Brutus*, 31).[19] The Lycians find in the death which they seek in inspired madness that unity with the universe which is achieved only momentarily by Hyperion, for whom it is similarly "the summit of thoughts and joys" "in blissful forgetting of self to return into the totality of Nature" (III. 9). Ajax too chooses a voluntary death, but only after he has recovered from the madness which is here seen as the state of being "outside himself," an interpretation which is not merely the fortuitous result of Sophocles' choice of words, for in the chorus in *Antigonä* addressed to "Spirit of Love" the words "und es ist, / Wer's an sich hat, nicht bei sich (and whoever possesses it is not with himself)" are a translation of ὁ δ' ἔχων μέμηνεν: "he who possesses you is mad" (*Ant*. 818 f. (790), v. 238).

Additional evidence that Hölderlin saw this passage in the same terms as Plutarch's report of the siege of Xanthos is provided by his translation of συντρόφοις ὀργαῖς. It was not unnatural that he should think of the commoner meaning of ὀργή, "anger," and so understand the phrase to mean "unstable because of his anger" rather than "unfaithful to

---

[18] Hölderlin's interpretation is supported by Liddell and Scott, who supply ἑαυτοῦ and understand the phrase to mean "wanders outside [himself]," i.e. "beside himself, out of his wits." Jebb, op. cit., p. 101, supplies συντρόφων ὀργῶν from the previous line and translates "is true no more to the promptings of his inbred nature, but dwells with alien thoughts."

[19] Translated by Perrin.

his natural character,"[20] but the misunderstanding must have been encouraged by the sense of "openness to the divine" which Hölderlin gives the notion of anger, and which we have already examined in relation to "the angry excess" of Oedipus. That Hölderlin had in mind a Greek quality is suggested by his choice of the epithet "angeboren (innate)," for it provides a link with the vocabulary of the letter to Böhlendorff in which he sees "the fire from heaven," "beautiful passion," as characteristic of the "Apolline realm" of the Greeks: "The peculiarly national will become always the lesser advantage as culture progresses. For that reason the Greeks are to a lesser extent masters of holy emotion because it was innate" (Br. 236, VI. 426).[21] And that Hölderlin thought of Ajax as exhibiting this national characteristic is shown by his statement in the "Notes on Antigone" that Ajax and Odysseus are "opposed . . . like National and Anti-National" (v. 268f.).[22]

The Juntine text of the first three lines of this passage is corrupt:

$$\kappa\rho\epsilon\hat{\iota}\sigma\sigma o\nu \ \gamma\acute{\alpha}\rho \ \text{'}\text{A}\ddot{\iota}\delta\alpha \ \kappa\epsilon\acute{\upsilon}\theta\omega\nu, \ \mathring{\eta} \ \nu o\sigma\hat{\omega}\nu \ \mu\acute{\alpha}\tau\alpha\nu,$$
$$\mathring{o}\varsigma \ \mathring{\epsilon}\kappa \ \pi\alpha\tau\rho\acute{\omega}\iota\alpha\varsigma \ \mathring{\eta}\kappa\omega\nu \ \gamma\epsilon\nu\epsilon\hat{\alpha}\varsigma$$
$$\pi o\lambda\upsilon\pi\acute{o}\nu\omega\nu \ \text{'}\text{A}\chi\alpha\acute{\iota}\omega\nu.[23]$$

In particular, the corresponding line of the strophe shows that a word is missing here at the end of the second line of the antistrophe. If with Jebb we accept Triclinius' insertion of ἄριστος we find Ajax described as "noblest of the Achaeans by his descent from the line of his fathers."[24] However, Sophocles' meaning was not accessible to Hölderlin, who sees Ajax simply as "one from the native race of the trouble-laden

---

[20] Literally "inbred impulses." For the same misunderstanding see *Ant.* 906 (875), v. 241, where αὐτόγνωτος ὀργά (self-willed disposition) is translated "das zornige Selbsterkennen (the angry recognition of self)."

[21] Though this letter was written in December 1801, the same questions were occupying Hölderlin's mind in the period of the *Ajax* translations, for in March 1804 he wrote to Leo von Seckendorf of his "Study of the Fatherland" and his interest in "the national, so far as it is different from the Greek." After drawing Seckendorf's attention to the Sophocles translations about to be published Hölderlin remarks, "The different fates of the heroes . . . how they serve Fate . . . I have understood in general terms." (Brief 244, VI. 437 f.).

[22] In the action which precedes the play they are opposed in the contest for the arms of Achilles. At the opening of the play Odysseus accepts from Athene her warning against human pride (*Aj.* 118ff.), and at the end his balanced and provident arguments in favour of granting his enemy Ajax burial lead the chorus to acknowledge his wisdom (1332 ff.). This moderation and prudence can indeed be seen as representing the "Nüchternheit (sobriety)" of which Ajax has no share.

[23] The corrections κρείσσων "Αιδαι and ὁ νοσῶν do not alter the general sense of the first line.

[24] Jebb, op.cit., p. 101. The O.C.T. has Wecklein's reading, ἄριστα.

Achaeans. " The omission led him to interpret the lines as stressing
Ajax's Greek origin before going on to ascribe to him the most characteristic of Greek attributes, for he was less interested in Ajax as an individual than as a Greek hero. Thus he instinctively translated πατρώιας
as "vaterländisch (belonging to the fatherland)" (v. 512) rather than
"väterlich (paternal)," before changing this to "heimatlich (native)," for
he was portraying Ajax as typical of "das Vaterländische (what belongs
to the fatherland)," which in the later foundation of "A Realm of Art"
was

> Versäumet und erbärmlich gieng
> Das Griechenland, das schönste, zu Grunde.
> ("... meinest du /Es solle gehen...," II. 228)
> [Neglected, and pitifully, went Greece, the most
> beautiful, to its end. (... "do you think it should go?
> ..."]

The interpretation of these lines throws light on Hölderlin's translation of Ismene's words in *Antigone*:

> οὐ γάρ ποτ', ὦναξ, οὐδ' ὃς ἂν βλάστηι μενεῖ
> νοῦς τοῖς κακῶς πράσσουσιν, ἀλλ' ἐξίσταται.[25]

> Es bleibt kein Herz, auch nicht das heimatliche
> Im Übelstand, mein König, außer sich geräth es.
> [No heart stays, not even the native heart,
> when times are ill, my King; it goes outside itsefl]
> (*Ant.* 585 f. (563 f.), v. 228)

Antigone has made it clear that she regards herself as no longer belonging to the land of the living: "my soul / is long since dead, so that I
serve the dead." Creon protests that she is "senseless" (ἄνους), and in
Ismene's rejoinder Hölderlin, by translating νοῦς with "heart" and using
"stays" absolutely, connects the derangement of reason with the "passion
for death" evident in Antigone's declaration.

The interpretation here of madness as the state of being "outside
oneself" and its connection with the lack of a "staying" form a link
between the situations of Antigone and Ajax.[26] Ajax's madness is promi-

---

[25] "Yes, King, not even such reason as may have been inborn stays with those
who are unfortunate, but it leaves its place."

[26] The length of line 586 supports the idea that it owes its present form to the
revision of the translation in 1803, which was probably responsible for the inclusion of
six-foot lines (cf. Beißner, *Hölderlins Übersetzungen aus dem Griechischen*, pp. 98,

nent in the passages Hölderlin translated and is given special emphasis. His complaint that he can find no "staying" is thus supported in the translation by a reference to his madness:

> wo geh ich hin
> Und bleibe?
> Wenn dierseit es welkt, ihr Lieben
> Und ganz in andrem ich
> In wilder Narrheit liege.
> [Where am I to go and stay? If on this side
> all withers, you dear friends, and right
> on the other I lie in wild folly (madness).]
>   (v. 277 (*Aj*. 404 ff.))

The Juntine has:

> ποῖ μολὼν μενῶ;
> εἰ τὰ μὲν, φθίνει, φίλοι
> τοῖς δ᾽ ὁμοῦ πέλας
> μωραῖς δ᾽ ἄγραις προσκείμεθα

The metre of an antistrophe suggests that the words τοῖς δέ are corrupt, and in any case emendation is needed as well as correction of the punctuation in order to make the text intelligible.[27] However, the last four words of the Greek are sound: "I devote myself to mad hunting." Nevertheless, Hölderlin mistranslates them in accordance with his own view of the situation: he exchanges adjective and noun as if the text read μωρίαις ἀγρίαις, and thus arrives at the emphatic phrase "in wild folly (madness)." This result is facilitated by the translation of the verb

---

122), and with which Hölderlin excused the delay in sending Wilmans the manuscript: "I wanted, since I was able to take a freer overall view of the matter, to make some further alterations in the translation and notes" (Br. 242, VI. 435). In that case the words which Hölderlin puts in Ismene's mouth belong to the same period as the *Ajax* translations, to which Hölderlin probably turned his attention in the months after finishing his revision of the two completed plays (cf. Beißner, op. cit., pp. 107f.). Further evidence that this passage was subjected to the revision is the occurrence in Creon's lines of "einheimisch (native)," a word which Hölderlin only started to use in this period: cf. "Chiron," II. 57 (the word does not occur in the earliest changes made to "Der blinde Sänger" after Hölderlin's return from France in 1802 and may only have entered the text as late as December 1803 when the "Nachtgesänge" were revised for publication (cf. Br. 243, VI. 436)); v. 277 (*Aj*. 396); "Aus Pindars erster Pythischer Ode," v. 291.

27 Jebb, op. cit., p. 71, has for line 406 τοιοῖσδ᾽ ὁμοῦ πέλας and translates: "If my past fame is destroyed, my friends, along with such victims as these near me . . ." The O.C.T. has τίσις δ᾽ἐμοῦ πέλας: "If . . . my punishment is near . . ."

πρόσκειμαι as if it were πρόκειμαι, which is used at the end of the antistrophe and which in *Hyperion* Hölderlin rendered with "liegen (lie)" (III. 240).

In the first stasimon, however, there is greater justification for the stress Hölderlin places on Ajax's madness. The words of the chorus, "Dem / Sein Haus ist göttlicher Wahnsinn (for him his house is divine madness)" (v. 278 (*Aj.* 611)), reminiscent of the "holy madness" spoken of in the "Anmerkungen zur Antigonä" (v. 267), are a graphic but close translation of θείαι μανίαι ξύναυλος. And when the chorus visualize the grief of

> Die Mutter, wenn von seiner Krankheit sie
> Dem Wahnsinn etwas höret,
> [His mother, when she hears of his illness, the madness]
> (v. 279 (*Aj.* 625 f.))

the faulty reading νοσοῦντα φρενομώρως hardly distorts Sophocles' meaning.[28]

At the end of the stasimon the chorus turn from Ajax's mother to his father:

> Ausduldender Vater! wie erwartet
> Zu erfahren von dem Kinde
> Dich unerträglich ein Schade.
> Niemals erzogen hat so etwas bei den Aeakiden
> Die Zeit, diß ausgenommen.
> [Long-suffering father! How there is waiting for you
> to learn of it, unbearably, the harm suffered
> by your child. Never has Time reared any such thing
> among the Aeacids, except for this.]
> (v. 279 (*Aj.* 641 ff.))

In his translation of

> ἄταν,
> ἂν οὔπω τις ἔθρεψεν
> αἰὼν Αἰακιδᾶν, ἄτερθε τοῦδε.[29]

_____

[28] Jebb: φρενομόρως; O.C.T.: φρενοβόρως.

[29] "A fate such as no life of the sons of Aeacus has ever yet known except this one."

Hölderlin disregards the connection between Αἰακιδᾶν and αἰών (essentially a period of time, hence a lifetime, an age, eternity) and makes "Time" responsible for Ajax's fate. The same thought seems to recur in the second stasimon, in which, in the Sophoclean tragedy, the chorus rejoice at Ajax's apparent readiness to forget his quarrel with the Greek leaders: πάνθ' ὁ μέγας χρόνος μαραίνει τε καὶ φλέγει.[30] Hölderlin translates:

> Alles ziehet hinweg die große Zeit damit es
> vergehet.
> [Great time draws everything away for it to perish.]
> (v. 280 (*Aj.* 714))

He appears to see in these words a reference to "die reißende Zeit (time that tears away)," which Oedipus follows ("Anm. Oed." v. 198), "der Geist der Zeit und Natur, das Himmlische, was den Menschen ergreift (the spirit of Time and Nature, the Divine, which seizes Man)," of which Antigone is a victim ("Anm. Ant." v. 266). "Ziehen" can here be regarded as a synonym of "reißen" as it is in the description of the cascading river gripped by an urge to which the "passion for death" is compared:

> so stürzt
> Der Strom hinab, er suchet die Ruh, es reißt
> Es ziehet wider Willen ihn von
> Klippe zu Klippe den Steuerlosen
> Das wunderbare Sehnen dem Abgrund zu.
> [So does the stream plunge downward: it looks for rest;
> against its will wonderful longing for the abyss tears it and pulls it on
> from rock to rock, rudderless.]
> ("Stimme des Volks" (I), II. 49)

The last three words of the Greek are in fact an interpolation,[31] but Hölderlin can only have regarded them as supporting his interpretation, for they seem to describe destruction by the "Flame of the Time-God" ("An Eduard," II. 40) in accordance with the vision of the "blazing up" of God's "wrath" in the second version of "Der Einzige (The Only One)," which describes man's retreat from destructive union

---

[30] "Great time makes all things fade (μαραίνει) and burns them up."

[31] The sentence is quoted without them in the anthology of Stobaeus, and their retention would presuppose a lacuna in the strophe. Cf. Jebb, op. cit., p. 112.

with God, "den Augenblik / Das Geschik der großen Zeit auch / Ihr Feuer fürchtend (fearing the moment, the fate of great Time and its fire too)" (II. 158). Hölderlin first translated the words literally: "and burns" (v. 513), but no doubt revised this version in order to make clear the destructive purpose of the divine power. Such "a holy end" in a period of the activity of "Nature" in its extreme form ("Stimme des Volks" (II), II. 51) can be contrasted with the manner of death "seit . . . böser Geist sich / Bemächtiget des glüklichen Altertums": "Langher währt Eines, gesangsfeind, klanglos, das / In Maasen vergeht (since . . . an evil spirit has made itself master of happy antiquity: There has lasted for a long time the one thing, an enemy of song, that produces no tone, that perishes in moderation)." ("Der Einzige" (II), 159).[32]

In so far as Hölderlin saw these words in their context he must have interpreted them as tragic irony, for at this stage of the play the chorus believe that Ajax has abandoned his decision to kill himself and that he has now carried out his intention of washing off in the sea the stains both of the slaughter and, symbolically, of his guilt. They assume that his new deference to the gods will now have led him to sacrifice to those deities whom he had offended.[33] This is the source of their joy:

> da Ajax,
> Der Mühe vergessend, wieder, auch der Götter
> Den schönen Rauch der Opfer
> Vollendet, gesezlich dienend
> Mit Hoheit.
> [as Ajax, forgetting his trouble, again, even
> performs the gods' fine smoking sacrifices (*lit.*
> the fine smoke of sacrifices), serving them in
> accordance with law with nobility.]
> (v. 280 (*Aj.* 710ff.))

In his translation of

> ὅτ' Αἴας
> λαθίπονος πάλιν, θεῶν δ' αὖ
> πάνθυτα θέσμι' ἐξήνυσεν, εὐνομίαι
> σέβων μεγίσται.[34]

---

[32] Hamburger's translation of the last clause: "that perishes in masses" (*Hölderlin*, p. 192) is excluded not only by the text, but also by the context, for Hölderlin is writing here of people who "Nicht gehn den Weg des Todes und hüten das Maas" (II. 158), who avoid the destruction brought about by union with the divine.

[33] Cf. *Aj.* 654 ff., 666f.

[34] "Since Ajax, forgetting his troubles again, has celebrated with all kinds of sacrifices the rites of the gods, honouring them with the greatest respect for the laws."

Hölderlin separates the noun εὐνομίαι from its adjective and makes of it an adverb describing the manner of Ajax's submission to the gods. The chorus believe that his life is no longer endangered by "the spirit of Time and Nature," but that he is ready to sacrifice to the gods in accordance with the laws of the sphere of "Art," adopting the attitude of Creon, "the honouring of God, as a lawful power" ("Anm. Ant." v. 266, 268).

The "smoke of sacrifices" also occurs in *Antigonä* as "the sacrificial smoke," whose epithet στέροψ (flashing; the noun λιγνύς means a smoky flame) is translated "wohlgestalt (well-shaped)" (*Ant.* 1174 (1127), v. 253). Discussing this passage and Hölderlin's use of the word "Gestalt (shape)," Beißner comments, "the undiluted etymological sense of the word . . . is detectable: "shape" not as "appearance" or "a thing shaped," but as a thing "set" or "erected." "[35] The evidence that the word does have the latter sense cannot be disputed, but Beißner's conclusion fails to take account of the fact that the former meaning is not for that reason lost. The word repeatedly contains an allusion to the sphere of "Art," the sphere which the poet, addressing Jupiter, refers to as "was du gestaltetest (what you shaped)" ("Natur und Kunst," II. 37). Indeed, the very word "wohlgestalt" is used in this sense in the "Grund zum Empedokles," where in order to describe the harmonious opposition of "Natur" and "Kunst" Hölderlin ascribes to each pole the characteristics of its opposite, speaking of the moment "when . . . the generalized . . . 'aorgic' man and the fair shape of Nature meet each other" (iv. 153).

When the sphere of "Art" loses its predominace, "it goes terribly disordered" ("Mnemosyne" (I), II. 193) and

unrecht,
Wie Rosse, gehn die gefangenen
Element' und alten
Geseze der Erd.
[Like steeds, the bound elements
and old laws of the earth go crookedly]
("Mnemosyne" (III), II. 197)

As this negation implies, its characteristic features are "shape/order" and "law," so that it is not insignificant when, in the list of misprints in *Oedipus der Tyrann*, Hölderlin replaces "hochwandelnd (walking on

---

[35] Beißner, op. cit., p. 145, whose argument is supported and developed by Zuberbühler, *Hölderlins Erneuerung der Sprache aus ihren etymologischen Ursprüngen*, pp. 62 f.

high)" (ὑψίποδες) with "gestaltet (shaped or ordered)" (v. 459) as the epithet of "laws" (*Oed. Tyr.* 884 (866), v. 162), a combination which also occurs in the late draft "Dem Fürsten," where he writes of

> die süße Heimath wo
> Viel Blumen blühen gesehn
> Als im Geseze deiner Gärten, in der Gestalt
> Des Erdballs.
> [the sweet homeland where many flowers bloom
> seen as in the law of your gardens,
> in the shape of the globe]
>
> (II. 248)

Similarly in Creon's words in *Antigonä*,

> wärs die Stadt allein, die haben,
> Nachdem in großer Fluth sie die geschüttert,
> Nun wiederum gestaltet unsere Götter,
> [if only the city were concerned,
> after tossing it in a great flood our gods
> have now once again given it back its shape]
>
> (*Ant.* 168 ff. (162 f.), v. 211)

"gestaltet (shaped)" as a translation of ὤρθωσαν is a synonym of "errichtet (established)," as the same verb is translated four lines below, but the deeper significance of the use of the word is that the city has again been granted "Gestalt" after the destructive irruption of the gods of "Nature," as which the attack of the Argive army, like the "restless deeds in the wide world" of Hölderlin's own period ("Dichterberuf," II. 47), is seen.[36]

The "smoke of sacrifices" therefore, which is described in *Antigonä* as "wohlgestalt," and which Ajax is thought to have offered the gods, is seen by Hölderlin as the appropriate response of one who is now regarded as "serving in accordance with the law." The gods to

---

[36] In the case of the other examples Beißner gives of "Gestalt" used in its root meaning it is important to notice that here too the form and restraint characteristic of the sphere of "Art" succeed the wild activity of "Nature," e.g. "Wenn aber die Himmlischen haben / Gebaut, still ist es / Auf Erden, und wohlgestalt stehn / Die betroffenen Berge . . . Wo inne stehet, beruhiget, da / Und dort, das Feuer (But when the heavenly ones have built, it is quiet on earth, and the mountains affected stand finely shaped, where there ceases, stilled, here and there the fire.)" (II. 222); "Und kaum mit einem Zaume weiß ich, daß gestellt / Die grausamweitgestrekten Rosse wer-den (And I know that the cruelly stretched galloping steeds are scarcely brought to order with a bridle)" (*Ant.* 495 f. (477 f.), v. 224) (cf. "Mnemosyne" (III), II. 197, where under the influence of "Nature" the "Laws of the Earth" bolt "wie Rosse [like steeds]. ").

whom sacrifice is offered are the Olympian gods, for Hölderlin above all
Zeus and Apollo, who allow man to remain in contact with the powers
of nature without threatening his individual existence. In an earlier line
of the same stasimon already discussed these gods are given an epithet
which distinguishes them from the actual gods of nature: the chorus
address Pan as "Der eingesezten Götter König! versammelnder! (King of
the appointed gods! Convoker!)" (v. 280 (*Aj.* 697 f.)). In this translation
of ὦ / θεῶν χοροποιὲ ἄναξ (king, dance-maker of the gods) Hölderlin
interprets θεῶν as an objective genitive after ἄναξ (it must in fact be
possessive or partitive), and incorporates Pan into his own view of the
Greek gods as assembler of "the heavenly choir" ("Brod und Wein," II.
94). Ajax, however, did not sacrifice to the "appointed gods," but
became the victim of "great Time."

At the beginning of the examination of the *Ajax* translations it
was shown how Hölderlin found in Sophocles a picture of nature which
he was able to expand into an image familiar in his earlier work.
Similarly he understood the Greek text in such a way that he saw Apollo
and Zeus portrayed in terms which corresponded to the conception he
had already formed of them. It then emerged that this approach was
characteristic of the translation as a whole and that his interpretation of a
number of significant passages was uniformly consistent with his views
on the nature of Greek tragedy. It remains therefore to draw together the
different threads and to attempt to establish how Hölderlin saw the play
as a whole.

Sophocles is concerned with the punishment of Ajax's arrogance.
In his tragedy Calchas is reported as explaining that Ajax has incurred
Athene's anger because of his excessive pride. Not only had he
announced his intention of winning victory without the help of the gods,
but he had also expressly rejected the support of Athene (*Aj.* 748ff.).
Ajax's madness, depicted at the beginning of the play, is the divine
retribution for this attitude, and on recovering his sanity he decides that
he can only retrieve in death the honour he has thus lost in life.

How then does Hölderlin appear to have interpreted this version
of the legend? The evidence contained in the passages translated is sufficiently consistent to allow us to form a conjecture. With the reservations
therefore which must accompany such a procedure we may surmise that
Hölderlin saw Ajax as representing, like the Agrigentines in the "Grund
zum Empedokles," the sphere of "Art" in its extreme form. This is suggested not only by his self-sufficiency, but also by the words addressed
to Salamis by the chorus:

Den hattest du ausgesandt einst
Wohl herrlich in wildem
Kriegsgeist.
[Him you had once sent forth truly magnificent
in his wild warlike spirit.]
(v. 278 (*Aj.* 612 f.))

We are reminded of "the wild war-like quality" of the men of southern France (Br. 240, VI. 432), which, it has been suggested, was the expression of the rootedness in this sphere which accompanied their union with Apollo. Ajax's rejection of the help of the gods in general and of Athene in particular may then be interpreted as his opposition to the sphere of "Nature," reminiscent of the ungrateful repudiation of Saturn by Jupiter, the representative of "Art" ("Natur und Kunst," II. 37).

This opposition to the goddess is the cause of her anger, so that, as in *Oedipus der Tyrann*, "the power of nature and the innermost part of Man become one in anger [Zorn]." ("Anm. Oed." v. 201). She is in fact seen as the representative of Zeus since Ajax complains,

es peitscht
Mich auch, verderblich
Des Zevs gewaltige Göttin.[37]
[there lashes me too, ruinously, Zeus' mighty goddess]
(v. 277 (*Aj.* 401 f.))

It is union with Zeus that Danae survives in her "stay before changing time," but just as Antigone follows "the spirit of Time and Nature" ("Anm. Ant." v. 266), so Ajax too becomes the victim of "Time" (v. 279 (*Aj.* 645)): "Great Time draws everything away for it to perish" (v. 280 (*Aj.* 714)). The chorus feel exposed to the same danger:

Ich aber duldend
Schon eine lange Zeit
Bin bei dem Ida auf
Der grasichten Waide der Schaafe,
Unausgezählet, auf der immergeordneten
Abgezehret von der Zeit, die schlimme
Hoffnung habend, daß ein Ende werde
Bald mir der flüchtende

---

[37] Sophocles refers to her as the daughter of Zeus: ἁ Διὸς . . . θεός.

Unfaßliche Hades.
[But I, suffering for a long time now, am on Ida,
on the grassy sheep pasture always ordered, not
counted, wasted away by Time, having the
wretched hope that my end will soon be the
fleeting impalpable Hades.]

(v. 278 (Aj. 600 ff.))

They, like Ajax, must fear the inability to achieve the security assured
for herself by Danae when

Sie zählete dem Vater der Zeit
Die Stundenschläge, die goldnen.
[She counted for the Father of Time
the striking hours, the golden ones.]

("Anm. Ant." v. 268)

Representing "Art" in its extreme form Ajax is united with
"Nature" in madness. We have already seen how Oedipus is united with
God at the moment when, with the discovery of his own identity, he
arrives at the extreme point of the pole of "Art." Although there is no
direct justification for it in the text the idea of madness is introduced in
the "Anmerkungen zum Oedipus" when Hölderlin writes of "the wild
foolish quest" and "the mentally sick search for a consciousness" (v. 199
f.). Similarly in the "Anmerkungen zur Antigonä" we have seen that
"holy madness," the state in which Antigone "in the highest consciousness avoids consciousness," may be interpreted as the taking on of
"aorgische Gestalt (inorganic form)" by "das Organische (the organic)"
(v. 267). Again there is little enough evidence in the Sophoclean text for
the idea of Antigone's madness, which seems to have its main support in
the fate of Lycurgus: "Und kennen lernt er, / Im Wahnsinn tastend, den
Gott mit schimpfender Zunge (and he learnt, groping in madness, to
know the god with insulting tongue)" (Ant. 998 f. (960 ff.), v. 246).

It almost seems as if the Ajax, in which madness forms an important element in the plot, influenced Hölderlin's interpretation of Oedipus
Tyrannus and Antigone. It is at any rate clear that in his interpretation
the Ajax exemplifies more completely than the other two tragedies the
scheme worked out in the "Grund zum Empedokles," even though there
the phenomenon of madness plays no part. Ajax's madness, resulting
from his opposition to the goddess, clearly represents "that moment
when the 'organic' casts off in a real, intense struggle, its selfhood, its
particular existence, which had reached an extreme" (IV. 153). In apply-

ing this interchange of the opposite poles to Empedokles himself Hölderlin writes: "In this way his spirit had to assume 'aorgic shape' (aorgische Gestalt) in the highest sense, to tear itself from itself and its centre, always to penetrate its object with such success that it lost itself in it, as in an abyss." (IV. 159). It is this "excess of objectivity and being outside oneself" (IV. 162) to which the chorus refer in saying that Ajax "nicht des angebornen / Zorns mächtig, sondern außer sich ist (is not master of his innate anger, but is outside himself)" (v. 279 (*Aj*. 639 f.)).[38] It also seems likely that Ajax himself is referring to his exchange of the sphere of "Art," to which man properly belongs, for that of "Nature" when he is to find a "stay,"

> Wenn dieserseit es welkt, ihr Lieben
> Und ganz in andrem ich
> In wilder Narrheit liege.
> [if on this side all withers, you dear friends,
> and right on the other I lie in wild folly]
> (v. 277 (*Aj*. 405 ff.))

Ajax's recovery from his fit of madness then corresponds to that part of the process "where then the 'organic' element which has become 'aorgic' seems to find itself again and to return to itself" (IV. 153). He is no longer "outside himself," but, as in *Antigonä* as well as the "Grund zum Empedokles," the death of the individual is necessary before a true reconciliation of "Nature" and "Art" is achieved.[39]

We can only regret that Hölderlin was not able to complete his translation of the *Ajax*, a tragedy which had not only always attracted him, but which demonstrates so fully the process by which "Nature" and "Art" are reconciled that one is tempted to believe that it influenced not merely his earlier translations but even the thought recorded in the

---

[38] Cf. *Hyperions Jugend*, III. 203, for the use of "lose oneself," "forget oneself," and "be outside oneself" as synonyms: "Never lose yourself! . . . Do not forget yourself in the feeling of wretchedness! Love, which . . . is always outside itself, in how many ways does it not go astray, yet how easily!"

[39] That Sophocles regarded Ajax's death as the means of reconciliation between Ajax and Athene is suggested by Jebb, op. cit., p. xxxviii: "At his first return to sanity, he had thought of death only as a refuge from disgrace and a recovery of honour. He has now come to view it also as an atonement due to Athene. He recognizes the sin of his former over-weening self-confidence. In this sense he dies reconciled to the gods." But the play also provides evidence of the wider reconciliation which, for Hölderlin, follows the death of the individual. Odysseus not only persuades Agamemnon to obey the laws of the gods by allowing Ajax to be buried, but is also reconciled with Teucer (*Aj*. 1332 ff., 1376 ff.). He thus heeds the warning of Athene to show arrogance neither to gods nor to men (127 ff.).

"Grund zum Empedokles." But the interest which the play had for Hölderlin was not restricted to that part of it which precedes Ajax's death and from which the three choric passages he translated come. The last part of the play deals with the question whether Ajax is to receive burial, on which Teucer insists, claiming for his brother the grateful memory due to the dead (*Aj.* 1266 ff.). It is this memory that is the subject of "Mnemosyne," the hymn which reveals the significance Hölderlin's Sophocles translations had for him.

The Bride of Messina

Florian Prader

The Narbonne fragment therefore remains an attempt, Schiller's attempt, to realise, in a drama written and devised by him, his reflections on the technique and style of the drama as paradigmatically realised by *Oedipus Rex*. In doing so Schiller relies on his model so that the plot almost exactly matches the events in *Oedipus Rex*, whilst the content and spirit of the play belong to a modern world.

The Bride of Messina seeks, however, to take us another step closer to the ancient tragedy. "With this work I have tried like the very devil; it is the first, as far as I know, that has been written in modern languages following the strict rules of ancient tragedy," Schiller wrote on 11 February 1803 to his publisher Friedrich Cotta. And in a letter to Wilhelm von Humboldt we read: "My first attempt at tragedy in strict form will give you pleasure: you will be able to judge from it whether or not I, as a contemporary of Sophocles, would also have won a prize with it. I have not forgotten that you called me the most modern of all new writers and so thought of me as being the absolute opposite of everything that is called ancient. It would therefore give me double the pleasure if I could wring from you the admission that I could also make this foreign spirit my own."[1] Indeed Schiller feels himself directly involved in a "little competition with the ancient tragedian."[2] Yet he does however admit that he was thinking more of himself than of an audience beyond himself, and that means that he will not consciously address his ideas on the nature of the drama with regard to the stage as he did in the

---

[1] 17 February 1803
[2] To Iffland, 22 April 1803

"Narbonne," but will let himself be directly influenced by antiquity, and draws directly on the spirit of the ancient tragedians. For he knows that their art cannot fail to achieve the desired effect. Only in the treatment of the chorus does he seem consciously to have followed his own artistic plan with a view to the audience, as the preface to the play attests. He enters into a competition, then, with the ancient tragedians in seeking to make the "alien spirit" of Sophocles his own. The question is: how does he fare in this competition?

Whenever there is mention of a "simple tragedy according to the strictest of Greek forms," one traditionally expects some consideration of the Aristotelian unities. Schiller referred to these from the very beginning of *The Bride of Messina*. By contrast with all of Schiller's other dramas the play only has five characters on stage, the duration of the action is restricted to the minimum, and although the scene of the action is not uniform, there is a definite symmetrical order to the scene changes: the play begins and ends in the columned hall in the palace, the middle being indicated by a room in the palace, with the two garden scenes in between. It is also noticeable that initially there is no division into acts, which is intended to place particular stress on the play's unity. The division into acts customary in our editions is based on the Hamburg theatre manuscript and was only intended by Schiller for the purposes of the performance, not for publication. Thus far, Schiller has adhered to the strict form of the original. All that the outward form requires in terms of overall concentration and uniformity has been fulfilled, so that Schiller can write about his new play to Iffland: "I have done it along the strict lines of ancient tragedy, a simple plot, few characters, little change in place, a simple duration of one day and one night."[3] Furthermore we are dealing with an action pure and simple "because the interest does not lie in the characters on the stage so much as in the action itself, as in Sophocles' *Oedipus*."[4] Added to this is the fact that the action is accompanied by a chorus throughout, which according to Schiller's own statement underlines perfectly the ancient style of the piece. The plot was thought up entirely by Schiller, and when we look at it more closely we can see that it also cannot deny the ancient spirit and that it shows parallels to *Oedipus* in the structure as well as the execution. A comparison with Sophocles' *Oedipus Rex* is inevitable here as in the Narbonne fragment. We shall attempt to take the comparison through in three stages, by first discussing the plot, then the intellectual content, and finally the chorus. If we have already recognised that the external

---

[3] 24 February 1803

[4] To Körner, 13 May 1801

prerequisites necessary for a drama in the severe Greek style have been satisfied, undoubtedly much better than in the Narbonne fragment, then our question in the following comparison must always be on our lips: How does Schiller fare in his competition with Sophocles?

1. The Plot

One need only look as far as the story to see that *The Bride of Messina* is a "play in the style of *Oedipus Rex.*" The birth of Beatrice, just as that of Oedipus, is under the sign of a disastrous prophecy. The child, cursed by fate, is to be exposed, but through her mother's wish to escape the promised doom is rescued and grows up in a different place without knowing who she is. Thus the child's connection with the royal house of Messina is effaced. Precisely this fact, however, leads to the house's downfall, just as Oedipus, ignorant of his own origin, falls into ruin when he unwittingly murders his own father and marries his mother. As in *Oedipus Rex* the action on stage concentrates on the shattering realisation of the true situation in which the main characters are involved. In the course of the action the terrible abyss that the rulers of Messina have fallen into through their intention of avoiding disaster must be revealed.

In the beginning of the play we are informed of the feud between the brothers Don Manuel and Don Cesar, which since the death of the old prince has transformed the entire town of Messina into an arena of a bloody civil war. Just as the priest in the prologue to *Oedipus Rex* pleads to the king in the name of the people to protect them against the visitation of the plague, so, as we learn from Isabella's speech, the elders of Messina demand from the royal mother the settlement of her sons' pernicious conflict. Isabella announces the immediately coming reconciliation of the hostile brothers, and the spectator is left wondering how lasting this will be. After this question there follows a further moment of tension when the princess charges her servant Diego to bring her from a distant convent a precious treasure that will make her motherly happiness complete. With that a secret is placed in our hands, whose disclosure we await.

The first exposition, presented to us before the arrival of the chorus, takes us up to this point. As in the prologue of *Oedipus Rex* we also have here the crucial moment. The question of the identity of Laius' murderer and that of the brothers' reconciliation respectively is put in the foreground, and yet the seed for the entire development and conclusion of what has gone before is already contained therein. As will emerge, the secret of the hidden valuable treasure in the convent also ties in with

Isabella's reconciliatory work; Beatrice is to unite the brothers in love, but has in reality already divided them: in her, disaster already waits. The secret that still surrounds her is the bud of the crucial moment that will arise through Beatrice being let out of the convent. So the exposition's first foreground question must develop into the background question of Beatrice's identity, and thus the aim of the drama—the recognition scene—is already signposted.

This simple exposition is dealt with more quickly and impressively than the conversation between the priest and the king and Creon returning from Delphi in *Oedipus Rex* is able to do. Isabella's powerful and brilliant monologue to the elders of Messina, and immediately afterwards the secretive mission for Diego offer us all the facts of the exposition and sweep us into the tension of the play with a powerful artistic force. The monologue is a masterpiece of a dramatic opening to a tragedy based on the ancient model.

The development up to the salient point following on from here is as a whole no longer comparable to the Sophoclean original. The oracle which already in the first scene of *Oedipus Rex* unmistakably anticipates the end, and clearly reveals the background to the spectator, in this case does not appear until the middle of the play, towards the end of the second act. Up to that point we are, however, informed of the situation in the house in broadly calculated, very careful stages. Next to take place is the promised reconciliation of the brothers. It is carried out with passionate love, yet is not free from quiet mysterious hints that lead us to suspect a possible sinister background. It seems significant when Don Cesar declares anyone who rekindles the flames of brotherly hate to be his mortal enemy. Perhaps one already notices here that this oath, as with Oedipus, could also apply to the speaker. We hear further of the lover that Don Manuel has abducted from a hidden convent, of the refound lover of Don Cesar and of the precious treasure, of the sister, that Isabella wishes to bring to meet her sons. The audience's premonition of the fatal identity of the sister with the two lovers grows steadily, and the threatening doom is already in sight when Isabella finally tells of the sinister oracle which she received in the form of various dream interpretations before the birth of her daughter.

Now we are still awaiting the development that reveals the true situation to the characters, and in this there are plenty of parallels to Sophocles' drama. The revelation scenes start with the news of Beatrice's abduction. The two brothers are to take up the chase of the abductors immediately, which forces Isabella to reveal more about her daughter and her hiding place. At this point Don Manuel comes very close to discovering the actual secret. King Oedipus has the task of finding Laius' murderer, and must discover himself to be the wanted man. Don Manuel must clear up the abduction of his sister and is on his own trail. All of Isabella's details about her daughter and all of Don Cesar's remarks about his lover seem to apply to his own bride, and when the name "Beatrice" is said it seems, as in *Oedipus Rex* through the reference to the crossroads, that the word that gives it all away has been uttered. But as in that case the shepherd's testimony can possibly quash the apprehension that has arisen, so here too there is a way of dampening down the pressing suspicion. The sister secretly attended the dead prince's funeral, and that fact can hardly apply to Don Manuel's lover. Her testimony will prove it.

The clear copying of *Oedipus Rex* extends still further, into Don Manuel's actual recognition scene. After Jocasta has mentioned those crossroads, Oedipus is no longer dispassionate, and, already shocked, enquires as to Laius' looks, whereupon Jocasta answers:

> Jocasta: Tall, the first soft bloom of silver in his hair.
> Oedipus: Oh woe is me! Have I hurled
> The terrible curse without knowing upon my own head?[5]

Don Manuel is also no longer unaffected after he has heard his sister's name, and when Beatrice is deeply shocked by his noble birth and descent, he asks her to describe her mother, and on her description he answers:

> "Oh woe! Her very self!"[6]

He thinks of his own mother, whose image has been described to him by Beatrice and asks once more in a premonition of horror:

> Don Manuel: Is my mother not unknown to you?
> Beatrice: Oh woeful and dread tidings.
> Oh had I never seen this day![7]

In both pieces it needs only one more word at this place to bring about the discovery. With Oedipus the word is delayed, whereas Don Manuel knows it immediately from Beatrice's confession of having been to the prince's funeral. The scene rushes with gripping precipitation to

---

[5] V.742–45
[6] V.1852
[7] V.1862–64

its end, where it reaches its climax in Don Manuel's recognition and
Don Cesar's fratricide.

And now the action presses on relentlessly towards further revelations of the tangled relationships. At the beginning of the fourth act the
hermit scene parallels the scene with Teiresias in *Oedipus Rex*. Isabella
is fearful for her abducted daughter Beatrice, and has called for a hermit
and asked for a prophecy. A messenger has brought word from the
hermit and reports that the lost girl has been found by Don Manuel. That
seems to be welcome news, but the hermit seems like Teiresias to have
hesitated to share his entire knowledge, and as a symbol of the tragically
disturbing misfortune he has set light to his hut with the candles dedicated by Isabella. For Oedipus Teiresias' ominous words are
incomprehensible. Similarly Isabella cannot explain the hermit's actions,
but the gruesome gesture in its mysterious and powerful symbolic
strength must have an effect on her and the spectators.

Terror and tension are maintained and increased in masterly fashion in the next scene. Don Cesar's Chorus bring Beatrice into the
columned hall. At first Isabella is relieved to see her daughter alive, just
as Jocasta shouts for joy when she hears of the death of Polybus. For her
a hope still exists. But the fear is immediately rekindled and sets her
before an impenetrable secret: according to the hermit's prophecy it was
Don Manuel who found Beatrice, and now it is Don Cesar who is sending her her daughter. As inexplicable as this contradiction and much
more frightening is Beatrice's shrinking back when she recognises her
mother as the princess of Messina. The spectator knows what has happened, but awaits in great suspense the coming discovery in which
Isabella and Don Cesar have to find out and come to terms with the terrible events.

At the first sight of Don Manuel's body, which is carried into the
hall accompanied by a funeral procession, the anxious princess and
mother is once more sure she is right. The catastrophe is obvious; all her
effort, based on trust in the heavenly powers, collapses. She has been
deceived by the oracles, and can only save herself from collapse with a
blasphemous outburst against the gods.

> Is it so you keep your word to me, you heavenly powers?
> Is this your truth? Woe to him.
> Who trusts you with an honest heart![8]

> The seers' art, it is an empty nothing,

---

[8] V.2326-28

Deceivers are they or have been deceived.
No truth can be discovered of the future,
Were you to draw upon hell's rivers,
Or draw upon the very source of light.[9]

Three times the oracles did not keep their word with her: not Don Manuel, but Don Cesar brought her her daughter; Don Manuel has been killed, she assumes, by robbers and not as she was told through the life of her daughter: and finally Beatrice can no longer, as her dreams promised, unite the brothers in love.

This scene must remind us of Jocasta, who mocks the gods with similar sophistry. Again three times the prophecies of the gods did not come true for her: her husband Laius was killed by robbers and not by her son; her child was put out in the wild as a baby so that the curse that he would become his father's murderer cannot have found fulfilment with him; and finally Polybus also did not die by the hand of his son, who was destined to parricide by the oracle of Delphi. So also Jocasta boldly calls up to the heavens:

> . . . —Oracles of the gods!
> Where are you now? . . .[10]

Isabella's certainty that she is right leads her still further into delusion. As Don Cesar comes up to her, she curses the murderer's hand and the mother who bore him, and urges her living son to avenge his brother. Just as Oedipus does not know that his curse actually applies to himself, so Isabella does not suspect that in Don Cesar she is looking at her elder son's murderer. The spectator, however, recognises the tragedy in her curse, which is especially effective and shocking in its irony. This tragic irony, of which we shall have more to say later, is already prefigured in *Oedipus Rex*, and copied here in *The Bride of Messina*.

At the end of fifth scene the discovery is complete. Don Cesar recognises his lover as his sister, throws this terrible discovery in his mother's face, and curses the womb that carried him. At this point we think of the curse that Jocasta throws as a last word to her husband, but there have already been enough parallels to the Sophoclean play uncovered to prove that the entire recognition scene mirrors that in *Oedipus Rex* step by step. The behaviour of the characters overlaps. As in *Oedipus Rex* they assume that the dead person was killed by robbers.

---

[9] V.2371–75
[10] V.946–49

And as in the ancient drama no attempt is made to pursue the murderers—the identity of the killer emerges of its own accord. The self-certainty of the deluded characters must lead them to recognition and bring the guilt to light. What is said of the Narbonne fragment can also apply here: the characters pick up the "Gorgon's head" themselves. Shocked to the core at the terrible fate that has befallen all of them, they finally stand there knowing, as Isabella puts it, that the gods have won and their honour has been saved. This is also attested at the end of *Oedipus Rex*.

These recognition scenes in the fourth act form the salient point. We have seen how the essential momentum is directed towards this point, which brings together again all that has taken place: here we can also understand the salient point to be the "hostile convergence of things," since the recognition is only made possible because the plot brings together all the characters in an unfortunate, fatal situation. Isabella meets Beatrice as princess and mother, and this "fatal competition" leads to the recognition. Isabella confidently steps up to the dead Don Manuel, the proud murderer Don Cesar, and Beatrice her daughter as well as Beatrice her son's bride, so that she cannot fail to press forward step by step towards the discovery, and the fear and tension increases up to the climax of the catastrophe.

Up to now we have only looked at the one side of the plot, the side that would be unthinkable without the model of *Oedipus Rex*. In that side Schiller attempts to copy the theatrically effective aspects of the Oedipus plot and thus places himself directly alongside the ancient author. The play, however, has a second plot that differs fundamentally from Sophocles' drama. We must now turn our attention to it.

At the start of *Oedipus Rex* everything has already taken place, and needs only to be wound up analytically on stage. The hero's irrevocable atrocities are no longer avoidable, since they lie far in the past; that is to say, the events are already set. In *The Bride of Messina* on the other hand, the decisive deed is not yet done and only takes place at the end of the third act. Alongside the *analytical* action which takes its point of departure in the keeping secret of Beatrice and the consequent confusion of family relationships, and reaches its goal in the shocking unravelling of the relationships through the recognition scenes, there is also a secondary, literally *actual* plot that starts with the brothers' feud between the two princes, reaches its peak with the murder of Don Manuel and finds completion in the expiatory death of Don Cesar. The oracle, which will be spoken of later, is a part of both sides of the action and thus binds the two plots together. In it rests the prerequisite for keeping Beatrice secret, and it is a means to a higher, mysterious tension in the analytical development. At the same time, however, it belongs to the actual plot because through it the macabre prophecy is fulfilled. Both plots share the same crucial moment, both grow consistently from the already discussed exposition. At the salient point, however, they part. The analytical action presses on in every way towards the discovery of the fatal situation, whereas after the fratricide the actual plot heightens the anticipation as to the fate of the murderer.

Schiller himself noted that in this way there are two different developments going on at the end, as we can tell from a letter to Goethe. Schiller writes: ". . . and the last sixth, which is usually the true feast of the tragic author, also gets a good onward movement. It serves the final action very well that I have now completely separated the burial of the one brother from the suicide of the other, and that this event brings that act to a close as a matter that is totally expected, and only when it is over, at the brother's graveside, does the last action take place, the vain attempt by the chorus and the mother to preserve Don Cesar. Thus all confusion and in particular all mixing of theatrical ceremony with the seriousness of the plot are avoided."[11] It is characteristic of Schiller that he ascribes the specifically theatrical effects to the recognition scene influenced by Sophocles, whilst Don Cesar's more modern expiatory death fits in with the realistic rather than the theatrical seriousness of the plot. The separation of the two plots in the interests of dramatic clarity and effect at the end of the play is a fortunate device by the author. In the development of the play, however, the analytical and the actual plots are tightly woven together, which threatens the play's artistic organisation. The two plots interfere with each other in their effect, as we shall see.

In the first section of the play the analysis cannot be carried out in direct succession of events, one precipitating the other, as in Sophocles. This is because of the way the oracle is used and the fact that the decisive deed has not yet been done. In *Oedipus Rex* already in the first episode the whole situation is unambiguously disclosed to the spectator through Teiresias' prophecy. That is not possible in *The Bride of Messina* because the main characters, particularly Don Cesar, cannot know of it. The actual plot could otherwise be threatened and the murder appear avoidable. Because the spectator cannot be informed of the background to the exposition all at once, the poet has to let him into the secrets in detail and successively of the relationships of the two brothers to their unknown sister.

Every precaution must be taken that in the confrontations in the first and second Acts, which are planned with an eye to the direct unroll-

---

[11] 26 January 1803

ing of the pre-history, the explanation of the relationships should not occur too early, because otherwise the murder would no longer be possible. The discovery must therefore be carefully delayed over a long period, and that prevents the precipitation of the analysis, and hides the doubtful reason for its meticulous gradation.

In the presentation of the situation, which of necessity has to be done on a broad scale, and in the artificial delaying of the prepared recognition, the author does not succeed in giving a credible motivation to every detail. The many psychological unlikelihoods in the first part of the piece have often been pointed out.[12] We will not dwell on these; a few points will suffice. Why does Don Manuel refrain from asking his unknown lover about her dark past? How can he leave the abducted girl unprotected in her hiding place in Messina? How can Don Cesar's first words to his lover be as if she were his wife, without afterwards looking into the reason for her grave consternation? The answer to these questions can only be found in the construction of the plot, caused by the design of the piece. This construction becomes particularly critical in the sixth scene of the second act. Here it can only appear arbitrary when Don Cesar leaves the stage before Diego tells of Beatrice's secret visit to the funeral, and when Don Manuel is no longer present when the name of Beatrice's hiding place, which he has been asking for so fervently, is given in the presence of Don Cesar. Don Manuel may only know the one piece of evidence, and Don Cesar the other, for the development of the drama to be still able to take place. The secret that surrounds Oedipus is incomparably more powerful; it can safely be spoken aloud, because nothing more can save him from his doom. In the *Bride of Messina* on the other hand it must be protected, through artificial motivation, so that it cannot be discovered before time. We recall at this point Goethe's comment in the conversations with Eckermann, that careful motivation was not something Schiller concerned himself with.[13] In other ways that may, as Goethe thought, be an advantage leading to greater theatrical effect, but here its consequence is that some scenes are disturbingly unbelievable. The linking of events suffers from appearing artificial.

In this unhappy manner the analytical action must be delayed until the decisive act, and that means that the murder itself as well does not follow on with absolute necessity from previous action. The two actions affect each other reciprocally.

---

[12] In the most detail in Joseph Kohm: Schiller's "Bride of Messina" and Sophocles' "Oidipus Tyrannos," Gotha 1901.

[13] 25 May 1831

It is only in the middle of the drama that we learn about the oracle, from Isabella's account of the two dreams. The oracle has a sustaining function in Sophocles. Without the oracle *Oedipus Rex* could not exist. In *The Bride of Messina* on the other hand it has lost that function. The action following Isabella's report could just as easily be carried on without the prophecies. Certainly here too they have the task of heightening the tragic tension, but this is broken shortly afterwards by Don Manuel's death. After the murder it is already clear that the dreams in their doom-laden meaning did speak the truth. They are already half carried out, and with Don Manuel's death the crisis in the city state is already over. The oracle thus only serves to heighten the tension momentarily, and from its fundamental significance in the Sophoclean drama has declined to a dramatic accessory.

Similarly the hermit scene no longer has the same effect as its parallel in Sophocles. Through his prophecy Teiresias leads the king into the self-confident blindness that with its tragic irony raises the entire succession of scenes to tragic intensity. Isabella, however, who hears of the hermit's symbolic, disaster-threatening behaviour, is already gripped by overwhelming suspicions, and is only more deeply shocked by the hermit. Unlike Oedipus, she does not react by self-confidently rejecting it, because the plot has already gone too far for that. The hermit scene therefore cannot bring about a dramatic act that sets in motion the quiescent plot with heightened tension and precipitation, and presses towards the dangerous revelation. The Teiresias scene gives great impetus to the development, whereas the hermit scene is only a decorative episode that skilfully picks up the threads of the analytical plot after Don Manuel's murder.

Similarly Isabella's blasphemous speeches no longer stand in the right place. They, too, compared with Jocasta's sophistry, have lost that dramatic function. Jocasta must, in her blindness, hopefully hold up the threatening revelation through her denial of the oracle, so that the next blow against the king can hit even harder. Isabella, in the face of Don Manuel's death, has nothing left to hold up. The oracle's fulfilment stands now clearly enough before her eyes. All that is left is the literal interpretation of the prophecy; its validity can no longer be disputed. Next to the body of her son, Isabella can no longer oppose the fated destiny like Jocasta. Her resistance can at the most protect her for a while from the catastrophe, and is, for the play, no more than powerful rhetoric in the frame of this scene.

The curse that she hurls on the head of the murderer also has no major significance in its tragic-ironic effect, as it does in *Oedipus Rex*, where, pronounced at the beginning of the piece, its sinister echo rings throughout the development. Its function too is limited to the moment, and is almost immediately vitiated by Don Cesar's self-discovery.

So all the aspects of the plot that are copied from *Oedipus Rex* come to stand at the wrong place because of the necessary consideration for the actual plot, and, however much they resemble their model, for that reason they forfeit the important effect which in *Oedipus* they so magnificently possess for the unrolling of the whole action. And, looked at the other way round, the analytical technique is not well suited to prepare the real plot; in the first part it constantly threatens to endanger the latter's feasibility, and at the end it must be artificially separated from it. The poet must also do without the unified legal process which in *Oedipus Rex* assigns each separate action its place with dramatic consequentiality, and allows each to grow naturally from the other, because such a thing would only make sense after the fourth act. Instead he is under an obligation in two directions: he must construct in both directions, and has not got a unified plan after which he could order the elements of the piece in a natural and dramatically effective manner. The construction is as a whole flawed.

*   *   *

3. The Chorus

"The use of the chorus, as it is found in the ancient tragedies" was counted by Schiller as one of the most essential elements of the strict form of tragedy. For when he sends the manuscript of *The Bride of Messina* to Iffland for the purposes of a performance in Berlin, he adds a note that the main effect of the tragedy is predicated upon the chorus.[14] How are we to understand that? Wherein does this so important effect of the chorus lie? This is the first question we must consider. Again we find the answer in Schiller's letters, and especially in his Preface to the book edition of *The Bride of Messina*. As the title already states, this is a consideration "of the use of the Chorus in tragedy," but, more than that, it is a renewed effort to define the goal of tragedy.[15]

It thus states: "True art has as its object not merely transient amusement; its point is not merely to transport mankind into a momentary dream of freedom, but in actual reality to make him free, and to do so by awakening, exercising and expanding within him a power to relegate to the objective distance the world of senses which

---

[14] 24 February 1803

[15] XVI, 118ff.

otherwise only burdens us as raw material and presses upon us as a blind force; and to transform it into a free work of our spirit and to govern the material through ideas."[16]

As we know, the organisation of the material according to plan, following the principle of the balancing of the emotions, shows the means by which Schiller confronts the "blind force" which presses down on us, in order to set us free. Here we must remember that precisely this balanced art awakens the spectator's independent activity. This will become—as we have read in Schiller—particularly stimulated, and can best put the emotionally stirred power of the imagination within bounds, when it can raise itself up "to help spiritual, moral ideas." This help can offer "general truths or moral maxims," that is to say reflective comments which relate moral events to general ideas, and so break up the material effect. So if a man succeeds in relating the material to the world of ideas, he proves himself above the reach of ordinary emotions, and freedom is secured. Now we understand better when further on in the Preface it says that a work of art "must be idea-based in all its parts if it is, as a whole, to have reality and accord with nature." The agreement of art and nature, according to Schiller's exact interpretation, is never attained through the general copying of nature, the awakening of an illusion, but only by art shaping the actual, particular, individual and changing side of nature in the light of the ideal, and raising it to something general, valid and lasting. So nature in art possesses a higher reality and truth than in itself.[17]

The reflection is, however, only an artistic method of leading the audience from the specialised to the general, from the restrictive into freedom. Yet the work of art may not be disturbed by reflection; it must "earn its place" and "win back through performance what it lacks in sensory life." And it is the chorus that makes that happen, in whose utterance and performance the ideal and the sensory, the distancing and the establishing of a rapport are intimately combined. In the chorus the balancing is brought about which Schiller achieves in another place through putting polar opposites against each other: the pure against the impure, the attractive against the repulsive, the children of the house against the villain. Through the careful dispensing of the extreme separating tendencies of the elements that beguile and enchant, the spectator is ensnared and finds his own independent activity. The chorus, then, is for Schiller the ancient means of setting the emotions side by side in a

---

[16] XVI, 120

[17] This is also the case for history: "As he (Aristotle) compares Poetry and history with each other and allows the former a greater truth than the latter, that too pleased me a great deal from such a man of understanding."—to Goethe 5 May 1797.

floating balance.

*   *   *

3c. Comparison with the Sophoclean Chorus

If we wish to bring Schiller's chorus into a relationship with the ancient drama, the most obvious comparison is with Sophocles. On the 28th July 1803 Goethe, in a note to Zelter,[18] divided the chorus in Greek tragedies into four epochs. The first two epochs, which particularly have to do with the work of Aeschylus, the rulers and the gods are only characters that accompany the chorus, and in the fourth epoch, that of Euripides, the chorus is no longer full of life, often appearing as an "inherited piece of the inventory." Neither of these uses of the chorus can really be compared to its use in *The Bride of Messina*. The third epoch, however, represented by the works of Sophocles, is characterised, according to Goethe, by the fact that the chorus accompanies the action:

"Inasmuch as the multitude must only watch the hero and fate, and can do nothing against specific or general nature, it turns to reflection and takes up the role of the qualified and welcome spectator." The comparison with Sophocles seems to us to be the most justified. We were reminded of Goethe's formulation, that the chorus is a "qualified spectator" in Schiller's own exposition, and so the comparison is easily made.

In Sophocles too the chorus is a reflecting spectator. It contemplates and weighs the circumstances, pacifies those who are in conflict, supports the understanding, calls the deluded to their senses, warns of misfortune with anguished apprehension, mourns disasters with sympathy, turns to the gods with pleas and prayers, and conscious of the ruling power of the gods, draws a lesson from what has happened.

Not that we should give too much weight to the reflections of the chorus in Sophocles. If we think of the peculiar choice of words and the complicated syntax in the language of the ancient chorus, we can hardly assume that the chorus's reflections would really have been understood at first hearing. The chorus's pronouncements must very likely have been largely obscure for the Greek spectator too. With repeated reading we shall naturally understand the chorus's meaning, and at the same time we are particularly struck by their *penchant* for reflection and moralising. The ancient tragedians however, as Ernst Howald[19] puts it, were not

---

[18] Goethe, Artemis Gedenkausgabe Vol.19, p.441f.

[19] Ernst Howald: *Die griechische Tragödie*, München & Berlin 1930, p. 22.

intent on "ratiocination"; they wanted to seize us in the fullest sense of the word. And this "seizing" consists, so far as the chorus is concerned, precisely in the fact that we are struck by the dark and secretive nature of their speech. Hidden within are the awful fear and respect that the men of antiquity felt before the sublimity of the gods. The chorus mean to spread a sense of holy solemnity, and it is under their guidance that the chorus watch the action. Hence the language of the chorus is in its atmosphere almost more important than what it says.

The language of the chorus in Schiller is entirely clear: Sophocles' mystery and solemnity have yielded to light: everything is clear and intelligible. True, the chorus's songs are kept in the ancient free rhythms, and so in the metre that is usually reserved for subjects that are unfathomable, immeasurable, powerfully striding onward, gripping: the hymnic style. In Schiller's case however the free rhythms are rhymed, and in such a manner that the rhyme cannot fail to be heard and marks the crucial point of every line: so that the line presses forward and comes to rest at its end. Furthermore, as the songs have not got strophe and antistrophe as in the ancient drama, the speech of the chorus moves with a speed that betrays the hand of the dramatist and writer for the theatre. Through the harmonies of the rhyme and the onward motion, the free rhythms do, however, lose their peculiar characteristics: they now hurry along, and in their freedom of movement no longer give expression to the solemn sacred atmosphere. The modern German rhyme takes their solemnity away from the rhythms, and conversely the free rhythms often seem to take away from the rhyme its due effect of melody. The mixture of old and new forms conceals an inner dichotomy, even though the "lyrical flow" is in places of moving grandeur.

Now Schiller in no sense intends, in these matters, to shore himself up on the poetry of the ancients. He knows so little Greek that the metre and sound of the Greek dramas, and their linguistic and rhythmical peculiarities, must be alien to him. There can therefore be no question of copying. We only wish to establish that the flourish of the language, the sensory atmosphere that the chorus breathes forth, is completely different in Schiller from Sophocles, and that reflection is far more prominent in the modern compared with the Sophoclean chorus. That is still no criticism of Schiller's chorus.

There is another difference that is of far more consequence with *The Bride of Messina*. Whom does the chorus actually represent? That is the question we must ask.

In the ancient tragedy it represents the general public, in which most of life takes place. The chorus is concerned with the situation and well-being of public life, in the middle of which the main characters stand. The chorus is, as it were, the court to which men are answerable. This court itself possesses no individual character; it has no subjective judgement and feeling, as it must speak the word of sympathy or censure that is generally valid.

In medieval Messina, however, Schiller feels he has to motivate the chorus differently. Here the life we are interested in is not played out among the general public. The chorus would no longer have a realistic function; it would no longer be a natural court but only an ideal person, an artificial mouthpiece. We agree with Wilhelm von Humboldt[20] that that would adequately legitimise Schiller's chorus as an artistic instrument, particularly in a piece such as *The Bride of Messina* which is so much directed against the theatre of illusion. And when Schiller says of French tragedy that the chorus has been replaced by a confidant who could take over this function in a richer fashion, Humboldt rightly expresses misgivings whether that would not be too much motivation: a "modern depravation, that again originates from the tiresome concept of illusion."[21]

But we can in fact sense the figure of a confidant in Schiller's chorus. That becomes especially clear in Act I scene 7, where Don Manuel confides to his chorus that he has found a bride and abducted her from the confines of a convent. In the "Maltese fragment" the chorus has hardly any other role than to accompany and be the confidant of Grand Master La Valette. A note in the fragments even goes so far as to suggest the possibility that La Valette could tell the chorus a secret under the seal of confession.[22] Modern drama needs the confidant figure: in Schiller we only have to think of Seni, Hanna Kennedy, Diego and Rudolf Harras. When the author talks disparagingly of the "pitiful confidant" of French tragedy, we must include the whole series of Schiller's confidants amongst these "pitiables," and we understand why Schiller is much inclined to give this thankless task to the more amply effective chorus.

But can the chorus really take over this function? Is its general significance not affected by this? Does not a confidant already have too many close personal ties to allow him to look at things rationally and objectively? Can he still be a court at all?

We will withhold the answer and pursue the comparison with the ancient example further. Of course one cannot talk of the Greek chorus

---

[20] cf. Humboldt's letter to Schiller of the 22 October 1803.

[21] Kettner II, 38 n.1

[22] Kettner II, 38 n.1

in terms of a modern confidant. There are no intimate secrets told that are to be kept from the general public, nor are any intimate feelings told that others should not know.[23]

If Schiller loads the role of the modern confidant on to the chorus, we recognise in that the sign of the playwright. On the one hand he wishes to give the "pitiful confidant" greater depth, and on the other to give the abstract concept of the chorus the real life that theatrical representation requires. The chorus of antiquity, and especially Sophocles', is too quiet for Schiller's theatrical temperament: there is too little movement; it lacks the lively effect necessary for the stage.

Körner points to the fact that Schiller's treatment of the chorus is closer to that of Aeschylus, because with Aeschylus one can detect more feeling. And in reference to *Oedipus Rex* Schiller declares to Iffland that he would like to translate and stage it—"just as it is, only treating the choral songs more freely."[24] It is typical of Schiller to treat the chorus in general more freely.

In *The Bride of Messina* he takes the liberty of dividing the chorus into two halves and having them appear on stage as the two brothers' entourage: "Although I have divided the chorus into two parts and portrayed it in conflict with itself, that is only the case when it takes part in the action, as an actual person and as a blind crowd. As a chorus and an ideal person it is always at one with itself."[25] The chorus therefore has a "double character," "one that reacts in a normal human fashion when in a state of calm reflection, and a specific one, when it becomes passionate and turns into a stage character itself." This is how Schiller himself describes his chorus in a letter to Körner.[26]

But what does this double character mean? In its general function the chorus is wise and superior, and enunciates the lessons of life, and in its specific form it represents "the masses' utter blindness, narrowness, dull passion"[27] that takes sides without prejudice. How can these two characters be united? How can a chorus embody a blind mass and a sublime wisdom in the same form? How do obtuse and limited vision and valid reflection co-exist in the same person? How can men take sides blindly and passionately and at the same time represent a valid, public

---

[23] So, too, monologues as conversations with oneself, like for example Beatrice's splendid monologue, are unthinkable in ancient tragedy. Monologues are communications to the citizens that are connected with the good or bad fortune of the speaker.

[24] 12 July 1803

[25] XVI, 128

[26] 10th March 1803

[27] *ibid.*

court? We may perhaps have some doubts whether the chorus in its general significance may not none the less in some respects count as a confidant, but here we must recognise the contrasting tendencies as totally irreconcilable. Through its property of taking part in the action the chorus takes on the appearance of reality, and through precisely that loses all artistic or natural reality.

A few examples will serve to make clear to us the unfortunate double character. Isabella calls the chorus a wild set and a false and heartless tribe.[28] The chorus does not contradict her as we would expect; instead quite the contrary: it praises the princess's calm clarity and at the same time acknowledges that its own efforts are confused, blind and pointless.[29] And three scenes later the chorus which has borne insult without demur is the sympathetic and wise confidant of Don Manuel, looking with calm superiority over the dark and doom-laden fate of the entire royal house. At another place Isabella urges the sons to unite, and the chorus supports her in her efforts:

> Hear the mother's warning speech:
> Truly, she speaks words of high import!
> Let it be enough and end the feud,
> Or if you wish, continue it![30]

This last line in such an earnest exhortation is wholly unexpected. It shows the characterless indifference which is intended to underline the special significance of the chorus. The main intention of the chorus, fully to support the mother's weighty words is however destroyed, indeed made ridiculous. And if the chorus is really indifferent as to whether feud or peace shall reign, it cannot say, thirty lines later, with credible passion

"You are brothers! Think of the end!"[31]

It would be easy to find more examples that show the incompatibility of the chorus' dual function. Karl August, Prince of Weimar, clearly recognised the duality in the chorus's attitude and very aptly described Schiller's choral figures as "armed poets." Schiller's chorus is a contradiction in itself.

---

[28] vv.336 and 349
[29] vv. 370–75
[30] vv.433–36
[31] v.465

Schiller is wrong to point to the division of the chorus in Aeschylos's *Eumenides* and Sophocles' *Ajax*, for in both these pieces, which are anyhow exceptions in Greek tragedy, there is no question of the chorus being in conflict with itself. The division only serves the physical arrangement of the scenes, and never threatens the chorus's inner unity. Schiller can not look for precedents here in the ancient tragedians. Only in its general function can the chorus be brought into a direct relationship with antiquity, and Schiller brilliantly knows how to interpret it so that it becomes fruitful for German classical drama. But just as already in the plot and the mixing of religions, so here too the material of ancient tragedy which has been artistically and faithfully taken over is mixed with a new conception, and through that is robbed of its overwhelmingly powerful effect.

*　*　*

5. Conclusion

How then does Schiller fare in his competition with the ancient tragedian Sophocles? This is the question that, in conclusion, we shall take up once again. Without doubt *The Bride of Messina* is a wonderful testimony to German classicism's artistic archaising tendencies. It should, however, have become clear too that Schiller did not create his drama out of the spirit of antiquity. The classical spirit eludes him: he cannot deny the modernity which Humboldt attributes to him of his own composition. What he faithfully copies from ancient drama and makes his own clashes with his own contribution put in alongside it, and the two spheres cannot be made to coincide, however much the external prerequisites for drama in the strict style have been fulfilled. Only the chorus seems to have been admirably moulded in its general function for use in German classic drama, but even here Schiller spoils his achievement by letting his theatrical temperament give in to the demand of giving the chorus a heightened liveliness and real significance in its specific use. The harmonious unity that we see in *Oedipus Rex* is just what is missing in Schiller's drama.

All the same Schiller himself was very moved by the first performance of his Greek drama. He writes to Körner that for the first time he had gained the impression of a true tragedy. But indicatively this impression goes back above all to the recognition scene which bears the stamp of antiquity. Schiller's sister-in-law, Karoline von Wolzogen, tells us about the first performance: "Schiller was very happy and touched, and in the last scenes where the dead prince was carried on he said to us;

'Now that really is a tragedy'."[32] And in a letter to Körner he adds: "Goethe experienced the same thing; he felt that this manifestation has initiated the boards of the theatre into something higher."[33] The classical orientation of the Weimar stage may have made its own contribution to this verdict. We can only really explain it by saying that both classicists were so much caught up in their enthusiasm for Greek tragedy that they could not yet clearly recognise what really separated the two. They allowed themselves to be too greatly impressed by the ancient elements, and were too close to their model to see the problem in their own classicism, namely that their art stands in danger of losing touch with real life.

Now evidence that is calculated to throw some light on the questionable nature of his endeavour is to be found in Schiller's letters from the time before *The Bride of Messina* was begun.

In the much-quoted letter to Goethe of the 2nd October 1797 we read: "But I fear that *Oedipus* is in a category of its own, and there can be no second such specimen. Least of all would one be able to find a counterpart to it from less mythical times. The oracle has a part in the tragedy that simply cannot be replaced by anything else, and if one wanted to keep the essential part of the story, with other characters and times, what is now fruitful would seem ridiculous." We must count the Middle Ages too among the less mythical times. For something to be called mythical it must be ideal, but no longer capable of life and reality. It is not the oracle *per se* that comes into it, but the complete trust in fate which is what gives the oracle its decisive and terrifying power, and which also determines its dominant part in the tragedy. This mythical element Schiller, as he correctly supposes in this passage, cannot capture in *The Bride of Messina* when he is altering characters and times and replacing the oracle with dreams.

All the same he attempts to create a counterpart to the "own category" of *Oedipus Rex* by inventing a tragic family "similar to that of Atreus and Laius though which a chain of misfortune" is perpetuated.[34] We already come across this attempt in the Narbonne fragment, and we find it again in the *Bride in Mourning* which, as a sequel to *The Robbers*, is intended to show an invented family whose fortunes are dogged by a chain of ill-luck. Schiller thinks up his material for the purpose of emulating *Oedipus Rex*, although on the 5th of January 1798 he writes to Goethe: "I am prepared to be told not to choose anything but historical

---

[32] Petersen 347

[33] 28 March 1803

[34] Petersen 348

material, and that I will founder on freely invented material. Idealising the realistic is a completely different operation from realising the ideal, and the latter is the case in freely invented subjects." So great is the attraction of ancient tragedy that he risks foundering on a known reef by inventing a plot for a Greek drama. And its production does, as he predicted, prove problematic.

In a letter of the 26th July 1800 to Johann Wilhelm Süvern he says, "I share with you unqualified admiration of Sophoclean tragedy, but it was a phenomenon of its time, which cannot return, and to force the living product of an individual, particular present on to a quite heterogeneous time, to be its yardstick and pattern, would mean the death rather than the life of art, which must always originate and have its effect as something dynamic and lively." Schiller undoubtedly thinks that his work originated in a dynamic and lively fashion, and we find very many signs of this everywhere where Schiller's ideas, his linguistic and dramatic creative power unmistakably come to the fore; and yet it still seems that in *The Bride of Messina* he made too much use of the Sophoclean tragedy, a phenomenon of its own time, as a yardstick and pattern. At any rate he was not able to create and shape it as a unified product of the New Age.

Now before and after this composition the poet retains his dynamic power and vitality for dramatic work. No other piece stands in such proximity to the much admired ancient model as *The Bride of Messina*. No other is so subject to the classicist's archaising tendency. But the same effort, which is at work here in extreme form and with "diabolical pains" also finds expression, with greater freedom and more fortunate success, in the poet's other works.

Life and Political Character of Sophocles— Character of His Different Tragedies

August Wilhelm von Schlegel

The birth of Sophocles was nearly at an equal distance between that of his predecessor and that of Euripides, so that he was about half a life-time from each: but on this point all the authorities do not coincide. He was, however, during the greatest part of his life the contemporary of both. He frequently contended for the ivy-wreath of tragedy with Aeschylus, and he outlived Euripides, who, however, also attained to a good old age. To speak in the spirit of the ancient religion, it seems that a beneficent Providence wished in this individual to evince to the human race the dignity and blessedness of its lot, by endowing him with every divine gift, with all that can adorn and elevate the mind and the heart, and crowning him with every imaginable blessing of this life. Descended from rich and honourable parents, and born a free citizen of the most enlightened state of Greece;—there were birth, necessary condition, and foundation. Beauty of person and of mind, and the uninterrupted enjoyment of both in the utmost perfection, to the extreme term of human existence; a most choice and finished education in gymnastics and the musical arts, the former so important in the development of the bodily powers, and the latter in the communication of harmony; the sweet bloom of youth, and the ripe fruit of age; the possession of and unbroken enjoyment of poetry and art, and the exercise of serene wisdom; love and respect among his fellow citizens, renown abroad, and the countenance and favour of the gods: these are the general features of the life of this pious and virtuous poet. It would seem as if the gods, to whom, and to Bacchus in particular, as the giver of all joy, and the civilizer of the human race, he devoted himself at an early age by the composition of tragical dramas for his festivals, had wished to confer immortality on him, so long did they delay the hour of his death; but as this could not be, they loosened him from life as gently as was possible, that he might imperceptibly change one immortality for another, the long duration of his earthly existence for the imperishable vitality of his name. When a youth of sixteen, he was selected, on account of his beauty, to dance (playing the while, after the Greek manner, on the lyre) at the head of the chorus of youths who, after the battle of Salamis (in which Aeschylus fought, and which he has so nobly described), executed the Paean round the trophy erected on that occasion. Thus then the beautiful season of his youthful bloom coincided with the most glorious epoch of the Athenian people. He held the rank of general as colleague with Pericles and Thucydides, and, when arrived at a more advanced age, was elected to the priesthood of a native hero. In his twenty-fifth year he began to exhibit tragedies; twenty times was he victorious; he often gained the second place, but never was he ranked so low as in the third. In this career he proceeded with increasing success till he had passed his ninetieth year; and some of his greatest works were even the fruit of a still later period. There is a story of an accusation being brought against him by one or more of his elder sons, of having become childish from age, and of being incapable of managing his own affairs. An alleged partiality for a grandson by a second wife is said to have been the motive of the charge. In his defence he contented himself with reading to his judges his *Oedipus at Colonos*, which he had then just composed (or, according to others, only the magnificent chorus in it, wherein he sings the praises of Colonos, his birth-place,) and the astonished judges, without farther consultation, conducted him in triumph to his house. If it be true that the second *Oedipus* was written at so late an age, as from its mature serenity and total freedom from the impetuosity and violence of youth we have good reason to conclude that it actually was, it affords us a pleasing picture of an old age at once amiable and venerable. Although the varying accounts of his death have a fabulous look, they all coincide in this, and alike convey this same purport, that he departed life without a struggle, while employed in his art, or something connected with it, and that, like an old swan of Apollo, he breathed out his life in song. The story also of the Lacedemonian general, who having entrenched the burying-ground of the poet's ancestors, and being twice warned by Bacchus in a vision to allow Sophocles to be there interred, dispatched a herald to the Athenians on the subject, I consider as true, as well as a number of other circumstances, which serve to set in a strong light the illustrious reverence in which his name was held. In calling him virtuous and pious, I used the words in his own sense; for although his works breathe the real character of ancient grandeur, gracefulness, and simplicity, he, of all the Grecian poets, is also the one whose feelings bear the strongest affinity to the spirit of our religion.

One gift alone was denied to him by nature: a voice attuned to song. He could only call forth and direct the harmonious effusions of other voices; he was therefore compelled to depart from the hitherto established practice for the poet to act a part in his own pieces. Once only did he make his appearance on the stage in the character of the blind singer Thamyris (a very characteristic trait) playing on the cithara.

As Aeschylus, who raised tragic poetry from its rude beginnings to the dignity of the Cothurnus, was his predecessor; the historical relation in which he stood to him enabled Sophocles to profit by the essays of that original master, so that Aeschylus appears as the rough designer, and Sophocles as the finisher and successor. The more artificial construction of Sophocles' dramas is easily perceived: the greater limitation of the chorus in proportion to the dialogue, the smoother polish of the rhythm, and the purer Attic diction, the introduction of a greater number of characters, the richer complication of the fable, the multiplication of incidents, a higher degree of development, the more tranquil dwelling upon all the momenta of the action, and the more striking theatrical effect allowed to decisive ones, the more perfect rounding off of the whole, even considered from a merely external point of view. But he excelled Aeschylus in something still more essential, and proved himself deserving of the good fortune of having such a preceptor, and of being allowed to enter into competition in the same field with him: I mean the harmonious perfection of his mind, which enabled him spontaneously to satisfy every requisition of the laws of beauty, a mind whose free impulse was accompanied by the most clear consciousness. To surpass Aeschylus in boldness of conception was perhaps impossible: I am inclined, however, to believe that is only because of his wisdom and moderation that Sophocles appears less bold, since he always goes to work with the greatest energy, and perhaps with even a more sustained earnestness, like a man who knows the extent of his powers, and is determined, when he does not exceed them, to stand up with the greater confidence for his rights.[1] As Aeschylus delights in transporting us to the

---

[1] This idea has been so happily expressed by the greatest genius perhaps of the last century, that the translator hopes he will be forgiven for here transcribing the passage: "I can truly say that, poor and unknown as I then was, I had pretty nearly as high an idea of myself and of my works, as I have at this moment, when the public has decided in their favour. It ever was my opinion, that the mistakes and blunders both in a rational and religious point of view, of which we see thousands daily guilty, are owing to their ignorance of themselves. To know myself, had been all along my constant study. I weighed myself alone; I balanced myself with others; I watched every means of information to see how much ground I occupied as a man and as a poet; I

convulsions of the primary world of the Titans, Sophocles, on the other hand, never avails himself of divine interposition except where it is absolutely necessary; he formed men, according to the general confession of antiquity, better, that is, not more moral and exempt from error, but more beautiful and noble than they really are; and while he took every thing in the most human sense, he was at the same time open to its higher significance. According to all appearance he was also more temperate than Aeschylus in his use of scenic ornaments; displaying perhaps more of taste and chastened beauty, but not attempting the same colossal magnificence.

To characterize the native sweetness and gracefulness so eminent in this poet, the ancients gave him the appellation of the Attic bee. Whoever is thoroughly imbued with the feeling of this peculiarity may flatter himself that a sense for ancient art has arisen within him; for the affected sentimentality of the present day, far from coinciding with the ancients in this opinion, would in the tragedies of Sophocles, both in respect of the representation of bodily sufferings, and in the sentiments and structure, find much that is insupportably austere.

When we consider the great fertility of Sophocles, for according to some he wrote a hundred and thirty pieces (of which, however, seventeen were pronounced spurious by Aristophanes the grammarian), and eighty according to the most moderate account, little, it must be owned, has come down to us, for we have only seven of them. Chance, however, has so far favoured us, that in these seven pieces we find several which were held by the ancients as his greatest works, the *Antigone*, for example, the *Electra*, and the two on the subject of *Oedipus*; and these have also come down to us tolerably free from mutilation and corruption in their text. The *Oedipus Tyrannus*, and the *Philoctetes*, have been generally, but without good reason, preferred by modern critics to all the others: the first on account of the artifice of the plot, in which the dreadful catastrophe, which so powerfully excites the curiosity (a rare case in the Greek tragedies), is inevitably brought about by a succession of connected causes; the latter on account of the masterly display of character, the beautiful contrast observable in those of the three leading personages, and the simple structure of the piece, in which, with so few persons, everything proceeds from the truest and most adequate motives. But the whole of the tragedies of Sophocles are separately resplendent with peculiar excellencies. In *Antigone* we have the purest display of feminine heroism; in *Ajax* the sense of manly honour in its full force; in the *Trachiniae* (or, as we should rather name it, the *Dying Hercules*), the female levity of Dejanira is beautifully atoned for by her death, and the sufferings of Hercules are portrayed with suitable dignity; *Electra* is distinguished by energy and pathos; in *Oedipus Coloneus* there prevails a mild and gentle emotion, and over the whole piece is diffused the sweetest gracefulness. I will not undertake to weigh the respective merits of these pieces against each other: but I own I entertain a singular predilection for the last of them, because it appears to me the most expressive of the personal feelings of the poet himself. As this piece was written for the very purpose of throwing a lustre on Athens, and his own birth-place more particularly, he appears to have laboured on it with a special love and affection.

Ajax and *Antigone* are usually the least understood. We cannot conceive how these pieces should run on so long after what we usually call the catastrophe. On this subject I shall hereafter offer a remark or two.

Of all the fables of ancient mythology in which fate is made to play a conspicuous part, the story of Oedipus is perhaps the most ingenious; but still many others, as, for instance, that of Niobe, which, without any complication of incidents, simply exhibit on a scale of colossal dimensions both of human arrogance, and its impending punishment from the gods, appear to me to be conceived in a grander style. The very intrigue which is involved in that of Oedipus detracts from its loftiness of character. Intrigue in the dramatic sense is a complication arising from the crossing of purposes and events, and this is found in a high degree in the fate of Oedipus, as all that is done by his parents or himself in order to evade the predicted horrors, serves only to bring them on the more surely. But that which gives so grand and terrible a character to this drama, is the circumstance which, however, is for the most part overlooked; that to the very Oedipus who solved the riddle of the Sphinx relating to human life, his own life should remain so long an inextricable riddle, to be so awfully cleared up, when all was irretrievably lost. A striking picture of the arrogant pretension of human wisdom, which is ever right enough in its general principles, but does not enable the possessor to make the proper application to himself.

Notwithstanding the severe conclusion of the first Oedipus we are so far reconciled to it by the violence, suspicion, and haughtiness in the character of Oedipus, that our feelings do not absolutely revolt at so horrible a fate. For this end, it was necessary thus far to sacrifice the character of Oedipus, who, however, raises himself in our estimation by his fatherly care and heroic zeal for the welfare of his people, that occasion him, by his honest search for the author of the crime, to accelerate his own destruction. It was also necessary, for the sake of contrast with his future misery, to exhibit him in his treatment of Tiresias and Creon, in all the haughtiness of regal dignity. And, indeed, all his earlier proceedings evince, in some measure, the same suspiciousness and violence of character; the former, in his refusing to be quieted by the assurances of Polybos, when taunted with being a suppositious child, and the latter, in his bloody quarrel with Laius. The latter character he seems to have inherited from both his parents. The arrogant levity of Jocasta, which induces her to deride the oracle as not confirmed by the event, the penalty of which she is so soon afterwards to inflict upon herself, was not indeed inherited by her son; he is, on the contrary, conspicuous throughout for the purity of his intentions; and his care and anxiety to escape from the predicted crime, added naturally to the poignancy of his despair, when he found that he had nevertheless been overtaken by it. Awful indeed is his blindness in not perceiving the truth when it was, as it were, brought directly home to him; as, for instance, when he puts the question to Jocasta, How did Laius look? and she answers he had become gray-haired, otherwise in appearance he was not unlike Oedipus. This is also another feature of her levity, that she should not have been struck with the resemblance to her husband, a circumstance that might have led her to recognize him as her son. Thus a close analysis of the piece will evince the utmost propriety and significance of every portion of it. As, however, it is customary to extol the correctness of Sophocles, and to boast more especially of the strict observance of probability which prevails throughout this *Oedipus*, I must here remark that this very piece is a proof how, on this subject, the ancient artists followed very different principles from those of modern critics. For, according to our way of thinking, nothing could be more improbable than that Oedipus should, so long, have forborne to inquire into the circumstances of the death of Laius, and that the scars on his feet, and even the name which he bore, should never have excited the curiosity of Jocasta, &c. But the ancients did not produce their works of art for calculating and prosaic understandings; and an improbability which, to be found out, required dissection, and did not exist within the matters of the representation itself, was to them none at all.

The diversity of character of Aeschylus and Sophocles is nowhere more conspicuous than in the *Eumenides* and the *Oedipus Coloneus*, as both these pieces were composed with the same aim. This aim was to glorify Athens as the sacred abode of law and humanity, on whose soil the crimes of the hero families of other countries might, by a higher mediation, be at last propitiated; while an ever-during prosperity was predicted to the Athenian people. The patriotic and liberty-breathing

Aeschylus has recourse to a judicial, and the pious Sophocles to a religious, procedure; even the consecration of Oedipus in death. Bent down by the consciousness of inevitable crimes, and lengthened misery, his honour is, as it were, cleared up by the gods themselves, as if desirous of showing that, in the terrible example which they made of him, they had no intention of visiting him in particular, but merely wished to give a solemn lesson to the whole human race. Sophocles, to whom the whole of life was one continued worship of the gods, delighted to throw all possible honour on its last moments as if a more solemn festival; and associated it with emotions very different from what the thought of mortality is in general calculated to excite. That the tortured and exhausted Oedipus should at last find peace and repose in the grove of the Furies, in the very spot from which all other mortals fled with aversion and horror, he whose misfortune consisted in having done a deed at which all men shudder, unconsciously and without warning of any inward feeling; in this there is a profound and mysterious meaning.

Aeschylus has given us in the person of Pallas a more majestic representation of the Attic cultivation, prudence, moderation, mildness, and magnanimity; but Sophocles, who delighted to draw all that is godlike within the sphere of humanity, has, in his Theseus, given a more delicate development of all these same things. Whoever is desirous of gaining an accurate idea of Grecian heroism, as contrasted with the Barbarian, would do well to consider this character with attention.

In Aeschylus, before the victim of persecution can be delivered, and the land can participate in blessings, the infernal horror of the Furies congeals the spectator's blood, and makes his hair stand on end, and the whole rancour of these goddesses of rage is exhausted: after this the transition to their peaceful retreat is the more wonderful; the whole human race seems, as it were, delivered from their power. In Sophocles, however, they do not ever appear, but are kept altogether in the background; and they are never mentioned by their own name, but always alluded to by some softening euphemism. But this very obscurity, so exactly befitting these daughters of night, and the very distance at which they are kept, are calculated to excite a silent horror in which the bodily senses have no part. The clothing the grove of the Furies with all the charms of a southern spring completes the sweetness of the poem; and were I to select from his own tragedies an emblem of the poetry of Sophocles, I should describe it as a sacred grove of the dark goddesses of fate, in which the laurel, the olive, and the vine, are always green, and the song of the nightingale is for ever heard.

Two of the pieces of Sophocles refer to what, in the Greek way of thinking, are the sacred rights of the dead, and the solemn importance of burial; in *Antigone* the whole of the action hinges on this, and in *Ajax* it forms the only satisfactory conclusion of the piece.

The ideal of the female character in *Antigone* is characterized by great austerity, and it is sufficient of itself to put an end to all the seductive representations of Grecian softness, which of late have been so universally current. Her indignation at Ismene's refusal to take part in her daring resolution; the manner in which she afterwards repulses Ismene, when repenting of her former weakness, she begs to be allowed to share her heroic sister's death, borders on harshness; both her silence, and then her invectives against Creon, by which she provokes him to execute his tyrannical threats, display the immovable energy of manly courage. The poet has, however, discovered the secret of painting the loving heart of woman in a single line, when to the assertion of Creon, that Polynices was an enemy to his country, she replies:

My love shall go with thine, but not my hate.[2]

Moreover, she puts a constraint on her feelings only so long as by giving vent to them, she might make her firmness of purpose appear equivocal. When, however, she is being led forth to inevitable death, she pours forth her soul in the tenderest and most touching wailings over the hard and untimely fate, and does not hesitate, she, the modest virgin, to mourn the loss of nuptials, and the unenjoyed bliss of marriage. Yet she never in a single syllable betrays any inclination for Haemon, and does not even mention the name of that amiable youth.[3] After such heroic determination, to have shown that any tie still bound her to existence, would have been a weakness; but to relinquish without one sorrowful regret those common enjoyments with which the gods have enriched this life, would have ill accorded with her devout sanctity of mind.

On a first view the chorus in *Antigone* may appear weak, acceding, as it does, at once, without opposition to the tyrannical commands of Creon, and without even attempting to make the slightest representation in behalf of the young heroine. But to exhibit the determination and the deed of Antigone in their full glory, it was necessary that they should stand out quite alone, and that she should have no stay or support. More-

---

[2]This is the version of Franklin, but it does not convey the meaning of the original, and I am not aware that the English language is sufficiently flexible to admit of an exact translation. The German, which, though far inferior to the Greek in harmony, is little behind in flexibility, has in this respect great advantage over the English; and Schlegel's *"nicht mitzuhassen, mitzulieben bin ich da,"* represents exactly Οὔτοι συνέχθειν ἀλλὰ συμφιλεῖν ἔφυν.—Trans.

[3]Barthelemy asserts the contrary; but the line to which he refers, according to the more correct manuscripts, and even according to the context, belongs to Ismene.

over, the very submissiveness of the chorus increases our impression of the irresistible nature of the royal commands. So, too, was it necessary for it to mingle with its concluding addresses to Antigone the most painful recollections, that she might drain the full cup of earthly sorrows. The case is very different in *Electra*, where the chorus appropriately takes an interest in the fate of the two principal characters, and encourages them in the execution of their design, as the moral feelings are divided as to its legitimacy, whereas there is no such conflict in Antigone's case, who had nothing to deter her from her purpose but mere external fears.

After the fulfillment of the deed, and the infliction of its penalties, the arrogance of Creon still remains to be corrected, and the death of Antigone to be avenged; nothing less than the destruction of his whole family, and his own despair, could be a sufficient atonement for the sacrifice of a life so costly. We have therefore the king's wife, who had not even been named before, brought at last on the stage, that she may hear the misfortunes of her family, and put an end to her own existence. To Grecian feelings it would have been impossible to consider the poem as properly concluding with the death of Antigone, without its penal retribution.

The case is the same in *Ajax*. His arrogance, which was punished with a degrading madness, is atoned for by the deep shame which at length drives him even to self-murder. The persecution of the unfortunate man must not, however, be carried farther; when, therefore, it is in contemplation to dishonour his very corpse by the refusal of interment, even Ulysses interferes. He owes the honours of burial to that Ulysses whom in life he had looked upon as his mortal enemy, and to whom, in the dreadful introductory scene, Pallas shows, in the example of the delirious Ajax, the nothingness of man. Thus Ulysses appears as the personification of moderation, which, if it had been possessed by Ajax, would have prevented his fall.

Self-murder is of frequent occurrence in ancient mythology, at least as adapted to tragedy; but it generally takes place, if not in a state of insanity, yet in a state of agitation, after some sudden calamity which leaves no room for consideration. Such self-murders as those of Jocasta, Haemon, Eurydice, and lastly of Dejanira, appear merely in the light of a subordinate appendage in the tragical pictures of Sophocles; but the suicide of Ajax is a cool determination, a free action, and of sufficient importance to become the principal subject of the piece. It is not the last fatal crisis of a slow mental malady, as is so often the case in these more effeminate modern times; still less is it that more theoretical disgust of life, founded on a condition of its worthlessness, which induced so many

of the later Romans, on Epicurean as well as Stoical principles, to put an
end to their existence. It is not through any unmanly despondency that
Ajax is unfaithful to his rude heroism. His delirium is over, as well as
his first comfortless feelings upon awaking from it; and it is not till after
the complete return of consciousness, and when he has had time to
measure the depth of the abyss into which, by a divine destiny, his over-
weening haughtiness has plunged him, when he contemplates his situation, and feels it ruined beyond remedy:—his honour wounded by the
refusal of the arms of Achilles; and the outburst of his vindictive rage
wasted in his infatuation on defenceless flocks; himself, after a long and
reproachless heroic career, a source of amusement to his enemies, an
object of derision and abomination to the Greeks, and to his honoured
father,—should he thus return to him—a disgrace: after reviewing all
this, he decides agreeably to his own motto, "gloriously to live or
gloriously to die," that the latter course alone remains open to him.
Even the dissimulation,—the first, perhaps, that he ever practised, by
which, to prevent the execution of his purpose from being disturbed, he
pacifies his comrades, must be considered as the fruit of greatness of
soul. He appoints Teucer guardian to his infant boy, the future consolation of his own bereaved parents; and, like Cato, dies not before he has
arranged the concerns of all who belong to him. As Antigone in her
womanly tenderness, so even he in his wild manner, seems in his last
speech to feel the majesty of that light of the sun from which he is
departing for ever. His rude courage disdains compassion, and therefore
excites it the more powerfully. What a picture of awaking from the
tumult of passion, when the tent opens and in the midst of the
slaughtered herds he sits on the ground bewailing himself!

As Ajax, in the feeling of inextinguishable shame, forms the
violent resolution of throwing away life, Philoctetes, on the other hand,
bears its wearisome load during long years of misery with the most
enduring patience. If Ajax is honoured by his despair, Philoctetes is
equally ennobled by his constancy. When the instinct of self-preservation
comes into collision with no moral impulse, it naturally exhibits itself in
all its strength. Nature has armed with this instinct whatever is possessed
of the breath of life, and the vigour with which every hostile attack on
existence is repelled is the strongest proof of its excellence. In the
presence, it is true, of that band of men by which he had been
abandoned, and if he must depend on their superior power, Philoctetes
would no more have wished for life than did Ajax. But he is alone with
nature; he quails not before the frightful aspect which she exhibits to
him, and still clings even to the maternal bosom of the all-nourishing
earth. Exiled on a desert island, tortured by an incurable wound, solitary

and helpless as he is, his bow procures him food from the birds of the forest, the rock yields him soothing herbs, the fountain supplies a fresh beverage, his cave affords him a cool shelter in summer, in winter he is warmed by the mid-day sun, or a fire of kindled boughs; even the raging attacks of his pain at length exhaust themselves, and leave him in a refreshing sleep. Alas! it is the artificial refinements, the oppressive burden of a relaxing and deadening superfluity which render man indifferent to the value of life: when it is stripped of all foreign appendages, though borne down with sufferings so that the naked existence alone remains, still will its sweetness flow from the heart at every pulse through all the veins. Miserable man! ten long years has he struggled; and yet he still lives, and clings to life and hope. What force of truth is there in all this! What, however, most moves us in behalf of Philoctetes is, that he, who by an abuse of power had been cast out from society, when it again approaches him is exposed by it to a second and still more dangerous evil, that of falsehood. The anxiety excited in the mind of the spectator lest Philoctetes should be deprived of his last means of subsistence, his bow, would be too painful, did he not from the beginning entertain a suspicion that the open-hearted and straight-forward Neoptolemus will not be able to maintain to the end the character which, so much against his will, he has assumed. Not without reason after this deception does Philoctetes turn away from mankind to those inanimate companions to which the instinctive craving for society had attached him. He calls on the island and its volcanoes to witness this fresh wrong; he believes that his beloved bow feels pain in being taken from him; and at length he takes a melancholy leave of his hospitable cavern, the fountains and the wave-washed cliffs, from which he so often looked in vain upon the ocean: so inclined to love is the uncorrupted mind of man.

Respecting the bodily sufferings of Philoctetes and the manner of representing them, Lessing has in his *Laocoön* declared himself against Winkelmann, and Herder again has in the *Silvae Criticae* (Kritische Wälder) contradicted Lessing. Both the two last writers have made many excellent observations on the piece, although we must allow with Herder, that Winkelmann was correct in affirming that the Philoctetes of Sophocles, like Laocoön in the celebrated group, suffers with the suppressed agony of an heroic soul never altogether overcome by his pain.

The *Trachiniæ* appears to me so very inferior to the other pieces of Sophocles which have reached us, that I could wish there were some warrant for supposing that this tragedy was composed in the age, indeed, and in the school of Sophocles, perhaps by his son Iophon, and that it was by mistake attributed to the father. There is much both in the structure and plan, and in the style of the piece, calculated to excite suspicion; and many critics have remarked that the introductory soliloquy of Dejanira, which is wholly uncalled-for, is very unlike the general character of Sophocles' prologues: and although this poet's usual rules of art are observed on the whole, yet it is very superficially; no where can we discern in it the profound mind of Sophocles. But as no writer of antiquity appears to have doubted its authenticity, while Cicero even quotes from it the complaint of Hercules, as from an indisputable work of Sophocles, we are compelled to content ourselves with the remark, that in this one instance the tragedian has failed to reach his usual elevation.

This brings us to the consideration of a general question, which, in the examination of the works of Euripides, will still more particularly engage the attention of the critic: how far, namely, the invention and execution of a drama must belong to one man to entitle him to pass for its author. Dramatic literature affords numerous examples of plays composed by several persons conjointly. It is well known that Euripides, in the details and execution of his pieces, availed himself of the assistance of a learned servant, Cephisophon; and he perhaps also consulted with him respecting his plots. It appears, moreover, certain that in Athens schools of dramatic art had at this date been formed; such, indeed, as usually arise when poetical talents are, by public competition, called abundantly and actively into exercise: schools of art which contain scholars of such excellence and of such kindred genius, that the master may confide to them a part of the execution, and even the plan, and yet allow the whole to pass under his name without any disparagement to his fame. Such were the schools of painting of the sixteenth century, and every one knows what a remarkable degree of critical acumen is necessary to discover in many of Raphael's pictures how much really belongs to his own pencil. Sophocles had educated his son Iophon to the tragic art, and might therefore easily receive assistance from him in the actual labour of composition, especially as it was necessary that the tragedies that were to compete for the prize should be ready and got by heart by a certain day. On the other hand, he might also execute occasional passages for works originally designed by the son; and the pieces of this description, in which the hand of the master was perceptible, would be naturally attributed to the more celebrated name.

From *The Conversations of Goethe with Eckermann and Soret*

Wednesday, March 21, 1827

Goethe showed me a little book, by Hinrichs, on the nature of antique tragedy. "I have read it with great interest," said he. "Hinrichs has taken the Oedipus and Antigone of Sophocles as the foundation whereon to develop his views. It is very remarkable; and I will lend it to you that you may read it, and that we may be able to converse upon it. I am by no means of his opinion; but it is highly instructive to see how a man of such thoroughly philosophical culture regards a poetical work of art from the point of view peculiar to his school.[1] I will say no more to-day, that I may not influence your opinion. Only read it, and you will find that it suggests all kinds of thoughts."

Wednesday, March 28, 1827.

I brought back to Goethe the book by Hinrichs, which I had read attentively. I had also gone once more through all the plays of Sophocles, to be in complete possession of my subject.

"Now," said Goethe, "how did you like him? He attacks a matter well—does he not?"

"This book affected me very strangely," said I. "No other book has aroused so many thoughts in me as this; and yet there is none I have so often been disposed to contradict."

"That is exactly the point," said Goethe. "What we agree with leaves us inactive, but contradiction makes us productive."

---

[1]That of Hegel.—*Trans.*

"His intentions," said I, "appear to me in the highest degree laudable, and he by no means confines himself to the surface of things. But he so often loses himself in refinements and motives—and that in so subjective a manner—that he loses the true aspect of the subject in detail, as well as the survey of the whole; and in such a case one is obliged to do violence both to oneself and the theme to think as he does. Besides, I have often fancied that my organs were not fine enough to apprehend the unusual subtlety of his distinctions."

"If they were philosophically prepared like his," said Goethe, "it would be better. But, to speak frankly, I am sorry that a man of undoubted innate power from the northern coast of Germany, like Hinrichs, should be so spoilt by the philosophy of Hegel as to lose all unbiassed and natural observation and thought, and gradually to get into an artificial and heavy style, both of thought and expression; so that we find passages in his book where our understanding comes to a stand-still, and we no longer know what we are reading."

"I have fared no better," said I. "Still I have rejoiced to meet with some passages, which have appeared to me perfectly clear and fitted for humanity in general; such, for instance, as his relation of the fable of Oedipus."

"Here," said Goethe, "he has been obliged to confine himself strictly to his subject. But there are in his book several passages in which the thought does not progress, but in which the obscure language constantly moves on the same spot and in the same circle, just like the 'Einmaleins'[2] of the witch in my 'Faust.' Give me the book again. Of his sixth lecture upon the chorus, I scarcely understood anything. What do you say, for instance, to this passage, which occurs near the end:—

"This realization (*i.e.* of popular life) is, as the true signification thereof,[3] on this account alone its true realization, which as a truth and certainty to itself, therefore constitutes the universally mental certainty, which certainly is at the same time the atoning certainty of the chorus, so that in this certainty alone, which has shown itself as the result of the combined movement of the tragic action, the chorus preserves its fitting relation to the universal popular consciousness, and in this capacity does not merely represent the people, but is that people according to its certainty."

---

[2]This word, which signifies "multiplication table," refers to the arithmetical jargon uttered by the witch in her kitchen.—*Trans.*

[3]The word "derselben," in the passage as cited, seems to want an antecedent. The reader is requested not to be too critical with this almost unreadable passage, which Goethe only refers to as an instance of obscurity.—*Trans.*

"I think we have had enough of this. What must the English and French think of the language of our philosophers, when we Germans do not understand them ourselves." "And in spite of all this," said I, "we both agree that a noble purpose lies at the foundation of the book, and that it possesses the quality of awakening thoughts."

"His idea of the relation between family and state," said Goethe, "and the tragical conflicts that may arise from them is certainly good and suggestive; still I cannot allow that it is the only right one, or even the best for tragic art. We are indeed all members both of a family and of a state, and a tragical fate does not often befall us which does not wound us in both capacities. Still we might be very good tragical characters, if we were merely members of a family or merely members of a state; for, after all, the only point is to get a conflict which admits of no solution, and this may arise from an antagonistical position in any relation whatever, provided a person has a really natural foundation, and is himself really tragic. Thus Ajax falls a victim to the demon of wounded honour, and Hercules to the demon of jealousy. In neither of these cases is there the least conflict between family piety and political virtue; though this, according to Hinrichs, should be the element of Greek tragedy."

"One sees clearly," said I, "that in this theory he merely had Antigone in his mind. He also appears to have had before his eyes merely the character and mode of action of this heroine, as he makes the assertion that family piety appears most pure in woman, and especially in a sister; and that a sister can love only a brother with perfect purity, and without sexual feeling."

"I should think," returned Goethe, "that the love of sister for sister was still more pure and unsexual. As if we did not know that numerous cases have occurred in which the most sensual inclinations have existed between brother and sister, both knowingly and unknowingly!"

"You must have remarked generally," continued Goethe, "that Hinrichs, in considering Greek tragedy, sets out from the *idea*; and that he looks upon Sophocles as one who, in the invention and arrangement of his pieces, likewise set out from an idea, and regulated the sex and rank of his characters accordingly. But Sophocles, when he wrote his pieces, by no means started from an *idea*; on the contrary, he seized upon some ancient ready-made popular tradition in which a good idea existed, and then only thought of adapting it in the best and most effective manner for the theatre. The Atrides will not allow Ajax to be buried; but as in Antigone the sister struggles for the brother, so in the Ajax the brother struggles for the brother. That the sister takes charge of the unburied Polyneices, and the brother takes charge of the fallen Ajax, is a contingent circumstance, and does not belong to the invention of the poet, but to the tradition, which the poet followed and was obliged to follow.''

"What he says about Creon's conduct," replied I, "appears to be equally untenable. He tries to prove that, in prohibiting the burial of Polyneices, Creon acts from pure political virtue; and since Creon is not merely a man, but also a prince, he lays down the proposition, that, as a man represents the tragic power of the state, this man can be no other than he who is himself the personification of the state itself—namely, the prince; and that of all persons the man as prince must be just that person who displays the greatest political virtue.''

"These are assertions which no one will believe," returned Goethe with a smile. "Besides, Creon by no means acts out of political virtue, but from hatred towards the dead. When Polyneices endeavoured to reconquer his paternal inheritance, from which he had been forcibly expelled, he did not commit such a monstrous crime against the state that his death was insufficient, and that the further punishment of the innocent corpse was required.

"An action should never be placed in the category of political virtue which is opposed to virtue in general. When Creon forbids the burial of Polyneices, and not only taints the air with the decaying corpse, but also affords an opportunity for the dogs and birds of prey to drag about pieces torn from the dead body, and thus to defile the altars—an action so offensive both to gods and men is by no means politically virtuous, but on the contrary a political crime. Besides, he has everybody in the play against him. He has the elders of the state, who form the chorus, against him; he has the people at large against him; he has Teiresias against him; he has his own family against him; but he hears not, and obstinately persists in his impiety, until he has brought to ruin all who belong to him, and is himself at last nothing but a shadow.''

"And still," said I, "when one hears him speak, one cannot help believing that he is somewhat in the right.''

"That is the very thing," said Goethe, "in which Sophocles is a master; and in which consists the very life of the dramatic in general. His characters all possess this gift of eloquence, and know how to explain the motives for their action so convincingly, that the hearer is almost always on the side of the last speaker.

"One can see that, in his youth, he enjoyed an excellent rhetorical education, by which he became trained to look for all the reasons and seeming reasons of things. Still, his great talent in this respect betrayed him into faults, as he sometimes went too far.

"There is a passage in Antigone which I always look upon as a blemish, and I would give a great deal for an apt philologist to prove that it is interpolated and spurious.

"After the heroine has, in the course of the piece, explained the noble motives for her action, and displayed the elevated purity of her soul, she at last, when she is led to death, brings forward a motive which is quite unworthy, and almost borders upon the comic.

"She says that, if she had been a mother, she would not have done, either for her dead children or for her dead husband, what she has done for her brother. 'For,' says she, 'if my children died I could have had others by my new husband. But with my brother, the case is different. I cannot have another brother; for since my mother and father are dead, there is no one to beget one.'

"This is, at least, the bare sense of this passage, which in my opinion, when placed in the mouth of a heroine going to her death, disturbs the tragic tone, and appears to me very far-fetched,—to savor too much of dialectical calculation. As I said, I should like a philologist to show us that the passage is spurious."

We then conversed further upon Sophocles, remarking that in his pieces he always less considered a moral tendency than an apt treatment of the subject in hand, particularly with regard to theatrical effect.

"I do not object," said Goethe, "to a dramatic poet having a moral influence in view; but when the point is to bring his subject clearly and effectively before his audience, his moral purpose proves of little use, and he needs much more a faculty for delineation and a familiarity with the stage to know what to do and what to leave undone. If there be a moral in the subject, it will appear, and the poet has nothing to consider but the effective and artistic treatment of his subject. If a poet has as high a soul as Sophocles, his influence will always be moral, let him do what he will. Besides, he knew the stage, and understood his craft thoroughly."

"How well he knew the theatre," answered I, "and how much he had in view a theatrical effect, we see in his 'Philoctetes,' and the great resemblance which this piece bears to 'Oedipus, in Colonos,' both in the arrangement and the course of action.

"In both pieces we see the hero in a helpless condition; both are old and suffering from bodily infirmities. Oedipus has, at his side, his daughter as a guide and a prop; Philoctetes has his bow. The resemblance is carried still further. Both have been thrust aside in their afflictions; but when the oracle declares with respect to both of them, that the victory can be obtained with their aid alone, and endeavour is made to get them back again; Ulysses comes to Philoctetes, Creon to Oedipus.

Both begin their discourse with cunning and honied words; but when these are of no avail they use violence, and we see Philoctetes deprived of his bow, and Oedipus of his daughter.''

"Such acts of violence," said Goethe, "give an opportunity for excellent altercations, and such situations of helplessness excited the emotions of the audience, on which account the poet, whose object it was to produce an effect upon the public, liked to introduce them. In order to strengthen this effect in the Oedipus, Sophocles brings him in as a weak old man, when he still, according to all circumstance, must have been a man in the prime of life. But at this vigorous age, the poet could not have used him for his play; he would have produced no effect, and he therefore made him a weak, helpless old man.''

"The resemblance to Philoctetes," continued I, "goes still further. The hero, in both pieces, does not act, but suffers. On the other hand, each of these passive heroes has two active characters against him. Oedipus has Creon and Polyneices, Philoctetes has Neoptolemus and Ulysses; two such opposing characters were necessary to discuss the subject on all sides, and to gain the necessary body and fulness for the piece.''

"You might add," interposed Goethe, "that both pieces bear this further resemblance, that we see in both the extremely effective situation of a happy change, since one hero, in his disconsolate situation, has his beloved daughter restored to him, and the other, his no less beloved bow.

"The happy conclusions of these two pieces are also similar; for both heroes are delivered from their sorrows: Oedipus is blissfully snatched away, and as for Philoctetes, we are forewarned by the oracle of his cure, before Troy, by Aesculapius.''

*   *   *   *   *   *   *   *

The conversation then turned upon the 'Antigone' of Sophocles, and the high moral tone prevailing in it; and, lastly, upon the question—how the moral element came into the world?

"Through God himself," returned Goethe, "like everything else. It is no product of human reflection, but a beautiful nature inherent and inborn. It is, more or less, inherent in mankind generally, but to a high degree in a few eminently gifted minds. These have, by great deeds or doctrines, manifested their divine nature; which, then, by the beauty of its appearance, won the love of men, and powerfully attracted them to reverence and emulation.''

"A consciousness of the worth of the morally beautiful and good could be attained by experience and wisdom, inasmuch as the bad showed itself in its consequences as a destroyer of happiness, both in individuals and the whole body, while the noble and right seemed to produce and secure the happiness of one and all. Thus the morally beautiful could become a doctrine, and diffuse itself over whole nations as something plainly expressed.''

"I have lately read somewhere,'' answered I, "the opinion that the Greek tragedy had made moral beauty a special object.''

"Not so much morality,'' returned Goethe, "as pure humanity in its whole extent; especially in such positions where, by falling into contact with rude power, it could assume a tragic character. In this region, indeed, even the moral stood as a principal part of human nature.

"The morality of Antigone, besides, was not invented by Sophocles, but was contained in the subject, which Sophocles chose the more readily, as it united so much dramatic effect with moral beauty.''

Goethe then spoke about the characters of Creon and Ismene, and on the necessity for these two persons for the development of the beautiful soul of the heroine.

"All that is noble,'' said he, "is in itself of a quiet nature, and appears to sleep until it is aroused and summoned forth by contrast. Such a contrast is Creon, who is brought in, partly on account of Antigone, in order that her noble nature and the right which is on her side may be brought out by him, partly on his own account, in order that his unhappy error may appear odious to us.

"But, as Sophocles meant to display the elevated soul of his heroine even before the deed, another contrast was requisite by which her character might be developed; and this is her sister Ismene. In this character, the poet has given us a beautiful standard of the commonplace, so that the greatness of Antigone, which is far above such a standard, is the more strikingly visible.''

On the Irony of Sophocles

Connop Thirlwall

Some readers may be a little surprised to see *irony* attributed to a tragic poet: and it may therefore be proper, before we proceed to illustrate the nature of the thing as it appears in the works of Sophocles, to explain and justify our application of the term. We must begin with a remark or two on the more ordinary use of the word, on that which to distinguish it from the subject of our present enquiry, we will call *verbal irony*. This most familiar species of irony may be described as a figure which enables the speaker to convey his meaning with greater force by means of a contrast between his thought and his expression, or to speak more accurately, between the thought which he evidently designs to express, and that which his words properly signify. The cases in which this figure may be advantageously employed are so various as to include some directly opposite in their nature. For it will serve to express assent and approbation as well as the contrary. Still as a friend cannot be defended unless against an enemy who attacks him, the use of verbal irony must in all cases be either directly or indirectly polemical. It is a weapon properly belonging to the armoury of controversy, and not fitted to any entirely peaceable occasion. This is not the less true because, as the enginery of war is often brought out, and sham fights exhibited, for the public amusement in time of peace, so there is a sportive irony, which instead of indicating any contrariety of opinion or animosity of feeling, is the surest sign of perfect harmony and goodwill. And as there is a mode of expressing sentiments of the utmost esteem and unanimity by an ironical reproof or contradiction, so there is an ironical self-commendation, by which a man may playfully confess his own failings. In the former case the speaker feigns the existence of adversaries whose language he pretends to adopt: in the latter he supposes himself surrounded, not as he really is by indulgent friends, but by severe judges of his actions, before whom it is necessary for him to disguise the imperfections of his character. But where irony is not merely jocular, it is not simply serious, but earnest. With respect to opinion it implies a conviction so deep, as to disdain a direct refutation of the opposite party: with respect to feeling, it implies an emotion so strong, as to be able to command itself, and to suppress its natural tone, in order to vent itself with greater force.

Irony is so inviting an instrument of literary warfare that there are perhaps few eminent controversial writers who have wholly abstained from the use of it. But in general even those who employ it most freely reserve it for particular occasions, to add weight and point to the gravest part of the argument. There is however an irony which deserves to be distinguished from the ordinary species by a different name, and which may be properly called *dialectic irony*. This, instead of being concentrated in insulated passages, and rendered prominent by its contrast with the prevailing tone of the composition, pervades every part, and is spread over the whole like a transparent vesture closely fitted to every limb of the body. The writer effects his purpose by placing the opinion of his adversary in the foreground, and saluting it with every demonstration of respect, while he is busied in withdrawing one by one all the supports on which it rests: and he never ceases to approach it with an air of deference, until he has completely undermined it, when he leaves it to sink by the weight of its own absurdity. Examples of this species are as rare as those of the other are common. The most perfect ever produced are those which occur in Plato's dialogues. In modern literature the finest specimens may be found in the works of Pascal, and of Plato's German translator, who has imbibed the peculiar spirit of the Platonic irony in a degree which has perhaps never been equalled. One of the most unfortunate attempts ever made at imitating this character of the Platonic dialogue, is Bishop Berkeley's Minute Philosopher. Examples of a more superficial kind, where the object is rather ridicule than argument, will readily present themselves to the reader's recollection. The highest triumph of irony consists not in refutation and demolition. It requires that, while the fallacy is exposed and overthrown by the admissions which it has itself demanded, the truth should be set in the clearest light, and on the most solid ground, by the attempts made to suppress and overwhelm it.

Without departing from the analogy that pervades the various kinds of verbal irony, we may speak of a *practical irony*, which is independent of all forms of speech, and needs not the aid of words. Life affords as many illustrations of this, as conversation and books of the other. But here we must carefully distinguish between two totally different kinds, which, though they may often outwardly coincide, spring from directly contrary feelings. There is a malignant, or at least a wanton irony, in the practical sense, by which a man humours the folly of another, for the purpose of rendering it more extravagant and incorrigible, whether it be with the further aim of extracting materials for ridicule from it, or of turning it to some still less liberal use. Specimens of this kind are perpetually occurring in society, and ancient and modern comedy is full of them. But this same irony has a darker side, which can excite only detestation and horror, as something belonging rather to the nature of a fiend than of a man. Such is the flattery which, under the mask of friendship, deliberately cherishes passions, and panders to wishes, which are hurrying their unconscious slave into ruin. Such is the spirit in which Timon gives his gold to Alcibiades and his companions, and afterwards to the thieves: though in the latter case he is near defeating his own purpose by the irony of his language, which compels one of the thieves to say: "He has almost charmed me from my profession by persuading me to it." Such is the irony with which the weird women feed the ambitious hopes of Macbeth, and afterward lull him into a false "security, mortals' chiefest enemy," when they have been commanded to

> raise such artificial sprites
> As by the strength of their illusion
> Shall draw him on to his confusion.

Till

> He shall spurn fate, scorn death, and bear
> His hopes 'bove wisdom, grace, and fear.

Such, but more truly diabolical, is the irony with which in *Faust* the Spirit of Evil accompanies his victim on his fatal career, and with which, by way of interlude, he receives the visit of the young scholar.

But there is also a practical irony which is not inconsistent with the highest degree of wisdom and benevolence. A man of superior understanding may often find himself compelled to assent to propositions which he knows, though true in themselves, will lead to very erroneous inferences in the mind of the speaker, because either circumstances prevent him from subjoining the proper limitations, or the person he is addressing is incapable of comprehending them. So again a friend may comply with the wishes of one who is dear to him, though he foresees that they will probably end in disappointment and vexation, either because he conceives that he has no right to decide for another, or because he thinks it probable that the disappointment itself will prove more salutary than the privation. Such is the conduct of the affectionate father in the parable, which is a type of universal application: for in every transgression there is a concurrence of a depraved will, which is the vice of the agent, with certain outward conditions, which may be considered as a boon graciously bestowed, but capable of being perverted into an instrument of evil, and a cause of misery. It must have occurred to most men, more especially to those of sanguine temperament, and whose lives have been chequered with many vicissitudes, now and then to reflect how little the good and ill of their lot has corresponded with their hopes and fears. All who have lived long enough in the world must be able to remember objects coveted with impatient eagerness, and pursued with long and unremitting toil, which in possession have proved tasteless and worthless: hours embittered with anxiety and dread by the prospect of changes which brought with them the fulfilment of the most ardent wishes: events anticipated with trembling expectation which arrived, past, and left no sensible trace behind them: while things of which they scarcely heeded the existence, persons whom they met with indifference, exerted the most important influence on their character and fortunes. When, at a sufficient interval and with altered mood, we review such instances of the mockery of fate, we can scarcely refrain from a melancholy smile. And such, we conceive, though without any of the feelings that sometimes sadden our retrospect, must have been the look which a superior intelligence, exempt from our passions, and capable of surveying all our relations, and foreseeing the consequences of all our actions, would at the time have cast upon the tumultuous workings of our blind ambition and our groundless apprehensions, upon the phantoms we raised to chase us, or to be chased, while the substance of good and evil presented itself to our view, and was utterly disregarded.

But it is not only in the lives of individuals that man's shortsighted impatience and temerity are thus tacitly rebuked by the course of events: examples still more striking are furnished by the history of states and institutions. The moment of the highest prosperity is often that which immediately precedes the most ruinous disaster, and (as in the case not only of a Xerxes, a Charles the Bold, a Philip the second, and a Napoleon, but of Athens, and Sparta, and Carthage, and Venice,) it is the sense of security that constitutes the danger, it is the consciousness of power and the desire of exerting it that causes the downfall. It is not however these sudden and signal reverses, the fruit of overweening arrogance and insatiable ambition, that we have here principally to observe: but rather an universal law, which manifests itself, no less in the moral world than in the physical, according to which the period of inward languor, corruption, and decay, which follows that of maturity, presents an aspect more dazzling and commanding, and to those who look only at the surface inspires greater confidence and respect, than the season of youthful health, of growing but unripened strength. The power of the Persians was most truly formidable when they first issued from their comparatively narrow territory to overspread Asia with their arms. But at what epoch in their history does the Great King appear invested with such majesty, as when he dictated the peace of Antaleidas to the Greeks! And yet at this very time the throne on which he sate with so lofty a port, was so insecurely based, that a slight shock would have been sufficient, as was soon proved, to level it with the dust.

It was nearly at the same juncture that Sparta seemed to have attained the summit of her power: her old enemy had been reduced to insignificance: her two most formidable rivals converted into useful dependants: her refractory allies chastised and cowed: in no quarter of the political horizon, neither in nor out of Greece, did it seem possible for the keenest eye to discover any prognostics of danger: her empire, says the contemporary historian, appeared in every respect to have been now established on a glorious and solid base. Yet in a few years the Spartan women saw for the first time the smoke of the flames with which a hostile army ravaged their country in the immediate neighbourhood of the capital: and a Spartan embassy implored the pity of the Athenians, and pleaded the magnanimity with which Sparta in her day of victory had preserved Athens from annihilation, as a motive for the exercise of similar generosity toward a fallen enemy. The historian sees in this reverse the judgement of the gods against treachery and impiety. But when we inquire about the steps by which the change was effected, we find that the mistress of Greece had lost—nearly a thousand of her subjects, and about four hundred of her citizens, at the battle of Leuctra.

It would be impertinent to accumulate illustrations which will present themselves uncalled to every reader's mind: we might otherwise find some amusement in comparing the history of great cities with that of their respective states, and in observing how often the splendour of the one has increased in proportion to the weakness and rottenness of the other. The ages of conquest and of glory had past, before Rome began to exhibit a marble front; and the old consuls who in the wars of a century scarcely quelled the Samnite hydra, and who brought army after army into the field to be destroyed by Hannibal, would have gazed with wonder on the magnificence in the midst of which the master of the empire, in anguish and dismay, called upon Varus to restore his three legions. Yet Rome under Augustus was probably less gorgeous than Byzantium under Constantine, whose city was no unapt image of the ill which Dante deplored, as the consequence, though not the effect, of his conversion.[1] But instead of dwelling on the numerous contrasts of this kind which history suggests in illustrating the fragile and transitory nature of all mortal greatness, we shall draw nearer to our main point, and shall at the same time be taking a more cheering view of our subject, if we observe, that, as all things human are subject to dissolution, so and for the same reason it is the moment of their destruction that to the best and noblest of them is the beginning of a higher being, the dawn of a brighter period of action. When we reflect on the colossal monarchies that have succeeded one another on the face of the earth, we readily acknowledge that they fulfilled the best purpose of their proud existence, when they were broken up in order that their fragments might serve as materials for new structures. We confess with a sigh that the wonders of Egypt were not a mere waste of human labour, if the sight of them inspired the genius of the Greeks. But we should have been more reluctant to admit that this nation itself, which stands so solitary and unapproachable in its peculiar excellence, attained its highest glory, when, by the loss of its freedom and its power, it was enabled to diffuse a small portion of its spirit through the Roman world: had it not been that it was the destiny of this Roman world to crumble into dust, and to be trampled by hordes of barbarians, strangers to arts and letters. Yet we can believe this, and things much more wonderful, when we contemplate that new order of things, which followed what seemed so frightful a darkness, and such irretrievable ruin.

We must add one other general remark before we proceed to apply the preceding. There is always a slight cast of irony in the grave, calm, respectful attention impartially bestowed by an intelligent judge on two contending parties, who are pleading their causes before him with all the earnestness of deep conviction, and of excited feeling. What makes the contrast interesting is, that the right and the truth lie on neither side exclusively: that there is no fraudulent purpose, no gross imbecility of intellect, on either: but both have plausible claims and specious reasons to allege, though each is too much blinded by prejudice or passion to do justice to the views of his adversary. For here the irony lies not in the demeanor of the judge, but is deeply seated in the case itself, which seems to favour each of the litigants, but really eludes them both. And this too it is that lends the highest degree of interest to the

---

[1] Inf. xix. Ahi, Constantin, di quanto mal fu matre, Non la tua conversion, ma quella dote Che da te prese il primo ricco patre.

conflicts of religious and political parties. For when we believe that no principle, no sentiment, is involved in the contest, but that each of the rival factions is equally selfish, and equally insincere, we must look on with indifference or disgust, unless some other interests are likely to be affected by the issue. Our attention is indeed more anxiously fixed on a struggle in which right and wrong, truth and falsehood, virtue and vice, are manifestly arrayed in deliberate opposition against each other. But still this case, if it ever occurs, is not that on which the mind dwells with the most intense anxiety. For it seems to carry its own final decision in itself. But the liveliest interest arises when by inevitable circumstances, characters, motives, and principles are brought into hostile collision, in which good and evil are so inextricably blended on each side, that we are compelled to give an equal share of our sympathy to each, while we perceive that no earthly power can reconcile them; that the strife must last until it is extinguished with at least one of the parties, and yet that this cannot happen without the sacrifice of something which we should wish to preserve. Such spectacles often occur in human affairs, and agitate the bystanders with painful perplexity. But a review of history tends to allay this uneasiness, by affording us on many such occasions, a glimpse of the balance held by an invisible hand, which so nicely adjusts the claims of the antagonists, that neither is wholly triumphant, nor absolutely defeated; each perhaps loses the object he aimed at, but in exchange gains something far beyond his hopes.

The dramatic poet is the creator of a little world, in which he rules with absolute sway, and may shape the destinies of the imaginary beings to whom he gives life and breath according to any plan that he may choose. Since however they are men whose actions he represents, and since it is human sympathy that he claims, he will, if he understands his art, makes his administration conform to the laws by which he conceives the course of mortal life to be really governed. Nothing that rouses the feelings in the history of mankind is foreign to his scene, but as he is confined by artificial limits, he must hasten the march of events, and compress within a narrow compass what is commonly found diffused over a large space, so that a faithful image of human existence may be concentrated in his mimic sphere. From this sphere however he himself stands aloof. The eye with which he views his microcosm, and the creatures who move in it, will not be one of human friendship, nor of brotherly kindness, nor of parental love; it will be that with which he imagines that the invisible power who orders the destiny of man might regard the world and its doings. The essential character therefore of all dramatic poetry must depend on the poet's religious or philosophical sentiments, on the light in which he contemplates history and life, on the belief he entertains as to the unseen hand that regulates their events.

If any of these remarks should appear questionable as a general proposition, we may at least safely assume their truth as beyond doubt, when they are applied to Sophocles. Not even the most superficial reader of his works can fail to observe, that they are all imprest with a deep religious character, that he takes every opportunity of directing the attention of his audience to an overruling Power, and appears to consider his own most important function to be that of interpreting its decrees. What then was the religion of Sophocles? what was his conception of this Power whom he himself represents in conducting the affairs of his ideal world? On the answer we give to this question must evidently depend our apprehension of the poet's main design, and our enjoyment of the art he has exerted in its execution. Unquestionably the religion of Sophocles was not the religion of Homer, and the light in which he viewed destiny and providence was not that in which they are exhibited by the Homeric poems. In the interval which separated the maturity of epic and dramatic poetry, the human mind had taken some great strides: and men of a vigorous and cultivated intellect could no longer acquiesce in the simple theology of the Homeric age. The dogma which to the hearers of the old bard seemed perhaps the best solution that could be found for their moral difficulties, that the father of gods and men was, like the humblest of his children, subject to the sway of an irresistible fate, against which he often might murmur in vain: this dogma was supprest or kept in the back ground, and on the other hand the paramount supremacy of Jupiter was brought prominently forward.[2] The popular mythology indeed still claimed unabated reverence, even from the most enlightened Greeks. But the quarrels of the gods, which had afforded so much entertainment to their simplehearted forefathers, were hushed on the tragic scene: and a unity of will was tacitly supposed to exist among the members of the Olympian family, which would have deprived Homer of his best machinery. The tendency of these changes was to transfer the functions of Destiny to Jupiter, and to represent all events as issuing from his will, and the good and evil that falls to the lot of mortals as dispensed by his hand. It is evident that, so far as this notion prevailed, the character of destiny was materially altered. It could no longer be considered as a mere brute force, a blind necessity working without consciousness of its means or its ends. The power indeed still remained, and was still

---

[2] See Antigon. 600. τεὰν, Ζεῦ, δύνασιν τίς ἀνδρῶν ὑπερβασία κατάσχοι, τὰν οὔθ᾽ ὕπνος αἱρεῖ ποθ᾽ ὁ παντογήρως κ. τ. λ. Oed. C. 1035. ἰὼ παντάρχε θεῶν, παντόπτα Ζεῦ. El. 174. μέγας ἐν οὐρανῷ Ζεύς, ὃς ἐφορᾷ πάντα καὶ κρατύνει. Oed. T. 897. ἀλλ᾽ ὦ κρατύνων, εἴπερ ὄρθ᾽ ἀκούεις, Ζεῦ πάντ᾽ ἀνάσσων. The thought is still more forcibly expressed in Philoct. 979. Ζεὺς ἔσθ᾽, ἵν᾽ εἰδῇς, Ζεὺς ὁ τῆσδε γῆς κρατῶν, Ζεύς, ᾧ δέδοκται ταῦθ᾽.

mysterious in its nature, inevitable and irresistible in its operation; but it was now conceived to be under the direction of a sovereign mind, acting according to the rules of unerring justice. This being the case, though its proceedings might often be inscrutable to man, they would never be accidental or capricious.

How far these ideas had acquired clearness and consistency in the mind of Sophocles, it is impossible precisely and certainly to determine. But it seems indisputable that indications of them appear in his works, and it is interesting to observe the traces of their influence on his poetry. It has indeed been often supposed that some of his greatest masterpieces were founded on a totally different view of the subject from that just described: on the supposition that mankind were either subject to an iron destiny, which without design or forethought steadily pursued its immutable track, insensible of the victims which in its progress it crushed beneath its car: or else that they were at the mercy of reckless and wayward deities, who sported with their happiness, and sometimes destroyed it merely to display their power. We do not deny that the former at least of these suppositions may be adapted to the purposes of dramatic poetry, and that the contrast between man with his hopes, fears, wishes, and undertakings, and a dark, inflexible fate, affords abundant room for the exhibition of tragic irony; but we conceive that this is not the loftiest kind, and that Sophocles really aimed at something higher. To investigate this subject thoroughly, so as to point out the various shades and gradations of irony in his tragedies, would require much more than the space which can here be devoted to it. We shall content ourselves with selecting some features in his compositions which appear most strikingly to illustrate the foregoing remarks. One observation however must be premised, without which the works of Sophocles can scarcely be viewed in a proper light. That absolute power which we have attributed to the dramatic poet over his creatures, may be limited by circumstances: and in the Greek theatre it was in fact restricted by peculiar causes. None but gods or heroes could act any prominent part in the Attic tragedy; and as the principal persons were all celebrated in the national poetry, their deeds and sufferings were in general familiar to the audience. The poet indeed enjoyed full liberty of choice among the manifold forms which almost every tradition assumed: and he was allowed to introduce considerable variations in subordinate points. But still he was confined within a definite range of subjects, and even in that he could not expatiate with uncontrolled freedom. Now the legends from which his scenes were to be drawn, were the fictions, at least the tales, of a simple but rude age: the characters of his principal persons were such as had struck the vigorous but unrefined imagination of a race who were still children of nature: their actions were such as exhibited the qualities most esteemed in the infancy of society; and their fate corresponded to the view then entertained of the manner in which the affairs of the world are directed by natural or supernatural agency. While the poet's materials were thus prescribed for him, it was scarcely possible that he should infuse his spirit equally into all, and so mould and organize them, as never to betray the coarseness of their original texture. Duly to estimate the art of Sophocles, and rightly to understand his designs, we must take into account the resistance of the elements which he had to transform and fashion to his purposes. When we consider their nature we shall not perhaps be surprized to find that he sometimes contents himself with slight indications of his meaning, and that everything does not appear exactly to harmonize with it. We shall rather admire the unity that pervades works framed out of such a chaos, and the genius which could stamp the ancient legends with a character so foreign to their original import.

The irony in which Sophocles appears to us to have displayed the highest powers of his art, is not equally conspicuous in all his remaining plays, though we believe the perception of it to be indispensable for the full enjoyment of every one of them. We shall for this reason be led to dwell less upon some of his greatest masterpieces, than upon works which are commonly deemed of inferior value. But we shall begin with those in which the poet's intention is most apparent, and shall thus perhaps be enabled to find a clue to it where it is less clearly disclosed. We are thus led in the first place to consider two of those founded on the Theban legends.

Though it is not certain whether *Oedipus King* and *Oedipus at Colonus* were parts of one original design, it is at least probable that the contrast by which the effect of each is so much heightened entered into the poet's plan. Each indeed is complete in itself, and contains every thing requisite for the full understanding and enjoyment of it; and yet each acquires a new force and beauty from a comparison with the other. We shall therefore consider them successively.

The opening scene of the first Oedipus exhibits the people of Cadmus bowed down under the weight of a terrible calamity. A devouring pestilence is ravaging its fields, and desolating its city. The art of man has hitherto availed nothing to check its progress: the aid of the gods has been implored in vain. The altars have blazed, and the temples reeked with incense: yet the victims of the Destroying Power continue to fall on every side, frequent as ever. The streets are constantly resounding with the paean: but its strains are still interrupted by the voice of wailing. In this extremity of affliction however a gleam of hope shoots from one quarter through the general gloom. The royal house has been hitherto exempt from the overwhelming evil. The king, happy in the affection of his consort, and surrounded by a flourishing family, seems alone to stand erect above the flood of evils with which his people are struggling, and under which they are ready to sink. To his fortune and wisdom the afflicted city now looks for deliverance. It has not been forgotten that, on a former occasion, when Thebes was smitten with a scourge almost equally grievous, the marvellous sagacity of Oedipus solved the enigma on which its fate depended. There is therefore good ground for hoping that his tried prudence, aided by the favour of the gods, may once more succeed in penetrating to the mysterious cause of the present calamity, and may contrive means of relief. With this belief a throng of suppliants of all ages, headed by the ministers of the temples, has come in solemn procession to the royal palace, and has seated itself on the steps of the altars before its vestibule, bearing the sacred ensigns with which the miserable are wont to implore succour from the powerful. Informed of their approach, the king himself comes forth to hear their complaints, and receive their requests. His generous nature is touched by the piteous spectacle, and though himself unhurt, he feels for the stroke under which his people suffers. The public distress has long been the object of his paternal cares: already he has taken measures for relieving it: he has sent a messenger to the oracle which had guided his steps in other momentous junctures by its timely warnings, and had brought him to his present state of greatness and glory: the answer of the Delphic god is hourly expected, without which even the wisdom of Oedipus himself can devise no remedy.

At the moment the envoy arrives with joyful tidings. Apollo has revealed to him the cause of the evil and the means of removing it. The land labours under a curse drawn upon it by the guilt of man: it is the stain of blood that has poisoned all the sources of life; the crime must be expiated, the pollution purged. Yet the oracle which declares the nature of the deed is silent as to the name of the criminal; he is denounced as the object of divine and human vengeance; but his person is not described, his abode is not disclosed, except by the intimation that the land is cursed by his presence. The sagacity of Oedipus is still required to detect the secret on which the safety of his people depends; and he confidently undertakes to bring it to light. The suppliant multitude, their worst fears quieted, better hopes revived, withdraw in calm reliance on the king and the god; and the Chorus appearing at the summons of Oedipus, cheered yet perplexed by the mysterious oracle, partially soothed by its promises, but still trembling with timid suspense, pours forth a plaintive strain, in which it describes the horrors of its present condition, and implores the succour of its tutelary deities.

During this pause the spectator has leisure to reflect, how different all is from what it seems. The wrath of heaven has been pointed against the afflicted city, only that it might fall with concentrated force on the head of a single man; and he who is its object stands alone calm and secure: unconscious of his own misery he can afford pity for the unfortunate: to him all look up for succour: and, as in the plenitude of wisdom and power, he undertakes to trace the evil, of which he is himself the sole author, to its secret source.

In the meanwhile the king has deliberated with his kinsman Creon, and now appears to proclaim his will and publish his measures. To the criminal, if he shall voluntarily discover himself, he offers leave to retire from the country with impunity: to whoever shall make him known, whether citizen or stranger, large reward and royal favour: but should this gracious invitation prove ineffectual, then he threatens the guilty with the utmost rigour of justice; and finally, should man's arm be too short, he consigns the offender by a solemn imprecation to the vengeance of the gods. The same curse he denounces against himself, if he knowingly harbours the man of blood under his roof, and a like one against all who refuse to aid him in his search. The Chorus, after protesting its innocence, offers advice. Next to Apollo the blind seer Tiresias is reputed to possess the largest share of supernatural knowledge. From him the truth which the oracle has withheld may be best ascertained. But Oedipus has anticipated this prudent counsel, and on Creon's suggestion has already sent for Tiresias, and is surprized that he has not yet arrived. At length the venerable man appears. His orbs of outward sight have long been quenched: but so much the clearer and stronger is the light which shines inward, and enables him to discern the hidden things of heaven and earth. The king conjures him to exert his prophetic power for the deliverance of his country and its ruler. But instead of a ready compliance, the request is received with expressions of grief and despondency: it is first evaded, and at length peremptorily refused. The indignation of Oedipus is roused by the unfeeling denial, and at length he is provoked to declare his suspicion that Tiresias has been himself, so far as his blindness permitted, an accessary to the regicide. The charge kindles in its turn the anger of the seer, and extorts from him the dreadful secret which he had resolved to suppress. He bids his accuser obey his own recent proclamation, and thenceforward as the perpetrator of the deed which had polluted the land, to seal his unhallowed lips. Enraged at the audacious recrimination, Oedipus taunts Tiresias with his blindness: a darkness, not of the eyes only, but of the mind; he is a child of night, whose puny malice can do no hurt to one whose eyes are open to the light of day. Yet who can have prompted the

old man to the impudent calumny? Who but the counsellor at whose suggestion he had been consulted? The man who, when Oedipus and his
children are removed, stands nearest to the throne? It is a conspiracy—a
plot laid by Creon, and hatched by Tiresias. The suspicion once admitted
becomes a settled conviction, and the king deplores the condition of
royalty, which he finds thus exposed to the assaults of envy and ambition. But his resentment, vehement as it is, at Creon's ingratitude, is
almost forgotten in his abhorrence and contempt of the hoary impostor
who has sold himself to the traitor. Even his boasted art is a juggle and a
lie. Else, why was it not exerted when the Sphinx propounded her fatal
riddle? The seer then was not Tiresias but Oedipus. The lips then closed
by the consciousness of ignorance have now been opened by the love of
gold. His age alone screens him from immediate punishment: the partner
of his guilt will not escape so easily. Tiresias answers by repeating his
declaration in still plainer terms; but as at the king's indignant command
he is about to retire, he drops an allusion to his birth, which reminds
Oedipus of a secret which he has not yet unriddled. Instead however of
satisfying his curiosity, the prophet once again, in language still more
distinct than before, describes his present condition and predicts his fate.

   This scene completes the exposition that was begun in the preceding one. The contrast between the real blindness and wretchedness of
Oedipus and his fancied wisdom and greatness can be carried no further,
than when he contemptuously rejects the truth which he is seeking and
has found, and makes it a ground of quarrel with a faithful friend. The
Chorus, in its next song, only interprets the irony of the action, when it
asks, who is the guilty wretch against whom the oracle has let loose the
ministers of vengeance? Where can be his lurkingplace? It must surely
be in some savage forest, in some dark cave, or rocky glen, among the
haunts of wild beasts, that the miserable fugitive hides himself from his
pursuers. Who can believe that he is dwelling in the heart of the city, in
the royal palace! that he is seated on the throne!

   It does not belong to our present purpose to dwell on the following scenes, in which the fearful mystery is gradually unfolded. The art
with which the poet has contrived to sustain the interest of the spectator,
by retarding the discovery, has been always deservedly admired. It has
indeed been too often considered as the great excellence of this sublime
poem, the real beauty of which, as we hope to shew, is of a very different kind, and infinitely more profound and heartstirring than mere
ingenuity can produce. But the attentive reader who shall examine this
part of the play from the point of view that has been here taken, will not
fail to observe, among numberless finer touches of irony with which the
dialogue is inlaid, that the poet has so constructed his plot, as always to

evolve the successive steps of the disclosure out of incidents which either exhibit the delusive security of Oedipus in the strongest light, or tend to cherish his confidence, and allay his fears. Thus the scene with Jocasta in which his apprehensions are first awakened, arises out of the suspicion he has conceived of Creon, which, unjust and arbitrary as it is, is the only refuge he has been able to find from the necessity of believing Tiresias. The tidings from Corinth, by which he and Jocasta are so elated as to question the prescience of the gods, leads to the discovery which fixes her doom. Still more remarkable is the mode in which this is connected with the following and final stage of the solution. Oedipus has reason to dread that the arrival of the herdsman may confirm his worst fears as to the death of Laius. Yet he forgets this as a slight care in his impatience to ascertain his parentage: hence the Chorus bursts out into a strain of joy at the prospect of the festive rites with which Cithaeron—a spot to be henceforth so dear to the royal family—will be honoured, when the happy discovery shall be made: and Oedipus presses the herdsman on this subject with sanguine eagerness, which will bear no evasion or delay, and never ceases to hope for the best, until he has extorted the truth which shews him the whole extent of his calamity.

No sooner has the film dropped from his eyes than he condemns himself to perpetual darkness, to the state which, but a short time before, had been the subject of his taunts on Tiresias. The feeling by which he is urged thus to verify the seer's prediction, is not the horror of the light and of all the objects it can present to him, but indignation at his own previous blindness. The eyes which have served him so ill, which have seen without discerning what it was most important for him to know, shall be for ever extinguished.[3] And in this condition, most wretched, most helpless, he enters once more, to exhibit a perfect contrast to his appearance in the opening scene, and thus to reverse that irony, of which we have hitherto seen but one side. While he saw the light of day, he had been ignorant, infatuated, incapable of distinguishing truth from falsehood, friend from foe. Now he clearly perceives all that concerns him; he is conscious of the difference between his own shrewdness and the divine intelligence: he is cured of his rash presumption, of his hasty suspicions, of his doubts and cares: he has now a sure test of Creon's sincerity, and he finds that it will stand the trial. Creon's moderation, discretion, and equanimity, are beautifully contrasted in this scene, as in that of the altercation, with the vehement passion of Oedipus. The

---

[3] Hermann's correction and interpretation of the passage here alluded to, v. 1271-1274, seem indispensably necessary, and restore one of the most beautiful touches in the play.

mutual relation of the two characters so exactly resembles that between Tasso and Antonio in Goethe's *Tasso*, that the German play may serve as a commentary on this part of the Greek one. And here it may be proper to remark that Sophocles has rendered sufficiently clear for an attentive reader, what has nevertheless been too commonly overlooked, and has greatly disturbed many in the enjoyment of this play: that Oedipus, though unfortunate enough to excite our sympathy, is not so perfectly innocent as to appear the victim of a cruel and malignant power. The particular acts indeed which constitute his calamity were involuntarily committed: and hence in the sequel he can vindicate himself from the attack of Creon, and represent himself to the villagers of Colonus as a man more sinned against than sinning.[4] But still it is no less evident that all the events of his life have arisen out of his headstrong, impetuous character, and could not have happened if he had not neglected the warning of the god. His blindness, both the inward and the outward, has been self-inflicted! Now, as soon as the first paroxysm of grief has subsided, he appears chastened, sobered, humbled: the first and most painful step to true knowledge and inward peace, has been taken; and he already feels an assurance, that he is henceforward an especial object of divine protection, which will shield him from all ordinary ills and dangers.

Here, where the main theme of the poet's irony is the contrast between the appearance of good and the reality of evil, these intimations of the opposite contrast are sufficient. But in *Oedipus at Colonus* this new aspect of the subject becomes the groundwork of the play. It is not indeed so strikingly exhibited as the former, because the fate of Oedipus is not the sole, nor even the principal object of attention, but is subordinate to another half political, half religious interest, arising out of the legends which connect it with the ancient glories and future prospects of Attica, and with the sanctuary of Colonus. Still the same conception which is partially unfolded in the first play is here steadily pursued, and, so far as the Theban hero is concerned, is the ruling idea. In the first scene the appearance of Oedipus presents a complete reverse of that which we witnessed at the opening of the preceding play. We now see him stript of all that then seemed to render his lot so enviable, and suffering the worst miseries to which human nature is liable. He is blind, old, destitute: an outcast from his home, an exile from his country, a wanderer in a foreign land: reduced to depend on the guidance and support of his daughter, who herself needs protection, and to subsist on the scanty pittance afforded him by the compassion of strangers, who, when-

---

[4] 266. τά γ᾽ ἔργα μου Πεπονθότ᾽ ἐστὶ μᾶλλον ἤ δεδρακότα.

ever they recognize him, view him with horror. But a change has likewise taken place within him, which compensates even for this load of affliction. In the school of adversity he has learnt patience, resignation, and content. The storm of passion has subsided, and has left him calm and firm. The cloud has rolled away from his mental vision, and nothing disturbs the clearness and serenity of his views. He not only contemplates the past in the light of truth, but feels himself instinct with prophetic powers. He is conscious of a charmed life, safe from the malice of man and the accidents of nature, and reserved by the gods for the accomplishment of high purposes. The first incident that occurs to him marks in the most signal manner the elevation to which he has been raised by his apparent fall, and the privilege he has gained by the calamity which separates him from the rest of mankind. He has been driven out of Thebes as a wretch polluted, and polluting the land. Yet he finds a resting place in the sanctuary of the awful goddesses, the avengers of crime, whose unutterable name fills every heart with horror, whose ground is too holy for any human foot to tread. For him there is no terror in the thought of them: he shrinks not from their presence, but greets them as friends and ministers of blessing. He is, as he describes himself, not only a pious but a sacred person.[5] But the arrival of Ismene exhibits him in a still more august character. Feeble and helpless as he appears, he is destined to be one of Attica's tutelary heroes: and two powerful states are to dispute with one another the possession of his person and the right of paying honours to his tomb. The poet on this occasion expresses the whole force of the contrast, which is the subject of the play, in a few emphatic lines. Oed. *How speaks the oracle, my child?* Ism. *Thou shalt be sought by them that banished thee, Living and dead, to aid the common weal.* Oed. *Why, who may prosper with such aid as mine?* Ism. *On thee 'tis said, the might of Thebes depends.* Oed. *Now, when all's lost, I am a man indeed.* Ism. *The gods now raise the head they once laid low.*[6] In the following scenes the most prominent object is undoubtedly the glory of Attica and of Theseus. The contest indeed between the two rivals for the possession or the friendship of the outcast, the violence of Creon and the earnest supplication of Polynices, serves to heighten our impression of the dignity with which Oedipus is now invested by the favour of the gods. But still, if the poet had not had a different purpose in view, he would probably have contented himself

---

[5] 287. ἥκω γὰρ ἱερὸς εὐσεβής τε.

[6] 388. Οιδ. τί δὲ τεθέσπισται τέκνον; Ισμ. Σὲ τοῖς ἐκεῖ ζητητὸν ἀνθρώποις ποτὲ Θανόντ᾿ ἔσεσθαι ζῶντά τ᾿ εὐσοίας χάριν. Οιδ. Τίς δ᾿ ἄν τι τοιοῦδ᾿ ἀνδρὸς εὖ πράξειεν ἄν; Ισμ. Ἐν σοὶ τὰ κείνων φασὶ γίγνεσθαι κράτη. Οιδ. Ὅτ᾿ οὐκ ἔτ᾿ εἰμί, τηνικαῦτ᾿ ἄρ᾿ εἰμ᾿ ἀνήρ. Ισμ. Νῦν γὰρ θεοί σ᾿ ὀρθοῦσι, πρόσθε δ᾿ ὤλλυσαν.

with a less elaborate picture of the struggle. As it is, Creon's arrogance and meanness place the magnanimity of the Attic hero in the strongest relief. It is not quite so evident what was the motive for introducing the interview with Polynices, which seems at first sight to have very little connexion either with the fate and character of Oedipus, or with the renown of Theseus. In this scene Oedipus appears to modern eyes in a somewhat unamiable aspect: and at all events it is one which will effectually prevent us from confounding his piety and resignation with a spirit of Christian meekness and charity. But to the ears of the ancients there was probably nothing grating in this vindictive sternness, while it contributes a very important service to the poet's main design. That the resolution of Oedipus should not be shaken by the solicitations of Creon, backed by threats and force, was to be expected; we now see that his anger is not to be softened by the appeal which Polynices makes to his pity and his parental affection. He is for ever alienated from his unnatural sons and from Thebes, and unalterably devoted to the generous strangers who have sheltered him. Their land shall retain him a willing sojourner, and in his tomb they shall possess a pledge of victory and of deliverance in danger. Nothing now remains but that he should descend into his last resting place, honoured by the express summons of the gods, and yielding a joyful obedience to their pleasure. His orphan daughters indeed drop some natural tears over the loss they have sustained: but even their grief is soon soothed by the thought of an end so peaceful and happy in itself, and so full of blessing to the hospitable land where the hero reposes.

We have already remarked that the irony we have been illustrating is not equally conspicuous in all the plays of Sophocles. In the two Oedipuses we conceive it is the main feature in the treatment of the subject, and is both clearly indicated by their structure, and unequivocally exprest in numberless passages. On the other hand, in the *Electra* it may appear doubtful whether anything is gained by considering the plot from this point of view, and whether we are justified in attributing it to Sophocles. The poet's object may seem to have been merely to exhibit the heroine in a series of situations, which successively call forth the fortitude, the energy, the unconquerable will, and the feminine tenderness, which compose her character. This object however may not be inconsistent with others: and the arrangement of the action seems to point to an ulterior design; which we shall very briefly suggest, as there are no marks which absolutely compel the reader to recognize it. The lamentations of Electra at her first appearance are protracted to a length which can scarcely be considered necessary for the purpose of an exposition of her character and situation, and we are therefore rather led to connect them with the scene which precedes them: and so regarded they certainly assume an ironical aspect. In the former our attention was directed to the bloodstained house of the Pelopids, the scene of so many crimes, where guilt has been so long triumphant, where all is still hushed in secure unsuspecting repose. But already the Avenger is standing near its threshold, ready to execute his errand of retributive justice, his success ensured by all the aids of human prudence, and by the sanction of the god. The friends concert their plan in a manner which leaves no doubt in the mind of the spectator that the righteous cause will speedily prevail. After this Electra's inconsolable grief, her despondency, and complaints, are less suited to excite our sympathy, than to suggest a reflexion on the contrast between that apparent prosperity and security of the guilty which she in her ignorance deplores, and the imminent danger with which we see them threatened by the divine vengeance. And this contrast becomes still stronger when, by the device of Orestes, the last fear which restrained the insolence of the criminals is removed, the last hope which cheered Electra's drooping spirit is extinguished; at the same time that the punishment of the one, and the deliverance of the other, are on the point of accomplishment.[7] Clytemnestra's sophistical vindication of her own conduct also assumes a tone of self mockery, which is deeply tragical, when we remember that, while she is pleading, her doom is sealed, and that the hand which is about to execute it is already lifted above her head. Finally, it is in the moment of their highest exultation and confidence, that each of the offenders discovers the inevitable certainty of their impending ruin.[8]

Of all our poet's remaining works, that which stands lowest in general estimation appears to be *The Trachinian Virgins*. Its merit has been commonly supposed to consist in the beauty of detached scenes or passages: but so inferior has it been thought, as a whole, to the other plays of Sophocles, that a celebrated critic has not scrupled to express a doubt as to its genuineness, and to conjecture that it ought to be ascribed to the poet's son Iophon. This conjecture Hermann (Præf.) rejects with

---

[7] This scene affords a very happy illustration of the difference between practical and verbal irony. The poet makes Clytemnestra use what she conceives to be language of bitter irony, while she is really uttering simple truth: 795. El. ὕβριζε. νῦν γὰρ εὐτυχοῦσα τυγχάνεις. Cl. οὔκουν 'Ορέστης καὶ σὺ παύσετον τάδε; El. πεπαύμεθ' ἡμεῖς, οὐχ ὅπως σε παύσομεν. According to the punctuation and accentuation adopted by Brunck and Hermann, in l. 796, Clytemnestra only taunts Electra without any irony. For the purpose of an illustration, it is not material how Sophocles meant the line to be spoken; but in spite of Triclinius we prefer either οὔκουν with an interrogation (as Aj. 79) or οὐκοῦν, without one (as Antig. 91): and of these, the former.

[8] This is the meaning of the taunt, 1481: καὶ μάντις ὢν ἄριστος ἐσφάλλου πάλαι; see Hermann's note.

great confidence, founded on his long and intimate acquaintance with the poetical character of Sophocles. It would seem however as if his opinion was formed in consideration rather of the particular features of the play, in which he recognizes the master's hand, than of the entire composition, which, according to his view of it, is defective in some very important points. The interest, he conceives, is so unfortunately divided between Hercules and Dejanira, that though the fate of the hero was intended by the poet to be the main spring of the spectator's fear and pity, his sympathy is insensibly transferred to the unhappy victim of conjugal affection, who thus becomes in reality the principal personage. Hence when her fate is decided, the spectator's suspense is at an end: the last act appears superfluous; and the sufferings of Hercules, now that the heroine is gone to whom all his vicissitudes had been referred, can no longer excite any deep concern. This defect, Hermann thinks, would have been remedied, if the hero's sufferings had been exhibited in the presence of Dejanira, so as to aggravate her affliction: and he can scarcely understand what could have led Sophocles to neglect an arrangement so clearly preferable to that which he has adopted, unless it may have been the wish to introduce a little variation in the treatment of a somewhat hacknied argument.

To Hermann's judgement on the genuineness of the piece we most cordially assent; but for this very reason we cannot embrace his opinion of its supposed imperfections, and at the risk of being thought superstitious admirers of a great name, we are inclined to infer from his objections to the composition, not that Sophocles was on this occasion either deficient in invention, or willing to sacrifice beauty to the affectation of originality—a species of vanity which his other works afford no ground for imputing to him: but that his design was not exactly such as the critic conceives. It appears to us that in fact Hermann has overlooked one of the most important features of the subject, which, if duly considered, satisfactorily accounts for all that according to his view disturbs the unity and symmetry of the drama. The fate of Hercules is undoubtedly the point on which the interest of the play was meant to turn. To it our attention is directed from beginning to end. Compared with Hercules, Dejanira is a very insignificant person: not indeed in the eyes of a modern reader, of whom Hermann's remark may be perfectly true, that the sympathy of the spectators is directed more to her than to the hero. In her we find much to admire, to love, and to pity: in him we see nothing but a great spirit almost overpowered by the intensity of bodily suffering. But the question is, was this the light in which they were viewed by the spectators for whom Sophocles wrote? Now it seems clear that to them Hercules was more than a suffering or struggling hero:

he was a deified person, who had assumed a blessed and immortal nature,[9] had become an object of religious adoration, and was frequently invoked for aid and protection in seasons of difficulty and danger. It was from the funeral pile on the top of Oeta that he ascended, as Sophocles elsewhere describes,[10] all radiant with fire divine, to enjoy the company of the gods above. The image of his earthly career could never be contemplated by his worshippers without reference to this, its happy and glorious termination. And therefore it cannot be contended that the poet did not take this feeling into account, because in the play itself he has introduced no allusion to the apotheosis. It does not follow because there Hercules himself, according to Hermann's observation, is described as quitting life with reluctance, like one of Homer's heroes, whose soul descends to Orcus bewailing its fate, and the vigour and youth which it leaves behind,[11] that therefore the spectators were expected to forget all their religious notions of him, or to consider him abstracted from the associations with which he was habitually connected in their thoughts. But in fact his blissful immortality is manifestly implied in that consummation of his labours, that final release from toil and hardship, which was announced to him by the oracle, the meaning of which he did not understand till he was experiencing its fulfilment. This mysterious prediction it is, which at the beginning of the play calls up Dejanira's hopes and fears into conflict, and the marvellous mode of its accomplishment is the subject of the ensuing scenes.

The opening scene, which, though less artificial than those of the other plays of Sophocles, ought not to be confounded with the prologues of Euripides, while it unfolds to us the anxiety and gloomy forebodings of Dejanira, places her character in the point of view which is necessary to the unity of the piece. Her happiness, her very being, are bound up in that of Hercules. The most fortunate event of her life had once seemed to her the issue of the struggle by which Hercules won for his bride. Now indeed, on looking back to the past, she is struck with the melancholy reflexion, that this union, the object of her most ardent wishes, had hitherto been productive of scarcely anything but disappointment and vexation. The hero, for whom alone she lived, had been almost perpetually separated from her by a series of hazardous adventures, which

---

[9] Od. Λ. 602, αὐτὸς δὲ μετ' ἀθανάτοισι θεοῖσιν Τέρπεται ἐν θαλίῃς, καὶ ἔχει καλλίσφυρον Ἥβην.

[10] Phil. 726. ἵν' ὁ χάλκασπις ἀνὴρ θεοῖς πλάθει πᾶσιν, θείῳ πυρὶ παμφαής, Οἴτας ὑπὲρ ὄχθων.

[11] 1262. ὡς ἐπίχαρτον τελέουσ' ἀεκούσιον ἔργον. "Quamvis enim fortis anima, tamen invita ad Orcum abit, ὃν πότμον γοόωσα, λιποῦσ' ἀδρότητα καὶ ἥβην." Herm.

kept her a prey to constant alarm and disquietude. Short and rare as his visits had always been, the interval which had elapsed since the last had been unusually long; she had been kept in more than ordinary ignorance of his situation: she begins to dread the worst, and is inclined to interpret the ambiguous tablet, which he left in her hands at parting, in the most unfavorable manner. The information she receives from her son, while it relieves her most painful fears, convinces her that the momentous crisis has arrived, which will either secure, or for ever destroy her happiness with that of her hero. A last labour remains for him to achieve, in which he is destined either to fall, or to reap the reward of his toils in a life unembittered by pain or sorrow. Soon however she hears that the crisis has ended happily, and for a moment joy takes undivided possession of her breast. But the glad tidings are quickly followed by the announcement of a new calamity, the danger of losing the affections of Hercules, or of sharing them with another. He has reached the goal: but by the same turn of fortune she is removed farther than ever from the object of her desires: the same gale which has wafted him into the haven of rest, has wellnigh wrecked her hopes. Still even against this evil she has long had a remedy in store, which, if it succeeds, will unite her lot to that of Hercules by indissoluble bonds: no woman shall again dispute his love with her. But now the irony of fate displays itself in the cruellest manner: all her wishes shall be granted, but only to verify her worst fears. The labours of Hercules are at an end: she herself has disabled him from ever undertaking another. No rival will henceforward divert his love from her: his eyes will soon be closed upon all earthly forms. But all this is but a bitter mockery: in truth she has made him in whose wellbeing her own was wrapt up, supremely wretched; she has converted his affection for herself into deadly hatred. She, who was able to ruin him, has no means of saving him: the only proof she can give of her fidelity and love is, to die.

That the death of Dejainira is indispensably necessary, every one will acknowledge; but those who think, as Hermann, that with it the play really ends, will perhaps agree with him in his opinion, that it ought to have been reserved to a later period in the action. According to the view we have here taken of the poet's design, he could not have chosen a more seasonable time for it. Had it been longer postponed, it would merely have disturbed the effect of the last scene without any compensating advantage. This scene, if we are not mistaken, is so far from a superfluous and cumbrous appendage, that it contains the solution of the whole enigma, and places all that goes before in its true light. Hercules appears distracted not only by his bodily torments, but also by furious passions: by the sense of an unmerited evil, perfidiously inflicted by a

hand which he had loved and trusted. The discovery of Dejanira's
innocence likewise reveals to him the real nature and causes of his situation: it exhibits his fate, though outwardly hard and terrible, as the fulfilment of a gracious and cheering prediction. Henceforth his murmurs
cease, his angry passions subside. He himself indeed does not yet penetrate into the depth of the mystery; but when, as by a prophetic impulse,
he directed Hyllus to transport him to the summit of Oeta, and there,
without tear or groan, to apply the torch to his funeral pile, he leads the
spectators to the reflexion which solves all difficulties, and melts all dis-
cords into the clearest harmony. Dejanira's wishes have been fulfilled,
not indeed in her own sense, but in an infinitely higher one. The gods
have decreed to bestow on Hercules not merely length of days, but
immortality; not merely ease and quiet, but celestial bliss. She indeed
has lost him, but only as she must have done in any case sooner or later;
and instead of forfeiting his affection, she has been enabled to put the
most unequivocal seal upon her faith and devotedness.

That this last scene should appear tedious to a modern reader, is
not surprising: but this may be owing to causes which have nothing to do
with its dramatic merits. We are accustomed to view Hercules either
through the medium of the arts, as a strong man, or through that of some
system of mythology, as a political or ethical personification, or it may
be as a mundane genius, a god of light. But it is probable that a very different impression was produced by his appearance on the Athenian stage,
and that a representation of the last incidents of his mortal state, was
there witnessed with lively sympathy. This interest may have extended to
details which in us cannot produce the slightest emotion, and hence the
introduction of the concluding injunction about Iole, which is the most
obscure as well as repulsive passage in the whole piece, may have had an
adequate motive, which we cannot fully comprehend. It certainly ought
not to prevent us from enjoying the beauty of the whole composition,
which though perhaps inferior to the other works of Sophocles, is not
unworthy of the author of the greatest among them.

In the *Ajax* the poet may seem to have made a singular exception
to his own practice as well as to that of all other great dramatic writers,
by distinctly expounding the moral of his play, and that not at the end,
but at the beginning of it. If we should suppose him to have done so, we
must also believe that he at the same time determined the point of view
from which he meant the whole to be considered. The irony of Minerva
first draws Ajax into a terrible exhibition of his miserable phrenzy, and
she then takes occasion from it to pronounce a solemn warning against
the arrogance which had involved so great a hero in so dreadful a
calamity. The following scenes down to the death of Ajax, might appear

to have been intended merely to enforce this impression, by representing the language and the effects of his despair when restored to the consciousness of his real situation. The concluding part, that which follows the main catastrophe, would according to this view have been introduced with as little necessity as the part corresponding to it in the play last examined, though it might be allowed possible to find some excuse for the addition in national opinions and feelings foreign to our own. If however this were the correct view of the tragedy, it would certainly deserve to be considered as the most faulty in its composition of all the remaining works of Sophocles. The fault would lie not merely in the want of unity between the two portions, which would be only accidentally connected with one another and would have no interest in common, but also in the dramatic anticlimax, in the gradual abatement of the terror and pity which the opening of the play so powerfully inspires. For Ajax has no sooner recovered his senses than the thought of death occurs to him as absolutely necessary. But he contemplates it, not as an evil, but as a certain remedy and refuge. He finds consolation in the consciousness of his unalterable resolution not to survive his shame, and in the conviction that no human power can prevent the execution of his purpose. The nearer his end approaches the more collected and tranquil he becomes: so that we are led to view him in a new light, and forget the awful lesson inculcated by the goddess in the opening scene.

It would perhaps be presumptuous to assert that the taste of Sophocles was too pure, to admit an episode at the end of a play such as that of *Johannes Parricida* which disfigures Schiller's *Wilhelm Tell*. But on the other hand we ought not to impute such a defect to any of his compositions, without carefully examining whether the parts which seem to hang loosely together, may not be more intimately united under the surface. On the other point we may venture to speak more confidently, and to maintain that Sophocles could never have meant to concentrate the whole moral effect of a tragedy in the first scene, so that it should be gradually softened and weakened as the action proceeded, and that a construction of any of his works which implies such a conclusion must have mistaken his design. In the present instance it seems possible to shew that the poet's thought, when rightly conceived, leads to a point of view from which nothing appears either superfluous or misplaced in the piece.

The hero's first appearance exhibits him in the lowest depth of his humiliation. The love of glory is his ruling passion, and disappointment in the pursuit of honour has goaded him to phrenzy. Through the interposition of the gods his vengeance has been baffled in a manner which must for ever expose him to the derision of his enemies. The delight and exultation which he expresses at his imaginary triumph serve to measure the greatness of his defeat, and the bitterness of the anguish which awaits him with the return of reason. Ulysses himself cannot witness so tremendous a reverse, so complete a prostration, even of a rival, without pity. But the reflexions which the spectacle suggests to him and Minerva, tend to divert our thoughts from what is peculiar and extraordinary in the situation of Ajax, and to fix them on the common lot of human nature. All mortal strength is weakness, all mortal prosperity vain and transient, and consequently all mortal pride is delusion and madness. When a man is most elated with the gifts of fortune, most confident in his security, then is his fall most certain: he is safe and strong only while he feels and acknowledges his own nothingness. Ajax in the contrast between his fancied success and his real calamity, is only a signal example of a very common blindness. The design of these reflexions was probably not to extract a moral from the scene, which needed not the aid of language to convey its lesson, but to prepare us for the contemplation of the other side of the subject, which is immediately presented to us. For in the next scene the hero's position is totally changed. The past indeed is immutable, the future affords not a glimpse of hope; but now he has awoke from his dream, he is healed of his phrenzy: he knows the worst that has befallen him, and that can befall. The discovery, it is true, is attended, as Tecmessa says, with a new pain, one from which his madness had till now protected him: but it is likewise a medicine which restores him to new health, and the pain itself a symptom of his recovery from the long disease, of which his late phrenzy had been only the last and most violent paroxysm: it gives him a treasure which he never possest before, that self-knowledge and self-control which Minerva's last words declared to be the condition and earnest of the favour of the gods.

It is possible that many readers will think this a very exaggerated, if not a totally false description of the state of mind and feeling which Ajax discloses in the progress of the play. It has been very commonly supposed that the poet's aim was to exhibit in his character untameable pride and inflexible obstinacy, hardened and strained to the utmost by despair: a spirit which will not yield even to the gods, and instead of bowing beneath the stroke of their displeasure, rises the higher by the recoil, and asserts its own freedom and dignity by a voluntary death. If this be so, the first scene must present a totally different aspect from that in which we have hitherto considered it; it will be nothing more than the occasion which enables the hero to display this unconquerable energy of soul; and the more we sympathize with his stern and lofty nature, the less can we be affected by the moral reflexions of Ulysses and the goddess, which would thus appear to be either unmeaning commonplace, or to be designed not to indicate, but to counteract the impression which the whole action is calculated to produce. This however may be looked upon as a slight objection: the main question is, whether the language and demeanor of Ajax after his recovery justifies the common view of the temper and sentiments attributed to him by the poet, and the inferences that have been drawn from them as to the general design of the play. And on this it must be observed, that though it soon becomes apparent that the purpose of self-destruction is irrevocably fixed in the mind of Ajax, though he steadily resists both the friendly counsels of the Chorus, and the pathetic intreaties of Tecmessa; and though that which determines his resolve, is his quick sense of honour, and his impatience of a degrading submission, still there is nothing in his words or conduct, either in the scenes with Tecmessa and the Chorus, or in his concluding soliloquy, that indicates a hard, cold, sullen mood. On the contrary, when he has learnt from Tecmessa the whole extent of his calamity, he breaks out for the first time of his life into wailings which express the keenness of his grief: and again the sight of the Chorus draws from him a strain of piteous exclamations on the cruelty of his fate. After this transient burst of passion indeed he recovers his firmness and composure, gives directions for the fulfilment of his last wishes with calmness, and though inflexibly adhering to his purpose, repels all the attempts made to divert him from it without heat or violence. But so far is he from having retired into the stronghold of a selfish pride, and shut himself up from all human sympathy, that in the midst of his unalterable resolution his thoughts are more occupied with care for others than with his own fate. His parental affection rushes in a full stream into his heart, as he contemplates his approaching separation from its object, and expresses itself in that tender address, in which, while he provides for the security of his child, and rejoices in the prospect of leaving behind him an heir worthy of his shield and of his fame, who shall avenge his wrongs, he dwells with delight on the image of its early years, when the young plant, sheltered from every rude blast,[12] shall enjoy its careless existence, and gladden the heart of the widowed mother, and on the consolation and support it will afford to the declining age of his own parents, so soon to be bereft of their natural stay. Throughout the whole of this speech, though two occasions occur which lead him to mention his enemies, all angry and revengeful feelings are absorbed by the softer emotions of the parent and the son:[13] and even the appearance of harsh-

---

[12] An image ludicrously disguised in Francklin's translation: "May the breath of life meantime nourish thy tender frame," as if Eurysaces could grow up to manhood unless it did.

[13] Even the lines (556) ὅταν δ᾿ ἵκῃ πρὸς τοῦτο, δεῖ σ᾿ ὅπως πατρὸς Δείξεις ἐν ἐχθροῖς, οἷος ἐξ οἵου 'τράφης, on which the Scholiast remarks, ἀντὶ τοῦ δεῖ σε

ness with which at the close of this scene he cuts short the importunity of
Tecmessa, is a sign of anything rather than coldness and insensibility.
Again, when the fatal sword is already fixed in the ground, his last
thoughts are turned to Salamis, to the grief of his father and mother,
which alone he bewails, to the beloved scenes and friends of his youth:
even the parting look which he casts on the Trojan plains, and their
familiar springs and streams, is one of tenderness: his last words an
affectionate farewell.

All this is so evident, that it must have been at least partially felt
by every intelligent reader, and it would probably have produced a
greater effect than it seems to have done on the judgements that have
been formed on the play, if a strong impression of an opposite kind had
not been made on most minds by the intermediate scene, in which, after
the Chorus has deplored the inflexible stubbornness with which Ajax has
rejected the intreaties of Tecmessa, the hero in a single speech announces
the intention with which he finally quits the camp to seek a solitary spot
on the seashore. Till within a few years all critics, from the Greek
scholiast downwards, had agreed in their general view of the object of
this speech, which they have supposed to be an artifice by which Ajax
dissembles his real feelings and purpose. They have been equally unanimous on another point, of no great importance in itself, but interesting
from its bearing on the former: they imagine that, after the scene with
the child, both Ajax and Tecmessa retire from the stage, and that the former comes out of the tent after the Chorus has ended its mournful strain.
And now, according to the common opinion, in order to pacify his
friends, and to secure himself from interruption in the deed he is about
to perform, he affects to have been softened by the prayers of Tecmessa,
and to have consented to spare his life: in signifying this change of
mind, he at the same time declares his resolution of proceeding to purify
himself from the stain of his frantic slaughter, and to make his peace, if
possible, with the offended goddess, and of paying due homage in future
to the Atridae, whom he acknowledges as his legitimate superiors. He
then dismisses Tecmessa into the tent, and leaves the Chorus to give vent
to its delight in a strain of rapturous joy. This speech, if considered as
ironical, undoubtedly indicates not merely immovable firmness of
resolution, but a spirit of haughty defiance, a bitter disdain of all
restraints, human or divine, which would prove that, if any change had
taken place in his sentiments, it was only one by which his pride had

---

ἐκδικῆσαι τὸν πατέρα, do not seem to imply any definite prospect of revenge, so much
as a hope that the glory of Eurysaces might in time silence and confound his father's
enemies.

been raised, and his ferocity hardened: and such appears to have been the inference which has been almost universally drawn from it.

But a few years back this portion of the play was placed in an entirely new light by Professor Welcker, who has made the Ajax the subject of an elaborate essay in the *Rheinisches Museum*, 1829; which, after all that has been written on this branch of literature, may be considered as one of the most valuable contributions that have yet been made to the study of the Greek drama. Beside a most learned discussion on the sources from which Sophocles drew his materials, and on the peculiar motives which guided him in the selection of them, it contains the author's reasons for rejecting the current opinion on the two points just mentioned. He conceives in the first place, that Ajax remains on the stage during the song of the Chorus which follows his dialogue with Tecmessa, inwardly absorbed in thought, and together with her and the child presenting to the spectators what they would perhaps have looked upon as a group of sculpture, and we should call a living picture. The strongest argument for this supposition is, that no sufficient motive appears or can be assigned, which should have induced Ajax to re-enter the tent, after he had bidden Tecmessa retire into it and withdraw her grief from the public eye. As little should we be able to understand why, if she had once obeyed his injunction, she should have come out again with him. On the other hand, dumb shew, exhibiting the principal person of a piece in an expressive attitude, was a contrivance by no means unusual in the Greek theatre, as is proved not only by the celebrated examples of the Niobe and the Achilles of Aeschylus, but also by the practice of Sophocles himself, who for instance allows Antigone to remain silent on the stage during a choral song of considerable length;[14] and in this very play keeps Tecmessa and the child for a long time in a studied posture near the corpse. The difficulty that may seem to arise from the Chorus in our play, which according to this hypothesis speaks of Ajax in his presence without addressing him, disappears if we imagine that the silent group occupied the back ground, which would in itself be the most natural position for it; nor is the language of the song itself such as called for any answer. But the more important question is, whether the subsequent speech of Ajax is designed to conceal his real

---

[14] Welcker therefore conceives that Creon's command (Antig. 760) is obeyed forthwith: and certainly this opinion seems to be confirmed by v. 769 τὰ δ' οὖν κόρα τάδ' οὐκ ἀπαλλάξει μόρου. But perhaps it is not necessary to imagine the sisters present, and both the last words of the Chorus, 804, and those of Antigone at the beginning of her next speech, rather indicate that she had just made her appearance. He also refers to the silence of Pylades in the Electra, and to that of Tecmessa when deceived by the speech of Ajax.

sentiments and to deceive the hearers. Welcker contends that though couched in language which is here and there ambiguous, it merely expresses the speaker's feelings, and that it is only through the eagerness with which men usually interpret all they see and hear according to their wishes, that Tecmessa and the Chorus misunderstand its meaning. He thinks that the artifice which the common construction attributes to Ajax is inconsistent, not only with the generosity but with the strength of his character, and that none of the purposes which have been supposed to explain it are sufficient to account for it; and that it involves consequences which destroy all the unity of the play, and render the poet's design unintelligible.

In order to understand the points on which this question hinges, we must observe that both Tecmessa and the Chorus are actually deceived by the speech of Ajax, and consequently that the ambiguity which deceives them was undoubtedly designed on the part of the poet. And this fact not only renders the occasion of the prevailing opinion independently of its truth very conceivable, but raises a strong prejudice in its favour, and throws the burden of the argument on those who reject it. It does not, however, necessarily follow that the deception produced by the speech was intentional on the part of the speaker; and to determine whether the poet meant it to be so considered, we must examine the speech both by itself, and in connexion with the rest of the play. The first inquiry is, whether it contains any expressions which Ajax could not have used without intending to mislead his friends. But it would not be a fair way of trying this question, to consider whether he speaks exactly as he might have done if he had not been conscious of their presence. It might be admitted that he purposely avoids the use of direct and unequivocal terms in announcing what he knew to be dreadful and afflicting to them, without granting that he wished to disguise his intentions from them. Natural and common humanity would have forbidden him to shock the feelings of persons to whom his life was so dear, by a distinct declaration of his final resolution. On the other hand, to ask why then he touches on the painful subject at all, would be unfairly to call in question the undoubted conventional privileges of the dramatic poet. Ajax must give vent to the thoughts and feelings under which he is about to act: but he may be expected to do so with a considerate reserve dictated by his situation. If after making this necessary allowance we proceed to examine his language, we shall perhaps find that though it is certainly adapted to raise hopes that he had abandoned his design of self-destruction, it implies nothing but what he may be believed really to have thought and felt. The beginning indeed speaks of a marvellous change which has taken place within him: his iron soul has been unmanned by pity for Tecmessa. This change would seem to have been wrought during the interval occupied by the song of the Chorus: for at the close of the preceding scene he had resisted all the attempts to soften him with an obstinacy which appeared to be only exasperated by her importunity. Hence most critics have imagined that Tecmessa is supposed to have renewed her intreaties within the tent, and that Ajax, instead of silencing them as before with a peremptory refusal, now affects to be overcome by them. This however is a mere conjecture, and we are equally at liberty to suppose that during the pause in which he has remained silently wrapt in thought, the workings of conjugal affection have made themselves felt so as to cost him a painful struggle, though without being able to move him from his purpose. It does not however seem necessary to consider this in the light of an abrupt and almost praeternatural inward revolution. It would be very consistent with human nature, of which Sophocles everywhere shews a fine and intimate knowledge, to interpret those replies to the supplications of Tecmessa, which sound so rough and hard, as signs of awakened sympathy, which Ajax had endeavoured to suppress by assuming a harsher tone, but which, after it ceased to be enforced from without, had gained new strength in his heart. Welcker regards the change as more sudden, though perfectly natural, as the excitement of a feeling which had hitherto slept in the hero's breast, and had at length been roused by the shock with which the gods had humbled his pride, and had finally been called into distinct action by the contagion of female tenderness. He compares it to the effect produced on the temper of Achilles by the loss of his friend. The prayers of Tecmessa are not indeed the cause, but the occasion: yet they decide the mood in which Ajax henceforth contemplates his relations to the gods and to mankind, and in which he ends his life. He considers his blood as a libation with which he is about to appease the wrath of the offended goddess, and to atone for the violence he had meditated against legitimate authority. The hearers naturally mistake the nature of this purifying bath. The mode in which he mentions his purpose of burying his sword may perhaps seem more difficult to reconcile with this view, and Welcker's remark, that the alledged motive, the calamitous operation of an enemy's gifts, was a current opinion which Ajax again expresses in his last speech, seems hardly sufficient to remove the appearance which this passage at first sight presents of a deliberate intention to mislead. Ajax designing to fall upon his sword, speaks only of hiding it as an illfated weapon in the ground. Could he, it may be asked, but for the sake of deception, have raised an image so different from the act which he was meditating. The sword might indeed be said to be concealed, when the hilt was fixed in the ground and the blade lodged in his body: but since this hiding produced the most fatal consequences instead of averting them, would he have selected this mode of describing his intended deed, if he had not foreseen that it would be misunderstood? This seems scarcely possible if it had been only the fatality of the weapon that he had in his thoughts. But perhaps it may be more easily conceived, if we suppose him to have reflected on it rather as having been once the object of his pride, a tribute of respect to his valour from a respected enemy, and afterward the instrument of his shame. He was now about to expiate his pride, and to wipe off his shame: in both respects he might be truly said to hide his sword in the most emphatic sense, when he sheathed it in his own body. The last objection that the speech suggests to the view proposed by Welcker, arises from the professions which Ajax appears to make of his intention in future to yield to the gods and pay due reverence to the Atridae, and in general to regulate his conduct by maxims of moderation and discretion. These professions would certainly be mere dissimulation if they referred to anything but the approaching termination of his career, whereas they seem to imply a prospect of its continuance. Yet, if Ajax contemplated his death as a satisfaction both to divine and human justice, his manner of describing the lesson he had learnt and which he would thenceforth practise, is not unnatural, but strongly emphatic.

On the other hand the objections which the speech raises to the common opinion are very difficult to remove. If the aim of Ajax is to deceive his friends, admitting the contrivance to be worthy of his character, and consistent with his previous conduct, he cannot reasonably be supposed more in earnest in one part of the speech than another. It would imply in himself and would create in the reader an intolerable confusion of ideas and feelings, to imagine that he really pitied the condition of Tecmessa, and nevertheless only expressed his sentiments for the purpose of deceiving her. And yet who that has witnessed the scene of the parting from his child, can believe that he felt no pity for the mother? If so, since he couples her widowhood with its orphanhood, we should be forced to infer that he was equally indifferent to both. On the same principle if the passages relating to the anger of the goddess and the submission due to the gods are to be taken as ironical, we must consider Ajax in the light of a Capaneus or a Mezentius, who not only disregards but insults the gods. That he should be sincere in his professions of reverence for them, and yet use his piety for a cloak, would be a contradiction not to be endured. But in no part of the play is Ajax represented as an audacious blasphemer and contemner of the gods, though in the pride of his heart he sometimes has forgotten what was due to them. His last speech, where his sentiments continue the same and are exprest without disguise, breathes not only piety but confidence in the divine favour, grounded on the consciousness not indeed of perfect innocence, but of great wrongs suffered, and of ample reparation made for a slight transgression. So though it may seem natural that he should speak with bitter disdain of the Atridae, against whom we find him retaining his resentment to the last, it would be incredible that he should have made his profession of respect for their station if it was insincere, an occasion of introducing such a series of general reflexions as that which follows, in which he appears to be reconciling himself to the thought of obedience, by considering it as a universal law of nature. All this evidently proceeds from the depth of his heart, and so viewed is beautiful and touching: whereas if it be taken as a trick, to make his assumed change of mood more credible, nothing can easily be conceived more repulsive in itself, and less appropriate to the character of Ajax. Finally his parting directions to Tecmessa and the Chorus are so little like those of a person who was anxious to conceal his design, that as Welcker truly observes, one might rather be disposed to complain of the improbability that their meaning should have been mistaken: if it were not that a prejudice once caught is known to be capable of blinding us to the clearest intimations of the truth.

On the whole then we adopt with entire conviction Welcker's general view of this speech, which indeed harmonizes so well with that which has here been taken of one great feature in the poetical character of Sophocles, that we have thought it necessary to weigh the arguments on each side as cautiously as possible. Still if any one should find it impossible to believe that Ajax could be unconscious of the effect that his words were producing, we should not be unwilling to admit that he perceived the ambiguity of those expressions which bear a double meaning, so long as we are not called upon to give up the opinion that he is throughout and thoroughly in earnest. Before we quit the subject we will notice one or two passages, which either appear to contradict this conclusion, or have been so interpreted. The curse which Ajax, when on the point of death, pronounces against the Atridae and the whole army, may at first sight seem to be inconsistent with those sentiments of reverence for their authority which he expresses in the former scene, and thus to prove that they were not genuine. It seems however no more difficult to conceive that Ajax, while he acknowledged the debt which he owed to justice for a breach of social order, might still consider himself as an injured man, and invoke the Furies to avenge his wrongs, than that he might believe himself an object of divine favour, notwithstanding the offences against the gods which he was about to expiate. The curse itself, after the example of Oedipus, will not be thought an indication of peculiar ferocity. Only that it should have been extended to the whole army, may seem an excess of vindictive cruelty, and in fact this has proved a stumbling block to several critics. But it must be remembered, in the first place, that the army had sanctioned and shared the iniquity of its chiefs, in withholding from Ajax the honours he had earned in their service; and next, that the ruin of the king involves the calamity of the people. So Achilles can not distinguish between Agamemnon and the Greeks.[15] With the exception of this curse, which however answers the purpose of recalling the hero's wrongs to our recollection, and thus strengthening our sympathy with his sufferings, the whole speech is highly pathetic, so that any expression of arrogant impiety would jar most offensively with its general tenor. And hence it is of some importance to observe, that there is nothing at all savouring of such a character in the address to Jupiter, where Ajax speaks of his petition as requesting no great boon (αἰτήσομαι δέ σ᾽ οὐ μακρὸν γέρας λαχεῖν). Mr Campbell, in his Lectures on Poetry, has entirely mistaken the force of this expression, where he says that *we recognize the self dependence and stubbornness of his pride, when he tells the chief of the gods that he had but a slight boon to implore of him.* Not to mention how unseasonable such pride would have been, when Ajax was actually supplicating a favour to which, though little for Jupiter to grant, he himself attached great importance, and how inconsistent with the reverence exprest for Jupiter's majesty in the address: "Thou first, O Jove"—it is clear that the words in question contain nothing more than a touching allusion to the extremity in which he was now placed, when the only thing left for him to desire of Jupiter, was that his body might not be deprived of the rites of burial. Mr Campbell could scarcely have overlooked this, if he had not been prepossessed with the common opinion about the character of Ajax, as exhibited in the previous speech, which he too considers as a

---

[15] These considerations seem sufficient to remove the difficulty which Hermann finds in the common construction of the words (844) γεύεσθε, μὴ φείδεσθε πανδήμου στρατοῦ, which, if γεύεσθε is referred to στρατοῦ, appear to him to breathe the most atrocious inhumanity. The construction he proposes, referring γεύεσθε to the Atridae, is so harsh that one is glad to dispense with it, and yet is of very little use in softening the alledged atrocity of the imprecation. Another difficulty which has perplexed the commentators in this passage is less connected with our present subject. The curse manifestly contains a prediction which was meant to conform to the event: yet the words πρὸς τῶν φιλίστων ἐκγόνων ὀλοίατο, cannot be reconciled with history without great violence, as by distinguishing between φιλίστων and ἐκγόνων, in the manner proposed by Musgrave. Hermann's interpretation is intolerably strained and perplexed. There is no necessity for supposing that Ajax has Ulysses in view at all. From him he had received a provocation indeed, but no peculiar *wrong*, which he should call upon the Furies to avenge. Welcker thinks that the easiest solution of the difficulty is to suppose that a line has dropt out after αὐτοσφαγεῖς, containing an allusion to Clytemnaestra's crime and punishment.

feint, and endeavours to explain, but without perceiving the main diffi-culties which the supposition involves. He sees nothing in the tragedy but an exhibition of "the despair and suicide of a proud soldier, who has lived but for martial honor, and cannot survive the loss of it." Though we think this conception of the subject so inadequate as to miss what is most essential in the poet's design, we must do Mr C. the justice to observe, that he has shewn a lively sense of some of the beauties of the play, which is the more meritorious, as we learn from him that the English translators have been insensible to them. He complains with great reason that Sophocles should have fallen into the hands of persons so little capable of relishing him, as not even to be struck with the sub-limity of the opening scene of the Ajax: though, since such perceptions are the gift of nature, we do not understand why they are called *illiberal critics*. We collect however one rather melancholy inference from this fact, and from Mr Campbell's lectures: that the study of the poet's works with a view to the pleasures of the imagination, has not kept pace with the diligence bestowed on them as objects of philological criticism.

Most critics have felt a great difficulty in explaining the reasons which induced Sophocles to protract the action after the death of Ajax, with which, according to modern notions the interest expires. What has been said on this subject has for the most part been proposed in the lan-guage of apology, and in a tone which now and then raises a suspicion that the advocate is not thoroughly convinced of the goodness of his cause. Thus Hermann faintly defends the concluding scenes with argu-ments which in substance condemn them: and though Mr Campbell assures us that "the interest does not at all flag in the remainder of the tragedy," we want some better explanation of the grounds of this opinion, than is to be found in the remark: "that the Greeks attached an awfully religious importance to the rites of burial," which would apply equally to many other tragedies which do not end in like manner: or in the assertion: that "we feel the hero's virtues to be told with the deepest effect when his widow and child kneel as suppliants to heaven and human mercy, beside his corps: when his spirited brother defies the threats of the Atridae to deny him sepulchral honors: and when Ulysses with politic magnanimity interposes to prevent the mean insult being offered to his fallen enemy." The celebration of a hero's virtues after his death is surely not a legitimate object of tragedy: nor is it true that those of Ajax are more effectually told by his widow and child when they kneel beside his corps, than when they cling to him during his life: or by Teucer and Ulysses when they interpose in his behalf, than they had previously been in the first scene by the admission of an enemy, and afterward by the attachment and admiration exprest by his friends. Still less can the conclusion of the piece be defended on the ground that "it leaves our sympathies calmed and elevated by the triumph of Ulysses in assuaging the vindictiveness of Agamemnon, and attaching the gratitude of Teucer." Our sympathies with Ajax have already been calmed and elevated by the serenity and majesty of his departure: with Ulysses we have none sufficiently powerful to keep up our interest during the following scenes: if we had, this would imply a want of unity, which would be as great a defect as that which has been made the subject of complaint. In order to justify the poet by shewing the connexion between these scenes and the preceding part of the play, it is absolutely necessary to take into account a circumstance which Welcker, though not the first to notice it, has placed in a clearer light than any former writer: that Ajax was an object, not merely of human interest, but of religious veneration, with the audience for whom Sophocles wrote. The Athenians were proud of him as one of their heroes, who, since Clisthenes, gave his name to a tribe which was distinguished by some peculiar privileges.[16] They claimed his sons as their adopted citizens, the ancestors of their noblest families and some of their most illustrious men. But the hero's title to those religious honours which were paid to him in the time of Sophocles, commenced only from his interment: and hence no subject could be more interesting to the Athenians in general, and more particularly to the tribe which bore his name,[17] than the contest on the issue of which his heroic sanctity depended. Welcker very happily remarks that Menelaus and his brother fill the part of an *Advocatus Diaboli* at a process of canonization. On the other hand the injury which Ajax has planned against the army and its chiefs, was one which according to primitive usage, in ordinary cases, would have justified the extreme of hostility on their part, and consequently the privation of funeral rites. This was not in the eyes of the Greeks *a mean insult*, but a natural and legitimate mode of vengeance; though the violence and

---

[16] See the honours of the Aeantidae in Plut. Symp. 1. 10. 2. 3. They were peculiarly connected with the glory of Marathon. Marathon itself belonged to them: they occupied the right wing in the battle: they numbered the polemarch Callimachus among their citizens: Miltiades was a descendant of Ajax (Marcellin. Vit. Thuc.): the decree for the expedition was made under their presidency. At Plataea too they acquitted themselves so nobly, that they were appointed to conduct the sacrifice to the Sphragitides on Cithaeron. Their chorusses were never to take the last place. Plutarch thinks that this was not so much the reward of merit, as a propitiation of the hero, who could not brook defeat. One may compare the use made of this topic by the rhetorician whose funeral oration is printed among the works of Demosthenes: οὐκ ἐλάνθανεν Αἰαντίδας, ὅτι τῶν ἀριστείων στερηθεὶς Αἴας ἀβίωτον ἑαυτῷ ἡγήσατο τὸν βίον.

[17] To which Welcker with great probability refers the allusion in the line (861) κλειναί τ' Ἀθῆναι καὶ τὸ σύντροφον γένος. If the tribe furnished the chorus, the local application would be still more pointed.

arrogance with which it is prosecuted by the Spartan king is exhibited in an odious light, undoubtedly for the sake of suggesting to the Athenian audience a political application to their rivals, which was especially happy in a piece dedicated to the honour of an Attic hero, and which they would not fail to seize and enjoy. But this strenuous opposition serves to exalt the character of Ajax, and to enhance the glory of his triumph. And thus the contrast between the appearance and the reality is completed, as in the second Oedipus. At the beginning we saw the hero in the depth of degradation, an object of mockery and of pity: this was the effect of his inordinate self esteem, of his overweening confidence in his own strength. But out of his humiliation, his anguish, and despair, issues a higher degree of happiness and renown than he had ever hoped to attain. He closes his career at peace with the gods: his incomparable merit is acknowledged by the rival whose success had wounded his pride: he leaves a name behind him which shall be remembered and revered to the latest generations.

We have already observed that the length of our remarks would not be regulated by the value of the pieces to be examined. The *Antigone* and the *Philoctetes*, though perhaps neither of them is inferior in beauty to the Ajax, will detain us a much shorter time.

In the *Antigone* the irony on which the interest depends, is of a kind totally different from that which has been illustrated by the preceding examples. It belongs to that head which we have endeavoured to describe as accompanying the administration of justice human and divine, of that which decides not merely the quarrels of individuals, but the contests of parties and of principles, so far as they are clothed in flesh and blood, and wield the weapons of earthly warfare. The subject of the tragedy is a struggle between Creon and Antigone, not however as private persons maintaining their selfish interests, but as each asserting a cause which its advocate holds to be just and sacred. Each partially succeeds in the struggle, but perishes through the success itself: while their destruction preserves the sanctity of the principles for which they contend. In order to perceive this, we must guard ourselves against being carried away by the impression which the beauty of the heroine's character naturally makes upon our feelings, but which tends to divert us from the right view of Creon's character and conduct: a partiality, to which modern readers are not the less liable, on account of the difficulty they find in entering into the train of religious feeling from which the contest derives its chief importance. In our admiration for Antigone we may be very apt to mistake the poet's irony, and to adopt the sentiments which he puts into her mouth, as his own view of the question, and the parties, while he is holding the balance perfectly even. But to consider the case

impartially, it is necessary to observe, in the first place, that Creon is a
legitimate ruler, and next, that he acts in the exercise of his legitimate
authority. He had received the supreme power by the right of succession,
and with the full consent of his subjects, whom he had preserved from
their foreign invaders.[18] Haemon does not mean to dispute his
soverainty, but only to signify the conditions under which it ought to be
exercised, when in reply to Creon's question, whether any but himself is
governor of the realm, he says, that it is no city which belongs to one
man (737). Creon's decree is the law of the land. Ismene, remonstrating
with Antigone on her resolution, declares herself incapable of acting in
opposition to the will of her fellow citizens.[19] And Antigone herself in
her concluding appeal admits that she has so acted (907). Nor was the
decree a wanton or tyrannical exertion of power. Creon himself
professes to consider it as indispensable to the wellbeing of the state,
which is the sole object of his care (188–192), as a just punishment for
the parricidal enterprize of Polynices. And this is not merely Creon's
language, whom however we have no reason to suspect of insincerity: it
is also evidently the judgement of the Chorus, whose first song, which
presents so lively a picture of the imminent danger from which Thebes
has just been rescued, seems to justify the vengeance taken on its author.
The reflexions contained in the next song, on the craft and ingenuity of
man, are pointed at the secret violation of Creon's ordinance, as an
instance in which the skill of contrivance has not been coupled with due
respect for the laws and obligations of society: and the Chorus depre-
cates all communion with persons capable of such criminal daring.[20]
Antigone herself does not vindicate her action on the ground that Creon
has overstept the bounds of his prerogative, but only claims an
extraordinary exemption from its operation, on account of her connexion
with the deceased. She even declares, that she would not have
undertaken such a resistance to the will of the state, for the sake either of
children or husband (907): it was only the peculiar relation in which she
stood to Polynices, that justified, and demanded it. This too is the only
ground which Haemon alledges for the general sympathy exprest by the
people with Antigone: and in relying on this, he tacitly admits that the
same action would have deserved punishment in any other person. His

---

[18] 1162. σώσας μὲν ἐχθρῶν τήνδε Καδμείων χθόνα Λαβών τε χώρας παντελῆ
μοναρχίαν: that is, as he himself says, (174) γένους κατ᾽ ἀγχιστεῖα τῶν ὀλωλότων.

[19] 79. τὸ δὲ Βίᾳ πολιτῶν δρᾶν, ἔφυν ἀμήχανος.

[20] σοφόν τι τὸ μηχανόεν τέχνας ὑπὲρ ἐλπίδ᾽ ἔχων, ποτὲ μὲν κακόν, ἄλλοτ᾽
ἐπ᾽ ἐσθλὸν ἕρπει· νόμους παρείρων χθονός, θεῶν τ᾽ ἐνόρκων δίκαν, ὑψίπολις· ἄπολις,
ὅτῳ τὸ μὴ καλὸν ξύνεστι, τόλμας χάριν· μήτ᾽ ἐμοὶ παρέστιος γένοιτο, μήτ᾽ ἴσον
φρονῶν, ὃς τάδ᾽ ἔρδει.

general warnings against excessive pertinacity are intended to induce his father to give up his private judgement to the popular opinion. Creon on the other hand is bent on vindicating and maintaining the majesty of the throne and of the laws. No state can subsist, if that which has been enacted by the magistrate, on mature deliberation, is to be set aside because it thwarts a woman's wishes, (672–678) or because it is condemned by the multitude (734). Obedience on the part of the governed, firmness on the part of the ruler, are essential to the good of the commonwealth. These sentiments appear to be adopted by the Chorus. Notwithstanding its good will toward Antigone, and its pity for her fate, it considers her as having incurred the penalty that had been inflicted on her by an act, which, though sufficiently fair and specious to attract the praises of men and to render her death glorious, was still a violation of duty, and brought her into a fatal conflict with eternal Justice; a headstrong defiance of the soverain power, sure to end in her destruction.[21] It has appeared to several learned men, not without a considerable show of probability, that the numerous passages in this play which inculcate the necessity of order, and submission to established authority, may have had great weight in disposing the Athenians to reward the poet with the dignity of strategus which we know did not necessarily involve any military duties, though Sophocles happened to be so employed, but which would still have been a singular recompense for mere poetical merit.[22]

Nevertheless the right is not wholly on the side of Creon. So far indeed as Polynices is concerned, he has only shewn a just severity sanctioned by public opinion, and perhaps required by the interest of the state. Early however in the action we have an intimation that in his zeal for the commonwealth, and for the maintenance of his royal authority, he has overlooked the claims of some other parties whose interests were affected by his conduct. The rights and duties of kindred, though they might not be permitted to alter the course prescribed by policy and justice, were still entitled to respect. If Antigone had forfeited her life to the rigour of the law, equity would have interposed, at least to mitigate the punishment of an act prompted by such laudable motives. The mode in which the penalty originally denounced against her offense was transmuted, so as to subject her to a death of lingering torture, added mock-

---

[21] The Chorus first attempts to console Antigone by reminding her of her fame (817): οὐκοῦν κλεινὴ καὶ ἔπαινον ἔχουσ' Ἐς τόδ' ἀπέρχῃ κεῦθος νεκύων: and then answers her complaints by suggesting her fault (853): προβᾶσ' ἐπ' ἔσχατον θράσους ὑψηλὸν ἐς Δίκας βάθρον προσέπεσες, ὦ τέκνον, πολύ· and again (872) σέβειν μὲν εὐσέβειά τις· κράτος δ' ὅτῳ κράτος μέλει, παραβατὸν οὐδαμῇ πέλει, σὲ δ' αὐτόγνωτος ὤλεσ' ὀργά.

[22] Mr. Campbell very needlessly and groundlessly conjectures that Sophocles possessed considerable military experience when he was elected to the office.

ery to cruelty. But the rites of burial concerned not only the deceased, and his surviving relatives; they might also be considered as a tribute due to the awful Power who ruled in the nether world; as such they could not commonly be withheld without impiety. Hence Antigone, in her first altercation with Creon, urges that her deed, though forbidden by human laws, was required by those of Hades, and might be deemed holy in the realms below[23] Haemon touches on the same topic, when he charges his father with trampling on the honours due to the gods, and says that he pleads not on behalf of Antigone alone, but of the infernal deities (745–749). Creon, in pronouncing his final sentence on Antigone, notices this plea, but only to treat it with contempt. ''Let her implore the aid of Hades, the only power whom she reveres: he will perhaps deliver her from her tomb; or at least she will learn by experience, that her reverence has been ill bestowed.'' We must not however construe these passages into a proof that Creon, in his decree, had committed an act of flagrant impiety, and that his contest with Antigone was in effect a struggle between policy and religion. It is clear that his prohibition was consistent with the customary law, and with the religious opinions of the heroic ages, as they are represented not only by Homer, but in other works of Sophocles himself. The determination of Achilles to prevent Hector's burial, and his treatment of the corps, are related as extraordinary proofs of his affection for Patroclus, but still as a legitimate exercise of the rights of war. In the deliberation of the gods on the subject, the only motive assigned for the interference of Jupiter, is Hector's merit and piety. Juno, Neptune, and Minerva, are so far from finding any thing impious in the conduct of Achilles, that they oppose the intervention of the powers friendly to Troy on behalf of the deceased. So the dispute about the burial in the *Ajax* turns entirely on the merits of the hero, without any reference to the claims of the infernal gods. And as little does Electra seem to know any thing of them, when she desires Orestes, after killing Aegisthus, to expose him to such interrers as befit a wretch like him, that is, as the Scholiast explains it, to the birds and hounds.[24] Hence in the Antigone it must not be supposed that any of the speakers assume as a general proposition, that to refuse burial to a corps is absolutely and in all cases an impious violation of divine laws, though they contend that the honours paid to the dead are grateful, and therefore in general due to the infernal gods. Hitherto therefore Creon can only be charged with having pursued a laudable aim somewhat intemperately and

---

[23] 519. Αντ. Ὅμως ὅ γ᾽ Ἅιδης τοὺς νόμους τούτους ποθεῖ. Κρ. Ἀλλ᾽ οὐχ ὁ χρηστὸς τῷ κακῷ λαχεῖν ἴσος. Αντ. Τίς οἶδεν, εἰ κάτωθεν εὐαγῆ τάδε;

[24] 1487. κτανὼν πρόθες Ταφεῦσιν, ὧν τόνδ᾽ εἰκὸς ἐστὶ τυγχάνειν.

inconsiderately, without sufficient indulgence for the natural feelings of mankind, or sufficient respect for the Powers to whom Polynices now properly belonged. He has one principle of action, which he knows to be right; but he does not reflect that there may be others of equal value, which ought not to be sacrificed to it. It is not however before the arrival of Tiresias that the effects of this inflexible and indiscriminate consistency become manifest. The seer declares that the gods have made known by the clearest signs that Creon's obstinacy excites their displeasure. He has reversed the order of nature, has entombed the living, and disinterred the dead. But still all may be well: nothing is yet irretrievably lost; if he will only acknowledge that he has gone too far, he may retrace his steps. The gods below claim Polynices, the gods above Antigone: it is not yet too late to restore them. But Creon, engrossed by his single object, rejects the prophet's counsel, defies his threats, and declares that no respect even for the holiest of things, shall induce him to swerve from his resolution. Far from regarding the pollution of the altars, he cares not though it should reach the throne of Jove himself: and glosses over his profaneness with the sophistical plea, that he knows, no man has power to pollute the gods. The calamity which now befalls him, is an appropriate chastisement. Already the event had proved his wisdom to be folly. The measures he had taken for the good of the state had involved it in distress and danger. His boasted firmness now gives way, and on a sudden he is ready to abandon his purpose, to revoke his decrees. But they are executed, in spite of himself, and in a manner which for ever destroys his own happiness. Antigone dies, the victim whom he had vowed to law and justice: but as in her he had sacrificed the domestic affections to his state policy, her death deprives him of the last hope of his family, and makes his hearth desolate. She, on the other hand, who had been drawn into an involuntary conflict with social order by the simple impulse of discharging a private duty, pays indeed the price which, she had foreseen, her undertaking would cost: but she succeeds in her design, and triumphs over the power of Creon, who himself becomes the minister of her wishes.

   The character and situation of the parties in this play rendered it almost necessary that the contest should be terminated by a tragical catastrophe, even if the poet had not been governed by the tradition on which his argument was founded: though to the last room is left open for a reconciliation which would have prevented the calamity. In the *Philoctetes* the struggle is brought to a happy issue, after all hopes of such a result appeared to have been extinguished: and this is not merely conformable to tradition, but required by the nature of the subject. Our present object is only to exhibit the works of Sophocles in a particular point of view, and we therefore abstain from entering into discussions, which, though very important for the full understanding of them, are foreign to our immediate purpose. We cannot however help observing that the Philoctetes is a remarkable instance of the danger of trusting to a first impression in forming a judgement on the design of an ancient author: and that it ought at the same time to check the rashness of those who think that in such subjects all is to be discovered at the first glance, and to raise the confidence of those who may be apt to despair that study and investigation can ever ascertain anything in them that has once been controverted. The *Philoctetes* engaged the attention of some of the most eminent German critics, a Winkelmann, a Lessing, a Herder, for a long time in an extraordinary degree. Yet there are probably few points on which intelligent judges of such matters are more unanimous, than that these celebrated men were all mistaken on the question which they agitated, and that it is only in later times that it has been placed on a right footing and clearly understood. The bodily sufferings of Philoctetes are exhibited by the poet for no other purpose than to afford a measure of the indignation with which he is inspired by his wrongs, and of the energy of his will. It is no ordinary pain that torments him, but of a kind similar to that which extorted groans and tears from Hercules himself. Yet in his eagerness to escape from the scene of his long wretchedness, he makes an almost superhuman effort to master it, and conceal it from the observation of the bystanders. The difficulty of the exertion proves the strength of the motive: yet the motive, strong as it is, is unable to bear him up against the violence of the pain. He loses his self-command, and gives vent to his agony in loud and piteous exclamations. But all he had hoped for from Neoptolemus, when he strove to stifle his sensations, was not to be cured of his sore, but to be transported to a place where his sufferings might be mitigated by the presence and aid of compassionate friends. When he discovers the fraud that had been played upon him, he is at the same time invited to return to Troy, by the prospect of recovering health and strength, and of using them in the most glorious of fields. But long as he had sighed for deliverance from his miserable solitude, intolerable as are the torments he endures, ambitious as he is of martial renown, and impatient of wasting the arrows of Hercules on birds and beasts, there is a feeling stronger than any of these which impels him to reject the proffered good with disdain and even loathing, and to prefer pining to his life's end in lonely, helpless, continually aggravated wretchedness. This is the feeling of the atrocious wrong that has been inflicted on him: a feeling which acquires new force with every fresh throb of pain, with every hour of melancholy musing, and renders the thought of being reconciled to those who have so deeply injured him, and of lending his aid to promote their interest and exalt their glory, one from which he recoils with abhorrence. At the time when his situation appears most utterly desperate, when he sees himself on the point of being abandoned to an extremity of distress, compared with which his past sufferings were light, while he is tracing the sad features of the dreary prospect that lies immediately before him, and owns himself overcome by its horrors, the suggestion of the Chorus, that his resolution is shaken, and their exhortation that he would comply with their wishes, rekindles all the fury of his indignation, which breaks forth in a strain of vehemence, such as had never before escaped him:[25] a passage only inferior in sublimity to the similar one in the Prometheus (1045), inasmuch as Prometheus is perfectly calm, Philoctetes transported by passion.

The resentment of Philoctetes is so just and natural, and his character so noble and amiable, he is so open and unsuspecting after all his experience of human treachery, so warm and kindly in the midst of all his sternness and impatience, that it would seem as if Sophocles had intended that he should be the object of our unqualified sympathy. Yet it is not so: the poet himself preserves an ironical composure, and while he excites our esteem and pity for the suffering hero, guards us against sharing the detestation Philoctetes feels for the authors of his calamity. The character of Ulysses is contrasted indeed most forcibly with that of his frank, generous, impetuous enemy; but the contrast is not one between light and darkness, good and evil, between all that we love and admire on the one hand, and what we most hate and loath on the other. The character of Ulysses, though not amiable, is far from being odious or despicable. He is one of those persons whom we cannot help viewing with respect, even when we disapprove of their principles and conduct. He is a sober, experienced, politic statesman, who keeps the public good steadily in view, and devotes himself entirely to the pursuit of it. Throughout the whole of his proceedings, with regard to Philoctetes, he maintains this dignity, and expresses his consciousness of it. He is always ready to avow and justify the grounds on which he acts. From the beginning he has been impelled by no base or selfish motive; but on the contrary, he has exposed himself to personal danger for the public service. He had never borne any ill will to Philoctetes: but when his presence was detrimental to the army, he advised his removal; now that it is discovered to be necessary for the success of the expedition, he exerts his utmost endeavours to bring him back to Troy. He knows the character of Philoctetes too well, to suppose that his resentment will ever

---

[25] 1197. οὐδέποτ᾽, οὐδέποτ᾽, ἴσθι τόδ᾽ ἔμπεδον, κ. τ. λ.

give way to persuasion (103), and the arrows of Hercules are a safeguard against open force. He therefore finds himself compelled to resort to artifice, which on this occasion appears the more defensible, because it is employed for the benefit not only of the Grecian army, but of Philoctetes himself, who, once deprived of his weapons, will probably consent to listen to reason. Neoptolemus, though his natural feelings are shocked by the proposal of Ulysses, is unable to resist the force of his arguments, and suffers himself to be persuaded that, by the step he is about to take, he shall earn the reputation not only of a wise, but of a good man.[26] It is true that he retains some misgivings, which, when strengthened by pity for Philoctetes, ripen into a complete change of purpose. But Ulysses never repents of his counsels, but considers the young man's abandonment of the enterprize as a culpable weakness, a breach of his duty to the common cause. In his own judgement this cause hallows the undertaking, and renders the fraud he has practised pious and laudable.[27] And hence when assailed by Philoctetes with the most virulent invectives, he preserves his temper, and replies to them in a tone of conscious rectitude. "He could easily refute them, if this were a season for argument; but he will confine himself to one plea: where the public weal demands such expedients, he scruples not to use them; with this exception, he may boast that no one surpasses him in justice and piety." Such language accords so well with the spirit of the Greek institutions, according to which the individual lived only in and for the state, that from the lips of Ulysses it can raise no doubt of his sincerity. We see that he has adopted his principles deliberately, and acts upon them consistently.

But the doctrine that the end sanctifies the means, though in every age it has found men to embrace it, has never been universally and absolutely admitted. Ulysses has convinced himself by his own sophistry, but he cannot pervert the ingenuous nature of Neoptolemus, whose unprejudiced decision turns the scale on the side of truth. The intervention of Neoptolemus is not more requisite for the complication of the action, than for the purpose of placing the two other characters in the strongest light. He cannot answer the fallacies of Ulysses, but he more effectually refutes them by his actions. The wily statesman has foreseen and provided against all the obstacles that might interfere with the execution of his plan—except one: he has not reckoned on the resistance he might find in the love of truth, natural to uncorrupted minds, and which,

---

[26] 117.Οδ. ὡς τοῦτό γ᾽ ἔρξας, δύο φέρει δωρήματα. Νε. Ποίω; μαθὼν γάρ, οὐκ ἂν ἀρνοίμην τὸ δρᾶν. Οδ. Σοφός τ᾽ ἂν αὐτὸς κἀγαθὸς κεκλῇ᾽ ἅμα.

[27] Hence with the god of craft he invokes the goddess of political prudence, his peculiar patroness: (133) Ἑρμῆς δ᾽ ὁ πέμπων Δόλιος ἡγήσαιτο νῷν, Νίκη τ᾽ Ἀθάνα Πολιάς, ἣ σώζει μ᾽ ἀεί..

in his young companion, has never been stifled by the practise of deceit. He had calculated on using Neoptolemus as an instrument, and he finds him a man. And hence the unexpected issue of the struggle renders full justice to all. Philoctetes is brought to embrace that which he had spurned as ignominy worse than death; but by means, which render it the most glorious event of his life, and compensate for the sufferings inflicted on him by the anger of the gods. The end of Ulysses is attained, but not until all his arts have been baffled, and he has been compelled to retire from the contest, defeated and scorned. Neoptolemus, who has sacrificed every thing to truth and honour, succeeds in every object of his ambition to the utmost extent of his desires. The machinery by which all this is effected is indeed an arbitrary symbol, but that which it represents may not be the less true.

We are aware how open the subjects discussed in the foregoing pages are to a variety of views, and how little any one of these can be expected to obtain general assent. We can even anticipate some of the objections that may be made to the one here proposed. According to the opinion of a great modern critic, it will perhaps appear to want the most decisive test of truth, the sanction of Aristotle. And undoubtedly if it is once admitted that no design or train of thought can be attributed to the Greek tragic poets which has not been noticed by Aristotle,[28] this little essay must be content to share the fate of the greater part of the works written in modern times on Greek tragedy, and to pass for an idle dream. We would however fain hope either that the critic's sentence, investing Aristotle as it does with a degree of infallibility and omniscience, which, in this particular province, we should be least of all disposed to concede to him, may bear a milder construction, or that we

---

[28] "Hodie plerisque fati usus in Graecorum tragoedia necessarius videtur: de quo quum nihil ab Aristotele traditum sit, apparet, quamvis in plerisque tragoediis Graecorum fato suae sint partes, tamen scriptores illarum fabularum non cogitavisse de fato." Hermann. Præf. ad Trachinias, p. 7. A little further on he observes: "Qua in re autem illi tragoediae naturam positam esse statuerint optime ex Aristotele cognosci potest, qui et ætate iis proximus fuerit, et, ut ipse Graecus, Graecorum more philosophatus est." And so again in the Preface to Philoctetes, p. 11. "Tragici Græcorum eam habebant animo informatam notionem tragoediae, quae est ab Aristotele in libro de arte poetica proposita." Had they then all the same notion of it, and was there no difference between that of Aeschylus and those of Sophocles and of Euripides? And if they had, was it sufficient, in order to comprehend it, to be a Greek of nearly the same age, and a philosopher? How many contradictory theories have been proposed on Goethe's poetry by contemporary German metaphysicians! Even Hermann himself has not been universally understood in his own day. Many persons are still persuaded that his treatise *De Mythologia Graecorum antiquissima* is mere poetry, while the author himself protests that it is plain prose. But, joking apart, if Lord Bacon had written a treatise on the art of poetry, who would now think his judgement conclusive on Shakespeare's notion of tragedy, or on the design and spirit of any of his plays?

may venture to appeal from it to a higher tribunal. Another more
specific objection may possibly be, that the idea of tragic irony which we
have attempted to illustrate by the preceding examples, is a modern one,
and that instead of finding it in Sophocles, we have forced it upon him.
So far as this objection relates to our conception of the poet's theology,
we trust that it may have been in some measure counteracted by the distinction above drawn between the religious sentiments of Sophocles, and
those of an earlier age. This distinction seems to have been entirely overlooked by a German author, who has written an essay of considerable
merit on the *Ajax*, and who in speaking of the attributes of Minerva, as
she appears in that play, observes: "the idea that the higher powers can
only interpose in the affairs of mankind for the purpose of making men
wiser and better, is purely modern."[29] That which he conceives to be
repugnant to modern ideas in the theology of Sophocles is, that Minerva
is represented as inspiring the phrenzy of Ajax: an agency which appears
to him inconsistent with the functions of the goddess of wisdom.
According to the view we have taken of the play, this inconsistency
would be merely nominal. But even according to his own, it is an
inconsistency which need not shock a modern reader more than an
ancient one. We are familiar with a magnificent passage, in which it is
said of "our living Dread, who dwells In Silo, his bright sanctuary,"
that, when about to punish the Philistines, "Among them he a spirit of
phrenzy sent, Who hurt their minds." Minerva at all events does no
more, and according to our view she interposes for a purely benevolent,
not a vindictive purpose. Whether Sophocles would have scrupled to
introduce her as an author of absolute uncompensated evil, is a question
with which we are not here concerned. But the idea of a humbling and
chastening Power, who extracts moral good out of physical evil, does
not seem too refined for the age and country of Sophocles, however difficult it may have been to reconcile with the popular mythology.

As we have had occasion to refer to the *Samson Agonistes*, we
are tempted to remark that few plays afford a finer specimen of tragic
irony: and that it may be very usefully compared with the *Ajax* and the
second *Oedipus*. We leave it to the reader to consider, whether the poet,
who was so deeply imbued with the spirit of Greek tragedy, was only
imitating the outward form of the ancient drama, or designed to transfer
one of its most essential elements to his work.

---

[29] Immermann. *Ueber den rasenden Ajax des Sopocles*, p. 23: at p. 18, he
observes: "the way in which a superior Being steps in, and determines the hero's
destiny, is irreconcilable with our presumptions (Ahnungen) about the supreme
government of human affairs."

On the other hand we admit that it is a most difficult and delicate task, to determine the precise degree in which a dramatic poet is conscious of certain bearings of his works, and of the ideas which they suggest to the reader, and hence to draw an inference as to his design. The only safe method of proceeding for this purpose, so as to avoid the danger of going very far astray, and at the same time to ensure some gain, is in each particular case to institute an accurate examination of the whole and of every part, such as Welcker's of the *Ajax*, which may be considered as a model of such investigations. We are conscious how far this essay falls short of such a standard: and if we are willing to hope that it may not be entirely useless, it is only so far as it may serve to indicate the right road, and to stimulate the curiosity of others to prosecute it in new directions.

Lecture XXVIII

John Keble

I propose now to make some few remarks on the plays of Sophocles, and to consider the especial rank which we should accord this great writer among poets: and I perceive, indeed, that I have undertaken a task in which I run the risk of giving no slight offence. For you know how keenly people resent any question being raised concerning the merits of great poets, and especially in the case of those to whom they themselves have been devoted in their youth. For some reason they seem to take such criticism as a personal wrong or insult: just as if these writers with whose poems they had been familiar from childhood were connected with them either in blood or by some sacred bond; and this is indeed a proof how great is the influence of genuine and divinely inspired poetry, when any imitation of it, however deceptive, touches the mind so deeply.

And perhaps in the case of Sophocles there is a peculiar and special reason why any one who, at this time of day, shall question the right of one who has been so highly praised to the title of a primary poet should be unusually liable to give offence. For with Sophocles or Euripides the most part of our ingenuous youth make their first acquaintance with the real charms of the Greek tongue. It is mainly in the study of their writings that the minds of boys, who have become tired of light amatory poems, are wont to learn lessons of deeper quality. When they reach these studies they are urged to greater effort, in the hope of really understanding the beauty of ancient tragedy. No wonder, therefore, if they look back for the springs of poetry itself to those writers, thanks to whom they first began to see that there was anything real in poetry.

And there is this further difficulty that among all, without exception, who have ever written poetry, no one has ever earned more varied praise, whether from ancient or modern critics and readers. So that the "buskin of Sophocles" (as Virgil has called it[1]) has almost become a proverbial synonym for Tragedy.

But, put shortly, the position comes simply to this: we must admit that we have been expending our time and labour upon an idle fancy, unless we are prepared to apply our theory to the most renowned writers just as strictly as to one who is of small account and gifts. The central point of our theory is that the essence of all poetry is to be found, not in high-wrought subtlety of thought, nor in pointed cleverness of phrase, but in the depths of the heart and the most sacred feelings of the men who write. Consequently, nothing will tend more conclusively to strengthen our contention than if, selecting one or two of those poets who are held of highest account, we take them as a test of the theory. The inquiry will mainly resolve itself into two questions: first, whether Sophocles exhibits traces of those qualities which usually show the presence of the true vein and real force of poetry; and, secondly, if we decide that he cannot justly be ranked as a primary poet, we must explain what is the real ground of the praise which by general consent he has won. And should we fail to find any genuine spring of inspiration in his work, while there are not wanting amply sufficient reasons for his great reputation, then I apprehend that, though he cannot be called a primary poet, yet we may class him with those who have become poets in virtue of consummate skill and culture, rather than in virtue of natural instincts.

And, to begin with, I may as well frankly confess the truth, that hitherto, though a careful student of Sophocles, I have not been able to trace any one deep feeling and pervading passion running through the whole of his work. Thus I, necessarily, am doubtful whether anything of the sort possessed him. Of course, I am well aware that we can hardly infer the general disposition of a writer from the impression made upon a single reader. For what one critic is competent to gauge the varying genius of so many great poets? And I hope that some one else may be so fortunate, some time, as to trace some such constant vein of feeling, which hitherto has eluded my own careful search. I should certainly yield to none in pleasure and delight at the discovery. For do we not all count it as real gain when any new fact is brought to light concerning the sources of the best poetry and the inmost feelings of great men?

Still, I can hardly expect that any one will easily discover in our good Sophocles native springs of inspiration of this quality: I, indeed,

---

[1] *Eclog.* viii, 10.

entirely miss in him those glowing emotions of the mind which spring to birth spontaneously; and this, both in his choruses and in his discussions and dialogues. Let us see how he acquits himself in situations whose whole strength is wont to lie in generous warmth of feeling.

These are concerned either with strong human feelings, or with the whole aspect of sky, earth, and the changes of the seasons. Are we, then, to conclude, some one may ask, that Sophocles shows small power in all that relates to human feelings? Does he who placed before us on the stage Electra, Philoctetes, Hercules, and, above all, Oedipus, seem to you to have utterly failed in this region? Sophocles, who, in his presentment of Ajax, so happily blended a warlike and ungoverned arrogance with the consciousness of a frenzy which he cannot wholly shake off?

> Dost thou behold this once intrepid Ajax,
> The brave, the mighty, long for strength renowned,
> And dauntless courage in the bloody field,
> Dost thou behold him? O what laughter now,
> What vile reproach must he sustain![2]

I, for one, should most readily believe that many readers have found themselves moved in no small degree by these lines: for what affects us more deeply than the laments wrung from a noble and brave man, as he struggles against the hard conditions of his life? But the grounds on which I hesitate to allow that Sophocles, when he drew this picture, was wholly rapt and inspired, as those who are poets by Nature and necessity are wont to be, may be stated as follows. First, because all his labour and interest are expended on the single character of Ajax, to the almost complete disregard of those who play minor parts. For neither in Tecmessa, as far as I can see, nor in the Atridae, nor even in Ulysses as depicted by Sophocles, does anything whatever stand out as a clear distinguishing mark sufficient to separate any one of them from the ordinary run of mankind. They, one and all, simply say and do such things as may assist the plot, or contribute to a discussion on some question of casuistry, such as are constantly met with in the later Greek Drama: but of their real self and of all that belongs to it there is utter silence. On the contrary, in Shakespeare's plays, as we all know, even the characters playing the most insignificant parts successfully claim their author's interest—not, of course, in equal degree, but in a similar way. With him we never find a countryman who happens to be standing

---

[2] *Ajax* 363 (Francklin).

by, or a soldier or a common jester, or any other whosoever, but has assigned him, in the word or two he has to say, something which suggests a character of his own. Thus we accord to Shakespeare, as of preeminent right, the high commendation of holding nothing that is human alien to himself, seeing that he was able to enter into the mind, the character, the very features of all classes of men in all parts of the world. In this respect he may be compared to Nature herself, which is wont to frame and adorn with minute detail, not merely regions which are, by reason of their striking beauty, visited and admired by all, but even obscure nooks not easily penetrated by the rays of the sun or by the eye of the sightseer. One and the same Nature, with one and the same loving care, adorns alike majestic oak-tree and the minutest specimen of fungus or fern which springs up under the shadow of that kingly tree. And perhaps we may in the same connexion compare the careful love of detail which our ancestors showed when building their churches, taking pains to carve and ornament the highest nook of the ceiling, the hinder part of the pillars, and everything that was far removed from the sun's light and men's observation. Consequently, when a poet lavishes his whole care on a single character, we judge that he is not modelled in Nature's mould, but on some rules of art. Whether, indeed, in our good Sophocles' case there is really any room for doubt on this point I leave skilled judges to decide.

I will add another point: those writers who have had the power of sympathizing with all frames of mind and all emotions—a quality in which Shakespeare was preeminent, if not unique, among our own poets and Homer among the Greeks—have hardly been able to avoid introducing trivial and grotesque incidents in the very crisis of gravest events. For such is generally the case in real life: serious things and mere trifles, laughable things and things that cause pain, are wont to be mixed in strangest medley. It is necessary, then, that Tragedy, as being a mirror of life, must leave room for an element of comic humour. But Sophocles' taste was, it would seem, too severe, his fastidiousness too great, to allow him to admit such a blending, such a hotch-potch of opposite qualities. We find in him no character like the soldier of the *Agamemnon* or the nurse in the *Choephoroe*: each of which has the like motive—to impress upon us, namely, that even men of the lowest rank, the sansculottes, occupied with meanest tasks, share in and understand life's sorrows and misfortunes. With Sophocles all is ornate, solemn, of set and formal speech: whence it is clear enough that he did not possess that source of inspiration which those enjoy who are by nature both alive to, and indeed sympathize with, every care.

But, then, who more felicitously skilful than Sophocles, in depicting those who are tortured by extreme suffering? Only recall to mind Hercules on Mount Oeta, and the magnificent throng of words with which he himself describes the onset of the disease which gains on him every moment:

> For, cleaving to my side, it eats within,
> Consuming all my flesh, and from my lungs,
> Still winding in, it drains my arteries,
> Drinks the warm blood, and I am done to death,
> My whole frame bound with this unheard-of chain.[3]

These lines are, indeed, beyond all praise: and I remember how one who was amongst the most learned men that I can remember, having read this passage over again, impulsively exclaimed "Bravo, Sophocles! what perfect art!" And we certainly cannot deny it: yet I fear that testimony such as this rather snatches away the crown of primary rank from the poet's brow than places it there. For surely Sophocles has here with consummate art described the agony from without rather than seemed himself to weep with him that wept. Just compare these lines with the lamentations uttered by the Hebrew writers, such as those of David, Job, Hezekiah, who, moved by a Spirit higher than human, have recorded in poetic form the effect and result wrought upon wretched mortals by tortured limbs and drooping heart and the whole array of diseases and bodily pains. It will be found beyond all question that their bewailings correspond strikingly with the expressions met with every day in such cases in real life: short and agonized ejaculations being, one by one, wrung from their inmost hearts, as if by the very force of their suffering. Then they range sea and land, so to speak, in quest of comparisons, if by possibility they may describe in speech their secret feelings of utter misery: while the Hercules of Sophocles seems to state in set speech what any onlooker infers, rather than what he himself inly experiences.

It may be questioned, too, whether in Sophocles wholly different characters, when whelmed in similar calamities, exhibit sufficient difference, one from the other; whether they follow, that is, the rule and, as it were, inviolable decree of Nature, never so ordering her workings that any two living creatures, much less any two human beings, should correspond each to each in every detail. It is only one who not merely thoroughly grasps this principle, but furthermore, so expresses it in his poetry, that any reader may be conscious of a real bond of sympathy between him and each separate character, that can be adjudged and

---

[3] *Trachiniae*, 1070 (1053) (Plumptre).

classed as a primary poet by special right—so far, at all events, as concerns that domain of Poetry which touches men's feelings and emotions.

To dwell just a little more at length upon the point to which we have thus been led: notice how very slight is the difference between Hercules and Philoctetes as regards their bearing under stress of pain. If indeed we except one detail—the fact that with Hercules the thought repeatedly presses of his disgrace, as he feels it, at being betrayed to tears like a woman by stress of anguish—all the rest is simply like Philoctetes.

Perhaps I may be met here with the question, whether it is quite fair to draw conclusions from bodily pains: since such suffering affects every one in much the same manner, and that a very simple one: so that we need not expect to see any difference between one person and another. Let us test the question, then, in another way, though still keeping to Philoctetes. For as he is comparable to Hercules in respect of disease and bodily pain, so, as regards the contempt and slight he experienced from the Atridae, he resembles Ulysses. Well, each of them inveighs against his enemies, not merely to like effect, but even in identical phrase and expression. We are at once conscious that the writer has taken little pains to assign to each expressions of resentment appropriate to his character. Nor is this a solitary instance; if we compare Antigone with Electra, or Creon enraged and denouncing the augur, with King Oedipus in like passion, do we not there, too, utterly fail to trace that natural variety of tone and hue, and those true utterances which break from the depths of the heart? Once more, the Argive Chrysothemis and the Theban Ismene, actually, in almost the same set identical words, each disowns her sister's scheme. And it will be noticed by any one, that while only seven plays of Sophocles survive to us, three times does he employ the familiar device of an ominous silence on the part of high-born women who, on simply hearing of some calamity, forthwith hang or stab themselves. First, we are told of Jocasta:

> Why has thy queen, O Oedipus, gone forth
> In her wild sorrow rushing? Much I fear
> Lest from such silence evil deeds burst out.[4]

Then, in the *Antigone*, the Chorus is perplexed what to think of Eurydice, the mother of Haemon:

> What dost thou make of this? She turneth back,

---

[4] *Oedipus Tyr.* 1092 (1073) (Plumptre).

Before one word, or good or ill she speaks.[5]

Lastly, in the case of Deianira too, just the same formula for
dying (if I may so term it) is employed:

Why creep'st thou off in silence? Know'st thou not
That silence but admits the accuser's charge?[6]

Some writers, of course, through a kind of carelessness, often
repeat themselves, while they nevertheless show discrimination as to
their characters and evince by other indications, and especially by their
fully charged feeling, that they possess the native spring of Poetry. This
is notably so, unless I am mistaken, in the case of our own Shakespeare.
But, trust me, Sophocles laboured under no carelessness of this sort.
Who of all the poets is more exquisite in rhythm? What artist ever handled the Greek tongue with greater power, to make it express whate'er he
would? But I should say that the question stands much in this way;
Sophocles, as his contemporaries bear witness, was pre-eminently of
tranquil and easy temper, little liable to be deeply moved by grief, either
on his own account or for the sake of others. For this is what I
understand by that "easy temper" (εὐκολία) which is the special quality
of praise accorded to him by Aristophanes:

an easy-minded soul, and always was.[7]

Small wonder, then, if, in that region of Poetry which depends on the
more subtle motions of the soul, he should show himself less happily
gifted.

But I am far indeed from denying that the minds of all men, who
are not wholly wanting in appreciation, are most keenly affected from
time to time by his work, and, in especial, by perusal of the renowned
Oedipus. But this effect is, I think, produced less by any powerful feeling evoked in us by the actors than by the tenor of the plot. It is the
story itself, not the character of Oedipus, which seizes and captivates our
minds: and this interest is by no means without its own special charm:
but whether it can be justly attributed to the poet's art I shall not attempt
to discuss here.

Passing, then, from these for the present, let us next consider
what may be called the other province of the poetic kingdom: and in this

[5] *Antigone*, 1258 (1244) (Plumptre).

[6] *Trachiniae*, 826 (813) (Plumptre).

[7] *Frogs*, 82 (Frere).

(I will confess it) I am almost inclined to allow Sophocles primary rank: as you recollect, it is pre-eminently concerned with the influence of Nature and the charm of scenery. In the treatment of this theme the first place among the Sophoclean plays is held, by general consent, both on the ground of sweetness and impressiveness, by the *Oedipus at Colonos*. Indeed, the aged Sophocles, when conducting the aged Oedipus to his native Athens, where he was to find a destined resting-place, could hardly fail to be strangely moved and inspired by the thought of the familiar spots, by the memories of his boyhood, above all, by the presence of the deities whom in his boyhood he and his parents had worshipped. Then how sacred, how impressive, how far removed from the routine of daily life, was the fact that not merely his native country Attica, the common haven and asylum for all sufferers, but even his own town, his own native soil, nay, the rocks, fountains, and trees which had been familiar to him from his tenderest years, should have Guardian Spirits of special kindliness. So, he hastens at the very opening of the tragedy to make reference to the place most dear to him:

> My father, woe-worn Oedipus! afar,
> If I see right, are towers that shield a town;
> This spot is holy, one may clearly tell,
> Full as it is of laurel, olive, vine,
> And many a nightingale within sings sweetly.
> Rest thy limbs here upon this rough-hewn rock.[8]

In exactly the same spirit we have the frequent praise, throughout the play, of all that concerns Attica, and in especial the picture of the last resting-place of the dying old man, which is described almost by rule and line: so that any one who will may follow his footsteps and not diverge a hair's breadth from the hallowed spot:

> And when he neared the threshold's broken slope,
> With steps of bronze fast rooted in the soil,
> He stopped on one of paths that intersect,
> Close to the hollow urn where still are kept
> The pledges true of Perithos and Theseus;
> And stopping at mid-distance between it,
> And the Thorikian rock, and hollow pear,
> And the stone sepulchre, he sat him down.[9]

---

[8] *Oed. Col.* 14 (Plumptre).
[9] *Oed. Col.* 1661 (1590) (Plumptre).

By such indications of the actual spots and by obscure allusions frequently made to the near presence of guardian deities, the writer brings it about, that a tragedy which more than all the rest lags in plot and action and proceeds haltingly, yet attracts and long holds our attention with powerful grip: however often I read it, I am moved as deeply as were those who, when they first heard it, decreed the prize with fullest honours to Sophocles, though his powers seemed already to some to be failing through age. Hence, even to me, it appears almost sacrilege to deny inspiration to such a man. One is reminded of Virgil, and might almost believe that, all unknown to himself, some contributory streamlet of that part of his poetry which depends on the delight in natural things may have trickled down to him from Sophocles.

And we shall find not a little that strengthens this opinion, when we turn back to the *Ajax*. For in that play men's fates and emotions are exquisitely blended with the various beauty of sea, shore, and river. As when the sailors in quest of their lost leader invoke the spirits haunting the region:

> Who, then, will tell me; who
> Of fisher's loving toil,
> Plying his sleepless task,
> Or who of Nymphs divine
> That haunt Olympos' height,
> Or which of all the streams
> Where Bosporos flows fast,
> Will tell if they have seen him anywhere,
> Wandering, the vexed in soul.[10]

Again, the same men, more than once, with a sort of home-sick gaze, look back on their native land, not without a weary disgust of the Trojan soil:

> What joy remaineth for me?
> Would I were there, where the rock,
> Thick-wooded and washed by the waves,
> Hangs o'er the face of the deep,
> Under Sunion's broad jutting peak,
> That there we might hail, once again,
> Athens, the holy, the blest.[11]

---

[10] *Ajax*, 888 (879) (Plumptre).
[11] *Ajax*, 1232 (1215) (Plumptre).

We can fancy that we actually see the vessel sailing along the familiar shore, the sailors standing up on the deck and joyfully hailing their native land.

Then this too:

> O glorious Salamis!
> Thou dwellest blest within thy sea-girt shores,
>   Admired of all men still;
> While I, poor fool, long since abiding here
>   In Ida's grassy mead,
>   Winter and summer too,
> Dwell, worn with woe, through months innumerable.[12]

Is not that an exact picture of the longing with which wanderers, far from home, turn their eyes back to their accustomed haunts? Islanders and used to the sea, they think slightly of the downs and meadows under Mount Ida, of that low-lying, tree-shaded region, those "meadowy pastures of the sheep," as compared with the open shore, the steep cliffs of their home, with the ocean breezes around them.

On this theme, however, there is another strange fact to be noted, namely, that men, far off from home and weighed down by some grief, are wont to consider the very regions themselves, which have become familiar by long association, as being comrades and sharers in their sorrow. Consequently, when bidden to leave them, even for their own country and for freedom, they will feel a certain regret at the prospect of being separated from the objects which had been, perhaps through many years, a solace and comfort to them. Whoever would thoroughly penetrate the secret causes of this fact of human nature will perhaps find himself inevitably compelled to rise to things higher and diviner, and to consider the whole subject of Poetry on that side of it where it touches the wisdom of Heaven. If you ask for illustrations, you will find the noblest in the story which is told about a castle on the Lake of Geneva,[13] when the one survivor among many captives was reluctant to be relieved of his chains, and could not, without wrench and effort, resign the bare walls, the plash of waters, the cell's cold stone floor, the cracked walls in many places admitting the light and air of heaven. With this single exception, which will to many perhaps appear incredible and like a morbid dream, I doubt indeed whether in any author we shall find more striking examples of this clinging affection, than in Sophocles' portrayal of Ajax and of Philoctetes.

---

[12] *Ajax*, 601 (596) (Plumptre).

[13] *The Prisoner of Chillon*.

And indeed, when Ajax has become weary of his life and looks
forward eagerly to his final rest in death, even then he is held back for a
while by an indefinable sense of sorrowful regret at the thought of leaving rivers, caverns, and woods which, by a campaign of ten long years,
had become almost as companions and friends to him:

> O ye paths of the wave!
> O ye caves by the sea!
> O thou glade by the shore!
> Long time, long time my feet
> On Troïa's soil ye kept;
> But never, never more
> Breathing the breath of life;
> Let the wise hear and heed.
> O streams, Scamandros' streams
> Hard by, to Argives kind,
> Never again shall ye see
> This man who calls to you now.[14]

By the very flow of the lines, sweet and wonderful as it is, Sophocles
has taught us here how deeply it touches a man's spirit to be wrenched
from regions made dear by long intercourse: and this is more striking, if
we remember Ajax's high spirit and indomitable temper.

Then, in the *Philoctetes*, nothing throughout the whole play so
touches us as the frequent mention of his cave, the mountains, the rivers,
indeed even the birds and beasts, by whose friendly influences the sorely
stricken exile had somewhat lightened the burden of his griefs. This is
why, at the very beginning of the poem, we have our attention carefully
drawn, in vivid outline, to his unlovely retreat, more like the lair of a
wild beast:

> But thy task it is
> To do thine office now, and search out well
> Where lies a cavern here with double mouth,
> Where in the winter twofold sunny side
> Is found to sit in, while in summer heat
> The breeze sends slumber through the tunnell'd vault;
> And just below, a little to the left,
> Thou may'st perchance a stream of water see,
> If still it flow there.[15]

---

[14] *Ajax*, 411 (Plumptre).
[15] *Phil.* 15 (Plumptre).

Hence, when betrayed by Neoptolemus, Philoctetes does not make the same appeals that others do in the same plight: he does not invoke the Gods, nor the Furies: he only appeals to his island, and the old familiar places:

> O creeks! O cliffs out-jutting in the deep!
> O all ye haunts of beasts that roam the hills!
> O rocks that go sheer down, to you I wail
> (None other do I know to whom to speak),
> To you who were my old familiar friends,
> The things this son of great Achilles does;
> ....
> O cave with double opening, once again
> I enter thee stript bare, my means of life
> Torn from me. I shall waste away alone
> In this my dwelling, slaying with this bow
> Nor wingèd bird, nor beast that roams the hills:
> But I myself, alas! shall give a meal
> To those who gave me mine, and whom I chased
> Now shall chase me; and I, in misery,
> Shall pay in death the penalty of death
> By me inflicted.[16]

Finally, when, as he believes, about to be left to languish in exile, it is by their companionship and comfort that he seeks to soothe his grief:

> O cave of hollow rock,
> Now hot, now icy cold,
> And I was doomed, ah me!
> To leave thee never more;
> But e'en in death thou still wilt be to me
> My one true helping friend.[17]

> O all ye wingèd game,
> And tribes of bright-eyed deer,
> Who on these high lawns fed,
> No more from this my home
> Will ye allure me forth.

---

[16] *Phil.* 959 (936) (Plumptre).
[17] *Phil.* 1109 (1081) (Plumptre).

> I wield not in my hands
> The strength I had of old
> (Ah me!) from those my darts;
> Full carelessly this place
> Is barred against you now,
> No longer fearful.[18]

Moreover, he shows that he shall feel regret for them in future days, even when he has achieved a triumphant release and full happiness. I shall quote once more the oft-quoted lines, both for their intrinsic beauty and because they are more appropriate than any to my present subject:

> Come, then, I leave this isle,
> And speak my parting words:
> Farewell, O roof, long time
> My one true guard and friend:
> And ye, O nymphs that sport
> In waters or in fields;
> Strong roar of waves that break
> On jutting promontory,
> Where oft my head was wet
> (Though hid in far recess)
> With blasts of stormy South:
> And oft the mount that bears
> The name of Hermes gave
> Its hollow loud lament,
> Echoing my stormy woe;
> And now, ye streams and fount
> Lykian, where haunt the wolves,
> We leave you, leave you now,
> Who ne'er had dreamt of this.
> Farewell, O Lemnos, girt by waters round,
> With fair breeze send me on
> Right well, that none may blame,
> Where Fate, the mighty, leads.[19]

We cannot help feeling that this most exquisite Farewell was due from Philoctetes, as much as it is due from a youth about to leave his country that he should seek a parent's embrace and blessing.

---

[18] *Phil.* 1146 (Plumptre).

[19] *Phil.* 1498 (1451) (Plumptre).

Who will deny that lines like these have a genuine inspiration and
are "sweeter than honey"? But I fear that they will be found too rare in
Sophocles to allow them to be taken as a test of the quality of his poetry
as a whole. Yet had it not been his lot to grow old in the shelter of a cul-
tured city life, such as was that of distinguished men at Athens, I believe
he would have afforded many more such illustrations; chiefly, because,
if we may trust tradition, such was his rooted attachment to his home
and native ground, so "extremely fond of the Athenians" (to use their
own description of him) was he, that he would accept no invitation, not
even of the greatest monarch, which involved leaving his own country.
If, then, any one wishes to place him in the circle of primary poets, on
the score of his love and devotion to his own country, I shall make no
objection, though I could wish for more numerous or more decisive evi-
dences of this sort, or at any rate that such as there are should bear
clearer marks of strong feeling, and should seem to gush forth freely
rather than to be fashioned and polished by art.

Moreover, may I not submit that his case is perhaps all the
weaker, because of the very praises which by general consent he has
won for himself? These praises, I should say, are hardly at all concerned
with any quality which is thoroughly cognate with and common to genuine poetry. For I note that Sophocles approves himself to the great
majority of readers mainly for two reasons: either because he is so finished and subtle in his diction, and easily stands out as the most learned
among the whole learned Greek race: or because he weaves the general
sequence of his plot so cleverly and cunningly. Of these two grounds, I
infer that the first specially commended itself to the ancient Greeks, the
other to our own times, and chiefly to the judgement of those who hold
with Aristotle that the chief merit of a poem lies in the action. But in
each case we may be allowed to question whether they necessarily touch
the real art and poetic gift, or may not merely be viewed as their formal
part and machinery.

First, then, let us consider the charm of his perfect Attic Greek,
his consummate use of words and sentences: as we all know, so far as
this is concerned, Sophocles was almost reverenced as divine in the critical judgement of the Greek ear: at least, if we may believe that the popular vote and taste is fairly reflected in the well-known and beautiful
epigram:

> Gently, where lies our Sophocles in sleep,
> Gently, green ivy, with light tendrils creep:
> There may the rose-leaf too and cluster'd vine

Climb round his honour'd tomb in graceful twine:
Sweet were his lays, with sense and feeling fraught,
Alike by Muses and by Graces taught.[20]

Observe that the ivy-leaves, "the meed of learned brows,"[21]
crown his head especially because "sense and feeling" are embodied in
"sweet lays": and how great was the power and attraction of this among
the Greeks, especially with the Athenians, can, I think, scarcely be con-
jectured, much less realized, in our own duller clime and by our less
sensitive ear. But to those who hold that "beauty of language" is one of
the very sources and fountain-heads of Poetry and must colour the whole
stream, I should be inclined to say that they fall into precisely the same
mistake as one who should maintain that we apprehend those objects
which touch our external sense with the body, not the mind: whereas all
philosophy which is at once sane and noble teaches us it is not with our
eyes we see the things we see, nor are sounds heard by the ear: but that
the mind withdrawn in its own dwelling makes use of these agents as
only messengers and reporters. In the same way Poetry uses both words
and metres as mere instruments, just like a queen employing her messengers: they are not dominant, not of first importance; the heavenly
flame is not by their means enkindled, but merely transmitted. Hence it
follows, with regard to any poet who by general consent is mainly
praised for the richness and beauty of his diction, that we may fairly
question if he has anything in common with those who are made poets
by Nature and true feeling before they occupy themselves with literary
style and metrical form.

With regard to the second ground of praise, which is given to
poets who cleverly construct their plots, who contrive intricate situations, and yet through them all guide the thread of the story to the point
which their scheme or truthfulness to facts requires, perhaps the question
will be more difficult: especially as we have to reckon with such weighty
authorities as Aristotle and his followers, who emphasize the "plot" or
story, as being of greater importance than all other elements of a drama,
and place Sophocles before all other tragedians as being the most skilled
and consummate artist in construction and plot. Moreover, almost the
whole of this line of argument is wont to be based upon the *Oedipus
Tyrannus*, as if it were the only or at least the main proof of their position. Now their authority would have greater weight with me, did I not
observe that they themselves defer too much to the popular judgement. I

---

[20] *Anthol.* (Macgregor).

[21] Hor. *Odes*, i. I. 29.

find that all through Aristotle's *Art of Poetry* there is an underlying
appeal to the people and the gallery: that, invariably, it is the external
form and feature of the poem, not the inner spirit of the poet, which is
looked to and considered: and that this is especially noticeable when
Aristotle develops his reasons for holding that in the composition of
Tragedy the plot should be assigned the chief place. Though he has the
air of offering many reasons, yet the sum of them all is contained in this
single one: "Those parts of Tragedy, by means of which it becomes most
interesting and affecting, are parts of the *fable*: I mean, *revolutions* and
discoveries."[22] As though, forsooth, the reputation of great poets is to
stand or fall by theatrical applause, by the number and lungs of the
shouters.

The man who has made up his mind to be governed by decrees of
this sort must needs rank some trivial story, such as may be met with
nowadays in any bookseller's shop, above the *Iliad* itself. Indeed, people
who take up such a book cannot relinquish it till read through to the end:
so enthralled are they by the skilful intricacy of its tangled skein. Such a
theory, I imagine, scarcely ever, if ever, happens in reading Homer or
Aeschylus: more truly inspired Poetry elects to be separated by a vast
gulf from mere skill in story-telling. But it is my deliberate opinion,
however, that true genuine Poetry may show itself also in the construction of the plot: if a writer of surpassing power were to set forth the
changes and chances of mortal life, the issues of conduct, and the mock-
ing sport of Fortune, not with intent that his books may be devoured by
boys and girls for mere amusement, but that he himself may enjoy a
profounder sense of the laws which silently control and govern all
things. This, I repeat, I acknowledge to be true Poetry: and most likely
to be found in men whose minds are thoroughly imbued with sacred
prophecy or history.

But to attribute so splendid and lofty an aim to Sophocles, even
in the *Oedipus*, is impossible, first and chiefly because the details of the
story are so shocking: indeed, to confess the truth, it has always seemed
to me to border on that class of story which Aristotle himself rejects as
being monstrous and repulsive, and it goes against our right feeling that
one who is innocent of any crime should be so harshly punished, and
should leave the stage without hope, without even an implied suggestion
that at some future time his fate may take a happier turn: just as if some
relentless Genie played with all men's fortunes as with his. Aeschylus,
unless I am mistaken, has a far higher religious sense: when cruel and
wicked deeds are wrought, he takes greater pains to hint at the real

---

22 Arist. *A.P.* vi. 17 (Twining).

presence of Deity and at the truth that One above will both exact due penalities and restore those who have suffered undeservedly. But when once we feel, in connexion with such an important element, any vague suspicion of this kind, I am afraid that our minds tend to turn with disgust from those oft-praised "revolutions and discoveries," and that all the more the more cleverly they are contrived. So, while I fully allow that no artist ever wrought the web of his story with greater art or skill: yet it may well be questioned if this very skilfulness may not somewhat detract from his praise as a poet: for he is without true religious feeling; without pity; and without that tender love of humanity with which Virgil is wont to trace the story of unhappy and suffering mortals.

Nor ought I to omit to add this: Sophocles excelled beyond all other dramatists in all that relates to scenic apparatus and device: and there is no need to demonstrate how perilous is such a gift, and how near it is to elaborate histrionic devices. Aeschylus also is said to have enlarged in many respects the machinery of the stage. But observe, how even here each is true to his own character. Aeschylus indeed, if I understand aright, was the first to substitute tragic representation for lyric songs, and only introduced such changes in the character and number of actors as was absolutely needed for a simple and dignified treatment. Sophocles brought on a third actor; he had his stage painted, and increased by one-fourth the number of the Chorus: the one effect of all the changes being to transfer the pleasure from the ear to the eye of the spectator. Indeed, it is said that he sometimes designedly wrote tragedies in order to suit this or that actor. Did time allow, I could point out many instances taken from his plays, which would wholly fail of their effect unless the scene were presented before the eye on the stage: and yet Aristotle himself declares that "the effect of Tragedy can be felt without representation and actors." But let me ask, what is the end and purpose of introducing in the *Electra* the shrouded body of Clytemnestra, just after the murder, as if it were that of Orestes: whereby Aegisthus is first deceived and then bewildered and appalled. To what purpose the feigned contrition of Ajax, the long-delayed contrition of Deianira and of Creon? What other justification of these changes of feeling can there possibly be but that they aimed at keeping the attention of spectators and readers in suspense? All such things have to do with the stage effect, not with the author.

Then we note that Sophocles from time to time presents on the stage, what is not merely hateful, but actually monstrous and horrible, such as Philoctetes' wound, the tunic of Hercules, the mangled eyes of Oedipus. Again, there is much too great elaboration of details, when any long narrative or casuistical discussion is introduced, with the result (and no result can be more offensive) that the poet very often is playing the part of a rhetorician or sophist, or even of some pushing demagogue or would-be politician. Assuredly, if Sophocles is open to blame in these particulars, any one may see that one simple explanation accounts for them all. Everything he wrote suggests a man whose poetry did not flow spontaneously as theme and feeling urged, but was with great effort and toil worked up to a point which would suit the stage and be more pleasing to the Athenian populace.

Then even the ancients bear witness that he was an imitator ("he culls beauties from each poet," says the Scholiast), and no one who has even dipped into Homer or Aeschylus before reading Sophocles can fail to notice it. This, indeed, is only an indication that a writer is without native poetic feeling, where it appears to result not from carelessness or rapid composition, but from art and design, and especially in passages which are introduced in order to touch the reader's feelings. Let those who claim primary rank for Sophocles tell us, whether we may not fairly assign to the latter class the dialogue of Ajax and Tecmessa, which closely follows Hector's well-known farewell to Andromache: or the whole conception of the *Electra*, which is almost exactly on the lines of Aeschylus' *Choephoroe*, except that Sophocles held it right to dispense with all the constant reference to religion, by which alone Aeschylus justified his story against the charge of impiety.

But if (and it is commonly alleged) we infer the celebrated "easy temper" (εὐκολία) of Sophocles to have been closely allied to the licence of his day, there will be less reason for surprise that such a distinguished and graceful writer was without genuine poetic inspiration. We all know that nothing more dulls and weakens sincere and genuine feeling than an indulgent and pleasure-loving way of life. The admirers of Sophocles, then, may be the less troubled if he be degraded from patrician rank, as we shall allow him to take the very first place among those who are poets made, not poets born: yet even in giving this verdict, we ought perhaps to make an exception in favour of that one special merit which has been before referred to, namely, that he seems often to have spoken with full and natural feeling whenever some nearer reference to places, especially those dear to himself, chanced to offer itself.

The Oedipus Complex

Sigmund Freud

We call the mother the first *love*-object. We speak of "love" when we lay the accent upon the mental side of the sexual impulses and disregard, or wish to forget for a moment, the demands of the fundamental physical or "sensual" side of the impulses. At about the time when the mother becomes the love-object, the mental operation of repression has already begun in the child and has withdrawn from him the knowledge of some part of his sexual aims. Now with this choice of the mother as love-object is connected all that which, under the name of *"the Oedipus complex,"* has become of such great importance in the psycho-analytic explanation of the neuroses, and which has had a perhaps equally important share in causing the opposition against psycho-analysis.

Here is a little incident which occurred during the present war. One of the staunch adherents of psycho-analysis was stationed in his medical capacity on the German front in Poland; he attracted the attention of his colleagues by the fact that he occasionally effected an unexpected influence upon a patient. On being questioned, he admitted that he worked with psycho-analytic methods and with readiness agreed to impart his knowledge to his colleagues. So every evening the medical men of the corps, his colleagues and superiors, met to be initiated into the mysteries of psycho-analysis. For a time all went well; but when he had introduced his audience to the Oedipus complex a superior officer rose and announced that he did not believe this, it was the behaviour of a cad for the lecturer to relate such things to brave men, fathers of families, who were fighting for their country, and he forbade the continuation of the lectures. This was the end; the analyst got himself transferred to another part of the front. In my opinion, however, it is a bad outlook if a victory for German arms depends upon an "organization" of science such as this, and German science will not prosper under any such organization.

Now you will be impatiently waiting to hear what this terrible Oedipus complex comprises. The name tells you: you all know the Greek myth of King Oedipus, whose destiny it was to slay his father and to wed his mother, who did all in his power to avoid the fate prophesied by the oracle, and who in self-punishment blinded himself when he discovered that in ignorance he had committed both these crimes. I trust that many of you have yourselves experienced the profound effect of the tragic drama fashioned by Sophocles from this story. The Attic poet's work portrays the gradual discovery of the deed of Oedipus, long since accomplished, and brings it slowly to light by skilfully prolonged enquiry, constantly fed by new evidence; it has thus a certain resemblance to the course of a psycho-analysis. In the dialogue the deluded mother-wife, Jocasta, resists the continuation of the enquiry; she points out that many people in their dreams have mated with their mother, but that dreams are of no account. To us dreams are of much account, especially typical dreams which occur in many people; we have no doubt that the dream Jocasta speaks of is intimately related to the shocking and terrible story of the myth.

It is surprising that Sophocles' tragedy does not call forth indignant remonstrance in its audience; this reaction would be much better justified in them than it was in the blunt army doctor. For at bottom it is an immoral play; it sets aside the individual's responsibility to social law, and displays divine forces ordaining the crime and rendering powerless the moral instincts of the human being which would guard him against the crime. It would be easy to believe that an accusation against destiny and the gods was intended in the story of the myth; in the hands of the critical Euripides, at variance with the gods, it would probably have become such an accusation. But with the reverent Sophocles there is no question of such an intention; the pious subtlety which declares it the highest morality to bow to the will of the gods, even when they ordain a crime, helps him out of the difficulty. I do not believe that this moral is one of the virtues of the drama, but neither does it detract from its effect; it leave the hearer indifferent; he does not react to this, but to the secret meaning and content of the myth itself. He reacts as though by self-analysis he had detected the Oedipus complex in himself, and had recognized the will of the gods and the oracle as glorified disguises of his own unconscious; as though he remembered in himself the wish to do away with his father and in his place to wed his mother, and must abhor the thought. The poet's words seem to him to mean: "In vain do you deny that you are accountable, in vain do you proclaim how you have striven against these evil designs. You are guilty, nevertheless; for you could not stifle them; they still survive unconsciously in you." And psychological truth is contained in this; even though man has repressed his evil desires into his Unconscious and would then gladly say to himself that he is no longer answerable for them, he is yet compelled to feel his responsibility in the form of a sense of guilt for which he can discern no foundation.

There is no possible doubt that one of the most important sources of the sense of guilt which so often torments neurotic people is to be found in the Oedipus complex. More than this: in 1913, under the title of *Totem und Tabu*, I published a study of the earliest forms of religion and morality in which I expressed a suspicion that perhaps the sense of guilt of mankind as a whole, which is the ultimate source of religion and morality, was acquired in the beginnings of history through the Oedipus complex. I should much like to tell you more of this, but I had better not; it is difficult to leave this subject when once one begins upon it, and we must return to individual psychology.

Now what does direct observation of children, at the period of object-choice before the latency period, show us in regard to the Oedipus complex? Well, it is easy to see that the little man wants his mother all to himself, finds his father in the way, becomes restive when the latter takes upon himself to caress her, and shows his satisfaction when the father goes away or is absent. He often expresses his feelings directly in words and promises his mother to marry her; this may not seem much in comparison with the deeds of Oedipus, but it is enough in fact; the kernel of each is the same. Observation is often rendered puzzling by the circumstance that the same child on other occasions at this period will display great affection for the father; but such contrasting—or, better, *ambivalent*—states of feeling, which in adults would lead to conflicts, can be tolerated alongside one another in the child for a long time, just as later on they dwell together permanently in the unconscious. One might try to object that the little boy's behaviour in due to egoistic motives and does not justify the conception of an erotic complex; the mother looks after all the child's needs and consequently it is to the child's interest that she should trouble herself about no one else. This too is quite correct; but it is soon clear that in this, as in similar dependent situations, egoistic interests only provide the occasion on which the erotic impulses seize. When the little boy shows the most open sexual curiosity about his mother, wants to sleep with her at night, insists on being in the room while she is dressing, or even attempts physical acts of seduction, as the mother so often observes and laughingly relates, the erotic nature of this attachment to her is established without a doubt. Moreover, it should not be forgotten that a mother looks after a little daughter's needs in the same way without producing this effect; and that often enough a father eagerly vies with her in trouble for the boy without succeeding in winning the same importance in his eyes as the mother. In short, the factor of sex preference is not to be eliminated from the situation by any criticisms. From the point of view of the boy's egoistic interests it would merely be foolish if he did not tolerate two people in his service rather than only one of them.

As you see, I have only described the relationship of a boy to his father and mother; things proceed in just the same way, with the necessary reversal, in little girls. The loving devotion to the father, the need to do away with the superfluous mother and to take her place, the early display of coquetry and the arts of later womanhood, make up a particularly charming picture in a little girl, and may cause us to forget its seriousness and the grave consequences which may later result from this situation. Let us not fail to add that frequently the parents themselves exert a decisive influence upon the awakening of the Oedipus complex in a child, by themselves following the sex attraction where there is more than one child; the father in an unmistakable manner prefers his little daughter with marks of tenderness, and the mother, the son: but even this factor does not seriously impugn the spontaneous nature of the infantile Oedipus complex. When other children appear, the Oedipus complex expands and becomes a family complex. Reinforced anew by the injury resulting to the egoistic interests, it actuates a feeling of aversion towards these new arrivals and an unhesitating wish to get rid of them again. These feelings of hatred are as a rule much more often openly expressed than those connected with the parental complex. If such a wish is fulfilled and after a short time death removes the unwanted addition to the family, later analysis can show what a significant event this death is for the child, although it does not necessarily remain in memory. Forced into the second place by the birth of another child and for the first time almost entirely parted from the mother, the child finds it very hard to forgive her for this exclusion of him; feelings which in adults we should describe as profound embitterment are roused in him, and often become the ground-work of a lasting estrangement. That sexual curiosity and all its consequences is usually connected with these experiences has already been mentioned. As these new brothers and sisters grow up the child's attitude to them undergoes the most important transformations. A boy may take his sister as love-object in place of his faithless mother; where there are several brothers to win the favour of a little sister hostile rivalry, of great importance in after life, shows itself already in the nursery. A little girl takes an older brother as a substitute for the father who no longer treats her with the same tenderness as in her earliest years; or she takes a little sister as a substitute for the child that she vainly wished for from her father.

So much and a great deal more of a similar kind is shown by direct observation of children, and by consideration of clear memories of childhood, uninfluenced by any analysis. Among other things you will infer from this that a child's position in the sequence of brothers and sisters is of very great significance for the course of his later life, a factor to be considered in every biography. What is even more important, however, is that in the face of these enlightening considerations, so easily to be obtained, you will hardly recall without smiling the scientific theories accounting for the prohibition of incest. What has not been invented for this purpose! We are told that sexual attraction is diverted from the members of the opposite sex in one family owing to their living together from early childhood; or that a biological tendency against in-breeding has a mental equivalent in the horror of incest! Whereby it is entirely overlooked that no such rigorous prohibitions in law and custom would be required if any trustworthy natural barriers against the temptation to incest existed. The opposite is the truth. The first choice of object in mankind is regularly an incestuous one, directed to the mother and sister of men, and the most stringent prohibitions are required to prevent this sustained infantile tendency from being carried into effect. In the savage and primitive peoples surviving to-day the incest prohibitions are a great deal stricter than with us; Theodor Reik has recently shown in a brilliant work that the meaning of the savage rites of puberty which represent re-birth is the loosening of the boy's incestuous attachment to the mother and his reconciliation with the father.

Mythology will show you that incest, ostensibly so much abhorred by men, is permitted to their gods without a thought; and from ancient history you may learn that incestuous marriage with a sister was prescribed as a sacred duty for kings (the Pharaohs of Egypt and the Incas of Peru); it was therefore in the nature of a privilege denied to the common herd.

Incest with the mother is one of the crimes of Oedipus and parricide the other. Incidentally, these are the two great offences condemned by totemism, the first social-religious institution of mankind. Now let us turn from the direct observation of children to the analytic investigation of adults who have become neurotic; what does analysis yield in further knowledge of the Oedipus complex? Well, this is soon told. The complex is revealed just as the myth relates it; it will be seen that every one of these neurotics was himself an Oedipus or, what amounts to the same thing, has become a Hamlet in his reaction to the complex. To be sure, the analytic picture of the Oedipus complex is an enlarged and accentuated edition of the infantile sketch; the hatred of the father and the death-wishes against him are no longer vague hints, the affection for the mother declares itself with the aim of possessing her as a woman. Are we really to accredit such grossness and intensity of the feelings to the tender age of childhood; or does the analysis deceive us by introducing another factor? It is not difficult to find one. Every time anyone describes anything past, even if he be a historian, we have to take into account all that he unintentionally imports into that past period from present and intermediate times, thereby falsifying it. With the neurotic it is even doubtful whether this retroversion is altogether unintentional; we shall hear later on that there are motives for it and we must explore the whole subject of the "retrogressive phantasy-making" which goes back to the remote past. We soon discover, too, that the hatred against the father has been strengthened by a number of motives arising in later periods and other relationships in life, and that the sexual desires towards the mother have been moulded into forms which should have been as yet foreign to the child. But it would be a vain attempt if we endeavoured to explain the whole of the Oedipus complex by "retrogressive phantasy-making," and by motives originating in later periods of life. The infantile nucleus, with more or less of the accretions to it, remains intact, as is confirmed by direct observation of children.

The clinical fact which confronts us behind the form of the Oedipus complex as established by analysis now becomes of the greatest practical importance. We learn that at the time of puberty, when the sexual instinct first asserts its demands in full strength, the old familiar incestuous objects are taken up again and again invested by the libido. The infantile object-choice was but a feeble venture in play, as it were, but it laid down the direction for the object-choice of puberty. At this time a very intense flow of feeling towards the Oedipus complex or in reaction to it comes into force; since their mental antecedents have become intolerable, however, these feelings must remain for the most part outside consciousness. From the time of puberty onward the human individual must devote himself to the great task of *freeing himself from the parents*; and only after this detachment is accomplished can he cease to be a child and so become a member of the social community. For a son, the task consists in releasing his libidinal desires from his mother, in order to employ them in the quest of an external love-object in reality; and in reconciling himself with his father if he has remained antagonistic to him, or in freeing himself from his domination if, in the reaction to the infantile revolt, he has lapsed into subservience to him. These tasks are laid down for every man; it is noteworthy how seldom they are carried through ideally, that is, how seldom they are solved in a manner psychologically as well as socially satisfactory. In neurotics, however, this detachment from the parents is not accomplished at all; the son remains all his life in subjection to his father, and incapable of transferring his libido to a new sexual object. In the reversed relationship the daughter's fate may be the same. In this sense the Oedipus complex is justifiably regarded as the kernel of the neuroses.

You will imagine how incompletely I am sketching a large number of the connections bound up with the Oedipus complex which practically and theoretically are of great importance. I shall not go into the variations and possible inversions of it at all. Of its less immediate effects I should like to allude to one only, which proves it to have influenced literary production in a far-reaching manner. Otto Rank has shown in a very valuable work that dramatists throughout the ages have drawn their material principally from the Oedipus and incest complex and its variations and masked forms. It should also be remarked that long before the time of psycho-analysis the two criminal offences of Oedipus were recognized as the true expressions of unbridled instinct. Among the works of the Encyclopaedist Diderot you will find the famous dialogue, *Le neveu de Rameau*, which was translated into German by no less a person than Goethe. There you may read these remarkable words: *Si le petit sauvage était abandonné à lui-même, qu'il conserva tout son imbecillité et qu'il réunit au peu de raison de l'enfant au berceau la violence des passions de l'homme de trente ans, il tordrait le cou à son père et coucherait avec sa mère.*

There is yet one thing more which I cannot pass over. The mother-wife of Oedipus must not remind us of dreams in vain. Do you still remember the results of our dream-analyses, how so often the dream-forming wishes proved perverse and incestuous in their nature, or betrayed an unsuspected enmity to near and beloved relatives? We then left the source of these evil strivings of feeling unexplained. Now you can answer this question yourselves. They are dispositions of the libido, and investments of objects by libido, belonging to early infancy and long since given up in conscious life, but which at night prove to be still present and in a certain sense capable of activity. But, since all men and not only neurotic persons have perverse, incestuous, and murderous dreams of this kind, we may infer that those who are normal to-day have also made the passage through the perversions and the object-investments of the Oedipus complex; and that this is the path of normal development; only that neurotics show in a magnified and exaggerated form what we also find revealed in the dream-analyses of normal people. And this is one of the reasons why we chose the study of dreams to lead up to that of neurotic symptoms.

Antigone

Käte Hamburger

One reason for presenting Antigone last in our analysis of the figures of Greek tragedy is that the story of this famous daughter of Oedipus follows his and that she, like him, was established in literature for all time by Sophocles. But over and above this, the unique nature of the Antigone theme and its literary constellation makes it particularly well suited to add a forceful finishing touch to our thesis.

Let us look first at the Sophoclean tragedy. The play and its interpretations are obviously a special case. Nothing, it seems, could be more monolithic and understandable than the plot, the heroine, the conflict, and the problem of Sophocles' *Antigone*. It is therefore all the more surprising that ever since Goethe, Hölderlin, and Hegel, almost no Greek tragedy has been more frequently and contradictorily interpreted than this one. Karl Reinhardt could even say in his fine book on Sophocles that one can only conclude, in view of "such numerous and contradictory attempts to characterize and categorize the figure of Antigone . . . that there is in fact something enigmatic in her, something beyond comprehension—and not only to Creon."

Yet the traditional literary view has seen Antigone's nature and conflict as clear and straightforward rather than enigmatic. She upholds, against her uncle Creon, King of Thebes, the unwritten divine law which requires her to bury her brother Polynices, who Creon has decreed is to remain unburied for having attacked his native city. But their brother Eteocles, ruler of Thebes since the death of Oedipus (who has been killed in single combat with Polynices) is given a state funeral as defender of the city.

Like all Sophoclean heroes and heroines, Antigone acts
absolutely. She accepts death, the penalty for disobeying the king's
decree:

> But all your strength is weakness itself against
> The immortal unrecorded laws of God.
> They are not merely now: they were, and shall be,
> Operative for ever, beyond man utterly.

Not for the sake of any man-made law, she says, will she incur the
punishment of the gods. The explanation of this has always seemed
straightforward enough; there are apparently no textual obscurities to
complicate it. Antigone's right, the duty required by love for her dead
brother, triumphs over Creon's right, which he defends against the arguments of his son Haemon, Antigone's future husband, as constitutional
right, maintaining that to make an exception for a relative would be an
infraction of the justice he is bound to exercise as king, and hence of the
order of the state:

> Of all the people in this city, only she
> Has had contempt for my law and broken it.
> Do you want me to show myself weak before the people?
> Or to break my sworn word? No, and I will not.
> The woman dies . . . .
>
> Show me the man who keeps his house in hand,
> He's fit for public authority . . . .
>
> Whoever is chosen to govern should be obeyed—
> Must be obeyed, in all things, great and small,
> Just and unjust! . . .
>
> Anarchy! Anarchy! Show me a greater evil!

Yet when Creon's eyes are opened by Tiresias to his injustice and he is
himself threatened with misfortune if he puts Antigone to death, he
decides to save her. But it is too late. She has already hanged herself in
the vault; at her feet Haemon drives his own sword into his side. Creon
remains, beaten, terribly in the wrong, defeated by Antigone in death.

Hegel, who called *Antigone* "the most excellent, the most satisfying work of art among all the splendors of the ancient and the modern
world," did not, to be sure, find it satisfying because of the absolute

victory of Antigone's right. For him both Antigone and Creon personify moral forces which come into conflict with one another: love of family and the rights of the state. Both are destroyed (Creon not physically but through the loss of his happiness), but they are destroyed only as individuals. Their ideas do not perish, but only the individuals who represent them, and they perish because they both represent only one side of the idea of eternal justice. Both of them are right and both of them are wrong, because both of them are right only one-sidedly. "It is only against one-sidedness that justice is aroused," says Hegel. One can of course raise the objection that even if he is right and Sophocles' tragedy does contain such a complicated philosophy of justice, Creon should still not give in and flout constitutional law when Tiresias threatens him with misfortune. If the state is more important to him than family love and his personal destiny, he should accept the consequences which Tiresias warns him will ensue from his actions toward Polynices and Antigone. But he tries to ward them off, to save Antigone at the last minute, to exempt her from the constitutional law he represents, so that Hegel's interpretation is not even consistent with the action. Other scholars, for instance Heinrich Weinstock, put Creon in the wrong because his concept of the state lacks piety and is unrelated to the divine, whereas Antigone bases her claim upon the gods of the underworld who dictate her acts.

However the critics may allocate the right and wrong between Antigone and Creon, Wolfgang Schadewaldt summed up the position when he said that the meaning of the work is ultimately a *metabasis eis allo genos*, that it moves into a sphere alien to the work, so that no rational interpretation, however well it fits, can encompass it. He makes this statement in an introduction to Orff's setting of Hölderlin's translation of the *Antigone* and remarks that it is a good thing that another mode of interpretation exists besides conceptual thinking—in this case music, which enters into a mystical unity with the flesh of the word in a way which cannot easily be explained.

In the case of *Antigone* there exists—perhaps through an accident of literary history, perhaps not—an interpretive work which in a certain sense stands between the abstract explanations of the literary critics and the philosophers and music, which arouses only an intuitive response. This is a work of literature: the *Antigone* by Jean Anouilh written in 1942. Besides being the only important play on the Antigone theme since Sophocles, this is a rare and remarkable instance of a modern presentation of an antique theme being at the same time an interpretation of it. It is therefore particularly meaningful in our attempt to uncover the germs in the Greek tragedies out of which the modern versions in their various forms have grown.

Anouilh's *Antigone* brings to light something in the *Antigone* of Sophocles which, as Reinhardt said, had remained enigmatic. As in the case of Hauptmann's *Iphigenia*, this is an archaic element which for good reason had been inaccessible to earlier interpreters. The relationship of Anouilh's *Antigone* to that of Sophocles, however, is quite different from the relationship between the Iphigenia plays of Hauptmann and Euripides. Hauptmann drew upon new, hitherto unknown material, new facts of archaic mythology. The case of Anouilh is much more complicated. Here we are not dealing with facts but with a sense of life—and an entirely modern one—which was able nevertheless to inspire a reinterpretation of Sophocles' *Antigone*. In this case the result is that the modern work illuminates the classical one and is illuminated by it to yield its own full meaning. This remarkable interaction (which of course emerges only from a fairly penetrating analysis of both works) is, to our knowledge, unique in the relationship between classical and modern Greek tragedies. Yet it entails no blurring of the differences and the lines of demarcation between the classical play and the modern one. On the contrary, this reciprocal clarification of meaning makes it possible to determine exactly where and in what sense Anouilh's *Antigone* represents a modernization of the *Antigone* of Sophocles.

There occurs in Anouilh a short sentence which seems to us to be the true key to the interpretation of this play and of Sophocles' *Antigone* as well, and to make comprehensible a whole series of passages in the latter that have always been difficult to interpret or have simply been passed over. After Antigone has been led away, Anouilh's Creon says: "Polynices was only a pretext." But before going into Anouilh's play, let us see where this remark of Creon's leads if we follow it back into the Sophoclean play.

What about Sophocles' Polynices? It is notable that the events of this historical episode of the Seven against Thebes, in which Polynices and his brother Eteocles killed each other in single combat, are mentioned, but nothing is said about the brothers' character and conduct, except that the chorus refers to them as two unfortunate wretches, born of the same blood, who raised their spears against one another. Only the fact that Polynices may not be buried has a structural function in the play, specifically in relation to Antigone's action and character. This function is what makes it clear that Antigone is not inspired to her rebellious act of self-sacrifice by particularly strong personal, sisterly love. To Antigone's famous words to Creon—"It is my nature to join in love, not hate," which for so long were taken to express loving feminine gentleness—modern scholarship has restored the meaning they held for Greek antiquity: that her love is not personal, individual love but is exclusively love of family, of blood relatives (which is in fact how Hegel understood it). This interpretation finally makes contextual sense of a passage which Goethe could never reconcile with Antigone's words about joining in love and which he found so repellent that he told Eckermann that he wished it might be proved unauthentic. This is the passage where Antigone says that she would never have assumed the burden of defying the king's decree for the sake of a child or a husband. She gives a very precise reason for this—one which appears very startling to modern sensibilities:

> What is the law that lies behind these words?
> One husband gone, I might have found another,
> Or a child from a new man in [the] first child's place,
> But with my parents hid away in death,
> No brother, ever, could spring up for me.

This passage clearly states that her love and self-sacrifice apply only to the blood relationship. It is also symptomatic that no thought of Haemon, the man she is to marry, crosses her mind and that it is only from him that we learn of the betrothal at all. There is no scene between Antigone and Haemon alone.

With this in mind, we now perceive another relationship between Antigone's death and the action which leads to it, the burial of Polynices, a relationship which is almost the reverse of the one uppermost in our mental image of Antigone. "Polynices was only a pretext"—these words actually shed much light on the Sophoclean Antigone figure and indeed on the structure of the play itself. The crucial passage here occurs in the central speech of the scene between Antigone and Creon, where Antigone refers to the unwritten law of the underworld gods who require that a blood relation be buried.

> I knew I must die, even without your decree:
> I am only mortal. And if I must die
> Now, before it is my time to die,
> Surely this is no hardship: can anyone
> Living, as I live, with evil all about me,
> Think Death less than a friend? This death of mine
> Is of no importance; but if I had left my brother
> Lying in death unburied, I should have suffered.
> Now I do not.
> (p. 203, Fitts and Fitzgerald translation)

The thing to notice here is the order in which the two motives are mentioned. "If I must die now, before it is my time to die, surely this is no hardship"—this expression of Antigone's readiness, one might even say her wish, to die precedes any mention of the action that will incur death. This might be taken to mean that she welcomes this action as the road that will lead her to Hades.

This passage alone of course would not suffice to confirm the hypothesis that behind Antigone's acknowledged motive for defying the king's decree, the obvious motive which precipitates the dramatic conflict, there is another one which, expressed as it is here, begins to look like the primary, more elemental one. There are, however, other passages which support the hypothesis. "You chose to live but I chose death," Antigone says to Ismene, when the latter offers to join her sister in her fate. A moment later she puts it even more strongly:

> Take heart. You live. My life died long ago.
> And that has made me fit to help the dead.
> (p. 178, Wyckoff translation)

This is the plainest passage. For here the connection of Antigone's death wish, her will to die, with her commitment to her blood relatives, to her "clan," is momentarily illuminated. The desire to die is in her because her relatives are dead, because "Persephone has called most of them home." Here we must refer again to the already quoted passage where Antigone says that she would not have defied the decree for anyone not related by blood, such as a husband or a child (which the mother does not feel to be a blood relative because, as she explains, she could conceive other children by other husbands).

But we must not jump to hasty conclusions. This relationship between Antigone's motives, in which the will for death is uppermost, is apparently suggested only in these few words, and we must ask whether they suffice to expose and explain the primacy of her death wish. Both the argument between Antigone and Creon and the one between Creon and Haemon hinge so absolutely on the question of justice that we are perhaps in danger of attributing a too crucial importance to what may be only casual words. But it is the outcome of the plot, the structure, and especially the ending of the play that show that Antigone's words are not casual or fortuitous; they lend these words a decisive weightiness and indeed shift the problem of *Antigone* to a more profound, more enigmatic level than the one of heroic action as such.

From this angle the Tiresias scene now takes on a new aspect. Tiresias appears after Antigone has been led away, and his appearance has always been related exclusively to Creon. Creon, caught in his own authoritarianism, is made aware of his injustice by Tiresias. The gods are angry with him because the dead man, who belongs to the gods of the underworld, is lying unburied and polluting the city and because Antigone, who belongs to the gods of the upper world, has been consigned to those of the netherworld. Only when calamity to his own house is prophesied does Creon capitulate and hurry to bury the dead Polynices and liberate Antigone. He comes too late; she has already hanged herself.

These elements in the action must not be disregarded. The fact that Antigone hangs herself before rescue arrives is a traditional fact of this epic legend. But a dramatist like Sophcoles could not retain this element of chance simply as chance. Thus the "coming too late" has also been the subject of interpretation which, however, like the Tiresias scene itself, has invariably been related to Creon. Creon, says Reinhardt, is "the man who realizes too late . . . he comes too late, not because events move faster than might have been expected but because he is such a limited man." In a similar vein Walter Jens holds that Creon "still thinks that by merely rescinding his decree he can put a stop to what has long been determined. . . . But it is too late. In the end there is nothing but the lament of 'one who is now no more than nothing.' " These explanations seem somehow unsatisfactory; in effect they read things into Creon's character and ignore the suicide motive as it applies to Antigone. Yet both the suicide and the "coming too late," as well as the whole Tiresias scene, acquire a more profound function, more firmly anchored in the structure of the tragedy, if they are seen in the light of Antigone's problem, that is, in the light of her will for death.

But we must read carefully and not disregard the factors which might contradict this view; we must pay particular attention to a major passage which indeed seems to do so—Antigone's lament, before she is led away, over having to depart from life before she has been a wife and mother:

> O tomb, vaulted bride-bed in eternal rock,
> Soon I shall be with my own again.
> > (p. 221, Fitts and Fitzgerald translation)
> No marriage-bed, no marriage-song for me,
> and since no wedding, so no child to rear.
> > (p. 190, Wyckoff translation)

Quite obviously these words contradict her earlier ones welcoming death. They contradict the idea that she is choosing death over life.

Interpretation of apparently contradictory passages like these always runs
the risk of explaining the contradictions psychologically and thus over-
looking the work's mode of being, which is by no means that of irrational life, with its innumerable inherent contradictions. Thus when
Reinhardt says that Antigone has "turned to face the realm of death"
and is standing, before the end, on the borderline between the conflicting
realms of the living and the dead, this is a psychological and thus an
essentially subjective explanation. According to Antigone's own words it
is true, yet it explains nothing. We must discover why Sophocles puts
into Antigone's mouth this affirmation of the will to live, which is to
some extent a contradiction of her earlier words. If this question is to be
satisfactorily answered, if, that is, it can be functionally fitted into the
total structure of the play, the nature of the work reveals itself, stripped
of everything accidental, and—by no means least important—the
apparently fortuitous "coming too late" proves to be a poetic necessity
and perfectly logical. Indeed, the construction of this play is so taut that
this ending, this "coming too late," together with the related Tiresias
scene, illuminates the earlier affirmation of the will to live and is illuminated by it; the one contributes to the understanding of the other.

Let us take the Tiresias scene as our starting point. What does it
mean if, instead of relating it *a priori* to Creon and his unmasking as a
man, we relate it to Antigone? It denotes the possibility that she may be
saved—a retarding element, or rather *the* retarding element, in the
action. The vault is still not death. Creon says to the chorus:

> Take her, go!
> You know your orders: take her to the vault
> And leave her alone there. And if she lives or dies,
> That's her affair, not ours.
> (p. 221, Fitts and Fitzgerald translation)

The Tiresias scene ends with Creon rushing off to save Antigone.
There is a good chance that she is still alive. So long as man lives, hope
for rescue from a desperate situation lives too. And here the connection
emerges between Antigone's affirmation of the will to live and the possibility of rescue. Those words are to be taken (or can be taken) as a
counterpoint, as it were, to suicide before she can be rescued, as a link
with the Tiresias scene, in which the possibility of rescue is implied, a
possibility which might have shifted the balance of events in favor of
life. The possibility of life is anticipated in Antigone's expression of the
life wish. But the fact that rescue comes too late, which is contrary to
what might be called the normal course of events, means in effect that

Antigone's will for death is after all stronger than her will for life. The expression of her will to live fulfils the structural function of revealing the absolute primacy of her readiness for death. Creon and his fate do not matter; Reinhardt rightly recognizes that his fate is "empty." "He is left overwhelmed by misfortune rather than stricken at the very root of his being." But the emptiness of Creon's fate is not intended merely as a contrast to the meaningfulness of Antigone's, as Reinhardt believes. What Creon had been threatened with had to come to pass; as we have tried to show, the function of the threat is to introduce the possibility of rescue which, coming too late, in its turn shows up the primacy of Antigone's readiness for death.

The viewpoint of our comparative analysis seems to have been long forgotten, for up to now interpretation has been confined to the *Antigone* of Sophocles. In every point, however, it has followed the lead of the suggestive words spoken by Anouilh's Creon: "Polynices was only a pretext." Creon goes on: "For her the most important thing was to die." This is a key sentence in two senses. First, it unlocks the classical work; second, it indicates the line which separates the modern play from the Greek one. The line is marked by the modernization of the death problem itself. For now it is of the utmost importance not to let Anouilh's *Antigone* tempt us to interpret Sophocles' tragedy in a modern way. It is always tempting to do this when we can see a plausible death problem complex in a classical play. So we must carefully re-examine the Sophoclean Antigone's will for death and try to determine its nature.

It originates—objectively—in the firm rooting of her existence in the family, the clan. Now that the family of her blood relations is no more, her existence is deprived of the roots which sustain it.

> . . . with no friend's mourning,
> by what decree I go to the fresh-made prison-tomb.
> Alive to the place of corpses, an alien still,
> never at home with the living nor with the dead.
> (p. 188, Wyckoff translation)

Words like these draw even dying into the lostness of existence. Dying is hard because there are no loved ones to mourn. This lament finds its complement in the comforting assurance that she will be allowed to join her dead again:

> I come as a dear friend to my dear father,
> to you, my mother, and my brother too.
> (p. 189, Wyckoff translation)

The objective reason for Antigone's readiness for death, the reason of which she herself is aware, is that she has been forsaken by her blood relatives. But her sense of clan is so deeply involved with her sense of life—in fact identical with it—that in this life situation her death wish and her clan feeling merge and lead to her dramatic action, in which they become one. In interpretation of this figure we can therefore say that she is a profoundly archaic one marked by a specifically chthonian sense of life. It is with good reason that she refers to the gods of the underworld, the chthonian gods whose commands she must obey.

We emphasize this again because it is at this point that Antigone's modernization begins or becomes noticeble: the antique Antigone's archaic, chthonian sense of existence, nurturing an objective, conscious will for death, widens into a sense of existence less determinate and less conscious, of which death is a constituent part, to the point that the death feeling rises to existential dominance.

The reslanting of Sophocles' *Antigone* through this existential broadening of the sense of life is also expressed stylistically by the slightly parodistic form of Anouilh's play. Characters who speak and think in modern terms act out the old play again, with its ancient plot and all the details which are not applicable to its modern setting. "Well, here we are," says the prologue, stepping forward in the Shakespearean manner. "These people are about to act out for you the story of Antigone. Antigone is the thin little creature sitting over there. . . . She is going to have to play her part through to the end" (pp. 9–10). And later Creon says to Antigone: "I'm cast in the bad role, of course, and you in the good one" (p. 77). This has a double meaning, one in the context of the present action and a different one in that of its famous classical model which it must still follow, repeating and parodying it, if it is to be an Antigone play.

Let us look now at Creon's role. The rescue problem of the Tiresias scene in Sophocles is recognizable in an expanded form in the modern play, in which from the outset Creon himself represents the possibility of Antigone's being saved from death. In Anouilh Creon is a thoroughly humane man, a kind uncle who gave Antigone her first doll, as he reminds her. The parodistic split in his personality—already indicated in the prologue's description of him as a robustly built man with wrinkles who is tired and given to meditation—consists in his having issued the decree concerning Polynices and being obliged to enforce it on account of public opinion. At the same time he is a wise, skeptical realist, by no means greedy for power, who finds his own official duty and Antigone's resolution equally absurd. "I'm not going to let you die for a matter of politics," he tells her, and he makes every effort to bring her to her senses. He himself reveals to Antigone that her brothers were degenerate playboys, one worse than the other, not worth giving her life for—never mind sacrificing it to bury Polynices. In fact Anouilh's conception of Creon sheds considerable light on the Sophoclean tragedy, not so much on Creon's character as on his role and function, which the completely different character of the modern Creon now exposes. Something which in Sophocles emerges only in Creon's last-minute attempt to save Antigone is elaborated by Anouilh into a clearly recognizable function of his role as a potential rescuer (and there is now of course no further need for Tiresias). But in the face of the modern Antigone's will to die this function is as powerless as is Creon's last-minute attempt in Sophocles.

The relationship between the Antigone figures in Anouilh and Sophocles is analogous to that between their Creons. The decisive point, as we have said, is the death problem underlying both characterizations, though in different forms. Seen this way, all the details of the modern play fit together, just as those of the classical tragedy combine in a unified structure.

Let us begin with the least accentuated element in Sophocles: Antigone's will to live, expressed toward the end in the lament that she will never be a wife or mother, and finally overcome by her will to die. This lament brings out the striking fact that Haemon, her future husband, has no part in her thoughts and that there is no scene between the two of them alone. This is indeed striking, but, as we believe we can show, for this very reason it confirms that Antigone's will to live is weaker than her will to die. In Anouilh her will to live is depicted more colorfully yet more vaguely, as though the girl herself did not quite understand it. Here Haemon plays a role in Antigone's feelings too. She loves this man, who has suddenly turned away from the beautiful, serene, worldly Ismene in favor of plain, scrawny, not to say ugly Antigone. She says she would have been proud to be his wife and even wanted to give herself to him before she died. She is under a compulsion; she is not wholly in control of her own being and willing. She admits to Creon that it is absurd to die for an unburied corpse, and when he asks her for whose sake, then, she is really making this gesture, she can find no answer but: "For nobody. For myself." This is the decisive admission; it is repeated again and confirmed in the farewell letter to Haemon that she dictates to the guard: "I don't even know any more what I'm dying for" (p. 119). This is the statement of the unconscious existential will for death which Creon's words "Polynices was only a pretext" confirm and by which they are confirmed. The very words of Sophocles' Antigone to Ismene—"You chose to live but I chose

death''—are repeated in Anouilh, and this in itself shows exactly how
and where the two works are linked. The sense of clan has become
irrelevant to the modern mind; it is completely eliminated through
Creon's exposure of Polynices and Eteocles, and it is this that brings into
the open the existential contingency of Antigone's death will.

Nevertheless there is an element in the sense of life of Anouilh's
Antigone which corresponds to the conscious, objective ground for the
Greek Antigone's will for death and which even points up the modern
Antigone's absoluteness of character. This element stands in the same
ambivalent relationship to her will for death as the clan feeling does in
the Greek Antigone, so that it is not quite clear which is cause and which
is effect. Antigone says an unconditional *no* where her uncle, making
concessions to life's eventualities, says a conditional *yes*. The discussion
of *yes* and *no*, which is the core of their argument, contains the whole
problem complex and dialectic of man's freedom and non-freedom.
Creon says with some justification that it is easier to say *no* than to say
yes. ''It is easy to say *no*. . . . To say *yes* you have to sweat and roll up
your sleeves, take hold of life with both hands and get into it up to the
elbows. It is easy to say *no*, even if it means dying. All you have to do
is sit still and wait'' (p. 86).

But this is the sensitive, problematical point. The *no* entails freedom from any duty in life, but it equally entails an absoluteness which,
if followed through to the point of sacrificing life, annuls this freedom.
Antigone wants everything or nothing—she would not even want or love
Haemon any longer (although she is in love with him) if she did not possess him totally and absolutely, if he ''stops growing pale with fear when
I grow pale, stops thinking I'm dead when I am five minutes late, stops
feeling that he is alone in the world and hating me when I laugh and he
doesn't know why'' (p. 98). She is the daughter of Oedipus and ''she
asks [her] questions to the bitter end,'' long after the tiny chance of hope
has vanished—''your dear, dirty hope!'' (p. 100)—the hope, say, that
she may still be saved. This is one of the grounds, one of the reasons,
that make life not worth living to the modern Antigone; it corresponds to
what makes it seem worthless to the Greek one. But it only corresponds
to it; it is not the same thing; it differs from it in proportion to the less
clearly defined sense of life that differentiates the modern mode of experiencing and its literary embodiment from the classical one. The sense of
life of Sophocles' Antigone is oriented toward death because her relatives are dead, that of Anouilh's Antigone is oriented toward death
because life itself does not meet the absoluteness of her demands, so that
she rejects it as contemptible, as Sophocles' Antigone rejects hers. But
when she says at the end that she no longer even knows what she is

dying for, this suggests a general attitude to life in which it is a simple fact that life may be dominant for one person, as it is for Ismene, and death for another, one case being just as irrational as the other. As the unidentified chorus finally puts it, when all those who had to die have died, it makes no difference what this man or that man believed, whether they understood any of it or not. If it had not been for little Antigone, they would all have had their peace. But her death too will be forgotten by those still alive; they will go on waiting for their own death, like Creon, or playing cards, like the guards.

These closing words of the modern French play are certainly a far cry from their Greek model, Sophocles. But the distance does not represent an absolute antithesis so much as a reshaping—an extreme one, to be sure—of an enigmatic element in the classical work in such a way that this modern reshaping brings it into focus. Such is the special interpretive function of Anouilh's *Antigone*, which for its own part is the Antigone of an age accustomed to thinking existentially. Being toward death is one of the fundamental existential principles in Heidegger's *Sein und Zeit*.

This concept and Anouilh's Antigone problem in particular bring up the name of Kierkegaard. Here again we venture to draw upon a theoretical and philosophical interpretation (as we did with Bloch's interpretation of Helen)—this time in order to confirm the value of Anouilh's modern Antigone for the interpretation of her classical counterpart.

Kierkegaard too developed the classical Antigone into a modern figure, and his interpretation and transformation of her is not altogether foreign to Anouilh's. Despite the differences between them, Kierkegaard's interpretation is in fact related to Anouilh's since it too centers on a tragic sense of life and not only on a tragic situation, as in Hegel. In the chapter entitled "The Ancient Tragic Motif as Reflected in the Modern" in *Entweder-Oder (Either/Or)*, he contrasts Sophocles' Antigone with a "modern" one, whom he calls "our Antigone, the bride of sorrow." For Kierkegaard, however, this sorrow "rests like an impenetrable sorrow over the whole family" (p. 153); it has pervaded its life since Antigone's father incurred his unhappy fate and tragic guilt. He holds that to take Antigone's defiance of the king's decree "as a isolated fact, as a collision between sisterly affection and piety and an arbitrary human prohibition" (p. 154) is to misunderstand the nature of the Greek tragedy. Precisely this, which most interpreters, following Hegel's lead, have taken to be the tragic situation of Sophocles' Antigone, Kierkegaard calls a modern tragic theme. By contrast "that which in the Greek sense affords the tragic interest is that Oedipus' sorrowful destiny re-echoes in the brother's unhappy death, in the sister's collision with a simple human prohibition; it is, so to say, the after effects, the tragic destiny of Oedipus, ramifying in every branch of his family. This is the totality which makes the sorrow of the spectator so infinitely deep'' (p. 154).

Kierkegaard does not quote any passages in support of this. But his whole case could be derived from Antigone's first words to Ismene:

> You would think that we had already suffered enough
> For the curse on Oedipus.
> (p. 185, Fitts and Fitzgerald translation)

This passage, however, contradicts the further conclusion—and this is perhaps why Kierkegaard did not quote it—which distinguishes his imaginary modern Antigone from the Greek one. The antique Antigone, he says, ''is not at all concerned about her father's unhappy destiny. . . . Antigone lives as carefree as any other young Grecian maiden . . . [so that] if it were not for the disclosure of this new fact [the burial of her brother] we might imagine her life as very happy in its gradual unfolding'' (pp. 153-154). This then is the point where the Greek outlook can be transformed into a modern one in an Antigone who is ''not turned outward but inward,'' that is to say, who is conscious in her inmost being of the sorrow, the hereditary sorrow, of the race and is formed by it. ''Her real life is concealed . . . [and therefore] although she is living, she is in another sense dead'' (p. 155). The bride of sorrow, ''she dedicates her life to sorrow over her father's destiny, over her own'' (p. 156).

Kierkegaard now gives a description of his imaginary Antigone, always mindful of her sorrow, which sounds like an analysis of an existing work. It is indeed a conception similar to Anouilh's modern Antigone, who is conscious of her death wish but not—or only vaguely—of its origin. In Kierkegaard's Antigone too there exists in this knowledge ''an ignorance which can always keep sorrow in movement, always transform it into pain'' (p. 159), but Kierkegaard explains this element of ignorance more precisely than Anouilh does. It applies to Antigone's uncertainty as to whether her father was aware of his guilt, a guilt which she believes she shares as his loving daughter and as a member of the family. Kierkegaard finds a modern motivating factor in this which does not exist in the antique Antigone, for whom ''her father's guilt and suffering is an eternal fact, an immovable fact, which her sorrow does not alter'' (p. 158), that is, it does not stimulate reflection, which is needed to make sorrow a completely inward ''substantial'' state—for this is how these associations are to be understood. This notion of the "substantial" probably approximates closely the notion of the "existential." We need not concern ourselves here with Kierkegaard's analysis of Antigone's sorrow, which on this particular point is somewhat abstruse. What is important for us is the fact that his modern Antigone is conceived in an existential instead of merely an ethical manner. Moreover, for him the classical Antigone already contains the germ of this conception. All the requisite elements for depicting her as "modern," as the bride of "substantial" sorrow, are present in her. Characteristically, she is said, in the passage already quoted, to be already dead, although still living. But the germ from which this interpretation springs shows itself to be closely related to an essential factor concealed in Sophocles' Antigone which, as we believe we have shown, accounts for her death wish: namely, her commitment to the family, to the clan. For Kierkegaard this bond is the source of the sorrow of family guilt, of Antigone's existence as a bride of sorrow, which already points to that leaning toward death which becomes her dominant sense of existence.

But this is just what separates the existential viewpoint of our own time from Kierkegaard's: Anouilh offers no specific factual explanation corresponding to Kierkegaard's attribution of Antigone's sorrow to her ignorance of Oedipus' relation to his guilt. Kierkegaard's "modern Antigone" is useful to the topic of this chapter if only because it shows in principle the possibility of existential interpretations of the Greek Antigone and thus helps to clarify Anouilh's play in its interpretive function and its significance for the Antigone problem.

Clearly these deeply existential versions of the Antigone theme do not exhaust the subject. It would indeed be curious if dramatists in a time like ours, who have experienced the problems of might and right in the stark reality of war and dictatorship, had missed the obvious aspect of the Antigone figure, her courageous personality. Antigone, whom Brecht called "the great figure of resistance," stands very much in the foreground of literary consciousness and it is easy to understand why both the first and the second world wars called attention to her. In 1947 Brecht adapted Hölderlin's translation of the Antigone; in 1917 Walter Hasenclever created a "figure of resistance" who without doubt possesses far more immediacy than Brecht's.

The latter point is not mentioned merely as a fact but as the point of departure for an assessment of the two versions. Exactly thirty years separate Hasenclever's work from Brecht's, and the times when the two plays were written are significant. Although Brecht called Sophocles' Antigone the great figure of resistance in classical tragedy, he added that in the year 1947 "her poem could not be written here." For the term "resistance," familiar to all those who lived through the Nazi era, had nothing in common with Antigone's resistance. "She does not represent the German resistance fighters who must seem most important to us," says Brecht. He thinks that "the ancient play, being so distant in time, did not invite identification with its heroine" (p. 100). But historical distance is perhaps not so essential as the type of resistance which Antigone represents. Pursuing Brecht's ideas, we might say that a personal confrontation with a tyrant, like Antigone's relatively straightforward action in defying Creon's prohibition, was a gesture of resistance unthinkable under totalitarian dictatorship, where resistance consisted in the attempt to eliminate that dictatorship, and in working clandestinely to that end. One might even say that the human, personal factor, which, despite all Creon's tyranny, still persists in his relationship with Antigone and in their discussion, is the very factor which in the year 1947 made any identification with Antigone impossible. Brecht evidently gave his adaptation the title *The Antigone of Sophcoles* to prevent its being taken as something possible in our time. Consequently he does not seek to make his Antigone play "worth seeing" as a demonstration of Antigone's problem but as an exemplification of "the role of the use of force in the collapse of top government," which is a far more abstract phenomenon.

These remarks of Brecht's in the preface to his Antigone play are almost more instructive than his treatment of the play itself, which formally might be called a composition (using Hölderlinian language), largely translated into the Brecht idiom and built around Hölderlinian thematic key words—a complex affair since Hölderlin's text is itself a translation. Behind the verbal lattice work of this Hölderlinian-Brechtian text the actual figure of Antigone emerges with little change; all its essential elements have been retained and are underlined in every case by the original words of Hölderlin's text. In some passages resistance to Creon's decree is already expressed as resistance to or a critique of the rule of dictatorship:

> Where you need force against others
> you soon need it against your own.
>
> (p. 44)

But the major change Brecht makes, in line with the intention stated in his preface, is that Antigone's problem is superseded by the more universal one of tyranny perishing in and of itself. For this purpose he introduces a situation of political warfare precipitated by Creon to divert attention from the domestic consequences of his rule—and here the topical allusion is obvious. The role of Tiresias as a prophet is limited to seeing through these events and their motives and foretelling the inevitability of ruin:

> What foolishness or evil have you done
> that you must go on committing foolishness and evil? . . .
> Robbery comes from robbery and hardness needs hardness
> and more needs more and in the end is nothing.
>
> (p. 80)

In a sense Brecht carries *ad absurdum* Hegel's old interpretation: that Creon also represents a rightful duty. And the objection to Hegel's view which already arises out of the Sophoclean plot—that Creon would have to stand by his decree even when the seer foretells disastrous consequences for him—is worked up into a capital theme by Brecht. For his Creon acts on purely utilitarian grounds; it is no longer fear of the gods' retribution that drives him to the vault to rescue Antigone but the necessity of securing Haemon's services as leader of his army, since he has been informed that his eldest son Megareus has been killed in battle.

The thirty years that separate the two German Antigones of Hasenclever and Brecht are, as we have said, symptomatic of their understanding of this great figure of resistance. For Brecht there was no connection between Antigone's resistance and the resistance movement of the 1940's, which fought not to defend human right against state right but to abolish a criminal dictatorship and to restore a nation's freedom and honor. Antigone's personal problem had to yield to the problem of power and its fate. In 1917 there was no analogous situation in any of the warring European countries. Resistance was not yet a reality but at best an idea, a genuine revolutionary idea (realized in Russia that same year) born of war weariness and directed against the form of government responsible for that war. In Hasenclever's *Antigone*, freely created on the Sophoclean model, the war plays this very role, its pros and cons argued out between "voices" loyal to the monarchy and revolutionary ones.

In Germany, however, World War I was also the era of literary Expressionism, and as an Expressionist dramatist Hasenclever was able to find in Sophocles, either in full view or immediately beneath the surface, everything which the Expressionists were hurling against society and their own time: resistance to the power of the state, resistance to the war, the proclamation of humanity and fraternity, love and life. Antigone's most famous line—"It is my nature to join in love, not hate''—can be taken as the key to Hasenclever's *Antigone*, as its revolutionary theme, though it is never cited in this sense. His Antigone becomes a revolutionary, rising above the personal deed of sisterly love to proclaim before the people the message of love for humanity. At first the people, still loyal to the monarchy, threaten her, only to kneel before her when she declares:

> I gave my brother back to the earth
> and celebrate with you resurrection.
> Now we are brothers in pain!
> Now I know: women can be immortal,
> when they water men's meaningless ways
> from the pitcher of love;
> when from tears of their poverty
> help sprouts;
> when the act of the living heart
> razes enmity's walls.

But even if it might look as though Antigone's death sacrifice for the sake of bringing love into this world is going to initiate a better, more humane era—the hope she expresses herself in the vault: "I have helped. My work is done"—this hope is extinguished again. When the people find themselves free after Creon's breakdown and departure, they want to storm and plunder the castle. Yet there is no doubt that this Antigone's doctrine of love and her self-sacrificial death point to the teaching and sacrificial death of Jesus, indeed to the Messianic hope of his second coming:

> Fellow men! In a thousand years
> I shall be walking among you.

But even though Hasenclever brings the light of the mystery of Christ to bear on his Antigone, it does nothing to illuminate the riddle of the great archetypal figure, who stands in the vast arena of world literature and the human consciousness looking more monumental than ever against an interpretation of this kind. And this is how she looks in the light of Anouilh's modern version, precisely because it has come closer to her secret than any other.

The Descendants of Labdacus in the Theatrical Works of Jean Cocteau

Démetrios N. Pantelodimos

In his *Lettre à Jacques Maritain* in 1926, Jean Cocteau tells how a Greek shepherd's crook, given to him by Picasso, inspired him to adapt classical tragedy to the rythms of the modern era. "I was attempting," he wrote, "a process of rejuvenation of the masterpieces so as to re-work and re-order them, removing the veneer and the dead wood; in short, to quote Stravinsky when taken to task for a lack of respect for Pergolesi, 'Where you revere, I love'; I wanted to marry them." This yearning of one who was a former pupil of the Lyceé Condorcet accords too with the theatrical *mores* of the end of the 19th and the beginning of the 20th centuries: from 1894, the year of the publication of Jean Moréas' *Iphigénie* and of the dedication of the ancient theatre of Orange as a cultural place of pilgrimage, classical drama was born and began to exert its influence over the literary circles of the time. The plays of Aeschylus, of Sophocles, and of Euripides were continually being translated into French to inspire contemporary authors. Alfred Poizat made use of the myth of Electra; Georges Rivollet took care of the *Phoenician Women* and of *Alcestis*, while Jean Giraudoux in 1929 presented *Amphitryon 38*. With regard to the plays dealing with the tragic story of the offspring of Adrastus, Sophocles' *Antigone* was, remarkably, translated three times on to the French stage in the first 25 years of this century, by l'abbé Bousquet in 1901,[1] by Dr. H. Mireur[2] in 1912, and

---

[1] Presented 23 June 1901 by the students of the class of humanity in the École Libre de l'Immaculée Conception, Paris-Vaurigard.

[2] Adaptation in French verse, Nice, 1912.

by Eugène Crespel[3] in 1919; it also served as a model for the *Antigones* of Alfred Poizat, Jean Réboul, and Louis Perroy, published in Paris in 1920, 1921, and 1922, respectively. Sophocles' *Oedipus Rex* was the prototype for Aubram and Fabrice's *King Oedipus* in 1900, and for *Oedipus, King of Thebes*, a play in three acts and thirteen scenes by St.-Georges de Bouhélier, which was put on at the Cirque d'Hiver by the Gémier Company on 17 December 1919. One can note also in passing, two adaptations of the play, one by Péladean called *Oedipus and the Sphinx*,[4] and the other, to which we shall return, by Cocteau. As for *Oedipus at Colonus*, three arrangements of that occur in the same period, one by Emmanuel des Essarts in 1900, one by Jules Gastambide, which was shown at the Théâtre de l'Oeuvre on 7 June 1904, and one by J. Rivollet rendered by the members of the Comédie Française on 21 July 1924.[5] André de Lille published at Nantes in 1912 a tragic poem after Sophocles entitled, *Oedipe à Colone*; the same title graces the play by Olivier Bournac and Boyer d'Agen, which is composed of a prologue, one act and two scenes, published in Paris in 1915.[6]

Among all the descendants of Labdacus, the one who held the greatest fascination for Cocteau was without question Antigone. On more than one occasion, the poet of the *Plaint-Chant* expressed his devotion to Sophocles' heroine: "Antigone is my patron saint." After the death in 1923 of his friend Raymond Radiguet, he became preoccupied by metaphysical considerations. In the previous year, he had sought in Antigone the epitome of revolt and reason. Later, in his *Lettre à Jacques Maritain*, he explained his decision: "Instinct always drives me against the law. That is the secret impulse behind my translation of *Antigone*. I should hate my love of order to benefit from the meaning the word is loosely credited with." A passion for acts of revolution, the blind refusal of all help, and the devotion of his temperament to spiritual superiority all act as spurs to Cocteau's attachment to the royal family of Thebes, whose members are endowed not only with great physical strength, but also with prodigious intelligence and a temper which impelled them inexorably into the grave.

---

[3] New translation in verse, Cherbourg, 1919.

[4] Péladan: *Oedipus and the Sphinx*, adapted after Sophocles, Paris, 1903.

[5] These three versions share the title of the ancient tragedy. The first was published at Clermont-Ferrand in 1900 and the second at Paris in 1905, while the third, a four-act piece in verse accompanied by the music of Guy Ropartz, appeared in Paris in 1925.

[6] The *Phoenissae* of Euripides formed the prototype to George Rivollet's four-act verse play of the same title, presented at the ancient theatre of Orange on 10 August 1902 and at the Théâtre Français de Paris 5 July 1905.

Cocteau's "contraction" was produced in the Atelier at Dullin on 20 October 1922 with the set by Picasso, costumes by Chanel, and music by Arthur Honegger, who would later distil from the play a 1942 opera staged with a set by Cocteau himself. Cocteau's intention was undoubtedly to condense the plot of Sophocles' *Antigone*, surveying a celebrated text to bring out its hidden qualities and awaken the interest of the youth infatuated with Modernism. In the words of André Fraigneau,[7] Cocteau subjected the forgotten works to an operation analogous to those carried on in beauty parlors in an attempted restoration of the sacred. Nevertheless, a detailed comparative study of the two texts reveals a curtailing on Cocteau's part of several of Sophocles' lines, especially in the stasimons of the chorus and the remarks of Tiresias. The Chorus' first song[8] is thereby reduced to 13 lines in a baroque style which already looks forward to several passages in the *Machine infernale*:

> CHORUS: Man is outrageous: he sails, he ploughs, he hunts, he fishes. He breaks horses, thinks, speaks. He invents codes, warms himself and keeps a roof over his head. He braves illness: death alone he cannot cure. He does good and evil. He is a good man when he heeds the precepts of heaven and the laws of earth but ceases to be so if he ignores them. Let no criminal be my guest. Ye Gods, what a strange marvel! It's unbelievable but true! Isn't that true, Antigone? Antigone! Antigone! Could you have disobeyed? Could you have been such a fool as to destroy yourself?[9]

From this example, it is very doubtful whether shrinking it can enhance a classical text or even hint at fresh beauties. Greek tragedy is a poem whose content requires learned comment and analysis to be appreciated in any depth: a summary will always fall short of the worth and beauty of the original.

What must be considered the most significant innovation of this French tradition is the language, which sets itself apart from the learned translations intended for the pupils of the *lycées* and the students at the Sorbonne. A consciously theatrical construct, it is colloquial without grating on the ear and avoids embarrassing anachronisms. Among the expressions used, two stand out: "anarchy" and "anarchists." On two

---

[7] A. Fraigneau, *Cocteau par lui-même*, (Paris, Écrivains de toujours, 1963) 51.

[8] Sophocles, *Antigone* 332-383.

[9] J. Cocteau, *Théâtre* (Paris, Gallimard, 1948), vol. 1, p. 18.

occasions, Créon labels Antigone's behaviour anarchic in conversation with his son Hémon. Curiously, the two words occur in propositions taking the form of maxims: "There is no greater sore than anarchy"[10] and "It is laudable to praise anarchists."[11] The original uses the terms ἄκοσμα and ἀκοσμοῦντας[12] which have less force than the words used by Cocteau. For him, Creon represents the passionately blind ruler desperate to hold on to power in the thick of the political crisis threatening the state. He goes so far as to compare Jocasta's brother with the revolutionary tribunal which sent defenders of liberty to the guillotine. He even thinks Charlotte Corday echoes Antigone's tone when she tells Fouquier-Tinville that she does not regret what she has done, because she has been successful.[13] Thus, the typically Sophoclean contrast between earthly and divine laws turns into a duel between two political tendencies, both of which are liberating.

One obstacle stands in the way of the tragic poets and playwrights who have sought to copy Greek antiquity or to compose in imitation of the unequalled precedents of ancient tragedy: the existence of the Chorus, whose presence enriched the text with lyric passages and kept the plot alive with its continual evolution on stage. French classical theatre had replaced it with the gentleman- and ladies-in-waiting (in conformity with 17th-century custom), who played a largely consultative role for the heroes of Corneille and Racine. Voltaire, who had a predilection for movement and the spectacular, introduced into his *Oedipe*[14] a two-man chorus from solely decorative motives. In retaining in his adaptation of Sophocles' *Antigone* a chorus which he himself played at the première, Cocteau seems to be demonstrating his approval of the arguments of the philosopher Ferney. At the play's revival in 1927, the production was notable for the presence of five plaster heads of young men, while the actors themselves wore transparent masks closely modelled on a fencing visor.[15] The overall effect is intended to evoke "a sordid royal carnival, a family of incest."[16] We should not lose sight of the fact that in the previous year, Cocteau had put on *Les Mariés de la Tour Eiffel* at the Théâtre des Champs-Elysées and the outsized scenery had provoked a scandal.

---

[10] J. Cocteau, *Théâtre*, p. 23.

[11] Ibid., p. 24.

[12] Sophocles, *Antigone*, 660, 730.

[13] J. Cocteau, *Théâtre*, p. 35. Antigone, Place de la Concorde, Notes written in 1926.

[14] Voltaire: tragedy in 5 acts (Paris, 1719).

[15] Cocteau, *Théâtre*, vol. 1, p. 11.

[16] Ibid.

After his experience of *Antigone* in the theatre, Cocteau, in collaboration with Stravinsky, tackled another ancient tragedy, *Oedipus the King*, and extracted from it an opera-cum-oratorio in Latin entitled *Oedipus Rex*. This first brush with Sophocles' unparalleled masterpiece was later to inspire a fresh "surgical operation" in Cocteau, the results of which were published in 1927 in the *Revue Hebdomadaire*.[17] Upon the retirement of Mounet-Sully, the tragic king of Thebes certainly appeared from time to time on the French stage, but was primarily of interest to the specialists of the Sorbonne. However, Cocteau's attempt "to rework an old masterpiece, to rejuvenate it, clear away the dead wood, strip off the veneer"[18] did not arouse much interest in the public at large, having as it did its first performance in 1936.

A producer and painter, Cocteau also brought his attentions to bear upon the scenery of his play, which was set of course in front of Oedipus' palace; yet he introduces a number of important modifications to underline further a particular aspect of the ancient myth, namely the trap set by the gods in their cruelty to man. Thus, the problems of predestination, fate, free will, and the critical relationship between divine nature and mankind which preoccupied Sophocles, are reduced in Cocteau to a game, a divine machination by the gods against a man innocent in the face of fate. Reading the stage directions, one could be forgiven for thinking one had happened upon a scene of enchantment, where the spectacle applies before its time the methods of avant-garde theatre. It is nonetheless appropriate to draw attention to the sense of realism that permeates the French adaptation. In the Greek play, the desperate Thebans implore the king right at the outset for his assistance, trying in a lucid and reasonable manner to rid Cadmus' city of the plague. Garlanded with laurel and full of hope and confidence, they help their leader to find the means of salvation. In Cocteau's scene, by contrast, the plague-ridden act out their agonies, while in front of the ramp the people's protestations are scrawled like slogans on the walls. The Chorus' place is taken by a golden statue draped in red in the shape of a youth resting outstretched on his elbow, his head upright and his mouth open. The actor playing this insignificant role must hide in the set and speak through the open mouth. The Theban populace's energetic action is transformed into a motionless being, a symbol of the deadly fate awaiting the whole city.

---

[17] Cocteau, *Oedipe roi, adaptation libre d'après Sophocle, Revue Hebdomadaire* 12 (1927) 391–414. This play was published by Plon in tandem with *Roméo et Juliette* in Paris in 1928.

[18] Cocteau, *Oedipe roi: Roméo et Juliette* (Paris, 1928), p. 2 (preface).

As regards the author's method of adaptation, we note in general that Cocteau was concerned to abbreviate the ancient text, whose length is perfectly suited to the exigencies of its performance on stage. He is in the habit of shortening the Chorus' lines, while remaining faithful to the words of Sophocles; he applies the same method to the long speeches. But he often removes entirely whole lines of dialogue, with no thought for the verisimiltude of certain episodes. At the start of Sophocles' play, while he waits for Creon's return from his mission to Delphi, the hero swears before the people to fulfil the oracle.[19] The king therefore finds himself obliged, when the plot reaches its crisis, to obey his own decrees which condemn him to the painful road into exile. Cocteau suppresses this passage, the moral justification for the unhappy Oedipus' last action. The majority of the modifications bear on the entry of Tiresias, who, on finding himself on the defensive, reveals all to stave off the king's anger. In Sophocles' tragedy, the annoyance of the two characters makes sense: the blind seer finds himself in a quandary and turns himself every which way in his struggle to avoid revealing the truth. The king, by contrast, takes Tiresias' silence and obstinacy as proof of guilt and treason. The truth, revealed during the course of the conversation, cannot gain acceptance with Oedipus and the tragedy's plot survives the first episode uninterrupted. Such formidable scenic economy has vanished clean away in Cocteau's adaptation, as he cares little for verisimilitude. The argument erupts out of the blue and the god's representative calls the king "foolhardy", "an impure beast,"[20] and "wicked."[21] Finally, by the removal of lines 433–436 in the original, Oedipus's question

by your account, whose son am I?[22]

is entirely unjustified, since Tiresias is not referring to his functions at the court of the father of the King of Thebes, who has begun an inquiry whose outcome will reveal his descent. In order better to understand the French version, it helps to compare the two texts, especially in the treatment of the beginning of Oedipus' and Tiresias' dialogue.

Tir.: Φεῦ, φεῦ, φρονεῖν ὡς δεινὸν ἔνθα μὴ τέλη
λύῃ φρονοῦντι· ταῦτα γὰρ καλῶς ἐγὼ
εἰδὼς διώλεσ'· οὐ γὰρ ἂν δεῦρ ἱκόμην[23]

---

[19] Sophocles, *Oedipus Tyrannos*, 76–77.
[20] Cocteau, *Oedipe roi*, p. 16.
[21] Ibid., p. 19.
[22] Ibid.
[23] Sophocles, *Oedipus Tyrannos*, 316–318.

[Alas, alas: what a terrible thing it is to
possess knowledge where knowledge can do no good
to the one who has it. I knew this well enough,
but I forgot it, otherwise I would not have come.]
Alas, I am a fool to have come.
There is nothing I can say, nothing. I cannot reveal
your misfortune.

OE: Τί φής; ξυνειδὼς οὐ φράσεις ἀλλ' ἐννοεῖς
ἡμᾶς προδοῦναι καὶ καταφθεῖραι πόλιν;[24]
[What do you mean? You are hugging the knowledge
to yourself, and won't disclose it, and have it in mind
to be false to me and to ruin the city?]

CH: You know and yet you are silent! Do you want to betray
your city? We beg you, speak. Speak! Speak, we beg you!

TIR: Ἥξει γὰρ αὐτά, κἂν ἐγὼ σιγῇ στέγω.[25]
[All will happen by itself, even if I shroud it in silence.]
You are rash and will learn nothing from me.
The truth will out despite my silence.

OE: . . . Ἴσθι γὰρ δοκῶν ἐμοί
καὶ ξυμφυτεῦσαι τοὔργον εἰργάσθαι θ' ὅσον
μὴ χερσὶ καίνων· εἰ δ' ἐτύγχανες βλέπων
καὶ τοὔργον ἂν σοῦ τοῦτ' ἔφην εἶναι μόνου.[26]
[Let me tell you that you seem to me to have plotted
the deed and executed it, except for not actually doing
the murder; and if you had sight, I would have said that this
deed was yours alone.]

Faithful to his *modus operandi*, Cocteau also foreshortens the
scene where Oedipus and Jocasta confide in one another,[27] and the inter-
jections by the Chorus, but he sticks faithfully to the Greek in the scene
of the two old men and in the climax, with the exception of the king's
lament on his re-appearance with his eyes pierced, after the tragic recognition inspired by *Oedipus Rex*:

I am night, deepest night. I am the king become night.
From day I am in night. O my boundless fog and
obscurity! Pins and memories pierce me.[28]

---

[24] Ibid., 330–331.
[25] Ibid., 341.
[26] Ibid., 346–349.
[27] Ibid., 707–862.
[28] Cocteau, *Oedipe roi*, p. 43.

This repeated opposition between night and the light of the sun corresponds in part to Oedipus' blindness and recognition, but in part also to the final brightening light of the truth which blinds eyes accustomed to the shadowy darkness of ignorance. Despite several poetic passages, the adaptation remains insignificant. Its sole interest is as a sketch of the masterpiece which appeared in 1934, since several subjects of this free translation are developed in *Machine Infernale*. The Chorus still remains reduced to a single character which recalls to failing memories at the beginning of each act the principal features of the myth and sets the scene. The greater part of the prologue is devoted to Oedipus' meeting with the Sphinx; this should have formed the subject-matter of a new play by Cocteau which eventually went to make up the second act of *Machine Infernale*. As it happens, this is the most interesting act, accommodating as it does metaphysical ideas, philosophical reflections, and symbolism, while at the same time treating the data of the ancient myth in an original manner.

The *Machine Infernale* had its premiere at the Louis Jouvet Theatre (Comédie des Champs-Elysées) on 10 April 1934, with sets and costumes by Christian Bérard. It was a double triumph. Following the path mapped out by his illustrious forebears, Corneille and Voltaire, Cocteau is not content as Sophocles had been, to portray the recognition of the King of Thebes, but exploits to the full other features of the ancient myth. The French tragedians of the 17th and 18th centuries resorted, in order to fill the requisite five acts of their plays, to episodes such as the love of Dirce and Theseus on the one hand and of Jocasta and Philoctetes on the other, which are wholly alien to the Oedipus myth and interrupt the flow of the tragedy. With the object of avoiding this stumbling-block (St-Georges de Bouhélier had already in 1919 introduced into his play the love of Antigone and Haemon), Cocteau bases three-quarters of his play on topics peculiar to the myth of Oedipus and antecedent in time to the ultimate climax. Thus, the play's first act, entitled "The Ghost," (which sets itself off against that by Gide[29] by its introduction of the picturesque, of a sense of playfulness, and the spectacular) owes much to Seneca, who had conjured up the spirit of the dead king Laius, although one can also detect the influence of the first act of *Hamlet*. Cocteau manages, however, to avoid the barren mimicry of his prototypes. In the Latin play, Laius' shade, conjured up by Tiresias, succeeeds in communicating his message charging Oedipus with the crimes of incest and murder; similarly Shakespeare's ghost conveys his secrets to Hamlet while the shade of the King of Thebes,

---

[29] André Gide, *Oedipe* (Paris, 1931).

invisible to Jocasta and Tiresias, cannot speak clearly before the two soldiers, leaving his words ineffectual. In addition, this ghost is not raised by Tiresias' magic art, but appears of his own volition to prefigure his family's impending downfall. Finally, in Creon's account of the necromancy, the modern drama's audience witnesses the apparition of the deceased king vainly trying to make himself understood. Honest and simple characters such as the two soldiers perceive the truth intuitively—in the second act the Nurse's son will almost make out the Sphinx in the guise of a young girl—but their low birth sadly does not allow them to assist their fellow-citizens, since they cannot put their intuitive talent to profitable use. Even Tiresias, whose very job it is to decipher mysteries and divine the truth, does not succeed in laying bare the holy secret in order to change the course of destiny.

The second act, entitled "The Meeting of Oedipus with the Sphinx," has more originality than the first. The Sphinx' character is split between a young girl questioning passers-by and the jackal-headed god Anubis who puts her victims to death; but what do these two symbolize? Roland Derche wondered whether it was Evil in general or War.[30] In fact, the key lies with Anubis: ". . . the gods have their gods. We have ours. They have theirs. That is what is known as infinity . . . Logic compels us, in order to appear to man, to take the shape they assign us; otherwise, they would see nothing but thin air."[31] The Sphinx and her executioner are therefore the tools of higher powers, symbols of the smooth operation of the machinery common to heaven and earth. Even a failure on the part of these two instruments of the gods, of Nemesis especially, could not derail the inexorable progress of destiny.

Tiring of slaughter, the Sphinx aspires to be loved of man. It is this weakness which entails Oedipus' false victory and throws him headlong into a deceptive happiness whose epilogue will be most painful. Cocteau is also concerned to emphasize the responsibility Oedipus bears: Laius' death apart, the ingratitude displayed towards his saviour justifies the misfortune which will soon strike him down. The poet of the *Plain-Chant* was the first, to our knowledge, among modern authors to formulate doubts on the young hero's victory by symbolizing the conquest of power. Softened by Oedipus' presence, yet still retaining certain aspects of her divine nature, the Sphinx reveals her secret and the solution to the riddle and unfolds in detail the scene that would ensue were Oedipus not to please her: ". . . Then I would ask you to come closer and I would help you by loosening your legs. There! And I'd question

---

[30] R. Derche, *Quatre mythes poétiques*, Paris, S.E.D.E.S., 1962, p. 63.

[31] Cocteau, *La Machine infernale*, pp. 82, 83, and 84.

you. I might ask 'What is the animal that walks on four legs in the morning, two at noon, and three in the evening?' And you would rack and cudgel your brains; and, by dint of hammering away at it, your mind would settle on a small vignette from your youth or you would repeat a number, or you would count the stars between those two demolished columns; and I would reacquaint you with reality by solving the riddle.

"The animal is man: As a child, he walks on four legs; in his prime, on two; and as an old man with the aid of a stick."[32]

Yet this scene is not wholly original, as Dio Chrysostom had already spoken of Oedipus' false victory over the Sphinx: σὺ μέν, ὦ Διόγενες, ἀναισθητότατον ἁπάντων ἀνθρώπων ἀποφαίνεις τὸν Οἰδίπουν· οἱ δὲ Ἕλληνες οἴονται οὐκ εὐτυχῆ μὲν γενέσθαι ἄνθρωπον, συνετὸν δὲ πάντων μάλιστα· μόνον γοῦν αὐτὸν λῦσαι τὸ αἴνιγμα τῆς Σφιγγός. καὶ ὁ Διογένης γελάσας, Μὴ γάρ, ἔφη, ἐκεῖνος ἔλυσε τὸ αἴνιγμα; οὐκ ἀκήκοας ὅτι ἄνθρωπον αὐτὸν ἐκέλευσε γνῶναι ἡ Σφίγξ; ὁ δὲ ἄνθρωπον μὲν ὅ ἐστιν οὔτε εἶπεν οὔτε ἔγνω· τὸ δὲ ὄνομα τὸ τοῦ ἀνθρώπου λέγων ᾤετο λέγειν τὸ ἐρωτώμενον· ὥσπερ εἴ τις ἐρωτηθεὶς τί ἐστι Σωκράτης, ὁ δὲ μηδὲν εἴποι πλέον τοῦ ὀνόματος, ὅτι Σωκράτης.[33]
[Diogenes, you make Oedipus out to be the least perceptive of all mankind. The Greeks, however, consider him as not the most fortunate, but the most intelligent: at any rate he alone solved the riddle of the Sphinx. Diogenes laughed: "Solved the riddle? Haven't you heard that the Sphinx told him to decide the answer was 'man'? But he neither said nor realized what 'man' actually was. In saying the word 'man' he thought he was saying what was being asked of him as if someone were asked 'What is Socrates?' and said nothing beyond the word 'Socrates.'"]

A bare comparison of the two reveals that Cocteau has admirably adapted for the theatre the passage from his ancient source.

The next act, entitled "The Wedding Night," is also original, but heavily coloured by Freudianism. Cocteau shows a certain daring in making us alive to maternal incest; in the first act, he had already stressed Jocasta's affectionate handling of the young soldier, but the sentiment was equivocal: a curious intermixture of feminine sensuousness and maternal affection. In the third act the situation becomes much more heavily charged, even stifling and suffocating because of the two spouses' nightmares, a host of portents, the drunkard's song (summarizing all that has come to pass) and Jocasta's terror in the face of the scars

---

32 Cocteau, *La Machine infernale*, pp. 118–119.

33 Dio Chrysostom 10.30–31.

which recall for her her son's adventure.   It is true that Sophocles'
renowned lines

πολλοὶ γὰρ ἤδη κἀν ὀνείρασιν βροτῶν
μητρὶ ξυνηυνάσθησαν[34]
[Many men have before now slept with their mothers
in their dreams.]

have caused much ink to flow. They amount, in fact, to an argument of
the Queen's as she uses every ploy, both concrete and abstract, to calm
Oedipus with her attempted demonstration that oracles are not infallible
in their outcome. By contrast, Cocteau's hero is open about his
incestuous intentions when Tiresias intimates that Jocasta might be his
mother:

I will reply that I have always dreamt of a love of that kind, of an
almost maternal love[35]

In this setting, Cocteau is already sketching his *parents terribles* under
the constant influence of Freud's psychoanalytical researches.
    The final act, while bearing similarities to *Oedipus Rex*, owes
much to Cocteau's genius. Although this section of the play deals with
the ultimate climax, i.e., the recognition of Oedipus' identity, it begins
with the arrival of the messenger from Corinth, who is the son of the
shepherd who had entrusted the child exposed on Mount Cithaeron to
King Polybus. Cocteau had had the happy idea of placing the quarrel
between Tiresias and Oedipus in the previous act, as well as the story of
the hero's victory over the Sphinx. Yet there is a defect in this final
episode: the revelation through the messenger of Oedipus' origins is
abrupt and without psychological foundation. Cocteau has erred in the
portrayal of his characters, as the son of Polybus' shepherd lacks
simplicity and naiveté, despite being full of good will and concern. By
contrast, Laius' herdsman is directly modelled on his ancient forebear,
although, as a result of the shortening of the scene and the suppression
of the clash of the two old men, he is not so clearly defined. The most
important innovations Cocteau brings to the myth are the presence in the
dénouement of Antigone, who insists on escorting her blind father into
exile; and the apparition of the ghost of Jocasta, finally purified in death,
who resumes her role as mother and guardian angel of her unhappy son.

---

[34] Sophocles, *Oedipus Tyrannos* 981–982.
[35] Cocteau, *La Machine infernale*, p. 154.

The myth of Oedipus, with its dramatic interest, its originality, its pathos, and the timeless problems it poses, has never ceased to provide a subject for playwrights. In adapting it to the *mores* and customs of his own time, Corneille seized the opportunity to convey his message on the problem of free will. Voltaire was more particularly concerned with dramatic movement and theatrical illusion, and made use of the same myth in his first play, which is full of philosophical allusions, a concession to his audience's laxer tastes. In addition to the question of free will and predestination, Gide placed the emphasis on the triumph both of Oedipus' gratuitous act and Antigone's religious virtue. Cocteau's philosophy is simpler. He grapples in particular with the timeless problem of destiny, of a fatalism whose yoke none can shake off. All man's attempts to pre-empt the future and change the course of destiny are futile and in fact oil the wheels of the infernal machine. The gods are content to lead mankind into misfortune without ever explaining the justification for their trials. They even multiply the portents of their doom so as to render the fall of mortals all the more painful and manifest. Any attempt at rebellion is in general destined to founder. Through the eyes of the blind seer, Oedipus sees only the happier side of his future life; husband and wife fall one after the other into the irrational, dreaming of the "outer battlements" and the "recalcitrant dog," while the shade of Laius seeks on several occasions to warn the Queen of the great danger she faces. Tiresias himself can neither save his fellow being nor comprehend the progress of the celestial system, since his final two words marking the end of the play preach total agnosticism.

Despite the hero's rebellion against his fate and his rejection of responsibility on to the shoulders of destiny, his punishment is essential to the dénouement and to the conclusion of what Tiresias calls "an horrific masterpiece." The same idea occurs later in *Les Chevaliers de la Table Ronde*, which was first produced at the Théâtre de l'Oeuvre on 14 October 1937: "It is destiny which prompted you to predict this visit. Destiny made you lay this trap. Destiny made you kill."[36] Yet, to re-establish moral order, it is necessary to expiate even one's unintentional acts: "You must pay, always pay. Pay for yourself, pay for your deeds."[37]

The descendants of Labdacus make regular reappearances in the works of Cocteau and in particular in the *Parents terribles*, put on at the Ambassadeurs Théâtre on 14 November 1938. Oedipus' place is taken by Michel, who, when he was small, wanted to "marry Mummy."[38]

---

[36] Cocteau, *Théâtre*, 1, p. 161.

[37] Ibid., p. 175

[38] Ibid., p. 230.

Open and honest, like the young conqueror of the Sphinx, he becomes the unwitting killer, not of his father, but of Jocasta. Aunt Léo imitates Créon and defends the social order. Yvonne combines Antigone's anarchic side and the unhealthy sensuality of Laius' widow. Like all Labdacus' unfortunate descendants, she is autocratic and longs for eternal love far from earthly change and decay. Meanwhile, the infernal machine, a symbol of the anguish of unavoidable misfortune, continues to set traps for mankind in all its impotence. Esther, one of the *monstres sacrés*, summarizes this philosophy of desperation, this blossoming of the absurd, which gives the taste of the torpid atmosphere of the inter-war years: "It was irresistible. There are forces pushing and dragging us towards catastrophe."[39]

---

[39] Ibid., 2, p. 51.

Ancient Tragedy on the Modern Stage

Wolfgang Schadewaldt

1

The appearance of the titles of Greek tragedies on our theatre programmes, and the performance on stage at not infrequent intervals of works by, especially, Sophocles and Aeschylus, but also Euripides, has become in our country a phenomenon no longer considered remarkable. At any rate I for my part have to confess—and others will have had the same experience—that in the forty years it will soon be since my boyhood and adolescence, during which I have taken a lively interest in the life of our theatre, I have never thought twice about the fact that in this period of time I have attended many important performances of Sophocles' Oedipus plays, the Sophoclean *Antigone*, and also Aeschylus' *Persians* and *Oresteia* as well as Euripides' *Medea, Trojan Women*, and *Suppliants*. Even when in the last decade it seemed to me, as a watchful observer, that I could detect such performances of the Greek tragedians becoming not only more frequent than before, but also more substantial, the observation in the first instance pleased me, but it did not take me altogether by surprise. Only after I became directly involved, with my own efforts at translation, in such modern performances of Greek tragedy on our stages, did I feel a great sense of wonder come over me one day: how it can possibly be that dramatic works which had their first performance before a completely different people, watched beneath a different sun and different gods some 2400 years ago, can still time and time again inspire theatre managers, directors, set designers, casts, and, connected with that, a modern public, in a way hardly different from the newest productions.

Now this phenomenon undoubtedly to some extent has its foundation in the great worth of these Greek tragedies, their inexhaustible
vividness; and just as in many other ways too we have to see our cultural
beginning—at a level perhaps not yet again attained—in the Greeks, so
too the history of our theatre takes its origin in the theatre of Dionysus at
the foot of the Acropolis of Athens in the fifth century B.C. However it
is not these chains of thought, which are more a humanist's chains of
thought, that I would like to pursue here. For the other side to this
phenomenon of an immediate stage presence of the Greek tragedians in
our time can only be understood from our own temporary historical position, which is also the position of our theatre today. It is that which I
wish to draw attention to in this lecture. In seeking to outline in broad
terms the history of the reception of Greek tragedy on the modern stage
in the last one hundred and fifty years, it is not my intention simply to
trace a so-called "phenomenon of its time" back to its historical roots.
What prompts us to take this course is the objective need to find our own
position, how this comes about at a time when there is cause for continuing to do something that one has hitherto been doing unconsciously—but
now with a clear awareness of the issues involved and a proper historical
perspective.

2

That we have gained a closer, more immediate and living relationship to Greek tragedy at all, is something which has only been made
possible in the last two hundred years, since the era of our classicism as
initiated by Winckelmann and brought to its peak by Goethe, Schiller,
Hölderlin and Kleist—I ignore the early attempt of late baroque classicism of a Martin Opitz, to translate *Antigone* into German
Alexandrines (1636)[1] and similarly I ignore the translation, excellent in
its own way, of Sophocles' *Electra* into Alexandrines, done by Johann

---

[1] Mart. Opitii, *Opera Poetica*. That is spiritual and worldly *Poemata*, last
revision and correction by the author himself. Amsterdam. Johan Iansson 1646, p.
164ff. Opitz had already translated Seneca's *Troades* in 1625. In the Latin preface to
Antigone Opitz speaks out against the view that tragedies were only written for *luxus*
and *voluptas*; the purpose of tragic art for him is a contemplative and moral one: "The
aim of tragic productions is to make us learn from the contemplation of some one else's
fortune, of whatever kind, to take more care in safeguarding our own, by good
behaviour, when it is flourishing; or to bear it more calmly and without becoming
depressed when it is against us and at a low point." More on Opitz's *Antigone* translation in Richard Alewyn's well-known book: *Vorbarocker Klassizismus und Griechische
Tragödie, Analyse, der Antigone-Übersetzung des Martin Opitz*, Heidelberg 1926: also
in *Neue Heidelberger Jahrbücher*, n.f. 1926 3-63 (Reprint: Libelli 79, Darmstadt
1962).

Elias Schlegel at Gottsched's suggestion during his studies at Leipzig (probably 1739)[2] But decisive as the breakthrough to Homer and the Greek tragedians was in that period of our classicism, in the sense of the recovery of the poetic *word*, this still did not lead to an immediate presence of Greek tragedy in the theatre. What was played on our stages[3] were the reworkings of the French classicising poets, Corneille, Racine, and above all Voltaire. People were captivated by the *opera seria* above all in the style of Gluck, and then came the German reworkings of a Goethe, Schiller, and Grillparzer. If Tobler, Stolberg, Solger, Hölderlin and also Humboldt were then translating Sophocles and Aeschylus, these poetic translators were struggling to wrest the tragic *word* for the German language; they did not achieve effectiveness on stage.[4]

---

[2] As Johann Heinrich Schlegel records in his edition of his brother's works, Part 1, Leipzig 1761, p. 387, Gottsched wished "to append Aristotle's *Poetics*, which he had previously resolved to publish, as further illustration of one of the best Greek tragedies in German translation." Apart from Johann Elias Schlegel one should mention for the pre-classical period Steinbrüchel's *Theater der Griechen*, published in Zurich, 1763. It contains the prose translations (some of them previously published individually) of Electra, Oedipus, Philoctetes, and Antigone of Sophocles, the Euripidean Hecuba, Iphigenia in Aulis, Hippolytus and Phoenissae: cf. Christian Heinrich Schmid, *Chronologie des deutschen Theaters*, 1775, new edition by Paul Legband Berlin 1902, 83, 143.

[3] I refer to the programmes of various German theatres in the eighteenth century: the Hamburg National Theatre, the Court Theatre at Gotha, the stage in Weimar, the old Burgtheater, as printed in the following works: Rudolf Schlösser, *Vom Hamburger Nationaltheater zur Gothaer Hofbühne*, Theatergeschichtliche Forschungen, published by B. Litzmann, vol. XIII, Hamburg and Leipzig 1895, 66ff.; Richard Hodermann, *Geschichte des Gothaer Hoftheaters 1775-1779*, Theater-geschichtliche Forschungen IX, Hamburg and Leipzig 1894, 130ff.; *175 Jahre Burgtheater 1776-1951* (continued up to the summer of 1954), published by the management of the Burgtheater, Wien 1955, 1ff. Perhaps the activities of a man like Friedrich Wilhelm Gotter can be regarded as symptomatic of the time, amongst whose works for the stage, mostly fashioned after the style of French models, is a tragedy *Orest und Elektra*, which is a reworking of Voltaire's *Oreste* (1750). This Electra play of Gotter's was first performed on the 7th of January 1772 by the Seyler company in Weimar, and then from 1777 onwards several times at Vienna's Burgtheater: cf. Rudolf Schlösser, *Friedrich Wilhelm Gotter. Sein Leben und seine Werke. Ein Beitrag zur Geschichte der Bühne und Bühnendichtung im 18. Jahrhundert*, Theater-geschichtliche Forschungen X, Hamburg and Leipzig 1894, 195f. We should also draw attention to the free adaptations frequently staged at this time, above all of Euripides, by Johann Elias Schlegel, and in particular his play *Orest und Pylades*; and also to the important repertoire planning by Conrad Ekhof at the time of his Actors' Academy in Schönemann's company: cf. Heinz Kindermann, *Conrad Ekhofs Schauspieler-Akademie*, Sitzungsberichte der Österreichischen Akademie der Wissenschaften, Phil.-Hist. Klasse, Band 230, 2 Abh., Wien 1956.

[4] It is noteworthy that Hölderlin, before he signed up with the publisher Wilmanns, tried in 1803 through his friend Schelling, "to have his translations of Sophocles' *Oedipus* and *Antigone* sent off to the Weimar theatre" (Letter 241, 28 Sept. 1803 Beck).

One revealing detail may illustrate this. Goethe, as director of the Weimar theatre in the years 1791 to 1817, only twice, out of the roughly six hundred plays that he staged during this period, attempted one of Sophocles' tragedies, and both times merely with a modern version by several hands. Thus in the spring of 1809 he staged *Antigone* in the version by Friedrich Rochlitz, and in 1813 *Oedipus* in the free rearrangement by August Klingemann.[5] He himself has no great expectations of the *Antigone* performance on the day before: "The play can no longer create what we nowadays call effect; but I still believe that it will fit in with and remain in the set of quietly noble representations that we perform from time to time."[6] And when the play had gone on stage: "The effect was what I expected. The play left behind a very agreeable, pleasing impression. Everyone was content and half-astonished, since people know hardly anything of this clarity and simplicity."[7] One notes the restrained, almost guarded tone. Perhaps even more indicative of the perplexity which even Goethe felt *vis-à-vis* the performance of one of Sophocles' tragedies, on 22 January 1809 he had written to Rochlitz: "*Antigone* is scheduled for the thirtieth. Unfortunately it does not fill the entire evening, and I have been forced to put in a little operetta afterwards." This "little operetta" which Goethe the theatre director had to put on after Sophocles' *Antigone* was by Seyfried and bore the title *At the Golden Lion*. It subsequently enjoyed many more revivals than Rochlitz's Sophoclean *Antigone* itself.[8]

---

[5] I take these dates of the Weimar repertoire as Carl A. H. Burkhardt presents it in his book, *Das Repertoire des Weimarischen Theaters unter Goethe's Leitung*, Hamburg 1891. Cf. also Heinz Kindermann, *Theatergeschichte der Goethezeit*, Vienna 1948, 681. Goethe's intentions of bringing more of Sophocles' tragedies to the stage went further, as his letter to Rochlitz of 26 December 1808 proves: "One thing seems imperative to me, that you make the same effort on *Oedipus* and *Oedipus at Colonus*: for *Antigone* is really only fully effective following on from these two plays. You could, to save yourself a bit of work, drop the Solger work and make these more accessible to only German ears. We should speak further of this when we get round to performing *Antigone*."

[6] To Rochlitz, 29 January 1809.

[7] To Rochlitz, 1 February 1809.

[8] We have remarkable evidence for the cultivated rhetorical style of this *Antigone* production of Goethe's from the lips of the actor Haake. After characterising the "free declamation," the "rhetorical beauty," as the highest rule of the Goethe school, which above all led to the cultivation of the "higher drama" of "declamatory tragedy," he continues: "In the year 1813 (?) I saw in Weimar a performance of *Antigone* in its most perfect form . . . but it was not the individual actors so much as the harmonious way in which they worked together that made this performance so attractive and memorable as the definitive highest example . . . *The Law of Rhetorical Beauty* everywhere took precedence over individual characterisation, the latter being something to which one almost had to lower oneself."—The quotation from Heinz Kindermann, *Theatergeschichte der Goethezeit*, Vienna 1948, 707.

With such facts in view one is forced to come to the conclusion that in the so-called classical age around the turn of the eighteenth century the theatre-supporting public, whether court society or the higher bourgeoisie, were not yet capable and ready for comprehending Greek tragedy in its genuine original form. The fresh reconquest of the Greeks took place at that time in the hearts of a few *cognoscenti* with vision, like Hölderlin, Keist, and basically Goethe as well where he really comes close to the Greeks, people with a deep inner knowledge about the nature of tragedy who were not necessarily understood and who remained alone. The wider public had been brought up on the eighteenth-century view of art: its taste, despite all the admiration for the Greeks, was rational and humanitarian, and just as unreceptive to the elemental natural force with which Greek tragedy puts before our eyes the truth of reality as it was, at first, to true Shakespearean tragedy. Even Goethe himself, when he got to know Aeschylus in Humboldt's translation, received the work with an admiration in which there was at the same time an unmistakable sense of alienation. His famous words about Aeschylus' *Oresteia*: "an ancient giant figure, shaped like a monster" gives proof of this.[9]

3

The intellectual movement that created the spiritual prerequisite for the reception on the German stage of Shakespeare as well as of Greek tragedy was Romanticism, and the deepened historical sense which, following Herder, was called for above all by the Romantics. This historical sense, in which the past was no longer seen as a massive archive of memorabilia, or a museum of great models, but as something which developed into a broad landscape, with many divisions and layers, implanted in our consciousness what I would like to call the sense for historical perspective. This historical perspective enables me to know something remote in time in its own place, in its own essence as something severed from me, something other, something removed, and yet through its perceived, measured distance from me still united with me again. And while historical detachment comes into my perspective on something distant in time, that historical perspective overcomes the detachment and makes possible a new qualified immediacy, a new closeness.

---

[9] The relevant sentence reads: "Such an ancient giant figure, shaped like a monster, appears before us and astonishes us, and we have to pull all our senses together to be able to do it anything like justice." To Humboldt, 1st September 1816.

August Wilhelm Schlegel's lectures on dramatic art and literature, which appeared in the years 1809 to 1811, and looked in detail at
the theatre of the Greeks as treated by the three great tragedians, helped
to prepare the way.[10] Then Karl Immermann took the first step towards a
performance of Sophocles during his impressive period in Düsseldorf
from 1832 (or 1834) to 1837. He organised dramatic readings of
Oedipus Rex, but during his few years of activity in Düsseldorf did not
manage to stage the performance he had in mind[11] The honour of the
first epoch-making performance of a Greek tragedy in its original form
falls therefore not to Karl Immermann but to the talented Romantic on
the royal throne, King Frederick William IV of Prussia. Inspired by a
circle of enthusiastic admirers of ancient tragedy, including the influential classical philologist August Boeckh, teaching in Berlin at the time,
the king organised a performance of *Antigone* on 28 October 1841
(repeated on 6 November) in the New Palace in Potsdam in front of an
invited circle of High Society. It was directed by Ludwig Tieck, called
from Dresden to Berlin by the king. They performed the Johann Jacob
Christian Donner's translation in a strict archaising style, on a stage that
had been raised five feet above the orchestra on which the chorus stood
and moved. Even today one can sense in the little book which the
organiser, aware of the epoch-making nature of this performance, had
printed, the feeling of amazement that "a play so foreign in content and
form" could have had such an immediate and convincing effect on all
those present.[12] August Boeckh in his valuable notice about the performance speaks of a "splendid and sublime" impression, an "uplifting and
powerful effect."[13] One should note that the performance "has become
an object of such general discussion and interest that it has become quite
an Event."[14] And in 1843 Ludwig Tieck writes as he looks back over
the performance: "The noble will of a great king has brought it about
that Sophocles' *Antigone* has been performed before the public. It had an

---

[10] Critical Edition by Giovanni Vittorio Amoretti, Bonn and Leipzig, 1923.

[11] Cf. Harry Mayne, *Immermann, Der Mann und sein Werk*, Munich 1921,
252; 350. Also Richard Fellner, *Geschichte der deutschen Musterbühne. Karl
Immermann; Leitung des Stadttheaters zu Düsseldorf*, Stuttgart 1888, 176.

[12] "*Über die Antigone des Sophokles und ihre Darstellung auf dem königl.
Schloßtheater im Neuen Palais bei Sanssouci*," *Drei Abhandlungen von August Boeckh*,
Ernst Heinrich Toelken, Friedrich Förster, Berlin 1842—the above quotation in the
Preface, p. xi f.

[13] Boeckh (op. cit.) 76; 86.

[14] Fr. Förster, (op. cit.) III. In his own way Heinrich Heine also attests to the
epoch-making nature of the performance in the poem "*Der neue Alexander*," supple-
ment to period poems, 3rd piece: . . . and Ernst Zinn kindly refers me to "*Verkehrte
Welt*," period poem nr. 42 "And a Puss in Boots (Tieck) brings Sophocles to the
stage."

uplifting effect on most of the spectators. A man of understanding said that is was remarkable how a work which school, lectures, and learned endeavour always relegated to a far, hazy distance in our imagination, now through this performance came convincingly close to us, fresh and lively as if it had been written today.''[15] Incidentally, it is again characteristic of the romantic spirit of this performance that Mendelssohn wrote the music for the chorus: movements and recitatives for many voices, as well as individual solos accompanied by the chorus.[16]

All in all the Potsdam performance of 1841 seemed to have proved that Greek tragedy could still have a place on our stages. More still, it was thought that ''it cannot pass without consequence that such a noble work of art, freed from the narrow confines of academia, the dusty schoolroom, comes out into the open and is made accessible to the general public's interest.''[17] And in fact the *Antigone* performance of 1841, which was in the following years itself repeated many times and, in a new translation, was even performed in Paris, according to Tieck, "with great effect," led to a whole series of performances of other tragedies of Sophocles as well as Euripides in Berlin, Potsdam as well as other German theatres (e.g. Hamburg 1844): *Oedipus Rex, Oedipus at Colonus* 1845, Euripides' *Medea* 1843 and Hippolytus 1851. Yet these other performances did not match the "great and excited interest" in *Antigone*. And Ludwig Tieck, who in 1851 still saw the performance of *Antigone* as a "step forward in our Theatre" has to admit, by contrast, on seeing *Oedipus at Colonus* that "the general public must first get used to such great manifestations if they are to be able to appreciate them."[18]

---

[15] Letter to the translator of "*Elektra*" in Ludwig Tieck, *Kritische Schriften* II, Leipzig 1848, 423f.

[16] It is perhaps worth noting that a critic like Tieck offers the opinion of Mendelssohn's "excellent music" that for him as a layman it had been "disturbing," "that the singing of the chorus had been isolated as a separate part, existing individually," as he thought "that the harmony of the whole thing is the fundamental objective of a work of art, but that the over-rich instrumentation makes the singing difficult to understand and isolates itself too much from the tragedy." *Kritische Schriften* IV, Leipzig 1852, 372. Apart from that the costumes were also criticised, about which Frederick Förster said that "perhaps learning had done too much and the tailor too little," op. cit. XIV.

[17] Förster, op. cit. VIII.

[18] Cf. for the last point in general Ludwig Tieck, *Bemerkungen über einige Schauspiele und deren Darstellung auf der Berliner Hofbühne*, 1851 in *Kritische Schriften* IV, Leipzig 1852, 369ff, the quoted passages pp. 373 and 379.

4

As Tieck's last cited verdict shows, archaising performances such as the one at Potsdam seem by their very nature to have been too exclusive to bring the real conquest of the stage as it developed, especially in the following period, in the course of the nineteenth century in tune with the great shifts in society. It was not until twenty years later, and then twenty years after that, that the next two decisive steps followed, at first through the spirit of historicism as well which intersected with late classicism; the first in 1866 by the Meininger Theatre, which one would perhaps describe as the historical theatre *par excellence*; the second with the *Oedipus Rex* performed on 29 December 1886 by the Burgtheater in Vienna, which in 1882 had already staged Sophocles' *Elektra*.

For this immediate revival of Sophocles' Greek tragedy on the stage of the time a man was needed who had such qualities that he could combine a timely true enthusiasm for classical antiquity, a living feel for the theatre and the necessary stage experience. This man was Adolf Wilbrandt, the subsequent director of the Vienna Burgtheater and the author of a great number of technically superbly constructed classical-epigonous dramas, among them the *Meister von Palmyra*. To give the bare dates first, it is best to let Wilbrandt himself speak, who in the introduction to the second edition of his translation of Sophocles in 1903 writes looking back on these performances as follows:[19] "Already in December 1866 the Meininger Theatre had performed my arrangement of *Oedipus Rex* and *Antigone* with great success; in April 1867 the whole trilogy [by which he understands *Oedipus Rex*, *Oedipus at Colonus* and *Antigone*] was performed on three consecutive nights and to great effect."

"That was the beginning; slowly other theatres and successes came. The first big step only came at the end of 1886: after the Munich Hoftheater had played the whole trilogy, *Oedipus Rex* was performed in the Vienna Burgtheater under my direction, and was found so powerfully moving and inspiring and provoked such a storm of applause as I have rarely experienced. It then became a box office draw and success for the Burgtheater [which put it on thirty times until 5 March 1899].[20] Since then it . . . has conquered many German stages and the irresistible force which is alive in this masterpiece of dramatic construction will win over many a stage yet."

---

[19] Adolf Wilbrandt, *Sophokles' ausgewählte Tragödien*, Munich 1903, p. IV, first published 1866 by Ch. Beck, Nördlingen.

[20] *175 Jahre Burgtheater, 1778-1951*, zusammengestellt und bearbeitet von der Direktion des Burgtheaters, Vienna 1954, 153.

As emerges from Adolf Wilbrandt's own words, it is mainly through his efforts as a man of the theatre, set against the background of the century's historical spirit, defining and overcoming distance, that the henceforth permanent transplantation of Sophocles on to our stages became a fact. Wilbrandt saw himself as the man who had restored Greek tragedy to the modern theatre, and notwithstanding all the important predecessors he had, he will still with good reason be so acknowledged by modern theatre historians.[21]

5

The external appropriation of ancient tragedy for the modern stage as such was achieved in the year 1886, but the internal appropriation of its essence was only now to begin. Adolf Wilbrandt had achieved his great success with a very opportune translation and adaptation of Sophocles' basic text, which he also had printed and about whose principles he expressed himself with all clarity in the introduction to his edition. We must look at this more closely, and, as is always necessary in tracing historical developments, together with the positive advances made on one level bring to light also limitations which are always bound up with every historical advance.

With great seriousness and honesty Wilbrandt struggles with the demand for fidelity to the original, in constant conflict with the "orthodox old school,"[22] and finds that true fidelity can never simply reside in literal exactness, or in a pure, archaising preservation of the transmitted text. "Only what works, is alive, and only what is alive is true!" he cries, and thereby introduces the effect on "today's" people as the measure for what is alive and for what is possible in the way of truth. Much of the original seems to him to be simply tied to its time, forever outlived and dead. This dead material must be firmly set aside, cut out or reworked, in order "truly" to preserve the real "life" of those immortal dramatic works of the Greeks. Significantly, as a child of his age he sees the Greek gods above all and their symbolism as outlived

---

[21] About the importance and the success of the introduction of Sophocles into the repertoire of the Burgtheater, cf. Rudolph Lothar, *Das Wiener Burgtheater*, Vienna 1934, 263 and Heinz Kindermann, *Das Burgtheater*, Vienna and Leipzig 1939, 125. In there is the report about the production by Speidel: "The success of the performance, which had been meticulously planned, was tremendous. The spectators, who approached the alien way of writing with sensitive understanding, and did not let any important part of the plot escape them, really deserve the greatest praise; Vienna has come of age for the great tragedy from which it formerly, with a greater or lesser degree of complaint, used to shut itself off."

[22] Wilbrandt, *op. cit.* 5ff.

and forever dead. And here he comes up against, in particular, the problem of the ancient chorus. "People are," he writes, "too much accustomed [i.e. from those performances in the ancient style] to seeing the chorus as an inevitable and irreplaceable constituent of Greek drama for them to accept without misgiving a version which got it out of the way."[23] Indeed, "if one of those festivals at which Sophocles and his fellow poets competed against each other before the whole people, before the city, sea and sky, were to be resurrected from the dead and repeated before our very eyes, no spectator would attend more devoutly than I, and no one would listen more piously to the chorus's solemn singing. But the dead do not rise again, and the Athenian chorus cannot be resurrected any more than any other dead people . . ." It stands "unexpectedly and without foundation like a pale theorem between the active participants." The old chorus "lies as if in an enchanted castle to which one can no longer find the entrance. Its *form* is petrified: it only remains to be asked: how can its *content* be rescued to live again?" And Wilbrandt answers: "By stripping it of its outworn symbolism, one confers on its general form a fitting *individuality*, and through this apparent violence restores its living relationship to the plot." Indeed, it can be that it is completely set aside, with only a quick word to make the necessary transition in the dialogue. Wilbrandt regards this radical method as called for in, for example, the fourth choral song in *Oedipus Rex*; that Dionysiac dance in which the chorus is swept along in Oedipus' euphoria before the catastrophe comes crashing in on him. "If I have any foresight and any knowledge and understanding, by Olympus, you shall not, O Cithairon, fail to be celebrated by us with dances on the morrow's full moon." Wilbrandt said that he had "seen very well how this choral song's incurably strange nature confuses our feelings and chills them with the undramatic pause it brings. Poetic value is not lost thereby [by its deletion]."[24] If one sets such radical solutions on one side, and asks how in practice in his adaptation Wilbrandt "confers a fitting individuality on a chorus stripped of its outworn symbolism," one example, typical of many, may give a demonstration.

The pivot, as it were, of the entire play about Oedipus the King is that middle choral song in which the poet makes his own voice heard, speaking from his own time, and expresses his deep concern about the decline of religion and morality as well as the threat to the role of the tragic chorus if "the divine passes away." A literal translation of this choral song goes as follows:

---

[23] Wilbrandt, *op. cit.* 8.

[24] Wilbrandt, *op. cit.* 17.

O, may Destiny be with me,
so that I carry with me the holy purity
in every word and deed
over which there are laws,
ranging on high, born in heaven's
ether, of whom Olympus alone
is father; no mortal nature of men
has brought them forth, and never shall
forgetfulness lay them to rest. Great
is the god in them, and grows not old.

Excess is the seed for the tyrant, Excess,
if it has vainly over-filled itself
with much that is untimely and not wholesome.
Ascended to the highest ridge,
it hurtles down to the sheer depths, Compulsion,
where it can put its foot to no good use.
But what is good for the state, that struggle,
may the god never extinguish it, is my prayer.
God I shall never cease
to hold as the one who stands before me.

But if some one proceeds presumptuously
in deed or word,
fearless before Justice and without awe
for the holy places of the gods,
may an evil fate overtake him
for his impious extravagance!—
If he makes his gains unjustly,
and does not hold apart from the unholy,
or tries to lay hands on the untouchable in a vain pursuit,
who shall in such a case, as a man,
have strength to keep the arrows
of his wild wishes from his soul!
If, forsooth, such actions are held in honour,
for what purpose shall I dance?

No more shall I go to the untouchable,
the navel of the earth, in prayer,
and not to the temple at Abai,
and not to Olympia:
if these things are not pointed out

and proved right to all mortals!—
No, mighty one, if that is how you are rightly called,
Zeus, ruler of all! May it not be hidden from you
and your reign which shall never die.
As Laios's old oracles are fading,
they are already erasing them!
Nowhere is Apollo manifest among the sacrifices.
The divine is passing away.[25]

In his version Wilbrandt to some extent retains the main ideas of
the choral song, but he mixes them up like a deck of cards, and above all
he breaks up the song of the chorus into a dialogue, between a first, second and third citizen. The choral song restored "truly" to its "real life"
now takes this form in Wilbrandt:

> *Second Citizen*
> *(looking at the queen and shaking his head)*
> Will it please the city?

> *First Citizen*
>   What do you mean?

> *Second Citizen*
> Arrogance! From which tyrants are born!—Arrogance,
> That fills itself on evil wantonness,
> That jeers at the old and good! From its peak
> Precipitately it falls, into the depths of need,
> and its stumbling feet carry it no more—
> They shall not malign what is holy,
> Not jeer at our gods. Have they no awe
> of the laws that range high in the ether,
> that guide our words and deeds?
> That eternal Olympus gave birth to,
> not thought up by men and mortal Nature?
> They never sleep, and forgetfulness does not
> lay them to sleep! The god that gives them life
> is ever awake and knows how to meet Insolence.

---

[25] Sophokles, *König Ödipus*. Deutsch von W. Schadewaldt, Berlin-Frankfurt
1955, 51f. New edition: Sophokles Tragödien, herausgegeben und mit einem Nachwort
versehen von W. Schadewaldt. Die Bibliothek der Alten Welt, Zürich-Stuttgart 1968,
201f.

Third Citizen

And so say I.
If they no longer honour the gods' temples,
or fear Justice; if, in wanton arrogance
they stretch out their hands to what is forbidden
and venture to do everything they please—if that
becomes respectable:
for what purpose then libation, prayer and sacrifice?
Why make the pilgrimage to Abai, to Olympia,
to the holy middle of the Earth?
Lord Zeus,
Ruler of all—if we address you with the right title—
May what they do not stay hidden from you!
The old oracles they cast away,
prophecy no longer counts. Apollo
is eclipsed, and everything divine
disappears!

First Citizen
(*anxiously making signs to him*)
Silence! The Queen!

What has happened here? With the most honest endeavour and remarkable skill a tragic chorus has, by this transformation, been preserved dramatically in conformity with the taste of the time and "rescued" by having its style changed and being levelled down into the form of a genre-type dialogue between citizens. At the same time, however, it is precisely this honesty and the skilfulness of this procedure which reveal how the real basic substance of the tragic play, the tragic message, was for Wilbrandt and the public of his day a book with seven seals, and it becomes clear how the effectiveness on stage which Wilbrandt had won for Sophocles' tragedy was bound up on the other hand with a renunciation of something which those "orthodox thinkers of the old school" had possessed when in the time of those first performances at Potsdam and Berlin they had left the choral songs untouched. For Wilbrandt that religious message was finally a "dead symbolism at last consigned to rest," a verdict which in reality is not so much a verdict on the possibility of renewal on stage, but rather a refreshingly candid self-judgement on the part of a man of the time on the man of what was then "today," the man who for all his enthusiasm for the "dramatic force" of *Oedipus Rex* as a work of art, through his views on what was alive and dead in a tragedy of Sophocles is only giving proof how he still lacked the responses necessary to appreciate the tragic religious sense of this tragedy. Or should I say, he lacked the need?

That perhaps is the nub of the matter. For what the history of the reception and reproduction of Greek tragedies on our modern stage basically shows us is not only the history of stage means and styles, not only the history of the kinds of society which, *qua* audience, support the theatre. All that has a role which belongs in and together with it. But the decisive element, which the history of the reception of the Greek tragedians on the modern stage is basically all about, is a piece of the history of religion, if I can so put it, or at any rate a piece of the history of the religious sense.

6

There is one man to whom Wilbrandt in the preface to his second edition[26] gives the highest praise as a translator of ancient tragedy, a man who came not from the field of the theatre and writing, but from that of philological scholarship, but who came remarkably close to Wilbrandt's principles and who must be briefly mentioned here: Ulrich von Wilamowitz-Moellendorff. He became known around the turn of the century through his translations of, above all, Euripides and then Aeschylus' *Oresteia*, and although he did not treat his texts as freely as Wilbrandt, but really meant to translate exactly what was there, none the less he was thinking as Wilbrandt did, in keeping with the relativising historicism of his time, when he conceived translation as fundamentally and decisively a transference, a change of clothing, a "travesty," and proclaimed: "The rule applies here too, to disregard the letter and to follow the spirit, not to translate words or sentences, but to take up and transmit thoughts and feelings. The clothing must become new, but its content remain. Every right translation is a travesty. Put more trenchantly, the soul remains, but changes its body: true translation is metempsychosis."[27]

The detail of Wilamowitz's practice has often been criticised, and indeed his style of translation is a curious mixture of Schiller, Geibel, Protestant church hymns, echoes of the late Goethe, Hebbel's dialogue, with strange lapses into everyday slang, and all of this together, quite unintentionally, and thus with all the more inner necessity, slipping into the mode of Naturalism then in its first upsurge with the Scandinavians,

---

[26] Wilbrandt, *op. cit.* ivf.

[27] "Was ist übersetzen" ["What is translation?"] 1899, now in *Reden und Vorträge* I, Berlin[4], 1925, 8.

with the young Hauptmann, and Otto Brahm's stage productions. It should not be forgotten what an important influence Wilamowitz exerted around the turn of the century, especially through his *Oresteia* translation. After the performance in Berlin by a student troupe on 6 December 1900[28] it was brought to the Vienna Burgtheater by *Paul Schlenther* with great success,[29] and contributed to the fact that since then Aeschylus has appeared time and again, and still appears, on the programmes of our theatres.

But even the Aeschylus that Wilamowitz made so effective for his time was an Aeschylus reduced to the level of a theatrical spectacle, which, just like Wilamowitz's translations in general, was very soon bound to lose its effect on the age when in the first decade of our century the new-romantic psychologistic Impressionism brought forth a true poet like the young Hugo von Hofmannsthal; and equally in the first decade of the century a great director was found in Max Reinhardt. Reinhardt, who, as is well known, began in an epoch-making manner in 1905 with Shakespeare's *Midsummer Night's Dream*, had already staged Hofmannsthal's version of *Oedipus Rex* in 1910,[30] which he several times put on later too, in the twenties, along with the *Oresteia* of Aeschylus (in the translation by Vollmöller) and Aristophanes' *Lysistrata*, in the Grosses Schauspielhaus in Berlin converted from the Schumann Circus. It was here that I myself saw *Oedipus* with Alexander Moissi in the leading role.

If I venture briefly to describe the impression made at the time by Sophocles' tragedy in these stagings, magnificent in themselves and supported by a distinguished company, it is not in the least my intention to in any way play down Reinhardt's great achievement as director or Hofmannsthal's as poet. (I am a great admirer of both.) We are trying here in a historical sense to define the actual limits of the possibilities of the time in the appropriation of Greek tragedy through the theatre. I have only to think of the opening scene of *Oedipus*, how, with the prayers of the people for help, and with the arrival of Creon, around one hundred extras, with their arms stretched out, were distributed around the system of steps, forming a giant pyramid, at whose summit was stationed Oedipus,[31] for it to seem pretty clear today how the brilliant sense of theatre of that great magician, who above all summoned up the full

---

[28] The "Theater des Westens" in Berlin was sold out six times.

[29] Cf. Wilamowitz's *Erinnerungen*, Leipzig 1929, 253f.; *175 Jahre Burgtheater* 177. Wilamowitz's translation of the *Oresteia* was put on thirteen times up to 1906, and then again in 1916. Cf. *175 Jahre Burgtheater* 178; 192.

[30] Cf. Julius Bab, *Das Theater der Gegenwart*, Leipzig 1928, 143f.

[31] Picture in Bab, *op. cit.* 143.

vitality of the theatrical with his manifold emotional as well as materially pictorial means, brought out in full force the Superdrama, if I may so put it, in Sophocles' tragedy, the *vis dramatica*, which does indeed lie within Sophocles, but not so much the seriousness of the real tragic content, the truth of the tragic action. In Hofmannsthal's version of the tragedy, however, there could be felt then, and there can still be felt today, that true Hofmannsthalian sense of the endless painfulness of existence, that giving of one's life-blood to oneself and the world, that over-refined, almost neurotic awareness of vitality, that suffering at one's own being alive, that is revealed in the nobility with which the poet in his utter truthfulness articulates it and reveals an ultimate humanity. But all this is entwined around Sophocles' tragedy so that even with Hofmannsthal the tragic substance is almost covered up. As proof of this one has only to look at how the same choral song from *Oedipus Rex* which we adduced before, "O, may Destiny be with me . . . ", is now, forty years later than Wilbrandt (1906,)[32] resolved in Hofmannsthal into a dialogue between seven old men:

The Old Men
(Enter)

First Man
Did you hear how they spoke of the Gods?
how impudent, shameless and naked
the words burst from their mouth?

Second Man
There must be a Something that binds our words,
that binds our acts, that binds criminal hands.
Weep, if nothing binds us!
When incontinence rages all round,
that is the end!

Third Man
Incontinence dwells in their hearts,
an eternal storm howls around their lives:
it drives them up to the dizzy heights,
where it is given to no man to stand.
When will it precipitate them down again,
into sorrow, humiliation, and the grave?

---

[32] Not but what it is clearly dependent on Wilbrandt.

Fourth Man

Into sorrow and the grave
it should cast them!
If they go unpunished,
their heads held high,
who is there still to believe?
If these men go on their way
in splendour and honour,
then none of us will offer any more sacrifices.

Fifth Man

If they insult the oracle,
the oracle of Laios,
the ancestral curse!
If they dare that, who shall offer prayers any more!

(A Pause)

First Man

To the navel of the Earth, the Delphic House,
to the illustrious temple of Abai,
my foot shall take me no more in pilgrimage.

The Seven
(together)

My foot shall take me no more!

First Man

If the Divine does not manifest itself here
so that I can grasp it in my hands.

The Seven
(together)

It is for you, you Gods, to bring awful change to this,
we want to grasp it, with these hands,
or else none of us will offer any more sacrifices.

It would be worthwhile to analyse more precisely Hofmannsthal's
version of this choral song, and indeed his entire version of *Oedipus*,
which he himself described as a "new translation."

Together with a nervous psychologising of the dialogue throughout, all the choral parts have been vigorously reduced, and made drama-

tic by a variety of changes. There is no doubt that we are no longer talking of a radical stripping away of dead symbolism. There is some trace of the demonic and divine running through this dialogue between the seven old men. But significantly its most powerful appearance is in that vague Hofmannsthalian "something." "There must be a Something that binds our words . . . that binds criminal hands.'' That means that a kind of piety, with a touch of the sensual and mystic, has in the meantime been revived in Hofmannsthal, but even as it makes itself felt, it draws back into itself and into the ill-defined again. This whole lyrical Impressionism, notwithstanding all the expressive power it achieved, is too psychologically self-absorbed, too occupied with itself, too individually and personally engrossed to let the great tragic reality come through. In Werfel's version of Euripides' *Trojans*[33] and Hasenclever's version of *Antigone*[34] the details are different, but in principle things are the same as with Hofmannsthal. But as for the director Reinhardt, in the end nothing is as indicative of his deep feeling for what is right as his move from the Deutsches Theater to the Schumann Circus, the Grosses Schauspielhaus, and from there to Salzburg, where he had expressly thought of bringing to the Festival Theatre there not only Mozart, Grillparzer, Raimund and Calderon but also Sophocles.[35] In the last decade of his work in Germany he felt more impelled towards the amphitheatrical space of the original Greek tragedy, which in his eyes would bring about the audience's sympathetic involvement in the play itself, and at the same time make the play monumentally imposing by drafting in actors *en masse*. If Reinhardt foundered on this course, even discounting the facts of his personal life, in this foundering there lay a forward-looking clue to a form of representation of Greek tragedy more filled from the inside out, possible not through some kind of monumentality, but only through a reaching back to the substance of Greek tragedy. This, however, required a change in direction which he was no longer capable of himself as he went on the course which, ever since the great achievements of his youth, was now indeed the course of his life.[36]

---

[33] Now newly brought out in S. Fischer's school editions. *Texte moderner Autoren*, Berlin 1952.

[34] Walter Hasenclever, *Antigone, Tragödie in 5 Akten*, Berlin 1917.

[35] Cf. Rudolf Lothar, *Das Wiener Burgtheater*, Wien 1934, 422.

[36] See further Julius Bub, *Das Theater der Gegenwart. Geschichte der dramatischen Bühne seit 1870*, Leipzig 1928, 117; 124ff., as well as Hans Rothe, *Max Reinhardt. 25 Jahre Deutsches Theater*, Munich 1930 (with copious illustrations). Further also Heinz Herald, *Max Reinhardt. Bildnis eines Theatermanns*, Hamburg 1953.

7

At this point, where during the thirties the progress of the historical development in any case experienced a sharp break, I would like for a while to leave the path we have been treading so far about the history of the representation of ancient tragedy in the theatre, and turn to the surprisingly similar course taken by the interpretation of tragedy in the same period in scholarship and literary criticism.

I may, I think, proceed in summary fashion, and so, broadly speaking, it can be said that after Goethe there were above all three kinds of concept through which people aimed to grasp the essence of the tragic:[37] the concept of the human, the concept of tragic fate, and the concept of tragic guilt or entanglement. The *human*, which after Lessing and the Enlightenment was still defined in terms of the humanitarian-philanthropic, by basing the effect of the tragic play on the three concepts derived by Lessing from Aristotle, of fear, pity and moral cleansing, but mainly that of pity.[38] *Fate*, which according to the words of Schiller "should uplift a man when it crushes him" and which the romantic tragedies of Destiny misunderstood in terms of the inescapable fate into whose net a man goes all the more surely as, in reliance on his human cleverness, he endeavours to extricate himself from it. And lastly *tragic guilt*, which, in conformity with the aesthetics of the schoolroom, and not just those, people narrowed down to the so-called *conflict of duties*, in which the tragic hero saw himself compelled, if he was to fulfil what was demanded of him on the one hand, to take upon himself on the other a burden of guilt for which he had to pay an incomparably heavier price. If in Hebbel's tragedy fate manifested itself on the one hand in the thought of a coming, necessary new era, on the other in the unchangeable "things must be so" idea of an individuality which asserted itself in an inner urge as well as conviction, one still recognised even then the tragic in the conflict area of personal individual relations, provided that one did not reduce it to the level of manners and morals. When at the end of the century, Naturalism, born of historicism, came in, placing in its assessment of the ancient tragedians Euripides by the side of and almost in place of the hitherto most favored "harmonious" Sophocles, a fresh wind also began to blow in the interpretation of ancient tragedy, and undoubtedly the psychological interpretation pursued by, in particular, the young Wilamowitz, lent at that time a new

---

[37] On what follows cf. my essay, *Das Drama der Antike in heutiger Sicht*, Universitas 8, 1953, 591ff.

[38] On this cf. my article, *Furcht und Mitleid?* Hermes 83, 1955, 129ff.

colourfulness to the faded late-classicistic categories. However, this led to people now seeing above all "character drama" in ancient tragedy. Even into our own century the philological commentaries were still expending much effort on reconstructing the characters of the main and secondary heroes from the mosaic-like piecing together of "places." The question of tragic guilt, as in the end an individual's moral guilt, continued to stand here too at the centre of interest. A man like Fontane had already protested against it in his theatre criticisms[39] on the occasion of a performance of *Oedipus Rex* in 1873.

The counter-movement against this view of the essence of tragedy which sought to analyse it from an internal, psychological standpoint, emerged during and after the first World War. Here it was the Sophocles book, still important today, by the son of Ulrich von Wilamowitz-Moellendorff, Tycho von Wilamowitz-Moellendorff,[40] who was killed in the first World War. It focused interest once again primarily on Sophocles the dramatist and, although overshooting the mark, none the less in general pertinently put the case for the dominant importance of action rather than character portrayal.

Basically Aristotle had already said all that was necessary, to which admittedly one had to find one's way back: *viz.* that in tragedy the first thing was not the characters but the story, what *happens*. These happenings, however, are not the simple *sequence of events* (as they could have been treated also in epic or novel form), nor are they the *action* in the narrower sense, which dramatically arranges and accentuates that sequence of events, but a third, something deeper: that which as "real happening" secretly, but with full tragic effect, makes itself known with unmistakable clarity in and through the action. What is meant by this *happening* can be best understood if I refer in the first place to something Goethe said:

> Strange is the prophet's song:
> Doubly strange, what is happening.[41]

A further decisive change in our relationship to Greek tragedy came in the time after the first World War, with renewed attention being paid to the actually much older recognition that tragedy, as a cult choral

---

[39] Theodor Fontane, *Plaudieren über Theater, 20 Jahre Königliches Schauspielhaus (1870-1890)*, Berlin 1905, 3f., discussion of the *Oedipus Rex* performance of 20 September 1873.

[40] *Die Dramatische Technik des Sophokles*, Philologische Untersuchungen 22, Berlin 1917.

[41] *Weissagungen des Bakis* JA 1, 228.

play, originally rested on the chorus, and only acquired its dramatic form through the addition of a second and finally a third actor in Aeschylus and Sophocles. Even on this path of ever stronger dramatisation tragedy with the Greeks remained the cult representation of the "enactment of holy story,"[42] first of the god Dionysus and his sufferings, and later of saga in general: that is, the history of the deeds and sufferings of the gods and heroes. But the chorus in the cult plays of Dionysus which had now evolved out of the old Dionysiac oratorio into dramatic tragedy, even if no longer the protagonist, was still a participant of full weight in what happened. Dramatic dialogue and lyrically-ecstatic choral songs together form in mature tragedy the tense structure which carries the tragedy as a whole: two realms of expression, two areas of human emotional behaviour, two realms of fulfilment of God, the World, and Man.

The action of ancient tragedy is based on the two forces of *conflict* and *suffering*. In conflict and suffering above all the old events of saga acquire in the area of tragic dialogue their new dramatic-dialectic effectiveness. At the same time the choruses create the cult relationship to the divine with their invocations, prayers, curses, litanies and laments for the dead. The "presence" of the divine, which expresses itself in the space of the dramatic dialogue in the course of what happens, gives immediate evidence of itself in the choruses. For that reason the chorus in no way represents the "ideal spectator" (as Schlegel taught) which could then justifiably appear as merely a dramatically disturbing "theorem." The choral sections in true ancient tragedy form, as it were, the gold background on which—as in Byzantine and early medieval paintings—the events of the holy story are represented in material form. And this mysterious gold background of the choral element is the very thing before which the dramatic events as consummation of the holy story lose their merely human, accidental, everyday qualities, and from which gain that other thing: religious relevance and validity. Anyone who could propose setting this golden background aside and replacing it with a naturalistic genre, might retain in what remained the humanly moving as well as the dramatically dynamic. He keeps, however, only the smallest part of the essence of tragedy. For what displays the essence of tragedy is definitely not simply the joys and sorrows of a man unshackled and dependent on himself, but those events which reach over man and god, in which along with mankind the god too is always in the picture.

---

[42] I owe this formulation to a lecture by Walther Kraus, Vienna. [Cf. Walther Kraus, Prometheus, *RE* 21. 1., 1957, 969. "Events that must have happened; the tragedy of Aeschylus has its essence in their solemn repetition."]

For tragedy is not simple drama, still less simple theatre. What tragedy is about, and how it always freshly restores to the theatre its highest calling, is simply the representation of that happening which is "stranger than the prophet's song." This happening is the way in which the *truth of reality* proves itself on man, on his noble yet confused actions, his great suffering, his downfall. It is divided in its nature, ambivalent—that inexplicable split of god within itself in the sense of that mysterious saying "No one is against God but God himself": *Nemo contra Deum nisi Deus ipse*, which is only to be survived by *the endurance* of suffering.

Man, just as he approaches the divine, being near God, shot through with God, is led in this essential split in the Truth of Reality, not into any measurable guilt: *guiltless* becomes *guilty*, and he has to bear this *guiltless guilt*, on which in reality tragedy rests, tragically in his existence, with his suffering, and indeed even his death. It is this happening, then, which fills us the attendant spectators, not with "fear" and "pity" (as Lessing) but rather (as the true Aristotle) with "horror" and "misery." Yet in as much as in all these happenings, with their sufferings, their annihilations, the existence of the gods is again and again freshly verified—that "and in all this there is nothing, that is not Zeus" the last words of a tragedy of Sophocles—we experience that tragic *cleansing* which, with the relief from horror and misery, finally puts the spectator back again into the blessed reality of the venerable Divine in all its awfulness.[43]

8

Having followed developments so far I have ended up, unremarked, at our most recent time in which, as even a superficial glance around will tell, there is a fresh effort in the most varied areas of intellectual activity as well as in the most varied countries to make ancient tragedy our own. Philological scholarship in the different countries of our continent is striving today to find the right interpretation of the essence of tragedy and the tragic.[44] Long forgotten insights of a

---

[43] Cf. also *Der König Ödipus des Sophokles in neuer Deutung*, Schweizer Monatshefte 36, 1956, 21–31.

[44] We may refer briefly to the works of Karl Reinhardt, *Sophokles*, Frankfurt 1933 (ed. 3 1947); *Aischylos als Regisseur und Theologe*, Bern 1949; G. Perotta *Sofocle*, Messina 1935; Mario Untersteiner, *Sofocle*, 1935; T. B. L. Webster: *An Introduction to Sophocles*, Oxford 1936; Cecil M. Bowra, *Sophoclean Tragedy*, Oxford 1945; Albin Lesky, *Die griechische Tragödie*, Stuttgart 1938; Emil Staiger, *Grundbegriffe der Poetik*, Zürich 1946; Hans Bogner, *Der tragische Gegensatz*, Heidelberg 1947; Benno v. Wiese, *Die deutsche Tragödie von Lessing bis Hebbel*, Hamburg, ed. 2 1952; Max Pohlenz, *Die griechische Tragödie*, Göttingen, ed. 2 1954; and also my

poet and thinker like Hölderlin (especially in his *Grund zum Empedokles* as well as his *Anmerkungen* to *Oedipus* and *Antigone*) are now beginning to regain prominence.[45] There is a strong productive use both of the materials and of the forms of ancient tragedy running through our most recent compositions for the stage, and Carl Orff in particular, through his important setting of Hölderlin's version of Sophocles' *Antigone* with new kinds of rhythms and means of musical expression, has contributed much to a fresh realization of the tragic word.[46]

There has also been a revival of activity in translating Greek tragedies; I name for example Rowan Woerner, Karl Reinhardt, Emil Staiger and Ernst Buschor. And in unison with all of this the last decade has seen a whole series of new performances of works by Aeschylus, Sophocles and Euripides on a great variety of German stages, in productions by Karl Heinz Stroux, Heinrich Koch, Heinz Arnold, Kurt Hübner, Heinz Dieter Kenter, Gustav Rudolf Sellner, Karl Heinz Streibing, Fritz Herterich, Heinrich Sauer, Ulrich Brecht and Wieland Wagner.

If we are to spend another word or two on these most recent developments, we step from the realm of watching, judging and evaluating into the realm of our own activity which for the time being eludes definitive judgement. For that reason there can be no talk of any such thing as today's achievements, but only of our present efforts; we, as, for the time being, the last generation, can have no thought of arrogating to ourselves the right to exalt ourselves above the efforts and achievements of the past. What we were attempting to trace in our historical outline was the change in the attempts, conditioning each other and always striving forward, to adapt ancient tragedy to our stage. Tragedy itself stood over all of these attempts as something quite simply unique and eternally unrepeatable, and it is only aspects of the tragic which the various epochs have in their own way won from Tragedy—in the course of which perhaps from the time of Hölderlin and Kleist to that of Wilbrandt and Hofmannsthal the progressive reception of tragedy as a dramatic work of art on the one hand was matched by an equally progressive distancing from its basic tragic content on the other. We too cannot claim any more than to have added through our efforts one more aspect to previous aspects. This much does, however, seem characteristic of this aspect of ours, that in tragedy today we no longer look so much

---

article *Sophokles und das Leid*, Potsdam 1944.

[45] More detail on this in my introduction to *Hölderlin, Die Tragödien des Sophokles*, Fischer-Bücherei 162, Frankfurt 1957.

[46] Reference may also be briefly made to such names as Gide, Giradoux, Sartre, Cocteau, Anouilh, Yourcenar, O'Neill, Eliot, Bert Brecht, and Caspar Neher (Antigone—model 1948, Berlin 1949).

for the visual element in the plays, or for the psychological drama of character, but for the objective tragic "happening."

A telling sign that, by comparison with the time of Wilbrandt and Hofmannsthal, there has been a change in our relationship to tragedy is our altered attitude to the ancient chorus all along the line. None of the recent translators and adapters has, so far as I can see, found it necessary to shorten, dramatise or level down the choral parts in the spirit of "contemporary fidelity" and for tragic effect. In Orff's musical interpretation of Hölderlin's *Antigone* it is above all in the choruses that there radiates something of the power of that old gold background. And similarly with regard to Sellner's production of *Oedipus Rex* at Darmstadt in 1952, the slightly exaggerated but revealing joke could be made that this *Oedipus* of Sellner's was a choral oratorio with dramatic intermezzi. Although the ancient chorus may still, today too, present many theatres with a difficult problem for them to overcome with their existing resources, none the less the problem is generally tackled with a fresh earnestness as something worth the effort. Our audiences too look at the chorus today with an open-mindedness quite different from thirty years ago. It seems that tragedy's message, its "happenings," meet with a direct interest. And this message and its realisation on stage seem fortuitously to match the intellectual capacities of present-day producers, as found in the contemporary theatrical style.

Now it may seem premature to speak of *the* theatrical style of the present day. There is much confusion in what is happening on our stages: the outmoded is being carted away, and over-ambitious experiments are attempted which are soon abandoned. But in these manifold efforts there can just the same be seen a basic direction, and this very thing seems to bring new possibilities *vis-à-vis* a new realisation on stage of the tragic happening. "Of the tragic happening" I say, that happening which is no more fixed in time than it transcends it, neither fixed in a particular historical Here and Now, nor elevated above all singularity of time, but which as Universal Happening, in which God and man confront each other and the truth of actuality breaks out in its necessary duality, eternally unique, that is to say *for the moment*.

To realise this *concrete momentariness* on stage was not the prime concern of the theatrical styles of the past which we have looked at up to now, for the very reason that they satisfied their own and once-and-for-all requirements. On the other hand contemporary theatrical style has to eschew much that is worth thinking about and was good in those endeavours. Yet it does seem once more to contain the possibility of giving the tragic events concrete momentariness a theatrical form, and so give a new freedom to much of tragedy's message. . . .

*   *   *

All this leads to forms which are far removed from what could be seen 2,400 years ago on stage and in the orchestra of the theatre of Dionysus at the foot of the acropolis of Athens. They are born from the situation of our time, and they do not archaise. Yet in exactly this way they may serve to aid that transforming assimilation which could, if it succeeds, draw attention to the concrete momentariness of tragedy which we spoke of earlier again in our Here and Now too.

For one thing is for sure: there can be no "preservation," no "repetition" of what once existed, in the sense of a preservation which is as correct as possible. What we call "correct" is itself always subject to the historical changes of our interpretations. There can only be, as the old Goethe so well put it, a new creation from the "extended elements of the past."[47] For that reason it is fairly obvious that we do not have in mind a more or a less of an "approximation" to Greek tragedy as it once itself was. Greek tragedy is, as the history of its subsequent influence to date has shown, inexhaustibly productive. One needs to differentiate—again fairly obviously—between what appears *regulative* and what is the realistically *achievable*. The total dedication to the original, the quest to emulate it, has had no small significance as a regulatory force for the creative efforts of copying. For actual success there is only that transforming assimilation which of course will become all the more real the less we take back in a spirit of usurpation what is of our own and of today to the reproduction of ancient tragedy, seeking rather to serve the original in the sense of that regulatory force with all the strength of our hearts and minds; and for the rest letting our own age— which is not necessarily identical with the picture one has of it—assert itself as something unspoken. One cannot therefore speak, in connection with the reception of Greek tragedy, of some kind of "restoration" of the so-called cult theatre. That is for the present fairly unrealistic. Today's actuality in the theatre is something which has grown up through the course of history. The old orchestra on the Acropolis at Athens is still the origin of our theatre, but much else has been added to it, and all of this has continued to develop, and in its passage through the centuries the theatre has taken on so many new tasks. It is only out of the totality of its historical growth that the theatre can continue to exist and (as a reality) develop in our own times. Yet to its further development as a mature whole there belongs that basic element too which was and is the old tragedy, and the continued fresh appropriation of it in

---

[47] To Kanzler Müller on 4 November 1823.

legitimate adaptations.[48]

"Are we to hope," Ludwig Tieck asked after the first performance of *Antigone* in Potsdam, "these efforts could have a good effect
. . . on our theatre?" To which he gave the answer: "We hope so, and
bend our efforts to undertaking the attempt."

---

[48] A complementary exposition of the history of tragic performances in our
schools would have been desirable; we had to limit ourselves here to the public stage.